Ted Grant

History of British Trotskyism

With an introduction and postscript by Rob Sewell

Wellred Publications
London

History of British Trotskyism
By Ted Grant

First published May 2002

UK distribution: Wellred Books, PO Box 2626,
London N1 7SQ, England
Tel: +44 (0) 20 7515 7291
E-mail: socappeal@easynet.co.uk

USA distribution: Wellred Books, PO Box 1331,
Fargo ND 58103, USA

Online bookshop sales: wellred.marxist.com
www.wellredusa.com

Typeset by Wellred and printed by Legoprint SpA, Lavis (Trento), Italy
Cover design by Jesus Llungueras

Trade distribution: Central Books, 99 Wallis Road, London E9 5LN
British Library Cataloguing in Publication Data
A catalogue record for this book is available from the British Library

ISBN: 1 9000 07 10 X

If you wish to contact the author for any comments or suggestions, please write via Wellred Publications. Additionally, for many of Ted Grant's writings and other material, there is a new website **www.tedgrant.org** which is being regularly updated.

Contents

Acknowledgments

The idea of writing a history of the Trotskyist movement was raised with me some forty years ago. Although somewhat delayed, all I can say is better late than never. In this project I would like to extend my gratitude to a number of people. In particular, I would like to give special thanks to Rob Sewell, whose dogged determination, invaluable assistance and great enthusiasm allowed this book to see the light of day.

I would like to express my deep appreciation to Espe Espigares for the laborious task of typing out the original manuscript and for the professional layout. My thanks also go to Alan Woods for his invaluable comments and suggestions, which have certainly served to greatly improve the book. Again, I would like to extend my gratitude to Al Richardson who kindly read over the original draft and suggested some changes, as well as for access to the archives of *Revolutionary History*. Ian Hunter has also provided invaluable help in pin-pointing documents as well as making very useful comments on the draft. Additionally, can I thank Emil Vaughan and Phil Mitchinson for proof-reading, Steve Jones for proof-reading and work on the biographical details, and Jesus Llungueras for the design of the cover. I want to also thank my old friend Millie Haston for her kindness and her permission to reproduce the vast bulk of the pictures contained in this book. Of course, my thanks go to those comrades, such as Doug Holmes, Terry Harrison, Pauline Wall, and others too many to mention, who have assisted in different ways. Last, but not least, I wish to thank Claudio Bellotti for his last minute help. *Grazie tanto!*

I must add, given the punishing schedule in which the book was produced, I take full responsibility for any factual errors that may have crept in.

Introduction

By Rob Sewell

The present work is a unique contribution to the history of British Trotskyism. Ted Grant became the chief theoretician of British Trotskyism during the Second World War, and was responsible for writing all the main political documents of the tendency. Ever since, for a period of something like six decades, he has been a central figure in the Trotskyist movement. This has given him colossal personal experience, which he has drawn upon to produce this book, which spans the origins of British Trotskyism to the break-up of the Revolutionary Communist Party in June 1949. These were tumultuous years of revolution and counter-revolution, depression, fascism and world war, which tested Trotskyism to the limit. The way in which the movement was able to face up to its historic tasks, its successes and failures, is outlined in this book.

Over the last 70 years, Ted has made a lasting contribution to the Trotskyist movement, and he is regarded by many as the foremost Marxist theoretician alive. Today, he remains an active and leading figure within the *Socialist Appeal* group in Britain and in the international Marxist current associated with the successful *In Defence of Marxism* website, which is attracting growing support internationally.

The early years

Ted Grant was born in South Africa, just before the First World War in a place called Germiston, just outside Johannesburg. His father had emigrated to South Africa from Russia, while his mother came from Le Marais in Paris. After a long marriage, his parents eventually divorced, and after a six-month stay with his father, Ted went to live permanently with his mother. While she ran a small grocery shop in Johannesburg, Ted was sent off to boarding school and his sisters to the convent to continue their education.

In his youth, he was inspired by events in Russia. But, as is so often the case, his first contact with the revolutionary movement had an accidental character. In order to supplement the family income, his mother took in lodgers, one of whom was Ralph (Raff) Lee, who had been a member of the South African Communist Party since 1922, but was expelled during the first Stalinist purges. A dedicated communist, Ralph had regular discussions with Ted, introducing him to the writings of Bernard Shaw, H. G. Wells, Maxim Gorky, Jack London and others. Within a short time, the reading material graduated to the writings of Marx and Engels, and also Lenin. By the age of fifteen Ted was a convinced Marxist.

Ted's elder sister Rae vividly remembers how her mother fed the family and friends, including Ralph, at a large household table - French stew seems to have been the favourite dish. Ralph, who became a close friend of the family, was six years Ted's senior. "Ralph and Ted were inseparable", said Rae. "Once Ralph convinced Ted about Marxism, that changed everything for him," she recalls. "I used to go on long walks with Ralph and he also tried to win me over to Marxism, but I was busy with another circle of friends, so he never succeeded." [1]

He did, however, convince Ted's younger sister Zena to join the Trotskyist movement. Lee with others, including the fifteen-year old Ted Grant, had made contact with the international Trotskyist movement in early 1929 via the American *Militant*, which had been dispatched to South Africa by the newly-founded Communist League of America. "It changed our lives completely", says Ted, "and I started on a political road that now spans more than seventy years."

Ted's sisters Zena (left) and Rae

The inspiring story of how the South African Trotskyists began their revolutionary work under the most difficult conditions imaginable is one of the most interesting parts of the present book. Their work in the Johannesburg Laundry Workers Union remains an inspiration today. But the conditions in South Africa made successful revolutionary work difficult, and in 1934 Ted left for England in the company of another young South African called Max Basch. He was never to return. They broke their journey in France where they met Trotsky's son, Leon Sedov, a member of the International Secretariat and co-ordinator of the work of the International Communist League, who was later murdered by Stalin's agents.

On their arrival in Britain in December 1934, Max Basch changed his name to Sid Frost and Ted changed his from Isaac Blank to Ted Grant - apparently "borrowed" from two of the ship's crew. In the same way, Trotsky had taken his name from one of his old tsarist jailors. Ted did this for personal reasons - to protect his family: whatever happened to him, he did not want anything bad to happen to his family back home in South Africa.

In London, they both joined the Marxist Group inside the Independent Labour Party. However, the possibilities for revolutionary work were becoming less and less, and within a matter of months, Ted Grant left the ILP to join the Trotskyists working within the Labour Party's youth organisation - the Labour League of Youth. From then on, Ted helped to develop the Bolshevik-Leninist Group within the Labour Party, which later became known as the *Militant* Group, after the name of its paper. At this time, their main work consisted of fighting the growing Stalinist influence within the youth movement. The Stalinists were striving to penetrate the Labour League of Youth and fuse it with the Young Communist League. Their faction was led by Ted Willis, who later became famous as the author of *Dixon of Dock Green* - a well-known television series in the 1950s portraying the life of a friendly British "Bobby" - and who was made a Lord for his services to the British Establishment. His colleague Jim Mortimer ended up as general secretary of the Labour Party. Ironically, Mortimer helped to expel Ted Grant from the Labour Party in 1983.

RCP comrades with placards blocking a fascist meeting at the Albert Hall

Shortly after his arrival in Britain, Ted also became actively involved in the struggle against fascism, engaging together with other comrades in running battles with the Moselyite Black Shirts in the East End of London. Here he participated in the famous battle of Cable Street, when the workers of the East End mobilised to stop the fascists in their tracks. There exists a photograph of Ted on a barricade in Long Lane, Bermondsey, South London, taken in 1937, which was reproduced in the 1948 edition of his pamphlet *The Menace of Fascism*, published by the Revolutionary Communist Party.

The Paddington Group

Ted Grant's early years in the South African group had given him a sound theoretical grounding in Marxism which placed him in good stead for the role he was to later play in the Trotskyist movement. After a few years, the failure of the leadership of the *Militant* Group to develop the tendency in any meaningful way, led to a growing dissatisfaction within its ranks. By the autumn of 1937, Ted's own branch in Paddington had become the most active section of the Group, selling the bulk of its newspapers, intervening in the wider labour movement, and engaging in extensive public activity.

Towards the end of the year, a row erupted over the election of the Group's leadership, where slanders were circulated about Ralph Lee. Lee had recently joined the *Militant* Group after arriving with others from South Africa during the summer. This episode led to a walkout and the formation of a new group, called the Workers International League (WIL).

Engels once remarked that sometimes a split could be a healthy thing. The 1937-38 split certainly came into this category, as subsequent events proved. It constituted a decisive step forward in the development of Trotskyism in Britain. The traditional party-building methods of the old groups - which were really a leftover from the methods of the pre-war socialist groupings - had become a barrier to growth. The cadres of the WIL turned their backs on the failed sectarian methods of the past and turned their faces firmly towards the broader layers of the organised working class. In reality, this marked the real beginning of British Trotskyism. Ted Grant played a leading role in this work, not only within the Workers International League but also within the Revolutionary Communist Party formed in 1944, which is fully covered in this book.

The war Years

The period covering the war years is also well documented in this book. It was a testing time. In the first few months of the war, a part of the leadership went to Ireland to establish a base in case the WIL was banned, leaving Ralph, Millie and Ted to run the organisation. In this period, Ralph Lee almost single-handedly produced a daily *Workers' Diary* for use in workplaces. However, by the end of 1940, Ralph had returned to South Africa for personal and health reasons, and the work of building the organisation fell on the shoulders of the other leading comrades.

Above all, the WIL enthusiastically embraced the new proletarian military policy when Trotsky first put it forward. This was in reality a development and deepening of the Internationalists' position during the First World War, and, while maintaining a principled opposition to the imperialist war, allowed the Trotskyists to connect with the working class. The interpretation of the new policy in *Youth for Socialism* did, however, lead to a dispute within the leadership in February 1941, with Ted and Healy (the "majority") on one side, and Millie, Jock Haston and Sam Levy (the "minority") on the other.[2] According to Millie, things got quite heated. But after a few articles in the internal bulletin the argument fizzled out. More pressing was the invasion of the Soviet Union by Hitler in June of that year. However, given the fact that the proletarian military policy was a new programme, such disagreements were likely, if not inevitable under the circumstances. In any case, the dispute showed that the WIL leaders could handle differences of opinion in a comradely and mature fashion.

The comrades of the WIL decisively challenged the attacks of the Stalinists, who after June 1941, took on a rabid chauvinist and strike-breaking role. The WIL, in a clear change in orientation, changed the name of its paper from *Youth for Socialism* to *Socialist Appeal*. The WIL energetically turned towards the factories, built up their position in industry and developed a national profile. In contrast, the official section of the International, the Revolutionary Socialist League, which rejected the proletarian military policy, collapsed. Eventually, its remnants fused with the WIL to form the RCP in 1944.

Soon afterwards, Jock Haston, Roy Tearse, Heaton Lee and Ann Keen were arrested for supporting a national unofficial strike of apprentices. After their release from prison, the RCP turned for the first time towards the parliamentary plane, and engaged in a by-election contest in the Welsh constituency of Neath. This allowed them to test out their ideas, build their profile and develop their organisation in South Wales. These great events are dealt with in detail in the book, and provide a heroic chapter in the history of our movement.

Without doubt, the WIL and the RCP played an outstanding role in the Second World War. Given their legal status, and correct policies, they were able to take advantage of the possibilities and connect with the advanced layers of the working class. Their success prompted the Home Secretary, Herbert Morrison, to supply the War Cabinet with a secret memo outlining the policies of the RCP, and giving brief biographies of its leaders. Although it was not carried through in the end, it is clear that the capitalist class was seriously considering banning the RCP. Due to their work, the British Trotskyists emerged from the war years with a solidly proletarian organisation greatly strengthened numerically and with important points of support within the labour movement. It can be said without any exaggeration that the WIL/RCP is likely to have conducted the most successful work in wartime of any Trotskyist organisation in the world.

The Post War Period

The immediate post war period opened up tremendous challenges before the international Trotskyist movement. The victory of the Red Army against German fascism greatly strengthened the USSR and the Stalinist parties internationally. They were able to use this dominant position, together with the Social Democrats, to derail the revolutionary wave that was sweeping Europe. Despite the revolutionary crisis, the bourgeoisie was able to save themselves by leaning on the workers' parties to carry through a counter-revolution in a "democratic form". This provided capitalism with a breathing space, and the political prerequisites for a certain social stability.

This new world situation, not foreseen by the Trotskyists, served to falsify their original war-time perspective of the movement of either a restoration of capitalism in the USSR or a political revolution, and a revolutionary crisis that would undermine the old parties and prepare the way for the creation of mass Trotskyist parties. In the words of Trotsky, "not one stone upon another would be left of the old organisations, and the Fourth International would become the dominant force on the planet." But the Trotskyists were far too weak to take advantage of the revolutionary situation that followed the war. Power fell into the hands of the Stalinist and reformist leaders, who, as in 1918, betrayed the movement and handed the power over to the bourgeoisie.

This new situation urgently required a new perspective to reorientate the international Trotskyist movement. The leadership of the RCP quickly came to an understanding of the new realities and changed their perspective accordingly. Ted Grant played a key role in this reorientation. It was his grasp of the Marxist method that permitted him to understand and explain what was taking place. By contrast, all the "leaders" of the Fourth International behaved like hopeless formalists and empiricists and were therefore incapable of grasping what was going on under their noses. Having completely failed to understand Trotsky's dialectical method, they simply repeated his past words and statements, which were not applicable to the new situation. Rather than change the original prognosis, they clung to it like grim death.

Of course, the RCP leaders were not the *only* ones who sought to disentangle and understand what was taking place. In the immediate aftermath of World War Two, other individuals also made a serious attempt to grapple with the new situation - at least to begin with. These included in particular David Rousset in France, and Felix Morrow and Albert Goldman in the United States. The latter two had carried on an intense correspondence with the RCP majority, and clearly helped, to a certain extent, to shape some of the views of Grant and Haston.

Unfortunately they represented minorities within their own national sections. They were forced to fight an unsuccessful rearguard struggle against the ideas of the International leadership. They were either subsequently marginalized or expelled, or both. Their isolated opposition reduced their ability to arrive at a fully worked-out position and they subsequently went off in different political tangents. The same was true of the later Vern-Ryan tendency within the American SWP. The leaders of the RCP had a great advantage. These "dissidents" in the International had the political majority within the British section. They were thus able to work out their views in a comprehensive form and to arrive at an accurate Marxist appraisal of what was developing in Britain and internationally.

As the leading theoretician of the RCP, Ted was able to extend and develop Marxist theory in a whole series of new directions after 1945. These ranged from the Marxist theory of the state to the defence of Marxist economic theory, from the peculiar development of the colonial revolution to Marxist tactics towards the mass organisations and party building. These documents are an important legacy that deserves to be far better known to the new generation of revolutionaries internationally.

The period of Ted Grant's memoirs contained in this book is a unique account by a leading participant and key theoretician of the Trotskyist movement. He examines the issues and difficulties facing the revolutionary tendency, and reveals the different positions taken at the time by its leading participants. However, this book is not simply a history, but an attempt to pass on the rich lessons from this turbulent period to the new generation of Marxists both in Britain and internationally.

Cannon's manoeuvres

It was inevitable that part of the present work should deal also with the intrigues perpetrated by the so-called leaders of the International against the leadership of the British Trotskyists. Brought out clearly are the key contributions of individuals such as Ralph Lee and Jock Haston, as well as the miserable role of Gerry Healy, James P. Cannon, Michael Pablo, Pierre Frank and Ernest Mandel.

From 1943, Cannon had conspired to remove the leadership of the British section and replace it with a more compliant set of individuals. Cannon was schooled in the methods of Zinoviev and regarded himself as a Zinovievite at least until 1928. He intrigued with Healy, who led a minority within the RCP, to destroy the Haston-Grant leadership. The International leaders supported a split in the RCP, with Healy's minority entering the Labour Party in late 1947, and the eventual fusion of the two groups in mid-1949, on Healy's terms.

As the book explains, their support for Healy and their sabotage of the British section - in which Pierre Frank also played a prominent role - resulted tragically in the break-up of the RCP in June 1949 and the destruction of a whole layer of experienced cadres. Cannon's stooge, Healy, together with their cronies in the leadership of the International, was directly responsible for this criminal state of affairs.

Once the fusion took place under Healy's leadership, he acted in the most dictatorial fashion, expelling people on the most trivial pretexts. As a result, Jock Haston was by now completely demoralised. The activities of Healy and the clique in Paris effectively drove him out of the movement. Roy Tearse, Jimmy Deane, together with other former leaders of the RCP, were expelled from the so-called fused group, known as the Club. By the end of 1950, the wrecking actions of Healy had destroyed the Party.

Tony Cliff and his supporters, who held to the false position of state capitalism, were never threatened with expulsion from the RCP because of their views. Now Healy unceremoniously booted them out of the Club. Those who failed to vote for the expulsions were themselves expelled! The Cliff group subsequently moved away from Trotskyism and organised themselves as the *Socialist Review* group. Their "state capitalist" position led them to take a neutral position in the Korean War, failing to defend the deformed workers' state of North Korea against the aggression of American imperialism.

Despite this and other fundamental disagreements, Ted Grant vehemently protested against the treatment of the Cliff group and the violation of their democratic rights. This was used by Healy as the pretext for Ted's own expulsion! He was expelled after 22 years membership of the Trotskyist movement. He was also a member of the Executive Committee of the Fourth International, and had his expulsion ratified at the Third World Congress on the motion of Ernest Mandel (Germaine). Scandalously, Mandel described Haston and Grant as "embodying the tendency of British Trotskyism, which obstinately refused to integrate itself into the International, to assimilate the new course of Trotskyism."

The destruction of the British section

A whole layer simply dropped out of revolutionary politics from sheer disillusionment with the "new course". The movement, which showed so much promise, was in ruins. "It now seems clear [sic]", says the then Healy follower Harry Ratner years later, "that Healy and his closest collaborators actually welcomed these defections as removing a threat to their own leadership, so much so that others who did not resign, such as Ted Grant, Roy Tearse and Jimmy Deane, were expelled on various pretexts. For example, when Jock Haston's expulsion was moved in the Political Bureau of the Club (comrades were not allowed just to resign, they had to be expelled), and Jimmy Deane asked that Haston be given the chance to produce a written statement in his defence before the vote of expulsion was put, he was told that 'it is necessary that you indicate in writing political support for the resolution condemning Haston without reservations immediately'. Refusing to do so, Deane was expelled for 'cryptic sympathy' with Haston. When Roy Tearse refused to break off personal relations with Haston he, too, was expelled." [3]

The events of 1950, which represented the destruction of the British section of the Fourth International, constituted a watershed in the development of British Trotskyism. This period marks the end of Ted Grant's history. The new chapter in the subsequent development of the Trotskyist movement, which brings the story up until the present day, is outlined in the postscript at the end of the book.

Marx explained that history is made by individuals. The colossal contribution by Ted Grant in the history of our movement is an inspiration to all those fighting to change society. This book is a valuable part of our heritage and deserves to be studied by the new generation awakening to the ideas of Trotskyism and the ideals of the socialist future.

18 March 2002

Notes:

1- Interview with Rob Sewell, Paris, 2 February 2002.

2- See WIL *Bulletin* articles, 28 February 1941, 20 March 1941, and 21 March 1941.

3- Harry Ratner, *Reluctant Revolutionary*, pp.144-5.

Ted Grant and Jimmy Deane, Neath 1945

1

Fighting Against the Stream - The Origins and Early Years

"Learning not to forget the past in order to foresee the future is our first, our most important task." Leon Trotsky, 27 July 1929.

Our movement - the Trotskyist movement - has a very rich history stretching back many decades. An understanding of our history is important from the point of view of appreciating the way in which a revolutionary movement develops. An understanding of the past sheds light on how a Marxist tendency grows and prepares itself for the titanic events of the future. The history of our tendency can be traced back directly to the great work of Leon Trotsky's Left Opposition in the 1920s and in fact stretches back even further to the heroic days of the Third International under Lenin and Trotsky.

The genesis of our movement in Britain was already rooted in the formation of the British Communist Party of Great Britain (CPGB) in 1920. At that time, the British Communist Party was very inexperienced and, in contrast to its European counterparts, very weak numerically and largely isolated from the broader labour movement. Although made up of courageous people who were inspired by the Russian Revolution, the young party was saturated with ultra-left and sectarian tendencies that had been the hallmark of the propaganda groups that came together to form the CPGB. Under the guidance of the Communist International, the party began gradually to overcome these shortcomings and turn its attention towards mass work and the serious task of building a mass revolutionary party.

This was not achieved without internal difficulty. Lenin had to use his personal authority to persuade the British leadership to abandon their sectarianism and, in order to influence reformist workers, apply for affiliation to the Labour Party. By 1923, significant changes in its approach and orientation had been carried through. The CPGB had gone through a re-organisation and was undertaking serious work in the trade unions through the creation of the Minority Movement, as well as creating points of support within the Labour Party. Everything seemed set for a big advance for the Communist movement in Britain.

However, just at this time, during 1923-4, the bureaucratic reaction within the Soviet Union was rapidly gaining ground within the state and the party. The isolation of the Russian Revolution in conditions of appalling backwardness gave rise to a huge bureaucracy keen to enjoy the fruits of victory. The opposition of the bureaucracy to world revolution had a material basis. The rising stratum of conservative officials wanted a quiet life, without the storm and stress of revolution and freed from the control of the masses. At each setback for the working class, this privileged caste composed of millions of officials - many of them former tsarist bureaucrats - gathered greater power into its hands, elbowing aside the exhausted working class.

This process found its reflection inside the Russian Communist Party where this upstart caste of officials gravitated around the figurehead of Stalin, who, with his narrow administrative and purely national outlook was best suited to reflect their conservative views and material interests. The theory of "socialism in one country", put forward in the autumn of 1924, was a reflection of the bureaucracy's disdain for the world revolution. They wished to be left alone to "get on" with the task of running the Soviet state - without the irksome interference of workers' democracy. Lenin was increasingly alarmed at the rise of the bureaucracy in state and Party institutions and formed a bloc with Trotsky to combat it. But from 1922 Lenin was incapacitated through a series of strokes, and behind the scenes the triumvirate of Stalin, Kamenev and Zinoviev was manoeuvring to isolate Trotsky. Lenin's Testament - in which he demanded Stalin's removal as general secretary and described Trotsky as the most able member of the Central Committee, was hidden from the Party membership, and a campaign of lies and slander was orchestrated against Trotsky and the Opposition.

After Lenin's last illness, Trotsky took upon his shoulders the struggle against Stalin and the growing bureaucratic menace, fighting for the Leninist programme of proletarian internationalism and workers' democracy. He launched the Left Opposition in late 1923 after the failure of the German Revolution in an attempt to defend the fundamental ideas of Lenin which were being systematically revised and discarded. The outbreak of this struggle within Russia between the Opposition and the Triumvirate of Stalin, Zinoviev and Kamenev was first of all contained within the leadership of the CPSU. However, the struggle had a momentum of its own, and with Lenin's death, the campaign to discredit Trotsky as Lenin's successor was soon taken into the ranks of the Communist International. As within the apparatus of the Russian Party, where Stalin had used his position to select personnel who were loyal to his faction, so Zinoviev selected leaders in the separate sections who proved more amenable to Moscow. Nevertheless, in these early days of the Communist movement the leadership was forced to allow a pseudo-democratic discussion on the issues raised by the Opposition that had broken out in the Russian Party.

The Stalin-Trotsky clash was first reported to the British Party in early 1924, soon after the death of Lenin. Reports were carried in the party press of the resolution passed at the Thirteenth Conference of the Soviet Communist Party condemning Trotsky's factionalism and classifying "Trotskyism" as a petty bourgeois deviation. By the end of the year, attacks on

"Trotskyism" became more frequent. Tom Bell, the general secretary, introduced a resolution condemning Trotsky at the Party Council on 30 November 1924. Completely ignoring the political issues at stake, he stressed Trotsky's failure to adhere to party rules as his main argument in condemning the Opposition. "The question of Trotsky, it seems to us, is a question of discipline. We are not arguing or discussing the ideological approach of Trotsky to the question as a whole. Our party is concerned fundamentally with the question of discipline," stated Bell. While there was disquiet at the Party Council with a number of voices challenging the position of the Party leadership, when it came to the vote, the condemnation of Trotsky was carried unanimously.[1]

A report of the Party Council was then given to a 300-strong London Aggregate in January 1925. JT Murphy, despite only having a summary of Trotsky's views, outlined the case against Trotsky and his violation of the decisions of the Russian Party and the International in reopening the debate on the Opposition views deemed "closed" by the party. In the meeting, Trotsky was defended by Arthur Reade, a member of the London District Committee, who moved a resolution regretting the "hasty vote of the Party Council" in condemning Trotsky and called on the CPGB to support the left wing of the Russian Party. After the discussion, Reade's motion received, according to the report of the *Weekly Worker,* 10 votes. (*Workers Weekly*, 23 January 1925). On 30 January, Reade wrote to the paper complaining that there were only 200 present, and that his motion for adjournment was only defeated by 81 to 65, and in the final vote, his motion received 15 votes.[2] In any case, the leadership won hands down.

The British CP, which had shown little interest in political theory or disputes over "socialism in one country", had fully swung behind the party leaders in Moscow. Around about this time, the Party issued a book, probably in May 1925 although it contained no date, entitled *The Errors of Trotskyism*, which printed Trotsky's *Lessons of October* and a series of replies from Zinoviev, Kamenev, Stalin, Krupskaya (who had initially been close to the Opposition) and others. The book was not intended as an analysis of Trotsky's ideas, but as the title clearly indicates, was an attack on "Trotskyism". JT Murphy, who was to replace Bell as the British representative on the International Executive Committee, wrote the introduction. At this time, given the prestige of Trotsky in Communist ranks, those who attacked Trotsky had to be somewhat cautious. "It is undoubtedly true", states Murphy, "that it came as a great surprise to the British working class when they saw the Communist International in the throes of a great controversy with Comrade Trotsky."[3]

Murphy was forced to recognise, even at this time, Trotsky's colossal reputation and authority within the ranks of the Comintern. In his preamble he states: "Comrade Trotsky's name has always been associated in our minds with Comrade Lenin. 'Lenin and Trotsky!' These were the names with which we conjured up in all our thoughts and feelings about the Russian Revolution and the Communist International. As the news of the Russian Revolution spread westward, these two figures loomed gigantically above our horizon and we never thought of differences... We saw only leaders, Soviets and masses, and over all the great historical giants, Lenin and Trotsky."[4] Nevertheless, a string of articles, which filled the majority of this book from Comintern leaders, were used to reinforce the myth of "Trotskyism".

It is interesting to note that every one of the people who wrote these anti-Trotsky articles was either expelled or in disfavour with Moscow in the following years. JT Murphy, who had moved Trotsky's expulsion from the Comintern, was himself ironically expelled on charges of

"Trotskyism". But the purge in the Communist International was only an anticipation of the far more monstrous purge whereby Stalin physically annihilated Lenin's Party. Even Lenin's wife Krupskaya found herself in danger. When she tried to protest against the expulsion and arrest of Zinoviev and Kamenev, Stalin rudely informed her that he could always find another widow for Lenin. One by one, Stalin murdered the entire Leninist Old Guard. At the end of the Great Purges, only Stalin remained.

The Stalinisation of the Communist International had serious effects in Britain. The British Communist Party, which had every possibility of turning itself into a significant force within the labour movement, was suddenly caught up in this faction fight with the Opposition. Although the British leaders lined up behind Stalin, they were forced to recognise Trotsky's past achievements. Even as late as the beginning of 1926, they published Trotsky's book *Where is Britain Going?* and were forced to defend it. So, in *Labour Monthly*, Palme Dutt, still not sure which way to jump, took up a robust defence of Trotsky in his review of the book. "Trotsky's book will be eagerly read, and will give stimulus and help; will help to break the chains of enslavement to old ideas and leadership, to give confidence and clearness and strength, and to show the plain path forward of the struggle", states Palme Dutt. "The English working class has cause to be grateful to Trotsky for his book; and to hope that he will not stay his hand at this short sketch, but will carry forward his work of interpretation, polemic and elucidation, and elaborate his analysis further, which is so much needed in England." (*Labour Monthly,* April 1926). Any hint of support had, however, completely evaporated by the time of Trotsky's criticism of the Anglo-Russian Trade Union Committee and his expulsion from the Russian CP in late 1927.

> "The book," wrote Trotsky later, "was aimed essentially at the official conception of the Politburo, with its hope of an evolution to the left by the British General Council, and of a gradual and painless penetration of communism into the ranks of the British Labour Party and trade unions."[5]

This was no mere speculation. At the Fifth Congress of the Communist International in 1924 Zinoviev, who was still in alliance with Stalin, after referring to the British CP as the most important section of the International, stated: "We do not know exactly when the Communist Mass Party of England will come, whether only through the Stewart-MacManus door or through some other door."[6] The "other door" was through a "deal" with the left wing of the Labour Party and trade unions, which was to have disastrous consequences in the Anglo-Russian Trade Union Committee and the disorientation of the British CP during the General Strike of 1926.

As a result of the acceptance of Stalin's policies, which now veered sharply towards opportunism, the British Communist Party increasingly lost sight of its independent role in the scheme of things. After a TUC delegation had visited the Soviet Union in 1925, Moscow looked increasingly towards these left bureaucrats for assistance. They had illusions that the "lefts" could help break Russia's isolation, and even introduce communism in Britain "by the back door." As a consequence, the Anglo-Russian Trade Union Committee was formed by representatives of British and Russian unions to promote trade union unity and serve as a means of protection against a possible military attack against the USSR. The chairman of the TUC, Purcell, together with Hicks, Bromley and Swales, became highly valued friends of the Soviet Union, and as a result, should be regarded as such by the British Communist Party. Such an approach was to have serious consequences in the 1926 General Strike. When the Strike broke out in May of that year, these "lefts" capitulated before the right wing, who in turn, capitulated before the Baldwin government. The right wing sold out the working class, which came as no surprise to the advanced workers. However, the betrayal of the "lefts" on the TUC, who had the support of the Communists, led to widespread confusion and disillusionment.

In the course of the General Strike, the Communist Party grew to around 10,000 members, but within a short time space of time, the bulk of the new recruits dropped away and left the Party. During the strike, the CPGB had failed to act as an independent revolutionary party, warning of the dangers from the left as well as the right. Despite the demands of the Left Opposition for the Soviet trade unions to break with the British TUC over their betrayal of the strike and resign from the Anglo-Russian committee, the Stalinists instead held on to their coat-tails, until they were unceremoniously dropped by their fair-weather friends. For the advanced workers, it was not only the treacherous actions of the left reformists that were discredited, but also the role of the Communist Party, which acted as a "revolutionary" cover for the fake lefts. This was the result of the opportunist line that was imposed on the British Communists by the Russian leadership.

A few months after Palme Dutt had written his article praising Trotsky, Thaelmann, the German Communist leader, remarked that the British CP was the only major party that had no differences with the Executive Committee of the Communist International (ECCI). It was regarded as the most "loyal" and its leaders, after a period of selection, considered the most pliable by the Kremlin. Pollitt and Co. simply followed every change in the party Line. On all occasions, they were with the "majority". The British Party accepted the official Line from Moscow as a necessary measure to consolidate socialism in Russia. They accepted the idea of the theory of "socialism in one country" without question. In February 1926, the resolution of the enlarged plenum of the Comintern executive praised the "absence of factional struggles in the British Party." It is no accident that Stalin regarded the British party as one of the best sections of the International.

The expulsion of the Opposition

The right-opportunist policy of the Stalinists in appeasing the "lefts" in the British TUC had seriously undermined the British Communists. But this betrayal paled in insignificance beside the terrible catastrophe of the defeat of the Chinese Revolution, which was caused by the policies of Stalin and Bukharin.

Between 1925 and 1927, the unfolding drama of the Chinese Revolution gripped the imagination of the Communist movement internationally. At this time, the Chinese CP was the only mass working class party in existence. It was poised to play a leading role within the revolution and had every chance of carrying through a Chinese "October". However, the opportunist policy pursued by Stalin was also affecting developments in China. His theory of revolution by stages, similar to that put forward by the Mensheviks in Russia, led to the subordination of the Chinese CP to the nationalist Kuomintang. This policy, sharply criticised by the Left Opposition, led to a terrible defeat in 1927 with the bloody suppression of the workers' movement by Stalin's one time friend, Chiang Kai-Shek. The defeat led to increased demoralisation within the Soviet working class, and was one of the major factors in the suppression of the Left Opposition at the end of the year.

Trotsky alone had warned against the policy of collaborating with Chiang Kai-Shek. But the defeat in China sealed the fate of the Left Opposition in Russia. The Russian working class, already exhausted by years of war and revolution, was disappointed and tended to fall into inactivity. The workers sympathised with the Opposition's policies but it was only a passive sympathy, and did not lead to active support. The workers were tired and apathetic, while the bureaucracy was increasingly emboldened by every step back taken by the world revolution. The Opposition was expelled in 1927, the same year that the Chinese working class was crushed. One year later, Trotsky was expelled from the USSR and deprived of Soviet citizenship. As it was still too early for Stalin to have him murdered, he was exiled to Turkey, from where he began to organise the International Left Opposition, dedicated to the fight to reform the Communist International and return it to the authentic ideas of Lenin and the October revolution.

The expulsion of the Left Opposition in November 1927 constituted a defeat for the genuine forces of Leninism within the Communist Parties. This opened the way for the shift to the left by Stalin and his elimination later of the Right Opposition of Bukharin. It marked a further step in the consolidation of the bureaucracy in the Soviet Union, and the elimination of all opposition elements within the Communist International. After the expulsion of the Russian Left Opposition, similar purges were carried out in every section of the Comintern. No criticism of Stalin was permitted. All the foreign Communist Parties were expected to jump when Moscow changed the Line. They learned to dance to Stalin's tune - or face the consequences.

From 1924 onwards, Stalin repeatedly carried out purges in one Communist Party after another. In France, the leadership of Souvarine and Rosmer, which sympathised with the Opposition, was replaced by the "left" leadership of Treint and Girault, who, in turn were expelled and replaced by Thorez and Doriot. In Germany, Brandler and Thalheimer were replaced by Fischer and Maslow, who, in turn were replaced by Thälmann and Neumann. In Poland, the Varsky leadership was replaced by Domsky, who was later removed. In China, the leader and founder of the party, Chen Tu-hsiu, was expelled for "Trotskyism". In Spain, leaders like Nin and Andrade were also expelled for "Trotskyism". And in the USA and Canada, Cannon, Abern, Shachtman and Spector suffered the same fate.

This development was in complete contrast to the situation in Britain. The impact of the Russian Opposition proved to have a far smaller effect. Here, the forces of a Trotskyist Opposition were slow to emerge. While there were certain murmurings and unease in the ranks of the Party concerning the internal disputes in Russia and the treatment of Trotsky and the Opposition, there was hardly a ripple compared to other European Parties. This was partly to do with the low political level of the party, and the inability of the Party cadres to understand what was really going on within the Russian Party.

From this time onwards, there was complete and uncritical support by the British leadership for the Stalinist Line. Among the most servile followers of Moscow were Palme Dutt, Harry Pollitt, William Gallagher (the same one who had criticised Lenin from the "left") and the other leaders of the CPGB. Among other things, this reflected the low political level of the British Party, including its leaders. Tom Bell was forced to recognise the ignorance of the British Party "as to what is actually transpiring in the Russian Party." J T Murphy also referred to the "general ignorance of international affairs prevailing amongst the membership in Britain."

This lack of understanding of theoretical issues had long been a hallmark of the British labour movement. As Marx and Engels noted, theory was never a strong point in the British working class, which tended towards empiricism and pragmatism. But without theory there can be no genuine Marxist-Leninist Party. The slavish support for the Moscow bureaucracy ultimately led to the destruction of the CPGB and all the other sections of the Comintern, but not before causing one catastrophe after another for the workers' movement internationally.

The 'Third Period'

By 1927, the balance of forces inside Russia was changing. All along, Trotsky and the Opposition had been warning of the dangers of capitalist restoration posed by the opportunist policy of Stalin and Bukharin of appeasing the rich peasants (the Kulaks). The Left Opposition demanded a reversal of this policy and instead proposed a programme of industrialisation based on five-year plans, the progressive taxation of the rich peasants and gradual collectivisation by example. Stalin and his faction ridiculed this, comparing Trotsky's proposal for electrification to "offering the peasant a gramophone instead of a cow."

However, by 1927-28 it was clear that there was a real danger of counter-revolution in Russia. The Kulaks, emboldened by the policy of the leadership, launched a grain strike that threatened the very basis of Soviet power. Alarmed, the Stalin faction broke with Bukharin and adopted a programme that was a caricature of that of the Left Opposition. In the process, the Stalinists swung over from opportunism to wild ultra-leftism. This entailed forced collectivisation of agriculture and adventurist targets in the five-year plans, under slogans like "carry out the five year plan in four years." This led to widespread disruption, a catastrophic fall in agricultural production and a terrible famine in which possibly ten million people perished. Nevertheless, the mass of Soviet workers welcomed the turn to industrialisation and five year plans. This provoked a crisis in the Opposition, in which many of its former adherents capitulated to Stalin - a mistake which they later paid for with their lives.

After burning their fingers with the previous right wing policy, the Stalin wing now swung one hundred and eighty degrees to the left and adopted an adventurist policy also on an international scale. Taking their lead blindly from Moscow, the Communist Parties internationally adopted the crazy ultra-left position of the "third period". The Stalinists proclaimed a new (third) period in which the collapse of capitalism was said to be imminent. The world slump of capitalism that began with the Wall Street Crash of 1929 was depicted as the final crisis of capitalism, completely ignoring what Lenin and Trotsky had explained many times - that there was no such thing as a "final crisis" of capitalism, and that capitalism will always manage to extricate itself from even the deepest crisis, until it is overthrown by the working class.

As a corollary to this lunacy, the Stalinists proclaimed that all other parties except themselves were "fascist". In particular, the social-democratic organisations were said to have become fascist - or "social fascist" - in character. "Social democracy and fascism", said Stalin, "are twins and not opposites." Social democracy was therefore considered the main enemy of the working class. As a result, everywhere, the Stalinists split and paralysed the working class movement. The worst results were experienced in Germany, where the ultra-left policies of the Stalinists rendered the working class powerless in the face of the Nazi menace. Instead of adopting Lenin's policy of the united front to achieve the united action of Communist and Socialist workers against the Nazis, they deliberately set out to split the workers' movement and thus allowed Hitler to come to power - as he later boasted "without breaking a window pane." The Stalinists collaborated with the Nazis in the Berlin tram strike and even made a bloc with the fascists during the so-called Red Referendum to bring down the Social Democratic government in Prussia. If they had succeeded, it would have meant that Hitler would have come to power two years earlier!

In Britain also we had the ludicrous position of the tiny Communist Party issuing ultimatums to the Labour Party, denouncing the Labour leaders as "social fascists", and even organising the breaking up of Labour Party meetings. They had to be broken up because the Labour leaders were the main enemy of working class, and were even more dangerous than the fascists! In the *Daily Worker*, Harry Pollitt, the leader of the Party, advocated that no Labour Party meeting should be allowed to take place in the open air. This ultra-left and sectarian line represented a complete abandonment of Lenin's policies. It served to completely isolate the CP. As a result of this madness the influence of the British Communist Party was completely undermined, and they were reduced to a small sect on the fringes of the labour movement.

The National Government

The second Labour Government, elected in 1929, was a government of crisis. The crisis hit Britain hard. Unemployment was soaring. The Labour leaders, who had fought the election on the issue of unemployment, were powerless to do anything about it. In order to solve the problem they would have had to take over the banks and big companies and instituted a socialist planned economy. Obviously, this was the last thing Ramsay MacDonald had in mind!

In 1931 the crisis manifested itself in the collapse of big banks and industrial concerns in Europe, beginning with the collapse of the Anstalt-Kredit bank in Austria. The American capitalists withdrew their funds from Europe, completing the financial debacle. Unemployment in Germany reached four million. The collapse of Britain's markets in the Dominions and other primary producing countries resulted in a deepening of the crisis on this side of the Channel. Unemployment, which had already been rising fast before 1930, now soared to intolerable levels. The pettifogging reforms of the Labour Government had no effect.

On the other hand, the ruling class now wanted to get rid of the Labour Government and replace it with a more reliable instrument for carrying out an all-out offensive against the working class. They set out to split the Labour Party, making use of the services of the right wing led by MacDonald. In 1931 they carried out a parliamentary coup that established a National Government, when MacDonald and the right wing of the Parliamentary Labour Party joined forces with the Tories and a section of the Liberals. They then organised a panic election on the "National Unity" ticket, which won an overwhelming majority later in the year.

In this election, the Labour vote fell sharply to 6,648,000, while the Tories got 11,800,000 - almost double the Labour figure - and the total "National" vote was 14,500,000. Labour seats that had been safe for 20 years were lost in the debacle. Every Labour minister lost his seat except for George Lansbury. Only 49 Labour MPs remained in Westminster, while the Tories had 417. Thus, after a severe defeat on the industrial front in 1926, the British workers now suffered a big defeat on the electoral plane. Nevertheless, despite the seriousness of the defeat, the Labour Party was not annihilated. It still had over six and a half million votes, and soon recovered. Moreover, the section which split away to join the National Government was a tiny minority of right wingers, mainly in the Parliamentary Party. At grass-roots level very few joined MacDonald. In opposition, Labour swung to the left and by 1935 it had recovered much of the lost ground.

However, in the short run, the labour movement was in a state of complete turmoil, which expressed itself in the rapid crystalisation of a mass left wing around the Independent Labour Party (ILP). The leaders of the ILP were insistently demanding the right to act as a separate party. In fact, they virtually had this right anyway, since Lansbury, the new leader of the Labour Party, was on the left and inclined to make compromises to keep them inside the Labour Party. However, as typical confused centrists, the ILP leaders made this organisational question into a question of "principle". They were convinced that the Labour Party was completely counter-revolutionary and that to accept its discipline in any way would be "treachery". The Stalinists who were attempting to win the ILP over encouraged this childishness. In actual fact, the programme and policy of the ILP was not qualitatively different from that of the Labour Party, which moved sharply to the left after 1931. By splitting away - which they did in Easter 1932 - the ILP leaders cut the advanced workers off from the mass, which was also moving to the left, but needed time to draw all the conclusions.

Up until this point those who had developed an interest and sympathy in Trotskyism in Britain were to be found in the Independent Labour Party (ILP) and in other radical circles, rather than within the Communist Party. The decline of the CPGB as a result of its ultra-leftism, cut itself off from developments inside the ILP, which was evolving as a mass left wing inside the Labour Party. The crisis that followed the economic collapse in 1929 and the formation of the National Government led to enormous ferment in the Labour Party. However, the Stalinists, blinded by their ultra-left madness, were initially incapable of taking advantage of this situation.

Towards the end of the 1920s, a couple of middle-class intellectuals, Frank Ridley and Chandu Ram, (the same Ridley who later on played a role as an adviser to the ILP leadership) got in touch with Trotsky with a view to founding a Left Opposition group in Britain. But Trotsky, although keen to establish a base in Britain, would not be rushed into an adventure. After examining the hopelessly confused material that they were putting forward Trotsky refused to have anything to do with them.

Ridley and Ram were wildly sectarian and ultra-left and had no idea of how to build a genuine movement. They saw the results of the 1931 general election as a transitional stage between bourgeois democracy and fascism. Trotsky answered their arguments point by point, rejecting their perspective of imminent fascism in Britain, as well as their characterisation of the trade unions as "imperialist organisations", and their premature call for a Fourth International. He simply advised them to "get into the trade unions and do something in relation to the mass movement." Trotsky immediately recognised that they were of little use in developing a real Left Opposition in Britain. At this early stage, therefore, one could only speak of individual sympathisers of Trotsky in Britain - not a Trotskyist tendency in any meaningful sense. The real development of British Trotskyism did not come about until after the experience of the world slump in 1929 and the rise of fascism in Germany.

The international situation had a profound impact on Britain. After the severe defeat of the General Strike, the workers were now struggling to come to grips with mass unemployment and the betrayal of the MacDonald Labour Government. There was a growing radicalisation within the mass organisations, especially around the Independent Labour Party. At this time,

Trotsky, from his place of enforced exile in Turkey, was waging an international campaign for a united front in Germany, as a means of achieving the united action of the Communists and Social-Democratic workers to prevent the coming to power of Hitler. Meanwhile, a small group of comrades within the British Communist Party in Balham, South London, began to move into opposition to the party leadership on a number of questions, including the need for united front tactics in Germany. It was from this small group that the first young forces of British Trotskyism were to emerge.

The International Left Opposition

From the small island of Prinkipo in Turkey, Leon Trotsky continued his lonely battle against Stalinism. Despite all the efforts of Stalin and his powerful apparatus to crush the Opposition and silence Trotsky, the voice of the Opposition was getting stronger and gaining new adherents among those Communists who wished to defend the real programme and traditions of Bolshevik-Leninism.

Sometimes, accidents can play an important role in history. Old Hegel long ago said that necessity expresses itself through accident, and what happened at the Sixth Congress of the Comintern was a good example of this dialectical law. In 1928, the American Communist James Cannon and his Canadian comrade Maurice Spector, while attending the Sixth Congress in Moscow, by accident got hold of a copy of Trotsky's brilliant document entitled the *Critique of the Draft Programme of the Communist International*, which sharply criticised the erroneous position of Bukharin and Stalin, and especially exposed the anti-Marxist theory of "socialism in one country", which had been put forward by Stalin at the end of 1924. This critique was a landmark in the ideological arming of the Left Opposition internationally. In a truly prophetic statement, Trotsky warned that if this position were adopted by the Communist International, it would inevitably mark the beginning of a process that would lead to the nationalist and reformist degeneration of every Communist Party in the world. Three generations later, his prediction - which was ridiculed by the Stalinists at the time - has been shown to be correct.

Stalin had no intention of circulating Trotsky's document. But by a strange accident of history, that is what happened. At that time, when the Stalinist regime had not yet been consolidated, the Communist International still had to observe certain norms of democratic centralism, which permitted the circulation of minority opinions. Although Trotsky had been expelled from the Russian Party a year earlier, he took advantage of the Congress to appeal to the Communist International. In the process he submitted his document on the *Draft Programme.* Through a blunder in the apparatus, they circulated Trotsky's document to the heads of the delegations, including members of the programme commission. It was here that James Cannon and Maurice Spector first saw and read Trotsky's document.

> "Through some slip-up in the apparatus in Moscow," recalls Cannon, "which was supposed to be airtight, this document of Trotsky came into the translating room of the Comintern. It fell into the hopper, where they had a dozen or more translators and stenographers with nothing else to do. They picked up Trotsky's document, translated it and distributed it to the heads of the delegations and the members of the programme commission. So, lo and behold, it was laid in my lap, translated into English! Maurice Spector, a delegate from the Canadian

> Party, and in somewhat the same frame of mind as myself, was also on the programme commission and he got a copy. We let the caucus meetings and the Congress sessions go to the devil while we read and studied this document. Then I knew what I had to do, and so did he. Our doubts had been resolved. It was as clear as daylight that Marxist truth was on the side of Trotsky. We had a compact there and then - Spector and I - that we would come back home and begin a struggle under the banner of Trotskyism." (*History of American Trotskyism,* New York, 1944, pp. 49-50).

The American comrades James Cannon, Max Shachtman and Martin Abern, who were members of the Central Committee of the American Communist Party, together with Spector in Canada broke with the Stalinists in 1928 and went over to Trotskyism. Within a short time, they were expelled from the Party and they organised themselves into the Communist League of America, together with a small grouping in Canada. This was an historic breakthrough as it served to break the isolation of Trotsky and the Opposition. This was a turning point in the fortunes of the Left Opposition and greatly facilitated the spread of Trotsky's ideas throughout the world - a fact that played a role in my own recruitment to Trotsky's International Left Opposition shortly afterwards.

The American Communist League began to publish a newspaper called *The Militant* in November 1928. Using some good old American enterprise, they got their hands on the Communist Party's mailing lists and then sent bundles of papers to as many progressive bookshops worldwide as they could, including in Britain, South Africa, and elsewhere. That is how the South African comrades, including myself, got in touch with the ideas of Trotskyism. We saw this material in the bookshop in Johannesburg, got hold of it and read it avidly from cover to cover. It contained all of Trotsky's criticisms of Stalinism, including his analysis of the aborted revolution in China in 1925-27. We used to wait eagerly for the arrival of each new batch of papers. The same happened in Cape Town. Out of this began, in around 1930, the development of Left Opposition groups in South Africa, in which I first got involved. The same was true in Britain. Material was sent to a left bookshop in London, and the comrades in Balham came across it, and this served to put them in touch with the international Trotskyist movement.

The Balham Group

In 1932, opposition arose in the two branches of the Communist Party in south London, Balham and Tooting. Certain local leaders, Reg Groves, Harry Wicks, Hugo Dewar and Henry Sara, who were on the district committee of the Party, came into political opposition to the CP national leadership. They had got hold of this Trotskyist material from the United States and agreed whole-heartedly with its political position. They recognised that what Trotsky was arguing for was absolutely correct, and that a united front in Germany between Social Democrats and Communists was essential to prevent Hitler's victory. In contrast to the Trotskyist sympathisers and individuals of the past, the Balham group represented the real genesis of Trotskyism in Britain. The Balham Group, as they became known, raised the question of Germany and the united front within the ranks of the Communist Party. During their interventions, they also raised the issue of applying the united front tactic to the party's struggle against fascism in Britain. From 1929 to the victory of Hitler in January 1933, the whole campaign of the International Left Opposition was focused on this vital question.

For Trotsky, Germany was the key to the international situation. The struggle in Germany was an elementary question of survival for the workers' movement. At all costs, the German workers had to prevent Hitler from coming to power. Failure would mean the total destruction of the strongest working class movement in Europe, if not the world. "Germany is now passing through one of those great hours upon which the fate of the German people, the fate of Europe, and in significant measure the fate of all humanity, will depend for decades", stated Trotsky.[8]

When faced with a Trotskyist opposition within the British CP, the leaders of the Party, Pollitt, Gallacher, and Palme Dutt naturally came down hard. They wrote material in The Communist, the theoretical journal of the CP, and in the pages of the *Daily Worker*, denouncing the united front of workers' organisations in Germany and Trotsky.

> "Question: Cannot the socialist and communists unite? Cannot all workers' organisations - the Communist Party, the Socialist Party and the trade union and the co-operatives come together and do something to resist the drive to fascism?
>
> "Answer: It is undoubtedly necessary to create working class unity but this must be unity between the workers in the factories and the streets, and not unity between the Communist Party and the Social Democratic Party, which is not a working class party.... For the Communist Party to unite with such a party would be to become an accomplice in the drive to fascist dictatorship." (*Daily Worker*, 13 August 1932)

On 11 February 1933, the *Daily Worker* stated: "He [James Maxton, ILP leader] presents the Social Democratic leadership as though it stood for the working class struggle against capitalism and was not in fact the chief support of capitalism. He conceals the fact that building the united working class front is only possible by a steady determined struggle against those whose policy is to split the front and disorganise the working class ranks - viz the Social Democratic leadership." (*Daily Worker*, 11 February 1933)

And again on 4 May 1933, three months after Hitler's victory: "The enormous treachery of the social democracy has called forth such a storm of indignation among the workers of all countries that other parties of the Second International have even declined to come forward in their defence.

> "But the social democrats have found one ally. And this is Trotsky. As a political cipher in the working class movement he has nothing to lose. He slobbers over the fascist jack-boot, calculating that he can make people talk about him, with the object of reappearing from his political oblivion for even one small hour at any price whatever." (*Daily Worker*, 4 May 1933)

For these Party hacks, faithfully following Stalin's Line, the social democrats were the main enemy of the working class, the main agency of capitalism within the ranks of the working class. The Stalinists talked glibly of a united front "from below", as if the rank and file could be easily separated from its leadership. This ultra-left policy lead to disaster. This suicidal policy pursued by the German Stalinists led in the end to the victory of Hitler and the crushing of the German working class, and prepared the way for the Second World War.

Trotsky took a personal interest in these developments in Britain, engaging in correspondence with the Balham comrades. He urged them repeatedly to organise and place their work on a sound footing. "The British Left Opposition must begin systematic work", wrote Trotsky to Reg Groves. "You must establish our staff-centre though a small one. You must build your publication, even on a modest scale...It is necessary to have a steady, uninterrupted activity, to educate our cadres, although in the first stages few. The fundamental power of history is in our favour. When, in Britain, more so than elsewhere, communism in a short time can conquer the consciousness of the wide masses, so can conquer; in the same short time, within the communist movement, the supremacy of the ideas of the Left Opposition, that is, the ideas of Marx and Lenin." [8]

In August 1932, the majority of the comrades in the Balham and Tooting branches of the CP were expelled for "Trotskyism". Excluded from the party, they had no alternative but to form themselves into an openly Trotskyist organisation, campaigning for a return to Leninist ideas. They called their group, made up of a dozen people, the "Communist League" and started to publish in May a monthly paper called the *Red Flag*. The founding of the Communist League represented a qualitative leap forward in the establishment of a genuine Trotskyist organisation in Britain. Following Trotsky's advice, they established themselves as an expelled faction of the Communist movement, and sought to fight for the party's return to its original ideas and programme.

As soon as the *Red Flag* appeared Trotsky wrote a letter on 22 July 1933 welcoming this "modest step forward", with the advice to study the policy of the CPGB alongside that of the Left Opposition in order to educate their ranks. "While persistently striving to widen our influence among the workers, we must at the same time concentrate on the theoretical and political education of our own ranks", wrote Trotsky. "We have a long and laborious road ahead of us. For this we need first-class cadres."

The expulsion of the Balham Group from the CP resulted in complete isolation from the ranks of the Party. Yet while the road to the communist workers was closed, new opportunities for revolutionary work opened up elsewhere. The world economic crisis and the experience of the Labour Government 1929 -1931 had produced a massive left current within the ranks of the Labour Party. This reflected itself in the sharp swing to the left of the ILP, an affiliated section of the Labour Party with some 100,000 mainly working class supporters. Led by the group of Clydeside MPs, Maxton, McGovern and Campbell Stevens, they had waged a struggle against the capitalist policies of the McDonald government. The ranks of the ILP, under the hammer blow of events, were in ferment and were moving in a revolutionary direction. They were in the process of shifting from reformism in a centrist direction, and were endeavouring to draw revolutionary conclusions from their experience. For Marxism, centrism signifies a confused spectrum of ideas somewhere between reformism and revolution, which is an inevitable stage in the process of radicalisation of the masses.

Trotsky and the ILP

The working class learns through its experience, and especially through the experience of great events that shake and transform the existing consciousness. Gradually, the class begins to draw revolutionary conclusions. But this process is not automatic. The mass cannot proceed immediately to a fully worked out revolutionary programme. In the first place, when the masses move into political action they always express themselves through their traditional mass organisations. In Britain that means the trade unions and the Labour Party, of which until 1932, the ILP was an affiliated part.

The crisis of capitalism therefore expresses itself in the formation of a mass left wing inside the existing mass organisations. This will at first inevitably have a left reformist or centrist character. The task of the Marxists is to participate in the mass left wing, to fertilise it with revolutionary ideas and assist the leftward-moving workers to draw revolutionary conclusions. Trotsky, who wrote in an article on the ILP, very well understood this: "Similar processes are to be observed in other countries. A left wing forms within the social-democratic parties which splits off at the following stage from the party and tries with its own forces to pave for itself a revolutionary path." [9]

At its Easter 1932 conference, after MacDonald's open betrayal and the formation of the National Government, the ILP took the decision to disaffiliate from the Labour Party. The disputed issue was over Labour's standing orders and the independence of ILP Members of Parliament. According to Trotsky, this decision to disaffiliate was a mistake, splitting for the wrong reasons, using the wrong methods and at the wrong time. Nevertheless, Trotsky recognised that this split represented an attempted break with reformism, and opened possibilities for the emergence of a mass revolutionary current. After the victory of Hitler, Trotsky entered into an energetic correspondence with the ILP with a view to drawing it closer to the Trotskyist movement. At this time, the ILP leaders had moved close to the Communist Party on the basis of a so-called united front, and were under the influence of Stalinism. Trotsky sought to counteract this pernicious influence in a series of articles written for the ILP press, urging the party to clarify its ideas and join the initiative of the International Communist League in an international venture for a new workers' international.

"The ILP can save the workers' movement of Britain from this new danger [from Stalinism]", wrote Trotsky in November, "only by freeing itself from all unclarity and haziness with regard to the ways and methods of the socialist revolution and by becoming a truly revolutionary party of the proletariat." [10]

Trotsky saw in these developments inside the ILP an enormous opportunity for the weak forces of British Trotskyism to overcome their isolation and connect with the mass movement of the working class. He was no stranger to the need for flexible tactics and a bold turn when events required it. Therefore, for the first time, in mid-1933 Trotsky raised the question of the entry of the Trotskyists into the ILP. His advice broadly speaking was that there were a hundred thousand workers moving towards revolutionary ideas, and it was therefore necessary that the comrades should actively participate in this mass movement in order to give it a revolutionary direction. The British Trotskyists should participate and try to win over the best elements if not the majority of the party to the programme of Bolshevism-Leninism, i.e. to the programme of Trotskyism.

Wicks, Groves, Dewar, and Sara largely influenced the newly-formed Communist League. Reg Groves was regarded as the main leader of the group. When Trotsky raised the question of entry into the ILP, it provoked an almighty row in the League. The discussion revealed that the leading lights of the group were very inflexible and had little grasp of revolutionary tactics. They simply stuck rigidly to the idea of an independent party, irrespective of its size or the circumstances. They dismissed Trotsky's position, arguing they could influence the best elements of the ILP from outside. In the end, their methods proved incapable of seizing the opportunities within the ILP.

Trotsky was scathing in his criticism of the sectarians who proclaim the independence of the party as a "principle" - whether it is a party of one or one million. "A Marxist party should, of course, strive to full independence and to the highest homogeneity", he wrote to the British comrades. "But in the process of its formation, a Marxist party often has to act as a faction of a centrist and even reformist party. Thus the Bolsheviks adhered for a number of years to the same party as the Mensheviks. Thus, the Third International only gradually formed itself out of the Second." He continued, "It is worth entering the ILP only if we make it our purpose to help this party, that is, its *revolutionary majority*, to transform it into a truly Marxist party." [11]

When it was necessary to have a flexible attitude, the leadership of the British group simply dug in its heels and reiterated the so-called principle of the independence of the revolutionary party. In reply to Trotsky, they maintained that they would build a mass revolutionary party outside of the ILP, and outside of the Communist Party, simply by raising their banner. The argument over this issue lasted almost a year, and therefore valuable time was lost. In the meantime the field was left open to the Stalinists, who had finally realised the possibilities of work in the ILP. Unlike these hidebound sectarians, the Stalinists quickly sent forces into the ILP and established their faction around the Revolutionary Policy Committee.

The dogmatic attitude of the leading comrades was therefore a big obstacle. They refused point blank to countenance entry into the ILP. "Doctrinaire intransigence is an essential trait of Bolshevism, but it makes up only 10 percent of its historic content; the other 90 percent is applying principles to the real movement; its participating in the mass organisations, above all the youth, who ask only for our support", warned Trotsky.[12] Eventually, after a prolonged and heated argument, the issue led to a split in the organisation. While the experienced majority stuck rigidly to their guns, the minority of younger and more inexperienced comrades took Trotsky's advice and entered the ILP.

The International Secretariat, rather than condemning the minority, under the circumstances urged both groups to see what they could do, once they had freed themselves from the factional atmosphere that had consumed the group over the previous period. For the time being, Groves, Wicks, Dewar and Sara carried on as before. They continued to proclaim their ideas and programme at open-air meetings, appealing to the masses to join them. However, their attempt to influence the ILP from outside led nowhere. They were ignored by the mass of workers, who began to move through the trade union movement, and into political activity.

As could have been predicted, these "principled" leaders, who had so haughtily rejected Trotsky's advice to enter the ILP, very rapidly performed a complete sommersault and ended up in the Labour Party on an entirely opportunist basis. This is a law with the ultra-lefts everywhere. Their opportunism was only the reverse side of their earlier ultra-left attitude. Very quickly they sank almost without trace. Groves was absorbed almost entirely into the Labour Party milieu, being selected as a Labour parliamentary candidate, while the others buried themselves in the National Council of Labour Colleges and the Labour Party. They had made their contribution in the early stage, but were to play no important role in the future development of the Trotskyist movement.

A small minority of comrades, led by Denzil Harber and Stewart Kirby, entered the ILP in March 1934. They clearly faced an uphill struggle. Valuable time had been lost. The ILP was already in decline, and rapidly losing membership. The Trotskyists were numerically small -

no more than a dozen strong. As a result of their political inexperience, but also - it must be said - of their middle-class composition and mentality, they failed to make the gains that Trotsky had thought possible. But not all was lost. Despite the difficulties, they did make certain progress. Their ideas had an effect on the best elements in and around the ILP and they managed to win over some talented individuals, such as CLR James. James was a West Indian who came over to Britain to play cricket, and decided to stay on as a cricketing correspondent for the *Manchester Guardian*. He came into contact with the group in London, was won over to Trotskyism and joined them inside the ILP. He wrote a book called *World Revolution* in 1937, and a year later his more famous book entitled *Black Jacobins*, about the slave rebellions during the French Revolution.

However, the evolution of British Trotskyism was influenced in a decisive way by the participation of new arrivals from South Africa, who pushed the movement in an entirely different direction. At this point it is therefore necessary to say a few words about the origins of Trotskyism in South Africa.

Trotskyism in South Africa

It is difficult now for people to realise the terrible difficulties that faced the workers' movement in South Africa in those dark days before the War. Even more difficult was the work of the revolutionary wing. It took a special kind of person to undertake such work, and such a person was my friend and comrade Ralph (Raff) Lee, the man who recruited me to the movement when I was still 15 years of age and who remained loyal to the ideas of Trotskyism until his tragic and premature death.

Ralph (or Raff, which is short for Raphael) played an important role in the birth of South African and British Trotskyism. He had been a member of the South African Communist Party since 1922, but was expelled during the first Stalinist purges. Ralph Lee had made contact with the international Trotskyist movement in early 1929 via the American *Militant* which had been dispatched to South Africa by the newly-founded Communist League of America. It was a revelation that changed our lives completely and I started on a political road that now spans more than seventy years.

Ralph Lee, himself still only in his early twenties, was also closely associated with another young Trotskyist, Murray Gow Purdy, who in turn had been a pupil of the very first South African Trotskyist, Frank Glass - a founding member of the Communist Party of South Africa (CPSA). Glass and his wife, Fanny Klennerman, had established a left-wing bookshop in Von Brandis Street, Johannesburg called Vanguard Booksellers, and it was here that I picked up my first copy of the American *Militant*. Like many others, Glass left South Africa for greater opportunities elsewhere. He ended up in China in 1930 where he played a pivotal role among the Chinese Trotskyists.

After leaving boarding school at 15, I got a job in a shipping company chasing up invoices. This allowed me to travel around and also gave me free time to read. This I put to full use studying the classics of Marxism. Ralph Lee organised a group of a handful of people - apart from myself there was Purdy, Millie Kahn - who later became Lee's wife - Raymond Lake, John Saperstein, Max Basch, as well as my sister Zena. In April 1934, we constituted ourselves as the Bolshevik-Leninist League of South Africa, and established links with another newly founded Trotskyist group in Cape Town. [13]

▶
Ralph Lee

▲ Millie Kahn (front left) in Nyasseland, May 1929

The Committee of the African Laundry Workers Union, with Murray Gow Purdy (holding hat), Johannesburg, 1934
▲

Millie had joined the Trotskyists, having been at first influenced by her mother who was a friend of Fanny Klennerman. Her sister, however, had joined the Communist Party, and they would not speak to one another for years. After joining the group, she moved to live with Lee in Johannesburg. My family also moved to Kerk Street in Johannesburg, where my mother ran the grocery store. Eventually, I left home and moved in with Ralph. From the centre of Johannesburg we were able to develop our political work more effectively.

In June 1934, Purdy had become Organising Secretary of a revived African Laundry Workers Union. In an attempt to build a base amongst the black working class, the group turned its whole attention to this work. This was the first practical initiative aimed at recovering the field of black trade union work, which the Stalinists had first wrecked and then abandoned. [14]

After they were married, Ralph and Millie moved into a shack next to the union headquarters, and began to raise funds for the union. "We lived next to the union offices", recalls Millie. "Sure, it was damned uncomfortable, but what did we care? They used to hold the union meetings in our back yard. We tried to raise money in various ways. I remember we collected bottles, cut off the tops, and then painted them. Raff was pretty good at art. But otherwise it was a dud financially." [15]

Within a matter of months, and after a successful recruiting drive, a strike took place towards the end of August, which resulted in the union winning recognition at a number of firms. Millie recalls marching with the black strikers through the streets of Johannesburg. "I was on my own as the other comrades were away I believe, and I got quite a lot of abuse from people shouting from the buildings. But we remained defiant." However, the agreement with the employers was broken, arrests were made and a number of strikers victimised. Purdy himself was imprisoned. It was, nevertheless, an historic struggle and a landmark in the history of the black South African working class. If nothing else, the struggle of the Laundry Workers' Union left behind an important tradition.

'Broader horizons'

Before the war, the black working class in South Africa was far smaller than today. The possibilities for our work were really very limited. The young South African Trotskyists looked for greater possibilities for socialist revolution in Europe, with its mighty working class and traditions. I took the decision to leave South Africa in the search for broader horizons for revolutionary work in Europe. Given the Commonwealth connections and language, Britain was the obvious choice.

Those who remained behind faced a very difficult time. The terrible problems are alluded to in the correspondence of the time. "The caretaker in the tenement where Mil and I live," wrote Lee, "has objected to the 'Kaffirs' who visit our room. We have been déclassé for a long time with our neighbours, the usual riff-raff of billiard room rats, odd jobs gentlemen, canvassers, taxi drivers and trollops that inhabit 'buildings'. So now we pack up and move again." [16]

Purdy, who was an adventurer and somewhat unstable, clashed repeatedly with Lee. "Our personal relations are now strained to the utmost", wrote Lee, "the way he glowers openly at me during branch meetings is ludicrous, and we can hardly exchange a civil word, let alone discuss any questions." [17] To add to the strains, Purdy latched onto the "French Turn" to create a fuss, increasing the internal difficulties of a small isolated group. In May Lee wrote, "I feel quite despondent at this moment about the immediate prospects of the International and the Workers Party of South Africa... Our immediate pressing task is to discover links with the masses of workers." [18] However in June, Lee wrote to Paul Koston, the secretary of the WPSA, "party affairs are in a hell of a mess here." [19] Eventually, Purdy was expelled and the group reorganised.

Between 1936-37, Lee acted as the general secretary of the WPSA, which was the official section of the International. Known to the Stalinists as "Johannesburg's chief protagonist and

Murray Gow Purdy with another Laundy Workers Union leader, Johannesburg 1934

defender of Leon Trotsky", the group was under tremendous pressure. Their turn towards the black working class led them into a close alliance with a number of metal workers, who began to take up some militant demands. In February 1937, the group provided invaluable support to these workers who went on strike for higher wages and better conditions. After ten days, the strike was broken with the connivance of the Stalinists and 16 strikers were arrested. Lee and another comrade, Max Sapire, paid the fines, but the strike had gone down to defeat.

The comrades had provided tremendous financial and moral support to the strike. Lee had "worked tirelessly... performing a score of tasks, approaching other organisations, collecting funds and even selling his few possessions to do so." The Africans also paid testimony to the support they had received from "coms. Heaton, Frieslich, Kahn, etc." [20]

Purdy, who had developed extreme ultra-left tendencies, went off to Abyssinia, and then on to India where he established a party called the Trotskyist Mazdoor Party. Muddled politically, Purdy developed an erroneous theory that India's untouchables were the proletarian vanguard. He was however fully involved in the struggle for national independence from Britain, and was sentenced in early 1946 to 10-years imprisonment as a result of a "revolutionary expropriation". On his early release after Independence in 1947, he was deported. Subsequently, in the same year he attended the Second World Congress of the Fourth International, and also visited me in London. But disillusioned with Trotskyism, he subsequently dropped out of the movement.

"Not long after the laundry workers' strike", writes Ian Hunter, "two of the youngest members of the group left Johannesburg to begin making their way to the centre of world action in Europe. These were Max Basch and Ted Grant. The Cape Town and Johannesburg groups had by then been in contact with each other for some time, and Grant and Basch were able to stop with the Cape Town Trotskyists whilst waiting for a suitable ship. Grant took the opportunity to deliver his first public speech, an account of the events of the laundry strike, to one of the Lenin Club's open air street meetings outside the Castle Street Post Office, and chaired on this occasion by Charlie Van Gelderen." [21] Unfortunately, as I remember, I didn't speak too well.

Together with Sid Frost (Max Basch), I took a German-owned passenger-cargo ship, which took about six weeks to reach Europe, stopping at numerous ports along the coast of West Africa. I recall one stop-off at Lagos, where we disembarked for a coffee. We followed the other passengers and ended up in a small coffee place, and we laughed like hell when the other South Africans sat down. They were horrified, being used to "white only" places, when blacks deliberately sat next to them. "Bloody Kaffirs!" they muttered, powerless to do anything about it. Oh, we had some great laughs then!

After a long journey, our ship reached its final destination in France. We took a train to Paris to meet with the French Trotskyists, who had adopted the "French turn" a few months earlier and, following Trotsky's advice, had just entered the French Socialist Party. Among others, we met Trotsky's son, Leon Sedov, who was a member of the International Secretariat and co-ordinator of the work of the International Communist League. He was later murdered by Stalin's agents whilst in hospital. We also met Jeanne Martin, Erwin Wolff, who was murdered in Spain, as well as Pierre Frank, Raymond Molinier and Erwin Bauer. The last-named, who was opposed to the "French turn", and looking for allies, was keen to speak with us. Molinier and Frank were expelled within a year on Trotsky's insistence, after breaking with the French group.

> "I came across to Britain with Ted in the autumn of 1934, arriving in England in December", recalled Sid Frost. "We sailed from South Africa in a ship that was German-owned, which the comrades thought a bit risky at the time, in view of Hitler's recent accession to power, but we docked safely in France and made our way to Paris in an eight-hour night train journey. We had been given details on how to make contact with the comrades there before we left South Africa. We were to walk along a famous boulevard (Montparnasse, I think) opposite a certain café, and after about an hour someone came out and made contact. The Trotskyists used to meet in the café there, and soon we met Leon Sedov, his wife [Jeanne Martin], Erwin Wolff, Pierre Frank, Bauer and Raymond Molinier." [22]

Trotsky was living in France at this time, and we were obviously keen to meet him, but we were doomed to disappointment. The political situation in the country was highly unstable. In February, the fascists had attempted to bring down the government, and the Stalinists were waging a constant campaign against Trotsky. Given the tight security surrounding his household, Trotsky was completely isolated in the mountain village of Domesne, near Grenoble. Under these circumstances, it was not possible for two unknown young comrades from South Africa to visit him.

Instead, Leon Sedov discussed a number of things with us, including the "French turn" and the situation in France and Britain. I had the impression that he wasn't very happy with the way things were progressing in Britain and in particular with the leadership of the group, who had only recently commenced work within the Independent Labour Party. My later experience showed me why.

The Marxist Group

Sid Frost and myself arrived in London at the end of 1934 and got a place to stay in Kings Cross. At this time, a number of other people in London and elsewhere were also won to the banner of Trotskyism. We had been in correspondence with the British comrades and had received copies of their earlier paper *Red Flag*. We joined the group straight away, ending up in the Holborn branch of the ILP. I immediately set about speaking for the group at ILP meetings about the "Labour Movement in South Africa", mainly drawing on the lessons of the recent laundry workers' strike in Johannesburg.

By this time, within the ILP the supporters of the Revolutionary Policy Committee had built up a significant left wing opposition to the leadership. They attempted to pull the ILP in the direction of Stalinism. While this group had some criticisms of the "third period" ultra-leftism, they leaned towards the position of Bukharin and the Communist Right Opposition. Their leading lights, Dr. CK Cullen and Jack Gaster, worked hard to influence the ILP towards a fusion with the Communist Party. These days, the Right Opposition of the Communist International, the supporters of Buharkin-Brandler-Lovestone, are totally unknown to most people even on the left. They have disappeared completely as a political current not only in Britain but internationally. However, at this time, they had quite big forces in the Soviet Union, Sweden and Germany. At one stage, they even had the majority of the Communist movement in America. Yet, as Trotsky had predicted, because they were not based on fundamental principles and a clear programme, they were doomed to disintegrate and disappear. The Right Opposition was only prepared to challenge the Stalinists on their ultra-left zigzag course in the Comintern, but tended to excuse Stalin's bureaucratic policies and regime within the USSR. Hand in hand with the Stalinists, they participated in the attacks on Trotskyism, and were our main opponents in the ILP, apart from the leadership, of course.

In contrast to the Right Opposition, Leon Trotsky, ever since his expulsion from the Soviet Union in 1929, had worked strenuously to build up a Leninist faction internationally. The Trotskyists saw their prime task as the reform of the Comintern, with the idea of bringing it back onto the road of Leninism as well as the reintroduction of workers' democracy in the Soviet Union. Trotsky right up until 1933 and the victory of Hitler defended this perspective. The victory of Hitler constituted an historic turning point for Trotsky. The utter failure of the German debacle, which was caused primarily by the ultra-left policies of the Stalinists, to stir up any opposition or criticism within the ranks of the Communist International, meant that the Comintern was dead. Incredibly, the leadership of the Comintern declared their policies absolutely correct. "After Hitler", they said, "our turn!" The actions of the Stalinists were comparable to the betrayal of the social democrats in 1914. Trotsky drew the conclusion that reform of the Comintern was no longer tenable, and that new revolutionary parties would have to be built and a new international prepared. "After the shameful capitulation of the Communist International in Germany", stated Trotsky, "the Bolshevik-Leninists, without hesitating a moment, proclaimed: the Third International is dead!" [23]

At this time, the ILP leadership, true to its centrist position, wanted to maintain its "independent" affiliation to the so-called London Bureau, an international body of centrist organisations. The ILP leaders, who had initially moved closer to the Communist Party, now pulled back in order to maintain their "independence", by which they meant the right of the ILP leadership to have control over their own internal affairs, which they wanted to conduct without any outside interference - including from Moscow. By the time of its Easter conference in 1934, the ILP had severed its links with the Comintern. This constituted a major blow to the Stalinists but it opened a window of opportunity for the Trotskyists to forcefully raise the question of support for a Fourth International.

However, the ILP was determined to maintain their customary centrist stance of a so-called middle road between two "extremes" - that is, to sink ever deeper into the centrist swamp. In the words of Brockway, "The ILP experimented in many directions, at one time approaching the Communist International, at another moving towards the Trotskyist position." For more than two years Trotsky had conducted a vigorous correspondence with the leaders of the ILP, hoping to break the best of them away from centrism and open the way for the development of a genuine revolutionary party. However, the ILP leadership chose to ignore Trotsky's arguments and led the ILP into a political and organisational blind alley.

Throughout this period, the inexperienced forces of Trotskyism tried their best to influence the ranks of the ILP. However, their lack of authority, as well as their lack of understanding of how to work, made it difficult for these young comrades to make significant headway. Nevertheless, over a period, the organisation managed to get a toehold within the ILP. It was a beginning, but the opportunities within the ILP were disappearing fast.

Bankruptcy of the ILP

The events in Germany fell like a thunderbolt in Britain. The entire labour and trade union movement was in a state of ferment. In the meeting of the TUC that was held after the victory of Hitler, there was uproar. The German labour movement had been one of the most powerful in the world, yet Hitler had been allowed to come to power virtually without a fight. The German unions had not even succeeded in organising a general strike. How could this be explained? Walter Citrine, replying from the platform, said: "If our German comrades would have fought, it would have meant civil war." He tried to frighten the delegates with the spectre of civil war, the streets running with blood and so on.

In reality, it would have been far better for the German workers to have fought - even if they were defeated, which is not at all certain - than to surrender without a fight, which is what happened. In such cases, the effect is total demoralisation. It explains why Germany was the only country on the European Continent where there was no organised Resistance movement against the Nazis. The workers were shattered and demoralised by the surrender of the leaders. Nor did this crime of the Stalinists and Social Democrats avoid bloodshed, as

Citrine and the others hypocritically maintained. On the contrary, the victory of Hitler led to the most terrible bloodshed. Millions of communists, socialists, trade unionists and Jews ended up in the concentration camps and within a few years the world was plunged into a war where 55 million people lost their lives. So much for the "realistic" policies of reformism!

The RED FLAG

Monthly Organ of the British Section, International Left Opposition

Number One. Vol. I. · One Penny. · May 1933

FOR LENIN AND TROTSKY!

On The Anti-Fascist Front.

A LETTER FROM GERMANY.

Why The RED FLAG Appears.

TO REGENERATE REVOLUTIONARY MOVEMENT.

THE MILITANT

(Incorporating "Youth Militant,") Organ of the Militant Group in the Labour Party

VOL. I. No. 1. JULY, 1937 ONE PENNY

"UNITY" MONGERS SURRENDER!

Now For A Real Left Wing!

In 1934, 1935 and 1936, the British Union of Fascists, led by Sir Oswald Mosley, went onto the offensive, lavishly supplied with money from big business and buoyed up by the victories of fascism in Italy, Germany and Austria. Mosley's Blackshirt thugs marched into working class and Jewish areas, provoking and beating up the people with no intervention by the police. At Olympia in June 1934 and the Albert Hall in March 1936, they violently assaulted opponents and even peaceful hecklers. Instead of dealing with the fascist bullies, the police instead attacked the anti-fascist demonstrators with baton charges.

Roused by the victory of Hitler, the British workers prepared to fight to defend their organisations. We waged an energetic campaign for a workers' united front against fascism. Together with workers from the Communist Party, Labour Party, ILP and trade unions, the Trotskyists, including myself, participated in the famous battle of Cable Street, where Mosley's Blackshirts were confronted by the organised might of the Labour movement and completely smashed. One hundred thousand people built barricades in the street to stop a march by 7,000 fascists. There was s real battle, with lorries upturned and the streets strewn with broken glass to prevent charges by mounted police. Finally, the Blackshirts were physically prevented from marching into the East End of London. It was a tremendous victory for the united front tactic, which Trotsky had advocated from the very beginning.

In October 1935 Mussolini's fascist troops marched into Abyssinia, provoking war between the two countries. The question of the attitude towards this war immediately assumed a great importance. Without hesitation, Trotsky gave critical support to the Abyssinian people in their colonial struggle against fascist Italy and imperialism. A defeat for Mussolini, noted Trotsky, would also constitute a massive blow against Mussolini and help undermine the Italian fascist regime. At first, the position taken by the ILP was generally positive, which was, in effect, to support workers' sanctions against Italy instead of the economic sanctions imposed by the League of Nations. However, Trotsky attacked the woolly position of the ILP parliamentary leaders, like McGovern, who wanted to cover up their bankruptcy under the fig leaf of pacifism. In the end the ILP, trailing after their parliamentary wing, took a neutral position, saying in effect that it was a conflict "between rival dictators".

In the run up to the general election of 1935 a dispute broke out within the Marxist Group over which Labour Party candidates to support. There wasn't exactly a split, but a massive argument over this issue that tended to paralyse the work of intervening in the election. A group of comrades adopted the position of the ILP leadership who only wanted to back those candidates who were against League of Nations' sanctions. They dressed this up by saying economic sanctions would lead to military sanctions and then to war. In effect, the ILP leadership portrayed these anti-sanctions candidates as the left-wing candidates. "How can we support candidates who support economic sanctions that could lead to imperialist war?" they said. So they ended up abandoning a class position and supporting the muddled position of the ILP leaders.

Trotsky intervened in the discussions to oppose this position. For Trotsky, whether one was for or against sanctions was not of fundamental importance. In seats where the ILP was not contesting, he insisted, the ILP must give support to the Labour Party candidates, whether they supported sanctions or not. It was a class question of supporting a workers' party against a bourgeois party. "Moreover", stated Trotsky, "the London Division's policy of giving critical support only to anti-sanctionists would imply a fundamental distinction between the social-patriots like Morrison and Ponsonby or - with your permission - even Cripps. Actually, their differences are merely propagandistic. Cripps is actually only a second class supporter of the bourgeoisie." [24] The Marxists wanted Labour to win the election in order to put the Labour leaders in power, so that their reformist policies could be put to the test. Here we can see the way in which Trotsky posed matters, very clearly, very soberly, very cautiously, but at the same time, posing a bold theoretical perspective for the movement.

By 1935, the Labour Party had recovered from the crushing blow of the 1931 defeat. The ILP on the other hand, as a result of its centrist politics, began to disintegrate and lose its active membership. Centrism is the most fatal position for a would-be revolutionary tendency. It was a halfway house that sought a middle path between Stalinism and Trotskyism, reformism and revolution. In the beginning, the ILP hankered after the Communist Party, which gave it a revolutionary aura. In doing so, it failed to turn its attention towards the mass organisations - the Labour Party and the trade unions. Trotsky said that the ILP, even with a hundred thousand members, was a very small organisation compared to the Labour Party.

Trotsky advised the ILP firstly to clarify their ideas and adopt a Marxist programme, secondly to face towards the workers in the reformist mass organisations - the unions and the Labour Party, and thirdly, to join the movement for a new Fourth International. He urged them to turn their back decisively on the Communist Party, which had dropped the old "third period" ultra-leftism, but was now leaning towards opportunism, as expressed in the theory of the Popular Front. This represented a serious danger to the leftward-moving workers. Instead, he recommended them to turn towards the Labour Party. The Labour Party, he argued, was based on the trade unions, and the trade unions were composed of millions of workers. He considered that the ILP leaders had split from the Labour Party prematurely - at the wrong time and on the wrong issue:

> "The ILP split from the Labour Party chiefly for the sake of its parliamentary fraction", wrote Trotsky. "We do not intend here to discuss whether the split was correct at that *given moment*, and whether the ILP gleaned from it the expected advantages. We don't think so. But it remains a fact that for every revolutionary organisation in England its attitude to the masses and to the class is almost coincident with its attitude towards the Labour Party." [25]

Trotsky sharply criticised the ILP leaders for their confused policies, their pacifism and their failure to face towards the Labour Party. Trotsky wrote many letters to the ILP explaining these issues and urging them to reconsider their position. But this advice fell on deaf ears. The ILP leaders simply ignored Trotsky's advice. "What does Trotsky know of the real position in Britain being so far away in Norway - on the heights of Oslo?" they jibbed. They appreciated his views against Stalinism - which they used to great effect - but completely ignored his revolutionary criticisms of centrism.

Although at the time of the split the ILP may have had the support of around 100,000 workers, they were soon reduced to impotence. The mass of workers could not see any fundamental difference between the confused centrist ideas of the ILP and the left reformist policies being advocated by Lansbury and Attlee, who, under the pressure of the working class, began to talk very "left". Where there are two reformist parties with no fundamental difference in programme and policy, the workers will always tend to support the bigger of the two.

The false policies and orientation of the ILP leaders eventually resulted in a sharp decline in their membership and support. From a large organisation - with the potential of becoming a mass movement - instead, the ILP became a rump. Thousands and thousands of members of the ILP simply drifted into inactivity, and moved out of the movement altogether. All that was left of the ILP in the end was an empty shell - and the enormous property the ILP had built up. They possessed a big apparatus. In every part of the country, in every district, there were ILP rooms and buildings. But that was all. The ILP, which started with so much potential for developing a mass revolutionary party, due to its false policies and sectarian approach, squandered everything. The hopes of hundreds of thousands of revolutionary-minded workers were dashed. Within a measurable space of time the Labour Party recovered and began to move to the left.

As early as April 1935, there were growing doubts about our work in the ILP and also about the functioning of the Marxist Group. Having worked closely with the British comrades for a number of months, we became increasingly dissatisfied with the leadership and the way in which the group was functioning. In April 1935, a joint letter, addressed directly to Leon Sedov, was sent to the International Secretariat (IS) in Paris, signed by myself, Stuart Kirby, Denzil Harber, Sid Frost and a few others complaining bitterly about the situation within the Group:

"Since the 1934 Annual Conference the decline in the membership and influence of the ILP has continued steadily", the letter explained. "A year ago the then secret Bolshevik-Leninist fraction in the ILP had a little under thirty members, almost all active. All these were in London, where some ten branches supported our line at the 1934 Winter Divisional Conference (which, by the way, was held in January, before most of the comrades of the Minority of the old Communist League had entered the party and before the fraction had been organised). At the 1934 Annual Conference held at Easter of last year, 20 branches voted for the Fourth International." A year later, "the vote for the Fourth International was so insignificant that no count was taken."

Regarding the real gains that were made in the ILP, the letter states: *"Since the entry of the Minority of the old Communist League into the ILP not one member of the party has been won over to our position in the London Division*, all our support having come from either new members (whom, in most cases, we had converted to Bolshevik-Leninism before they joined the ILP), or from old ILPers who had, to a greater or lesser extent, adopted our position before we had entered - in most cases owing to the propaganda carried out by the old Communist League." (Emphasis in original).

The letter then turned to the internal situation within the Marxist Group. "With regard to the internal position of the group of Bolshevik-Leninists, the position is far worse today than it was a year ago." We observed a dangerous growth of centrist tendencies within the group itself. There was a "fetish of doing ILP work and of 'loyalty' to the ILP leadership and constitution." As an example of this, it says "recently two South African comrades said in a private discussion with comrade [Margaret] Johns, a member of the committee of the Marxist Group, that they thought that under certain circumstances, the Labour League of Youth (youth organisation of the Labour Party) might be found to be a better field for our work than the ILP. At the next meeting of the Holborn Branch of the ILP (of which both comrade Johns and the South African comrades are members), comrade Johns, in the absence of the South African comrades, accused them of disloyalty to the ILP, in as much as they thought the Labour League of Youth a better organisation than the ILP, and on these grounds moved their expulsion from the branch and from the party [sic!]. Certain of our comrades managed to get this matter postponed for a time so that the comrades in question should have an opportunity for defending themselves."

The two South Africans referred to were Sid Frost and myself. We had been in Britain for less than six months before running into the crass opportunism of the leadership of the Marxist Group, who had adapted themselves to the ILP bureaucracy. The letter went on to accuse the leadership of the group of creating "a small clique of perhaps half a dozen, which designs to guide the policy of the Marxist Group and maintain relations with the IS." It informed the IS that the situation within the ILP was so bad, that Kirby and Harber had left the ILP and entered the Labour Party where they have established a Bolshevik-Leninist Group. "They left the ILP individually, since they felt that they could work there no longer, and are now working for Bolshevik-Leninist principles in a new environment." They now considered such individual resignations a "tactical error".

This letter must have influenced the views of the International Secretariat about the situation in Britain, and in particular the exaggerations of the group's leadership. There can be no doubt such correspondence would have been passed on to Trotsky, who at that time was closely following the situation within the ILP. The letter would surely have influenced his evaluation of the ILP and the question of a turn towards the Labour Party. In fact, towards the end of 1935, Trotsky drew the same conclusions about the ILP and called for a new orientation towards the Labour Party.

Trotsky and the Labour Party

In analysing the movement in Britain, Trotsky showed not only a profound understanding, but also a sensitivity to the mass movement and how it would develop. Above all, he was keen to educate the young forces of Trotskyism against sectarianism and ultra-leftism. Trotsky came to the conclusion that the experience of the ILP must be drawn to a close. There was nothing more to be gained by work in the rump that remained within the ILP. There were clearly more favourable opportunities opening up within the Labour Party, especially the Labour League of Youth. "Since the ILP youth seem to be few and scattered, while the Labour Youth is the mass youth organisation, I would say: 'Do not only build fractions - seek to enter'," advised Trotsky. "The British section will recruit its first cadres from the thirty thousand young workers in the Labour League of Youth." [26] This was the first time in the history of our movement that entry was posed, not into a centrist organisation, but into a reformist organisation.

Trotsky wrote to our comrades in the ILP urging them to make the necessary turn towards the Labour Party. He told them they should prepare the ground by campaigning for the ILP to affiliate to the Labour Party. If the ILP refused to re-affiliate to the Labour Party, or even consider the question seriously, we should call on all revolutionaries to leave with us and join the struggle within the Labour Party. In the process, we would need to explain that the ILP was doomed as a revolutionary force, and we needed to draw all the necessary conclusions. The ILP could not now play the role that they had once hoped it would play, and it was necessary now to take all revolutionary forces into the Labour Party. Above all, in Trotsky's view, it was from the Labour Youth that the future major forces of British Trotskyism would emerge.

At each historical turn in events, there tends to be a split in the movement. What happened in 1933 would be repeated again in 1936. Trotsky raised this question of entry into the Labour Party, but the majority of the ILP comrades, including the leadership, were opposed and not prepared to follow his advice. They had, in effect, adapted themselves to life within the ILP. They were again determined to cling to the corpse, maintaining that black was white and the ILP offered the only way forward. For them work in the ILP was a "principled question", when in reality it was a question of tactics, as the Old Man pointed out:

> "It is not enough for a revolutionist to have correct ideas", wrote Trotsky. "Let us not forget that correct ideas have already been set down in *Capital* and in *The Communist Manifesto.* But that has not prevented false ideas from being broadcast. It is the task of the revolutionary party to weld together the correct ideas with the mass labour movement. Only in this manner can an idea become a driving force...
>
> "To conclude: the Koran says that the mountain came to the prophet. Marxism counsels the prophet to go to the mountain." [27]

Denzil Harber, as we have already pointed out, had entered the Labour Party in early 1935 to set up the Bolshevik-Leninist Group. I had joined the Labour Party myself, following the line of Trotsky at that time. CLR James, Arthur Cooper and other comrades who were the leadership of the ILP faction completely rejected entry into what they regarded as a reformist swamp. As I was in touch with both groupings, I had discussions with James, but he had developed other ideas. James and Cooper had illusions that they could influence Brockway and build a big movement inside the ILP. They failed to recognise that years of centrism had produced a certain ossification within the party. For the centrist ILP leaders, it had become an organic way of life. To a certain extent, this outlook had even affected the ILP rank and file. So the best way to influence the ranks of the ILP, as Trotsky explained, was to go into the Labour Party and build a revolutionary tendency there. They had to show by deeds what could be done and the way in which such a movement would develop. "I deem it absolutely necessary", wrote Trotsky in the summer of 1936, "for our comrades to break openly with the ILP and transfer to the Labour Party where, as is shown especially by the experience in the youth, much more can be accomplished." [28] Again, "the most important thing is to get in", urged Trotsky impatiently. [29]

Trotsky's arguments produced a massive crisis within the Marxist Group. There was a split and over a period a growing minority drifted into the Labour Party and began the task of building the "Bolshevik-Leninist Group". Unfortunately, once again valuable time had been lost. Trotsky was very critical of this time-wasting. "In Spain, where our section is carrying out a miserable political line, the youth, who were just becoming interested in the Fourth International, were handed over to the Stalinists", he said. "In England, where our people were too slow to get involved, the Stalinists have become the most important force among the Labour Party youth and we are in second place." [30] The failure of Nin and the Spanish Trotskyists, in the name of "independence", to enter the Socialist Youth was to contribute directly to the defeat of the Spanish Revolution. "The lads who called themselves Bolshevik-Leninists", wrote Trotsky, "and who permitted this, or better yet, who caused this, have to be stigmatised forever as criminals against the revolution." [31]

In Britain, the new group inside the Labour Party began the publication of a monthly journal called Youth Militant, aimed at members of the Labour League of Youth. Already operating in the Labour Party was the Marxist League of Wicks and Dewar. They had entered on an opportunist basis. Ironically, this seems to be a social law. Those individuals who take an ultra-left attitude tend to swing from one extreme to the other. Because they do not possess a balanced attitude and a Marxist understanding of the processes that take place within the mass organisations, they burn their fingers at every stage, jumping from ultra-leftism to opportunism and back again.

The question of how revolutionaries should work within the mass organisations was dealt with many times by Trotsky, and not only in relation to Britain. Just as Dewar had entered the Labour Party on an opportunist basis, so had Naville in France entered the Socialist Party, having previously opposed the idea as "capitulation" when Trotsky had first suggested it. Both started out bitterly against entrism in "principle", then somersaulted to the other extreme. Trotsky commented bitterly:

> "He [Naville] called the entry 'capitulation' because basically he was frightened by the prospect of a ferocious battle against a powerful apparatus", states Trotsky. "It is much easier to defend 'intransigent' principles in a sealed jar.... Since then Naville has entered the Socialist Party. But he abandoned the banner of the organisation, the programme. He does not wish to be more than the left wing of the SP. He has already presented motions in common with the left wing, confused opportunist motions, full of the verbiage of so-called centrism." [32]

CLR James, who was a key leader of the Marxist Group, and had been expelled from the ILP for publishing *Fight*, suddenly, without any real preparation, discovered the "principle" of the independent party. Like so many others before and since, he became hooked on this so-called principle. So, James, together with Arthur Cooper, organised his supporters into an independent Marxist Group, which continued to publish the *Fight* as its paper. James moved closer to Wicks, who assisted him in the writing of his well-known book *World Revolution*. In early 1938 they fused the two disintegrating groups to produce the Revolutionary Socialist League. Naturally, this fusion was predictably to prove completely barren.

When Trotsky later reviewed James' *World Revolution* he commented on it in a generally favourable way, but then pointed out that its main failing was the lack of a dialectical method, an arbitrary and formalistic approach to history. The same undialectical formalism can be seen in the attitude towards tactics and party building, not only on the part of CLR James but also of all the others who rejected Trotsky's advice on the Labour Party. They all had the same defect - formalism instead of Marxist dialectics.

In late 1937, the Militant Labour League was set up by the Bolshevik-Leninist Group, as a front organisation for its work inside the Labour Party. The Bolshevik-Leninists had by this time become known as the Militant Group, after the name of their paper. The Militant Labour League was supposed to be a left-wing organisation, not completely Trotskyist, aimed at organising the left inside the Labour Party. But it proved to be a dead letter. Our position in the Labour Party was confused with the contradictory position of an outer organisation and an inner organisation. This was bound to lead to friction as all members of the Militant Labour League, the open organisation, realised that the inner group was taking all the decisions. It also meant a duplication of apparatus, because nine-tenths of the members of the Militant Labour League were also members of the Militant Group. There was only a tiny periphery in the Militant Labour League who was not already members. The whole thing proved to be an extra burden with no results.

Therefore, this Militant Labour League was stillborn and destined to play no practical role. It had one or two centrists, and one or two left reformists looking for a platform, but it had no real importance. On the other hand, the Militant Group had won over a considerable portion of the Marxist Group. They had managed to grow inside the Labour Party, and had won over a layer of supporters in London, Leeds, Liverpool, and Glasgow. This also included Starkey Jackson and Jock Haston. Jackson, a very able man, had joined the Labour League of Youth at the age of 14. He lost his job as a result of his activities during the General Strike, and in the same year was elected to the first Youth Delegation to the USSR. He then joined the YCL, but was soon disillusioned with Stalinism and joined the Trotskyists. He soon became a leader and secretary of the organisation. He lost his life at sea during the war. Jock Haston was an ex-seaman and he had been looking around for a revolutionary tendency. He was a disillusioned member of the Communist Party and he ended up joining our Militant Group with a group of others who were won from our activities in Hyde Park. Excellent recruits were also made in Liverpool, such as Gertie and Jimmy Deane.

The Deane family had a long and proud revolutionary history. Gertie's father had been a member of the old Social Democratic Federation, the original British Marxist organisation, and was Labour's first councillor in Liverpool. The Irish revolutionary trade union leader, Jim Larkin, a good friend of the family, made frequent visits to the Deane household. Gertie also knew James Connolly, Hyndman and Harry Quelch. She was an active suffragette, and later become a Marxist. Through her son Jimmy, she was won over to Trotskyism, and remained a committed revolutionary until the end of her life. Her other sons, Arthur and Brian also became members of the Workers International League and the Revolutionary Communist Party. Jimmy, an exceptionally talented man who was a model of a proletarian revolutionary, is now unfortunately in very poor health, but he remains a committed Marxist to this very day. He has always had a great feel for workers, especially the youth, and is a source of inspiration to all those who have ever known and worked with him.

In relation to work in the Labour Party, Trotsky rejected entry into the left reformist Socialist League, which was a remnant of the ILP that had remained in the Labour Party under the leadership of Stafford Cripps. Trotsky regarded it as a grouping composed of mainly middle class elements. He argued that we should turn our back on the Socialist League and concentrate the bulk of our work on other possibilities in the Labour Party and especially in the Labour League of Youth. In the course of this discussion, Trotsky made a remarkable prediction that Stafford Cripps, the leading left reformist, who at that time was demagogically talking about revolution, the abolition of the monarchy, and so on, would inevitably betray the movement and end up on the right wing. This was the case. Sir Stafford Cripps, as he later became known, was one of the most rabid right wing ministers in the post-war Labour government.

This is no accident. Inherent in reformism, explained Trotsky, is betrayal. As a consequence, it would be a profound mistake to put any faith in the "left" leaders of the Labour Party, any more than the right wing leaders. In fact, said Trotsky, the real danger to the movement is more often from the left than from the right, because they will sow even greater illusions. However, it is not a question of the bad faith or lack of sincerity of this or that individual. It is a political question. Both the right and the left wing of reformism accept capitalism. The difference is that the Lefts want a kinder, more humane capitalism with reforms and class peace. They do not understand that, if you accept capitalism, then you must also accept the laws of capitalism. In the end that must mean attacking the wages, jobs and conditions of the working class. As the Bible says: you cannot serve two masters; you cannot serve God and Mammon.

Needless to say, while maintaining complete independence from the left reformists, our arguments with them are never posed in the lunatic way of the sectarians who imagine that hysteria and abuse are a good substitute for argument. Our criticism of the reformist leaders is aimed at convincing the honest reformist workers, and is always put forward in a friendly fashion. We do not make concessions to reformism on principled questions. We always put forward a sharp and penetrating criticism of their policies based upon facts, figures and sound arguments.

On this question too, we follow the advice of the Old Man: "The greatest patience, a calm, friendly tone, are indispensable", said Trotsky. [33] Only in this way can you get the ear of the reformist workers and win them to a consistent revolutionary position.

The Paddington Group

In July 1937, Ralph Lee and his wife Millie, Heaton Lee (no relation to Ralph) and Dick Frieslich, who were members of the Trotskyist movement in South Africa, emigrated to Britain. Ralph was a very talented writer, a very talented speaker and a very talented organiser. He had been, together with Millie, the driving force in the Johannesburg group. He was the comrade, as we have seen, who won me over to Marxism in South Africa. He was certainly widely read, but not perhaps as theoretically developed as he could have been. But he had a great capacity in all other regards. He had been the general secretary of the Workers Party of South Africa, the united party of South African Trotskyism before leaving for Britain. I had been in correspondence with him and Millie while they were in South Africa and we had discussed in depth all the key questions of the movement. Ralph was a great personal friend of mine and he and Millie looked us up as soon as they arrived. I had left my digs at Kings Cross and was now sharing accommodation with Haston in Paddington, and so introduced him to the new arrivals.

Ralph wanted to see at first hand the different Trotskyist groups that existed in Britain. Of course, I urged him to join our group in the Labour Party, but Ralph hesitated and wanted to see things for himself. He didn't just take as read what I told him, or Jock Haston for that matter, who also went to discuss with him and Millie. First of all, Ralph wanted to discuss with James and all the people in his group. He even had discussions with Reg Groves. Apparently, Groves told him, "Don't publish any more material. There's too much material being published already... all you seem to want to do is use the duplicator, you know, turn the handle. You should stick to the material that was already turned out".

Ralph and Millie in Johannesburg in 1936

This was the typical sort of over-weaning remark of Groves, who had always had a reluctance to publish Trotsky's material. Groves' organisation had disappeared and he had lost the little rank and file he once had. At the time, Groves, Wicks and James were considered "the three little generals without an army". Their sectarian and opportunist attitudes and their inflexible approach, could have no attraction for these South African comrades who had worked hard to connect with the black working class back home in Johannesburg. So Ralph and Millie, and the other comrades who came from South Africa soon joined the Militant Group, and our political work became concentrated in the Paddington area of London.

Popular frontism

The Stalinists had by now abandoned the old discredited policy of "social fascism". Nevertheless, their policy of "fighting fascism" was thoroughly opportunist, although the ordinary CP workers were obviously sincere in their desire to fight fascism. At first the Stalinists raised the slogan of the united front, which they had so cavalierly rejected when Trotsky urged them to implement it in Germany. However, their version of the "united front" had nothing in common with Lenin's united front policy. In the struggle against fascism, the CP insisted in including all and sundry: pacifists, vicars, bishops, Liberals and even "progressive Tories".

They attempted to put on a respectable and "patriotic" image. On demonstrations they carried the Union Jack flag. On several occasions we had the ludicrous spectacle of Mosley's fascists and the Stalinists confronting each other in rival demonstrations, both waving the Union Jack - and both sides singing "God Save the King"! In other words, the CP had entirely abandoned a class position and became the most fervent advocates of a class collaborationist policy.

This fitted in with Stalin's policy, which after about 1935 consisted in appeasing the "Western democracies" - particularly Britain and France - allegedly as a means of defending the Soviet Union against Hitler. At one stage, they even included Mussolini's Italy in this putative anti-Hitler coalition. Apparently, it was a case of "good" Italian fascism against "bad" German fascism. When the Stalinists were pushing for a "Popular front", they used to sing a song (I think it was called the "United Front Song") which went:

Then left, two, three,
Then left, two, three,
To the work that we must do.
March on to the workers' united front,
For you are a worker too.

To which we used to answer:

Then zig-zag-zig,
Then zig-zag-zig.
There's a place, duchess, for you!
March on to the bourgeois united front.
For we are bourgeois, too!

However, their opportunism did not get them very far. The attempts of the Stalinists to unite with the Labour Party - having previously denounced the Labour Party as "fascists" - obviously met with a dusty answer. Herbert Morrison, who had been the target of the attacks in their ultra left period, subjected them to merciless mockery and carried the Labour conference easily. The Labour Party conference in effect threw out the Communist Party's proposal for a "united front" by 2,116,000 votes to 331,000.

Their opportunist policy was too much even for the ILP, which up till then had been flirting with Stalinism. As GDH Cole recalls: "Following the new Moscow policy of close alliances with all nominally democratic parties, and of throwing aside programmes which might antagonise them, the Communists were more eager to collaborate with Liberals than ILPers." [34] The antagonisms between the two became especially bitter at the time of the Spanish Civil War, when Stalin's GPU were murdering members of the POUM - the ILP's sister party in Spain. At this time the Stalinists even started calling the poor old centrists of the ILP "Trotskyists".

From 1935, Stalin had been preparing to move against all potential opposition within the party. With the murder of Kirov (by Stalin), a key Stalinist bureaucrat in Moscow, wheels were set in motion that would lead to the murder of all the Old Bolsheviks in notorious Purge trials extending over more than three years. These Old Bolsheviks faced horrendous charges of aiding the counterrevolution and even the attempted murder of Lenin! All this was supposedly organised by a terrorist centre abroad, led by Trotsky and his son Leon Sedov. Not only the leaders of the Party, but millions of suspected Trotskyists were tortured and murdered in the prisons and labour camps of Stalin's GPU. By means of these monstrous trials, the Stalinist bureaucracy consolidated its position over the corpses of Lenin's Party.

In 1936 Stalin began his purge of the Old Bolsheviks with the trial of Kamenev and Zinoviev. During the show trial, the defendants "confessed" to plotting the murder of Kirov and of conspiring with Trotsky and Hitler to overthrow Stalin and carry out a capitalist counter-revolution in the Soviet Union. Vishinsky, the State Prosecutor - and a former Menshevik opponent of Bolshevism - demanded the death penalty for two men who had been Lenin's close colleagues for many years. In the official court record we could Vishinsky's ravings: "contemptible, base, vile, despicable murderous scoundrels, not tigers or lions but merely mad Fascist police dogs, humanity's dregs, the scum of the underworld, traitors and bandits." He ended with the cry: "Shoot these mad curs, every one of them."

The *Daily Worker* followed the same theme under the editorial *The Malice of a Renegade.*

> "The revelations of the terrorist plot to assassinate the Soviet leaders, a plot instigated by Trotsky and engineered in all its details by Zinoviev and Kamenev will fill all decent citizens with loathing and hatred.
>
> "These people long ago abandoned every socialist principle, they worked energetically to retard, hinder and destroy socialist culture, they conspired to murder George Kirov, a Bolshevik leader beloved of the whole country, they accepted political responsibility for the murder, abjured their own view and deeds at their trial only in order to cover up the actual machinery of their murder organisation.
>
> "Crowning infamy of all this is the evidence showing how they were linked up with the Nazi Secret Police which provided false passports for their agents. So they stand revealed as tools of a world fascist attack." (*Daily Worker*, 17 August 1936)

Having been framed and forced to confess, the defendants were then shot. The Stalinists immediately applauded this monstrous frame-up internationally. Taking its cue from Moscow, the *Daily Worker* carried a heading in big letters: "Shoot the reptiles!" They described the accused in the vilest terms: "They are 'a festering, cankering sore' and we echo fervently the workers' verdict: Shoot the reptiles!" (*Daily Worker*, 24 August 1936)

Prominent British Stalinists like Campbell and Pritt wrote whole books, attempting to show that the Moscow trials were completely legal and fair. In fact, the victims were convicted purely on the basis of confessions which were beaten out of them by Stalin's GPU. They were not allowed any defence lawyers. And all the accusations made against them were proven to be false by the Dewey Commission. (See the two volumes *The Case of Leon Trotsky* and *Not Guilty.*)

The Purge Trials were a kind of one-sided civil war that Stalin and the bureaucracy waged against the Bolshevik Party. Stalinism and Bolshevism are completely incompatible, and Stalin could only consolidate his bureaucratic regime over the dead body of Lenin's Party. One crime led to another. The Trial of the Sixteen was followed the next year by the Trial of the Seventeen, including Radek, Sokolnikov and Piatakov. Later Stalin arrested the hero of the Red Army Tukhachevsky and other prominent Soviet generals, who were all executed. Pravda exulted: "The reptile of Fascist espionage has many heads but we will cut off every head and paralyse and sever every tentacle." In reality, by destroying the finest cadres of the Red Army, Stalin encouraged Hitler to attack the USSR and gravely weakened its defences - a fact that became all too clear in 1941.

The Spanish Revolution

One of the reasons for the murder of the Old Bolsheviks was the revolution that had broken out in Spain in July 1936. The uprising of Franco had created a revolutionary wave throughout Spain, and in Catalonia in particular. There, power was in the hands of the workers and the Republican government was suspended in mid-air. Stalin feared that a successful revolution in Spain would re-enthuse the masses in the USSR, and any of the Old Bolshevik leaders could become a pole of attraction under these circumstances. This could lead to the death-knell of the Stalin regime and the rebirth of workers' democracy in Russia. As a result, Stalin pursued a counter-revolutionary policy in Spain designed to betray the revolution and divert it into simply a military struggle with Franco. He supplied arms to the Republicans - at a price - and forced a policy upon the government to eliminate the revolutionary elements within their ranks. The Spanish CP became an open tool of counter-revolution under the slogan "First Win the War!"

The policy of the Stalinists - reflecting the Moscow Line - was openly pro-bourgeois and anti-revolutionary. In Spain, this led to the defeat of the revolution, although, as Trotsky pointed out, the Spanish workers could have made not one revolution but ten. They were betrayed by the leadership - not only the Stalinists but also the Socialists, the Anarchists and the centrists of the POUM - all of which played a fatal role. The supporters of Trotsky led by Andres Nin, broke from the Trotskyist movement in 1935 to enter an alliance with Catalan left nationalists around Maurin. This alliance produced the POUM, a centrist organisation, which veered between reformism and revolution. Despite breaking with Trotskyism and entering the Catalan government, they were regarded by the Stalinists as "Trotskyist". They became their main targets for elimination. After the May 1937 events, the POUM was declared illegal and its leaders arrested and murdered. This defeat in Spain laid the basis for the victory of Franco and prepared the way for the Second World War.

The Spanish events greatly intensified the antagonism between the ILP and the Stalinists. In May of that year the Spanish Stalinists staged a provocation in Barcelona where they seized the telephone exchange that had been captured from the fascists in 1936 by the CNT and the POUM. The Stalinists resorted to armed force to crush the revolution in Catalonia, where they kidnapped and murdered Andres Nin and other leaders of the POUM. Yet Pollitt had the brazen cheek to describe the actions of the POUMists in Barcelona as a "fascist counter-revolution". In his speech to the 1937 congress of the CPGB, Harry Pollitt was practically foaming at the mouth:

> "In opposition to the People's Front in France and Spain, its refusal to appreciate the difference between certain democratic states and open fascist states, its foul slanders against the Soviet Union, its support of the POUM which daily stabs the Spanish people in the back - all this forms clear evidence that certain elements inside the ILP have, while disclaiming the name of Trotsky, fully developed the whole stock-in-trade of the Trotskyists.
>
> "The support of the fascist rising in Barcelona by the New Leader, carried out under the

> flag of the POUM to whom the drunken fascist general de Lano wirelessed a message of support and sympathy, is a shameful episode.
>
> "[...] The Trotskyist criminals in Barcelona acted as the tools of the fascists, carried out the rebellion that the fascists wanted, and only by the steadfastness of the Catalan people [sic!] was this rebellion defeated.
>
> "It was this foul policy which received the support of a section of the ILP leaders." [35]

The British Trotskyists not only rallied to the support of the Spanish Revolution, but also denounced the counter-revolutionary role of the Stalinists. In particular, we waged a campaign to expose the Moscow Trials as the biggest frame-up in history. The ILP leaders played a scandalous role in refusing to support our initiative of an international committee of inquiry into the Moscow Trials. In May 1937, Fenner Brockway, in the name of the London Bureau, rejected the invitation to endorse the American Inquiry, because, he said, it was set up by a "partisan" Committee for the Defence of Trotsky. This hypocritical stance was even more scandalous since the London Bureau supported the centrist POUM in Spain, which was now being exterminated by the Stalinists. Wherever possible we raised this issue within the labour movement, and countered the lies of the Stalinists about "Trotsky-fascists".

The Paddington group

In the Paddington branch of the Militant Group, we had nine members. One of the new recruits at this time was Gerry Healy, who ended up a complete gangster. One amusing episode was the way in which Haston recruited Gerry Healy. Healy was a member of the Communist Party at that time, and he came across Trotskyism when he met Haston selling the *Militant* paper at Hyde Park. Gerry Healy introduced himself to Haston by saying "you bastard Trotskyist", and punched Haston on the jaw. Haston got hold of him, and, since he was twice the size of Healy, could have given him a really rough time, but instead of this he calmed him down. "Look, come and have a cup of tea and we'll discuss the question", said Haston. Sad to say, he managed to convince Healy to accept Trotskyism and he also became a member of the Paddington Group.

Although there were only nine of us in Paddington, out of a national membership of about fifty or so, we were by far the most active members of the organisation. Out of the 800 copies of the paper that were sold, 500 of them were sold by our group in Paddington. It may sound amazing but it is an actual fact. We sold at Speakers Corner and in Hyde Park. We sold in the local working class areas and around the housing estates every Sunday morning. We went out assiduously selling the paper on the doorstep. Sometimes we went out with a loudhailer, the whole lots of us, selling the paper and trying to win people. We succeeded in building up a regular sale in the working class areas around Paddington. So this one small group of comrades, with an abundance of energy and enthusiasm, was selling more papers than the rest of the organisation put together.

As a result of our energetic work and the extraordinary ability of Ralph Lee, it soon became obvious that the Paddington tendency, as you might call it, was playing the leading role in the organisation. Recognising this, Lee was co-opted onto the Executive Committee of the group. Haston was also elected to the EC. Given his leading role in South Africa, Ralph had in fact been proposed as secretary of the group. However, in the winter of 1937, when the elections for the leadership of the group were being held, we discovered by accident that there had been an intrigue by the existing leadership against him. An incredible fairy-tale had been spread around the organisation that Ralph had come from South Africa because he had allegedly stolen the funds of the Laundry Workers Union. This slander was all the more disgusting because, in fact, the exact opposite was true. Ralph and Millie had subsidised the union out of their own pockets as far as they were able, at considerable cost to themselves. Not a word of this allegation came out into the open. The story was simply spread behind our backs, which was a real scandal in a so-called Marxist organisation.

It was later established that the rumour had originated from the South African Stalinists. It had been picked up by Hermann Van Gelderen, a member of the Trotskyist group in Cape Town, and relayed by him to his brother, Charlie Van Gelderen, in London. He in turn stupidly passed the allegations on to the leadership who used them for its own purposes to discredit Lee. You must remember that this was late 1937, at the height of the Frame-up Trials in Moscow. There was a tremendous hate campaign being conducted by the Stalinists world-wide against us, using all kinds of disgusting slanders - "Trotsky-fascists" and such like. The Trotskyists were vigorously campaigning against the frame-ups and slanders at this very time. Ralph Lee had been a target for the South African Stalinists for a long time. They accused him of "counter-revolution" and all manner of things. Unscrupulous elements could easily acquire some of this dirt manufactured against Lee by our enemies.

Of course, as soon as we discovered this scandal we went through the roof. We demanded that the matter be raised openly at the next aggregate. So at the following aggregate in December, the allegations were brought out into the open and Lee raised charges of "irresponsibility" against the officers of the group. This, as expected, caused a terrible row. Lee demanded that there should be an inquiry into what had taken place. Immediately Harber and Jackson, who felt their positions threatened, launched a vicious attack on us, saying we were splitting, undermining and disorganising the movement by raising this question. In reality, they were responsible for the mess. In sheer disgust Haston walked out of the meeting in protest, and as a gesture of solidarity we all walked out. That is all we intended to do. There was no question of a split. We were absolutely disgusted, and that was all. But as soon as we had walked out the door, Harber moved that we should be expelled and in our absence this was passed! The very people, who accused us of being splitters, themselves split the organisation by immediately expelling us. This completely poisoned our relations with the old group.

Some time later, the truth came out. The secretary of the Workers' Party of South Africa condemned Van Gelderen as "an irresponsible person". The Johannesburg group's secretary, Max Sapire, wrote to exonerate Ralph, "Comrade RL had many enemies in this country - as have all genuine revolutionaries in all countries. It is only to be expected. And that these enemies should seize every opportunity to besmirch the past record of a revolutionary by lies, deceit and falsifications innumerable should also occasion no surprise. The disastrous blunder committed by your organisation by allowing itself to be tricked and side tracked by falsehood and intrigue is utterly indefensible.

> "The negligent manner in which this whole matter has been handled by responsible members of your group is thoroughly unbecoming a revolutionary organisation and we trust that you will give this communication the widest publicity in an endeavour to clear comrade RL's name of the slanders cast upon him. We also hope that you yourself will regard this

> communication in a very serious and sober light and will thereby avoid repetition of such catastrophic errors in the future." [36]

A letter was also received from RTR. Molefe, member of the Committee for the African Metal Trades Union, and signed by ten former strikers which outlined Lee's tremendous role in helping the union. "During the strike comrade RL and comrade Sapire worked their duties satisfactorily. Our secretary RL shall never be forgotten in our minds. Even today our members wished him back. Comrade RL left for England in June when the strike was three months over. Now comrades only lies you have been told there."

Even the IS condemned Harber and Van Gelderen. But while this cleared Lee's name, the whole atmosphere within the group had been thoroughly poisoned by the affair. How could we have any trust in such leaders in the future? The damage had been done.

The Workers International League

The question was immediately raised of what to do. We discussed this continually for three or four nights that week, and the discussions lasted for a full week or more. We knew that if we waged a struggle for re-entry into the organisation that we would be allowed back. But we asked ourselves, what would that accomplish. We came to the conclusion that the organisation at that stage represented only the embryonic stage of the Trotskyist movement. We needed to break out of that type of immature politics. We also knew that every great revolutionary movement in the beginning tends to attract mainly middle class types. The social composition of the Militant Group was pretty bad. It was composed to a large degree of bohemians and people of that sort. There were people who wore cloaks and sandals, and grew beards, which, at that time, was a sort of exotic fashion in certain "intellectual" circles. You can just imagine the type of individuals. They were your typical Bloomsbury bohemians.

We came to the conclusion that it would be pointless to return to the old group. Certainly, comradely and personal relations had become impossible and there was a huge amount of distrust as a result of the intrigue. If we re-entered this group, we would have a long and perhaps fruitless struggle to transform the internal life. So after considerable deliberations, we finally came round to the view expressed by Old Engels, that sometimes a split, even on an apparent organisational question, can reflect certain underlying major differences and tendencies. For example, the Bolshevik split from the Mensheviks in 1903 initially had nothing to do with political questions. There were no fundamental political differences at that stage. But the split revealed a difference in outlook, a difference in approach, and attitude. It was only later that fundamental political differences emerged between Mensheviks and Bolsheviks. Therefore, we concluded that a split from a dead organisation could give an impulse to the movement.

Trotsky also thought on similar lines. In dealing with the French Trotskyists five years earlier he favoured separating out the healthy elements from those who held the organisation back.

> "A revolutionary organisation cannot develop without purging itself, especially under conditions of legal work, when not infrequently chance, alien and degenerate elements gather under the banner of revolution. Since, in addition, the Left Opposition formed itself in the struggle with monstrous bureaucratism, many quasi-oppositionists have concluded that inside the Opposition 'everything is permitted'. In the French League and on its periphery

> prevail practises that have nothing in common with a revolutionary proletarian organisation. Separate groups and individuals easily change their political position or in general are not concerned about it, devoting their time and effort to the discrediting of the Left Opposition, to personal squabbles, insinuations and organisational sabotage…
>
> "To be able to cope with the new tasks, it is necessary to burn out with a red-hot iron the anarchist and Menshevik methods from the organisations of the Bolshevik-Leninists.
>
> "We are making an important revolutionary turn. At such moments inner crises or splits are absolutely inevitable. To fear them is to substitute petty-bourgeois sentimentalism and personal scheming for revolutionary policy… Under these circumstances, a splitting off of a part of the League will be a great step forward. It will reject all that is unhealthy, crippled and incapacitated; it will give a lesson to the vacillating and irresolute elements; it will harden the better sections of the youth; it will improve the inner atmosphere; it will open up before the League new, great possibilities. What will be lost - partly only temporarily - will be regained a hundredfold already at the next stage." [37]

There was only one thing to do. It was impossible for us to return to the poisoned atmosphere of the Marxist Group. We weren't going to abandon the movement, so we had no alternative but to organise a group of our own. And this we did - all nine of us. We gave the new group the name of Workers International League. Perhaps at a later stage even the question of unity between the two groups might arise. We did not discount it. But for the time being, we branched out on our own, determined to develop a healthy Trotskyist movement in Britain. Some have attacked us for our stand. We have even been called "unprincipled" for the split. It has been said that there was no political basis for it. The "Lee affair", as it became known, has been presented as a purely personal schism. This became Van Gelderen's position. But these critics could not see, or refused to see, the real situation. And events - which are decisive - were to prove who was correct.

As an interesting aside, one of those to walk out of the meeting and protest against the actions of the leadership of the Militant Group was a young musician by the name of Michael Tippet. He had joined the Militant Group after leaving the Communist Party before the war. He later joined the WIL, but developed pacifist leanings, for which he was expelled in 1940. I know we were still in touch with him up until his imprisonment for refusing to go into the army in 1943. Tippet later became a world famous composer. He was knighted and become the Master of the Queen's Music. He died a few years ago, and very few people suspected that Sir Michael Tippet was a one-time Trotskyist! Looking back on it, we may have been a bit hard on him.

At the time, Tippet protested energetically against the shenanigans of the leadership around Harber. "Why are GMM minutes to be declared correct or incorrect by an EC? And then by an EC which declared itself unconstitutional? What a further muddle and confusion! Is this going to be cleared up?" He went on, "They (the EC) deferred the original issue for a month, and proceeded to initiate censure and expulsion against the original sufferer of the provocation and his associates. The commencement of the proceedings to elect an EC were eminently revealing, and not being able to contain my disgust, I left." [38]

The International Secretariat had condemned the Militant Group's leadership for the mess they had created, but also attacked our split and called on us to return. The WIL replied that we had not split, but were expelled and rejected the advice of the IS. We wrote back to them:

"If the comrades of our group accepted the expulsion and did not appeal to the 'national membership', it was because:

1) The national membership is fictitious
2) Because the actions of the leadership after our expulsion reinforced the conclusion we formed before the expulsion that both leadership and membership were irresponsible..." [39]

In late December 1937 the Workers International League came into being. At the start there were myself, Ralph and Millie, Jock Haston, Betty Hamilton, Heaton Lee, Jessie Strachan, Dick Freislich and Gerry Healy. We were confident of the ideas and the responsibility that rested on our shoulders. With the world war looming, we engaged in an energetic campaign to build up our forces. The old methods had proved ineffective. It was time to cut a new path.

Notes:

1- See *The Comintern and its Critics, Revolutionary History,* vol.8, no.1, pp.34-39.
2- See idid., pp.40-43.
3- *The Errors of Trotskyism,* p.5.
4- Ibid.
5- Trotsky, *My Life*, p. 527.
6- Abridged Report, 17 June - 8 July 1924, quoted in MacFarlane, *History of the British Communist Party,* p. 142.
7- Trotsky, *The Struggle Against Fascism in Germany*, New York, 2001, p.152.
8- Trotsky's *Writings on Britain*, volume 3, London 1974, p.64.
9- Ibid., vol. 3, p. 68.
10- Ibid., vol. 3, p.72.
11- Ibid, pp. 87 and 89, emphasis in original.
12- *Writings of Leon Trotsky* supplement 1934-40, p. 540.
13- See Ian Hunter, *Raff Lee and the Pioneer Trotskyists of Johannesburg, Revolutionary History,* Volume 4, no. 4, Spring 1993, pp. 60-65.
14- Ibid.
15- Interview with Rob Sewell, London, 19 January 2002.
16- Lee to Koston, 12 April 1935.
17- Ibid.
18- Lee to Koston, 17 May 1935.
19- Ibid.
20- Quoted in Hunter, op. cit. p.76
21- ibid, p.65
22- Quoted in Bornstein and Richardson, *Against the Stream - a History of the Trotskyist Movement in Britain 1924-38,* London 1986, p.169.
23- Trotsky, *Whither France,* London, 1974, p.85.
24- Trotsky, *Writings on Britain,* vol. 3, p.119.
25- Ibid., p.107.
26- *Writings of Leon Trotsky* 1935-36, p.203.
27- Ibid., 1934-35, pp.33 and 38.
28- Ibid., 1935-36, p.366.
29- Ibid., p.379.
30- Ibid., p.322.
31- Ibid., p.368.
32- Ibid., supplement 1934-40, p. 553.
33- Ibid., 1935-36, p.268.
34- GDH. Cole, *The Common People*, p. 605.
35- *It Can be Done*, Report of the Fourteenth Congress of the CPGB, p. 61.

36- From the archives of *Revolutionary History.*
37- Trotsky, op. cit. 1933-34, pp. 90-91.
38- Quoted in *Revolutionary History*, vol.7, no.1, pp. 185-6.
39- Quoted by John Archer in his unpublished Ph.D. thesis on *Trotskyism in Britain 1931-37*, chapter 6, p.242, dated September 1979.

The first issue of the *Workers International News*

WORKERS' INTERNATIONAL NEWS

VOL.1 NO.1 — 1 JANUARY 1938 — TWO PENCE

G.P.U. STALKS ABROAD

Open Letter to All Working Class Orgahisations by Leon Trotsky

The international working-class movement is being consumed by a frightful disease. The carrier of the contagion is the Comintern or, to speak more exactly, the G.P.U., which uses the apparatus of the Comintern as its legal cover. The events of the last few months in Spain have shown what crimes the unbridled and utterly depraved bureaucracy of Moscow is capable of, supported by its servitors which it recruits from among the declassed dregs of humanity. It is a question neither of " occasional " assassinations nor of " occasional " falsifications. It is a question of a plot against the international working-class movement.

It is obvious that the Moscow trials were possible only under a totalitarian regime in which the G.P.U. dictated their conduct not only to the accused but also to the counsel for the prosecution and for the defence. But these judicial falsifications were from the very beginning conceived as the point of departure for a campaign of extermination directed against the opponents of the Moscow clique on the international arena. On the 3rd of March Stalin delivered a speech to the plenum of the Central Committee of the Russian Communist Party in which he proclaimed that " the Fourth International is composed, as regards two-thirds of its membership, of spies and saboteurs." This impudent declaration, typical of Stalin, already clearly shows at what the Cain of the Kremlin was aiming. His schemes, however, were by no means limited to the cadres of the Fourth International. In Spain, the P.O.U.M., which was waging an implacable struggle with the Fourth International, was counted among the " Trotskyites." After the P.O.U.M. came the turn of the Anarcho-Syndicalists and even of the Left wing Socialists. Anyone who protests against the repression of the Anarchists is now counted as a Trotskyist. Falsifications and crimes are multiplying in a hideous progression. Doubtless one can place certain particularly scandalous details to the account of the excessive zeal of isolated agents. But the work as a whole is strictly centralised and is being carried out according to the plan elaborated in the Kremlin.

On 21st April there met at Paris an extraordinary plenum of the Executive Committee of the Comintern at which were present the most trustworthy representatives of the 17 most important sections. The sessions were of a strictly secret character. Only a brief statement to the effect that the attention of the plenum had been concentrated upon the international struggle against Trotskyism found its way into the world Press. The instructions had been sent from Moscow, coming direct from Stalin. Neither the debates nor the decisions were published. It appears from all the information we have received and from the subsequent events that this secret plenum was in fact *a congress of the most responsible international agents of the G.P.U. whose object was to prepare the campaign of false accusations, delations, abductions and assassinations against the adversaries of Stalinism in the working-class movement of the whole world.*

2

Trotskyism of a New Type

We began first of all to publish a monthly called *Workers International News*, and our orientation was towards the Labour Party as Trotsky had urged. Britain was entering a pre-pre-revolutionary situation, and the British ruling class was making preparations not for war, but civil war. The development of such events, would lead to a crisis within the Labour Party and open up possibilities for the revolutionary tendency. However, while we conducted work in the Labour Party, we were at that same time energetically trying to promote our material everywhere we could, and attempting to influence people in the direction of Trotskyism. In this way, we managed to recruit members of the Young Communist League and the ILP. These new recruits then assisted our work inside the Labour Party, and in particular our work in the Labour League of Youth, where we were engaged in an almighty battle with the Stalinists.

When we began the work in developing our tendency, we decided, consciously and deliberately, to turn our back on the little squabbling sects, the Militant Group, the Marxist Group, and other remnants. Instead, we would face towards the mass movement. We would face towards the working class, and begin the real process of constructing of a strong Marxist organisation. Although we originally had only nine members, these nine were very dedicated people. Millie had private funds from South Africa and so both she and Ralph were able to work full-time for the new organisation. The other members were mainly unemployed, with only a couple of comrades actually working. Gerry Healy, I recall, had a job. The rest of us managed to get by on unemployment benefit. Well at least we got a meagre subsistence from the state for the purpose of revolutionary activity! As full-time professionals, we got about fifteen shillings a week. Those on national assistance got a rise to about seventeen shillings a week, which at that time, if you didn't drink or smoke, you could just about manage to live on.

So the nine of us began an energetic campaign to build the WIL. The first task was to publish our material. It was too expensive to get stuff printed commercially as we didn't have the money. However, Ralph managed to pick up and repair a battered old Ardena printing machine for next to nothing. Those of you who are familiar with such machines, which specialise in turning out small cards, will know that is more like a toy rather than a printing press. Anyway, we got a little Ardena and we found a typesetter to do the typesetting. We managed to do the compositing ourselves. Both Lee and Haston possessed some mechanical skills, so we soon learned how to do the printing work. But to say the least, the Ardena printing was a backbreaking job!

We wrote the articles, proof-read them, prepared them for printing, worked the printing machine and sold the magazine. As I recall, till perhaps one, two or three in the morning, we were busy, in Groves' words, "turning the handle". In this way we turned out the *Workers International News* every month, devoted largely to republishing Trotsky's material and articles from the international movement. Our first issue of *Workers International News* came off the press in January 1938, with a front-page article by Trotsky, entitled *GPU Stalks Abroad - Open Letter to All Working Class Organisations.* It was a proud moment for us, and an essential task in building the organisation.

We selected certain spots to sell the magazine: Hyde Park, Tottenham Court Road and Piccadilly, where we sold regularly every Saturday and Sunday. In that way we made contacts both nationally and internationally, as many people who visit London inevitably travel to Hyde Park and Speakers Corner. Also workers from London and the rest of the country going on a jaunt to the West End inevitably passed through either Piccadilly or Tottenham Court Road. Therefore, we made quite a number of contacts and actual members from our sales at that time. We intervened wherever possible in all the strikes that took place, and we made contact with industrial workers, and very slowly a trickle of workers began to join the organisation. Right from the beginning our tendency was working class in its composition. Industrial workers in particular were won from the engineering factories and we built a basis within the Amalgamated Engineering Union. We ignored completely the old sectarian tendencies, with their overwhelming petty-bourgeois composition, engrossed in their armchair politics, and began the work of rebuilding the movement.

After some time, we scraped together the money to buy a second-hand treadle-printing machine that was foot-operated. We manage to pick one up very cheap - about twenty pounds, I think. I am sure it would be very antediluvian by modern standards! But it was a tremendous leap forward when compared to the little handle-cranking Ardena machine. This treadle machine allowed us to publish a bigger size than the small magazine format. We also printed the bulletin of the Paddington branch of the Labour League of Youth, called *Searchlight.* Our comrades actually started this publication as a duplicated paper for the socialist youth as we politically controlled the Paddington youth branch. Later this became *Youth for Socialism*, which we maintained until 1941.

One of the first pamphlets we produced was *The Lessons of Spain* by Trotsky, in July 1938, for which Ralph and myself wrote the introduction. We sent Trotsky a copy, and he sent back an enthusiastic letter congratulating the WIL on this great achievement, and particularly the fact that we had got our own printing press. We felt we were on our way, and had grown within six months to 30 comrades. Although mainly based in London, we won over comrades in other areas, and in the end took about a third of the members of the Militant Group. We began to construct an organisation that was mainly working class in composition, young and very energetic.

I must say, even at that early stage we had already attracted the attention of the Special Branch. Although we had only a small group they became interested in our activities. Later on, MI5 actually sent people to penetrate our organisation, but even at this time they started sniffing around. I remember one chap called Jones who came along and said he was a gas worker and wanted to join our organization. Later, quite by accident, we found out he was a Detective Inspector Jones. But we had our suspicions straight away. We just took one look at the size of his feet and it was quite obvious where comrade Jones came from! At this time the headquarters of the organisation was in the basement of Ralph and Millie's house. As he said he had a job at the gas works, we made it our business to find out the truth. We fobbed him off, and for a few days we watched the gas works and asked the workers what shift Mr. Jones worked on. The workers were bemused. They had no knowledge of this Mr. Jones. He told us that he was a member of the CP - in fact he had a CP card in his possession - so he was obviously also doing work for the police in the Communist Party!

We continued to put him off from joining with one excuse or another. Firstly, before joining, we told him that he had to show his revolutionary integrity by giving money to the organisation. Of course, being a good agent we got money out of him. Then, having a sense of humour, we decided to play a trick on D.C. Jones. He showed a great interest in getting copies of every paper and leaflet we had published. He had to get his hands on these leaflets! We had just issued the first issue of *Searchlight*, when he got in touch with us. So we decided to skip issue number 2 and just put number 3 on the second issue. Poor old Detective-Inspector Jones was in a terrible panic over trying to trace the phantom issue No. 2! He must have been hauled over the coals at Scotland Yard for this failing, because he tried frantically to get hold of the missing number. For months he tried and, of course, failed miserably!

Having failed with him, the Special Branch next sent along a woman undercover detective. We also sized her up as just another agent and we told her the same story: "if you want to join the organisation you have to make a financial sacrifice." At that time we wanted to publish Trotsky's *Transitional Programme*, which cost £12 and 10 shillings. So she dutifully produced the £12 and 10 shillings, but, of course, we gave her the run-around as well. Afterwards, when Haston was arrested and being questioned by Detective Whitehead - the head of the Special Branch dealing with the Fourth International - Whitehead asked: "Where do you get your money from?" Haston replied: "Well, as far as I remember, you paid for the *Transitional Programme!*" which of course shut him up. Anyway, having given us the £12 and 10 shillings, she also failed to get into the organisation.

The role of Cannon

In the middle of 1938 plans were being laid by the International Secretariat in Paris for the first World Congress, the founding congress of the Fourth International. Since 1933, Trotsky had raised the idea of a new International to replace the bankrupt Internationals of the Stalinists and reformists as a weapon for world revolution. Throughout the 1930s,

Trotsky sought to prepare the ground for its launch. However, whereas the other Internationals were born in a period of working class advance and revolution, the Fourth International was being formed in a period of colossal defeats and retreat for the working class. Nevertheless, the founding of the Fourth International in 1938 was directly linked to the perspective of world war and revolutionary upheavals. On the basis of this perspective, Trotsky forecast that within ten years not one stone upon another would be left of the old organisations, and that the Fourth International would become the dominant force on the planet.

As a prelude to the founding Congress of the Fourth International in Paris, James Cannon, the leader of the American Trotskyists and delegate to the World Congress, came over from the United States to prepare the ground for a unified Trotskyist organisation in Britain. He imagined that he was going to brush away the differences and unify the movement in one fell swoop. At that time, there existed three separate groups claiming Trotskyist roots in the London area, and one in Scotland. There was the Militant Group, the Revolutionary Socialist League, the Revolutionary Socialist Party, and ourselves, the WIL. The RSP was a split-off from the Socialist Labour Party, a largely sectarian organisation in Scotland, with remnants in Glasgow, Edinburgh and a few individuals in Yorkshire, which had moved in the direction of Trotskyism.

So this was the state of things when Cannon came to this country. We looked up to Cannon, who had a long revolutionary history in the movement. He was the leader of the SWP and was in regular contact with Trotsky in Mexico. The comrades held him in very high regard. When we met Cannon he told us that his task was to unify the British groups before the founding congress of the Fourth International in September. That was the deadline and we couldn't wait until everything was right in everybody's head before carrying through this unification. For our part, we told him that we were in favour of unity, but it must be on a correct principled basis. At that time, given the fundamental differences between the groups, you had to face up to the immediate problem of how to work: entry or non-entry, independent work or work in the Labour Party. We told Cannon that before we could get unity we had to agree on one clear policy. Any united organisation would have to agree either a policy for entry or a policy for independent work. Added to this were, of course, the rights of the minority to put forward their position completely freely and to try and convince the majority within the framework of the organisation.

Cannon said, "Yes, but the RSP tendency and the James tendency would never accept that." So we countered: "If they're not prepared to accept that then, of course, there won't be any unity as far as we are concerned". Cannon tried to persuade us but failed to convince any of our leading comrades. We told Cannon that we would give him every opportunity to speak to the rank and file of our organisation, and we invited him to speak at our monthly aggregate meeting. He accepted the invitation and asked us how many members did we have? We told him we had thirty members. He looked at us, and figured American-style, if you had thirty members, you simply doubled it and say you had sixty; if you had sixty, you doubled it and say you had 120, and so on. So when we said we had thirty members, Cannon said, "you mean fifteen". This was clearly the method used elsewhere in calculating the membership. Cannon continued, "Well, I understood from others you had ten or fifteen members". This was probably the figure he had been told by Harber and Jackson, who had no idea of how fast we had grown.

As usual, they were completely out of touch. So we said firmly, "No, we have 30 members", and Cannon, who clearly didn't believe us, just nodded.

Our membership meeting was held in a room in Jock Haston's house in Warwick Avenue, where the print machine was also kept. Before the meeting, we proudly showed off the treadle machine to Cannon, and he was suitably impressed. Cannon sat down at the table at the front of the meeting. It was exactly half-past seven when the meeting was due to start. There were ten people present in the room, so Cannon asked if we should begin. We said, "No, hang on. Give us a few more minutes until all the comrades arrive." Cannon just smiled and said nothing and looked at his notes. Then after about ten more minutes there were twenty people in the room, so again Cannon asked if we should start the proceedings. Again, we said, "Hang on, give us a few more minutes." At a quarter to eight, to Cannon's surprise, there were thirty people in the room. So we told Cannon we could now start. He must have thought that we were very naïve or something. "They say they've got thirty, and they've actually got thirty", he must have said to himself in bemusement.

Cannon spoke forcefully to our members, arguing for unity at all costs. However, his arguments fell on stony ground and he failed to convince a single comrade. The WIL membership was homogeneous, firm, and clear on the unity question, both the leadership and the rank and file. We pointed out to him the weaknesses of the other groups. We said, "You haven't had a meeting with the rank and file of the Militant Group, or with the rank and file of the RSL. Only our tendency is prepared to let you meet with the membership and discuss things out openly." We told him that the reason for this was that the other tendencies were very loose, petty bourgeois and politically woolly.

In our discussions with Cannon, he told us that on the tactical questions, he could see we were not sectarian in relation to the trade unions, or in our attitude towards the Labour Party. According to him, our general approach was correct. We were just sectarian on this question of unity! We told him that on the contrary, we took a Marxist principled stand on the question of unity. After seeing he was getting nowhere, he asked if we would at any rate attend the Unity Conference that was about to take place. We said, "Certainly we'll come to the Unity Conference, and we'll put our position there". We had no objection to that, and neither did Cannon. In fact, we presented our own document on perspectives and tactics. The only ones to offer a clear and full political explanation.

The Unity Conference took place in South London, somewhere in Clapham. Our thirty comrades appeared, as well as large numbers of others, even the "political corpses" - those who had long dropped out of political activity. They had even fished out Harry Wicks and Henry Sara. I do not remember exactly how many were there, but the place was full. Sara took the chair of the meeting. He had been in the original Trotskyist tendency, the Balham Group. And therefore, despite their poor record in building the Trotskyist movement, a certain leniency and good will was extended towards them. As usual at these proceedings, the conference didn't start on time and there was a lot of shuffling about the place. Ralph Lee, who was a great wit, remarked, "It's like a French bedroom farce, with people moving all around, one door opening and the other door closing... its difficult to know what is going on". As expected, we were like pariahs at the Unity Conference. No one was talking to us. We were completely ignored. We ended up simply discussing among ourselves, waiting patiently in the hall for the conference to start.

Eventually it started about an hour late. They were still going round and round in circles from one room to another, trying even at that late stage to patch up an agreement that could be acceptable to everybody. At any rate they succeeded after an hour or so in getting the other groups together. Then, if you can believe it, it only took them about twenty minutes to patch up an agreement between the leaders. We heard afterwards that Cannon had persuaded James to come to America, promising him a position in the American SWP building up the black movement. He also managed to persuade Henry Sara of the benefits of a united organisation. On that basis they managed to arrive at some sort of compromise. The compromise was that *both* tactics would be legitimate, that they would carry out an open party tactic and an entrist tactic simultaneously. Of course, it was sheer madness, and we knew it.

The session was introduced by the young American, Nathan Gould, the IS representative in Europe. Rather than deal with the concrete differences and orientation, he spoke about the *Transitional Programme.* There was no political discussion on the tactics and strategy that separated us. When we saw the proposed Unity Agreement, we were amazed, and said openly, "How the hell can this work?" We made it clear we would have nothing to do with an unprincipled agreement like the one proposed. Lee gave a speech in which he said, "Cannon is like the man who tied the tails of the two Kilkenny cats together, and they will end up tearing each other to pieces." He predicted that by joining these three groups together, what you would be doing would be to "unite" three organisations into ten. That would be the upshot of it all. There was only a limited amount of resources, only a limited amount of money and comrades, and if both tactics were employed, it would destroy the organisation. The people in favour of the entrist tactic would say that the resources should go to them, and they would point to the conference resolution, the open group would do the same. It was therefore a formula for paralysing the organisation. Cannon was furious because we refused to accept the Unity Agreement. He got up and said, "We crush splitters like beetles". And Sara chipped in: "This is a scandal. Here is our guest comrade from the United States, and he is being treated shamefully!"

We rejected this assertion. At this point, I intervened. "Even if Comrade Trotsky himself had come here we would have acted no differently. The need to state differences clearly is a principle of our movement, as opposed to the Stalinists. Each comrade should be allowed to say what he or she honestly believes." And I concluded, "If Comrade Trotsky himself stood before us and put forward a position we did not agree with, we would have every opportunity of putting forward our case. And he would have been in favour of that." After that, the whole argument was dropped.

Cannon then got up again to put a stop to this infantile line of argument - I'll give him credit for that - and said that he didn't object to these attacks. He continued, "we can take it, but we can also dish it out". He then proceeded to "dish it out" to us, but without having any effect on our membership. We weren't the least bit bothered because we knew what was going to happen. The new united organisation, which claimed 170 members, took the name of Revolutionary Socialist League. However, the Militant Group was committed to entrism; the old RSL was for independent work, and the RSP was against entrism in principle. It was a dog's dinner, and would be shown to be so by events. Meanwhile, the 30-strong Workers International League, which refused to endorse the Agreement, continued to pursue its work within the Labour Party, as well as having a flexible approach to opportunities outside.

Haston and myself, but Haston in particular had a number of discussions with Cannon. He was clearly impressed with the WIL. After the conference he asked if we would see him and we agreed. Cannon told us frankly: "Well, you haven't joined the organisation, but I hope you will have good relations with the RSL." He asked us if we would send a delegate to the Founding Congress of the International on the condition that relations between ourselves and the united tendency would be harmonious. Obviously, we had absolute agreement with the programme and policy of the International. We agreed fully with the *Transitional Programme*, written by Trotsky, which put forward the idea of the International conducting mass work on the basis of transitional demands. We said that we agreed completely with the ideas, the methods, the policies and the programme of the International. We explained we would like very much to apply, at least for sympathetic affiliation to the International. So he asked if we would send a delegate to the World Congress, and we told him we would discuss the question, and do our best to send someone. If we could raise the money, which was always a stumbling block, we would certainly be represented. In his discussions with us, Cannon was emphatic that we should be present at the Congress. He must have wanted us to attend, as he probably thought that the Congress would have exerted sufficient pressure to push us into unification with the other groups. Anyway, that was probably the idea in the back of his mind.

However, when we came to discuss the question in our Executive Committee, we realised that we didn't have the money to send anyone to Paris. We were mainly unemployed and living on the breadline. We simply couldn't afford it. We were bitterly disappointed, but we decided instead to send a letter explaining our position and requesting sympathetic affiliation to the International. We drafted a letter and, in order not to duplicate the typing, Millie put the statement straight onto a stencil, which we copied to circulate to our comrades. We thought nothing of it and simply did it out of convenience, so it could be circulated widely inside our ranks. In fact, the letter was approved at a general members' meeting before being sent in a sealed envelope which Denzil Harber, who was attending the Congress for the RSL, was supposed to deliver.

The founding congress of the Fourth

At the World Congress in early September, the report of the British Section was presented. This contained a sharp attack on the WIL for refusing to unite with the other groups. I understand it was one of the French delegates who moved that we be treated as a sympathising group of the Fourth International. Then Cannon launched a vicious attack on us, accusing the "Lee group" of splitting on "purely personal grievances", obstructing unification, and refusing to send a delegate to the World Congress. He told a whole lot of lies, saying that our letter to the Congress was a statement to "the world at large", an open statement to our enemies, purely on the basis that it was duplicated and not typed. As a result of Cannon's attack on the WIL, sympathetic affiliation was rejected. From that time onwards, Cannon was to nurture a deeply held grudge against the WIL and its leadership, which was to have serious repercussions in the future.

Shortly after the Congress, on 12 October, Cannon wrote a report to Trotsky which referred to the "Lee Group".

"The Militant Group in the past six months had suffered from an unfortunate split led by Lee which resulted in the creation of another group without any principled grounds for the split (the *Workers International News*). This could only introduce confusion and demoralisation - the more so since both groups work exclusively in the Labour Party. At the same time the Liverpool branch had withdrawn from the Militant Group on opportunistic grounds. They wanted to work in the Labour Party simply as a left wing without any international connections...."

At the Unity Conference in London, "We carried on a strong crusade against irresponsible splits and made it clear that the international conference would do away with the possibility of a multiplicity of groups, and recognise only one section in each country...

"The Lee group consists of about thirty, mostly youngsters, who have been deeply poisoned with personal antagonism to the leadership of the Militant Group. They attempted to obstruct the unification but were pounded mercilessly at the Unification Conference, and their ranks were badly shaken. Their attitude was condemned by the international conference.

"Shachtman, during his visit in England, also had a session with this group. His opinion is the same as mine - that they will have to submit to the international decision and come into the united British section or suffer a split. It is only necessary for the British section to take a firm and resolute stand in regard to this group, and in no case to acknowledge its legitimacy.

"Unfortunately, this is easier said than done. The English comrades, alas, are gentlemen. They are not accustomed to our 'brutal' (i.e. Bolshevik) treatment of groups who play with splits. However, I think they learned something from our visit, at least they said they did.

"I will not attempt to prophesise the outcome of the British experiment in unification. Friction undoubtedly exists, and still worse, there are undoubted differences in conception. Some of the members of the James group were still debating the French turn from the point of view of Field-Oehler." [1]

As Cannon's report mentions, following the Congress, Max Shachtman arrived back in Britain to ask us to reconsider our position. He was quite indignant when he met us, asking why we had deliberately broken with the International in this manner. But when we heard a report of what had happened at the Congress, we were furious at Cannon and the others for spreading slanders about us. We then gave poor old Shatchman a roasting over the issue. I will say this for Shachtman; he was genuinely surprised when we told him what had really happened with Cannon over the Unity Agreement. Shachtman listened to what we had to say and he agreed to speak to our membership. We denounced the manoeuvres of Cannon at the meeting, but Shachtman defended him as best he could. "Well, it was a manoeuvre", he said, "but it was a good manoeuvre. Cannon wanted unity. He wanted to bring the tendency together", and so on and so forth. As if that was sufficient reason to stab us in the back. Although even at that time, there must have been frictions between him and Cannon that overshadowed the faction fight of 1939-40, he still defended Cannon.

As could be expected, Shachtman got a cool reception from the members, who were totally unconvinced by his arguments. After he left for America, we took the view that we were, in fact, the illegitimate child of the International. We would still continue the work of the International. In fact, we considered that we were the real Fourth International in Britain. Our view of the development of pre-war Trotskyism was summed up in a document produced by the WIL in late 1942. We saw it as a necessary preliminary stage in our development. But we regarded the formation of the WIL as a decisive break with the past, and the creation of the real beginnings of a genuine Trotskyist tradition in Britain.

"The initial cadres of the Left Opposition in the Communist Party of Great Britain, were in the main petty bourgeois", stated the WIL document. "While accepting the ideas and principles of the International Left Opposition, they made no attempt to concretise these ideas and apply them to the British movement. The spirit of a petty bourgeois discussion circle was fostered in the early meetings. No real attempt was made to acquaint the youth members and sympathisers of the theoretical differences between the Bolshevik-Leninists and the Stalinist bureaucracy nationally or internationally, or with the programme of the Left Opposition. The leadership showed the greatest incapacity to train the younger elements or to conduct any decisive political action.

"During the period of the campaign of the Left Opposition for re-entry into the Communist Parties, it was possible for a loose collection of individuals to hold together, for in this country it enabled them to appear in public as "critics" while binding them to no real programme of activity. However, when the German betrayal impelled the Left Opposition to consider the reform of the Comintern no longer possible and adopt the perspective of orientation towards the new Fourth International, the basic weakness of the British Bolshevik-Leninists was revealed.

"The directive given to the British comrades was to turn towards the centrist organisations as the main field of work. This perspective worked out by comrade Trotsky, was fundamentally correct. But due to the complete incapacity of the Trotskyists to carry out this tactic, the outcome resulted in failure. This turn towards the centrists marked the first of what was to be a series of splits. Incapable of acting as a unified body, the opposition burst asunder, one group entering the ILP, the other at first remained independent and later entered the Labour Party. This initial split took place without any thorough discussion or preparation, the factional lines running parallel to the personal alliances of the various individuals.

"From 1934 until 1938 a continuous series of splits took place. The political lines were as a rule, not fundamental in character, but on questions of tactics, which were raised to immutable principles. The factions were characterised by a core, which generally speaking, broke along lines of personal affiliation. The few who remained on the periphery of these factions - mainly fresh elements turning to the Trotskyist viewpoint - moved aimlessly from one group to the other seeking a lead.

"The French Party's turn to the Socialist Party and the Oehler split in America over the question of entry into the Socialist Party, created a new basis for the various factions. The 'principle' of the 'independence of the Bolshevik Party' became the centre of the new and 'higher' forms of political discussion.

"During the whole of this period, the International Secretariat was completely misinformed as to the real situation in the British movement - its strength, the forms of work it conducted, its support among the workers, and in every other aspect of its activities. The loose connection between the IS and the British movement facilitated this.

"The Trotskyist groups which evolved and disappeared were myriad. The Communist Left Opposition, the Marxist League, the Marxist Group, the Militant Group, the Chelsea Action Group, the Revolutionary Socialist League, the Unified Revolutionary Socialist League, the Militant Labour League, the Revolutionary Workers League, Workers International League - all these in the London area alone, and others emerged from time to time in the provinces.

"By September 1938 there were three distinct groups in existence in the London area as follows: (the names of the leaderships of those organisations are given to identify them as subsequently the names were changed). The Revolutionary Socialist League (James, Duncan, Lane - Wicks, Dewar), the Marxist League (Wicks, Dewar) had just entered into a unification with the RSL on the basis of the independent tactic. The Militant Group (Harber, Jackson) which was an entrist group in the Labour Party. Workers International League (Lee, Grant, Haston) - an entrist group in the Labour Party.

"There also existed the Revolutionary Socialist Party of Edinburgh, which was moving towards the Fourth International and was about to affect a unification with the RSL on the basis of the independent tactic. The leaders of this group were Maitland and Tait.

"Each year - and sometimes twice a year - a 'unity' Conference was called, but without any serious preparation or intention. The soft elements that had proved themselves incapable of any continuity of organised work, who had dropped out of the movement from time to time, appeared on the platform and played a predominant role in the 'discussions'. Each year it became more and more obvious that a genuine unification among the old elements was absolutely precluded, because of the determination of the 'leaders' to retain their independence and resist any encroachment on their positions, and most important, because of the absence of a genuine rank and file. It was evident that unification would only take place on the basis of a common programme of action, on the basis of common *work*.

"Such was the position in the British movement when the 'Peace and Unity Conference' took place in September 1938. In the bulletin circulated for pre-conference discussion, there were three theses submitted for discussion by the WIL, the RSL and the RSP. Representatives of these three groups, as well as a representative of the Militant Group attended the Conference. At this conference, the 'Peace and Unity agreement' was drawn up by and presented by the American comrade. There was no political discussion on the differences of tactics and perspectives for Britain, which had separated the groups for years. Only this 'Peace and Unity Agreement' which the groups were given twenty minutes to sign. All groups signed except WIL." [2]

We had turned our back decisively on the so-called united tendency, the RSL - as we had done with the old Militant Group. And, just as we expected, as soon as Cannon and Shachtman had gone back to America, the fun started. Within weeks of this so-called Unity Conference, the first splits appeared, and the organisation began to dissolve into its constituent parts. The RSP walked out when they saw what was happening. Henry Sara and Harry Wicks left, and a deep split took place at its conference where the majority of the old RSL split away to form the Revolutionary Workers League, followed by a series of individual resignations. The group that was left suffered from the formation of rival factions, especially with the outbreak of the Second World War, and their attitude towards the proletarian military policy advocated by Trotsky.

The RSL, seeing us as an enemy group, immediately declared war on us. We in turn went onto the offensive. Our wings weren't clipped and our hands weren't tied by any agreement, so we got stuck into a vigorous campaign to win over the best elements in the RSL branches, which were in a state of crisis. Very quickly, in the early part of 1939, we won over the comrades in Liverpool. We took the big majority of the Liverpool branch, including Jimmy Dean and Tommy Birchall and other key comrades. The same thing happened in Leeds, where we won over the majority of the RSP. We left Frank Maitland and Tommy Tate, who were the leaders of that tendency, almost completely high and dry. We soon won the majority of the RSP in Edinburgh, which had been their stronghold, and they entered the Labour Party under our guidance.

Up to the onset of the war, we had begun a systematic publication of Trotskyist pamphlets. For example, as I have already mentioned, we issued the *Lessons of Spain* by Trotsky with our own introduction. "The experience of Spain is a warning and a lesson to the workers of the world, above all to the British workers", we wrote. "Yesterday's drama in Spain is being rehearsed today in Britain. Tomorrow it will be enacted if the British workers have failed to realise the nature of the tasks which history has placed before them. And in preparing to tackle those tasks, the working class has need above all, of 'a party, once more a party; again a party'."

On re-reading it after many years, I must say, it was a very good introduction. Trotsky sent us a very enthusiastic letter in response. Although it wasn't very well printed, the Old Man was very encouraged by our small efforts. We were not the official section of the international, but Trotsky could see from the introduction that we had a very healthy approach and were a genuine Bolshevik-Leninist tendency, and not a sect. It is significant that the only split in the whole of our history in which Trotsky did not intervene, or denounce was our split with the Militant Group. We believe that this was for two reasons. Firstly, Trotsky knew the limitations of Cannon and didn't accept all his opinions at face value. Secondly, he was not prepared to pass judgement on groups until he was certain of how the different tendencies were developing. He would not intervene prematurely in Britain until things had crystallised sufficiently. In any case, he must have despaired about the way the RSL was splitting into fragments. For the moment, he left things alone in Britain, and concentrated on events in America, and the developing faction fight between Cannon and Shachtman.

We made sure Trotsky got our material, and I am sure he would certainly have compared it very favourably with the material of the RSL. Trotsky was waiting, if you like, to see which way the wind was blowing in Britain. This view is partially confirmed in the reply to questions put to Trotsky by CLR James in April 1939. James outlined a brief history of the British section, including the Unity Agreement. "The pact for unity and peace stipulated that each group was to continue its own activity and after six months a balance sheet was to be drawn", James told Trotsky. However, James went on to explain, "The last news is the friction has continued [sic] and that the Labour Party group is now dominant." This is diplomatic language for saying the "unity agreement" had fallen apart. James then goes on to inform Trotsky, "There is also another group - Lee's group in the Labour Party - which refused to have anything to do with fusion, saying that it was bound to fail. The Lee group is very active." Significantly, Trotsky in reply to James' points, made no reference to the Lee group, or its decision not to take part in the fusion. Trotsky preferred to wait and see.

British Trotskyism in the Second World War

Stalin's foreign policy - which was supposed to avoid war and defend the USSR - actually placed the Soviet Union in great danger. His betrayal of the Spanish Revolution made war inevitable. The attempt to woo Britain and France failed utterly. The "democracies" that Pollitt lauded so enthusiastically in 1937 were in fact allowing Hitler to build up his army and expand his borders in the belief that he was going to attack Russia.

The feebleness of Chamberlain in the face of Hitler at the time of the Czechoslovakia debacle was dictated by the weakness of British capitalism at the time. It is a fact that Britain was unprepared for war with Germany. In reality, the ruling class was more afraid of the British Labour movement than German fascism, which they saw as a bulwark against Bolshevism. Churchill, that great "democrat", had been an ardent admirer of Mussolini. A big section of the British ruling class had been sympathetic to the Nazis right up until the war. During the first days of 1939, Chamberlain and his minister Halifax were in Rome, feasting with Mussolini and raising their glasses in tribute to the new emperor of Abyssinia. Halifax told the Italian foreign minister Ciano that he hoped Franco would soon "settle the Spanish question". So much for the "British democrats"!

Finally, after the British imperialists had handed Czechoslovakia and its huge arms industries to Hitler on a plate, Stalin dropped the idea of a pact with the "democracies" and instead did a deal with Hitler. In August 1939 Germany and Russia signed a non-aggression pact. This made a European war inevitable, but ensured that Hitler would first strike westwards not eastwards. The USSR established friendly trading relations with Germany. In effect, as Trotsky said, Stalin assumed the role of Hitler's quartermaster. While it was permissible for the Soviet Union to manoeuvre between different capitalist powers to safeguard itself, Stalin's policy was a complete betrayal of the elementary principles of a Leninist foreign policy. After the signing ceremony was over, Stalin proposed a toast - to Adolf Hitler: "I know how much the German people love their Fuehrer", he said. "I should therefore to drink a toast to his health."

Shortly after this, the Germans and Russians occupied Poland and the Red Army moved into the Baltic States and Finland, where the Russians got a hotter reception than they had bargained for. They suffered terrible casualties in the Karelia campaign in the beginning of 1940 - perhaps a million were killed or wounded. The problems experienced by the Red Army in Finland showed the terrible damage that had been inflicted by Stalin's Purges. It was this more than anything else that made Hitler decide to attack the Soviet Union, believing - wrongly - that it would be easy to conquer.

These events caused considerable shock internationally. Ordinary members of the labour movement were shocked and disquieted by Stalin's Purges and scandalised by the Hitler-Stalin Pact. We made life as difficult as we could for the Stalinists, of course. And although these events were of a deadly serious character, we never lost our sense of humour. After all, humour also has a place in working class propaganda and agitation, and is especially effective in the British labour movement. I remember we lampooned them mercilessly in a song set to the music of "Oh my darling Clementine", which went like this:

"Leon Trotsky is a Nazi.
Yes, I know it for a fact!
First I read it, then I said it,
Before the Stalin-Hitler Pact.

Chorus:

Oh my darling, Oh my darling,
Oh my darling Party Line.
Never break thee or forsake thee
Oh my darling Party Line.

In the Kremlin, in the Kremlin,
In the Fall of thirty nine,
Sat a Russian and a Prussian,

Working out the Party Line.

In Siberia, in Siberia,
Where the Arctic son doth shine
Sat an old Bolshevik
Who they called a dirty swine.

Party comrade, Party comrade,
What a sorry fate is thine!
Comrade Stalin does not love you
'Cause you left the Party Line.

To this, we added a couple of lines to the tune of *Auld lang syne:*

And should old Bolshies be forgot
And never brought to mind,
You'll find them in Siberia
With a ball and chain behind.

A ball and chain behind, my dear,
A ball and chain behind,
For Stalin shot the bloody lot
For the sake of old lang syne.

Britain in war

In the second half of the 1930s there were signs of an upturn in the class struggle in Britain. After almost a decade of passivity on the industrial front following the defeat of the General Strike, trade union militancy was on the increase again. There was a spate of unofficial strikes, which the union leaders were powerless to control. The London bus strike of 1937 showed a high degree of militancy. *The Times* was warning the union leaders that if they could not keep their house in order, other methods would have to be found. This was a veiled threat of dictatorship. The army manoeuvres in the period before the war were, based not on the assumption of war with Germany but rather civil disturbances in Britain itself. For the first time the insurance companies were refusing to insure against the risk of civil war.

In September 1939 Britain declared war on Germany. Within a short space of time, Scotland Yard raided the WIL premises. This set the tone for the whole of the war period. Interestingly enough, the RSL were left untouched by the Special Branch. Due to their lack of activity and their sectarian approach, they were not considered as a potential danger nor given the slightest importance by the state. The raids only affected organisations that were active and posed some kind of threat to the war effort. Scotland Yard detectives came to our headquarters, which was in Haston's house, and searched the place from top to bottom. They were there almost all day, going through our material, every document, and every scrap of paper. They also questioned us repeatedly. We told them of our political position towards the war and other questions, and then they left. After that it became a regular thing that once a month we would have a visit from Scotland Yard. Sometimes, they became so familiar that we joked with them. "Come on", we said, "why raid us like this? If you'd only let us know, give us your address and we'll send you notices of the meetings". Despite this good humour, they disrupted our activity and turned everything upside down. Of course, in opposing the war we were considered a damn nuisance, but there was nothing they could do about it. In those days, the security forces were mainly interested in the CP and the fascist organisations that openly supported Germany.

As an anecdote, just after the war began, we were surprised by the sudden appearance in Britain of Pierre Frank. He was considered a political opponent, as he had broken with the Trotskyist movement in France, and Trotsky had sharply criticised his actions. He had came to Britain as a representative of the Molinier group - the PCI - that had split from the International. Whereas Trotsky had not attacked or criticised us for our split, he had denounced the Molinier/Frank tendency in the sharpest possible terms. With his customary wit Trotsky said that Molinier was like a cow that gives lots of milk and then kicks over the bucket! He characterised both Molinier and Frank as rotten opportunists and adventurers. A resolution written by Trotsky himself stressed, while his supporters would be welcomed back, any question of Molinier returning to the Trotskyist movement was entirely ruled out.

Frank had escaped to Britain to avoid capture by the French authorities. He attempted to promote the Molinier group in Britain and create an axis between this group and the WIL. We explained to Frank in no uncertain terms that although the WIL had been dealt with unfairly at the Founding World Congress, we nevertheless considered ourselves a loyal part of the Trotskyist movement and were not prepared under any circumstances to attack the International. We were confident that over time we would be recognised as the legitimate British section of the International. Therefore, we refused to have anything to do with Pierre Frank, who went away with his tail between his legs. He failed to convince a single comrade of the need to turn our back on the International or of trying to create some new sort of rival group. The British authorities later interned him. Of course, the WIL protested vigorously about his internment, but when he was released he caused us some bother for a while, when he provided a prop for Gerry Healy's factionalism.

Having failed to convince us on unity with Molinier, Frank tried every means possible to organise some sort of faction inside our group. He managed to convince one of our comrades, Betty Hamilton (who ended up with Healy), that we had an unhealthy internal regime within the WIL. This was supposedly due to the fact that we didn't have any real differences within our ranks. For Pierre Frank that was unhealthy! Frank, who was staying at her place, convinced her that an organisation without factions was un-Bolshevik. Even if there were no political differences, he argued, you must have factions within the organisation! In the end, we were not prepared to countenance this nonsense and we expelled Betty Hamilton for intriguing with a hostile grouping.

As a further aside, Healy, just a month or two before the war, announced he was starting a new career in Lever Brothers. He worked for them in some sort of scheme where leaflets were distributed round the houses, and he was about to net an important supervisor's job in the company. So he began to drift out of activity and was preparing to leave the movement altogether. Perhaps I shouldn't really confess this, but I managed to persuade him to stay! "Now look here, you can get a job as a supervisor. You might even go higher up. But what would be the use of it?" I told him. "The war is coming in a few months and what happens to your job then? Your job won't last. So the plan is a stupid idea." After the discussion, he chose to remain in the movement. At that time, Healy did positive work as an industrial organiser for the tendency. But that was not to last long.

Trotsky's military policy

From Mexico, Trotsky advanced the slogan of unconditional defence of the Soviet Union in the war. This brought to a head the crisis that had been simmering inside the American SWP. A minority led by Max Shachtman and James Burnham were opposed to Trotsky's position. They considered that the regime in the USSR had degenerated to the point where it was no longer a deformed workers' state - as Trotsky maintained - but was "state capitalism". This provoked a debate in which Trotsky intervened with some of his most brilliant and profound articles and documents, which were published as a book, In Defence of Marxism.

Needless to say, we were in complete agreement with Trotsky's position, which formed the basis for our later development and deepening of the idea of proletarian Bonapartism.

WIL opposed the imperialist war from the start. In the September 1939 issue of *Youth for Socialism*, I wrote an article under the banner heading of *Down With the War*. However, unlike the drawing room "Marxists" of the RSL, who were effectively paralysed by the war, we took our agitation to the factories and workplaces in an attempt to connect with the working class. Just before the fall of France in June 1940, in some of his last writings, Trotsky wrote some of the finest political material of his entire life. He was examining the attitude of the revolutionary movement towards imperialist war in general, and the Second World War in particular. As I pointed out at the time, "the Old Man gave the finest theoretical exposition of the Marxist-Internationalist attitude to imperialist war in general, and the present imperialist war in particular. These fragments will remain for all time the classical exposition of the Marxist approach to the problem and of the dialectical method as a means for determining the policy of the revolutionary party."

Trotsky pointed out that Lenin in the course of the First World War had laid down the Marxist attitude towards war. However, if the truth is to be told, because the revolutionary movement had been caught by surprise by the betrayal of August 1914, Lenin and the other leading internationalists had tended to pose things in a slightly ultra-left manner. The internationalists defended the ideas of internationalism, class solidarity and raised the question of revolutionary defeatism. They put forward the idea that in war, the defeat of your own ruling class is the lesser evil. Posed in a crude and unqualified way - which is exactly what the sectarians have been doing for the last 80 years - this policy can be interpreted as support for the foreign bourgeoisie. The ignorant sectarians have no idea of the concrete circumstances that determined Lenin's stance in 1914.

The reason why Lenin expressed himself in such a way was to draw a clear line between the revolutionary vanguard and the social patriotic traitors of the Second International. The betrayal of the leaders of the Second International was entirely unexpected - even by Lenin and Trotsky. It caused tremendous disorientation and confusion. For this reason, Lenin tended to bend the stick in one direction. However, his emphatic policy of revolutionary defeatism was aimed at the cadres of the International, and not the broad masses. Revolutionary defeatism was not the means whereby the working class would be won to the revolutionary party. Far from it. In 1917 the masses in Russia were won over with the slogans of peace, bread and land, and "All Power to the Soviets". Revolutionary defeatism could never have won the masses to the programme and banner of the revolution. That is why Lenin changed his views on slogans regarding the war when he returned to Russia in the Spring of 1917. He adapted his slogans to concrete circumstances. That is what ensured the success of the Bolshevik Party.

While the Second World War was an imperialist war, not qualitatively different to the war of 1914-18, nevertheless the concrete circumstances were different and this had to be taken into account as far as tactics and slogans were concerned. As Trotsky explained in an unfinished article, dictated just prior to his assassination in 1940:

> "The present war, as we have stated on more than one occasion, is a continuation of the last war. But a continuation does not signify a repetition. As a general rule, a continuation signifies a development, a deepening, [and] a sharpening. Our policy, the policy of the revolutionary proletariat towards the second imperialist war is a continuation of the policy elaborated during the last imperialist war, primarily under Lenin's leadership. But a continuation does not signify a repetition. In this case too, continuation signifies a development, a deepening and a sharpening. *We were caught unawares in 1914.*
>
> "During the last war not only the proletariat as a whole but also its vanguard, and, in a certain sense, the vanguard of this vanguard was caught unawares. The elaboration of the principles of revolutionary policy toward the war began at a time when the war was already in full blaze and the military machine exercised unlimited rule. One year after the outbreak of the war the small revolutionary minority was still compelled to accommodate itself to a centrist majority at the Zimmerwald Conference. Prior to the February Revolution and even afterwards, the revolutionary elements felt themselves to be not contenders for power but the extreme left opposition. Even Lenin relegated the socialist revolution to a more or less distant future...
>
> "In 1915 Lenin referred in his writings to revolutionary wars which the victorious proletariat would have to wage. But it was a question of an indefinite historical perspective and not of tomorrow's task. The attention of the revolutionary wing was centred on the question of the defence of the capitalist fatherland. The revolutionaries naturally replied to this question in the negative. This was entirely correct. But this purely negative answer served as the basis for propaganda and for training cadres but it could not win the masses who did not want a foreign conqueror.
>
> "In Russia prior to the war the Bolsheviks constituted four fifths of the proletarian vanguard, that is, of the workers participating in political life (newspapers, elections, etc). Following the February revolution the unlimited rule passed into the hands of the defencists, the Mensheviks and the SRs. True enough, the Bolsheviks in the space of eight months conquered the overwhelming majority of the workers. But the decisive role in this conquest was played not by the refusal to defend the bourgeois fatherland but the slogan: 'All power to the Soviets!' And only by this revolutionary slogan! The criticism of imperialism, its militarism, the renunciation of the defence of bourgeois democracy and so on could never have conquered the overwhelming majority of the people to the side of the Bolsheviks..." [3]

While it was necessary to maintain a principled and inflexible attitude of irreconcilable opposition towards the imperialist war, it was necessary to put our attitude towards the war in a way that would be understood by the broad masses. It was out of this approach, that the proletarian military policy of the Fourth International, put forward originally by Trotsky, was developed by the Trotskyist movement. Of course, the war was an imperialist war, and a continuation of 1914-18. As such, we were opposed to imperialism, capitalism and its war. In the words of Clauswitz, which Lenin was fond of quoting, "War is the continuation of politics by other means."

The Allied powers were simply using anti-fascist propaganda to cover up their war aims. Nevertheless, we had to take into consideration that the mass of workers genuinely wanted to defeat Hitler fascism. That is why they supported the war against Hitler. We also wanted to defeat Hitler, but with our own means and programme. This could only be achieved by the carrying through of a revolutionary war against fascism, which meant the working class taking power. The proletarian military policy was based on the conception that the capitalist class could not fight a real war against fascism. The British bourgeois had supported fascism before the war in its struggle against the socialist revolution. Only the working class could fight fascism, and so they would have to expropriate the ruling class, take over the country and conduct a genuine revolutionary war.

The Stalinists and the war

The Communist Party carried out a number of somersaults in the first period of the war. When the war broke out in 1939, the CPGB was still on the "popular front" Line. So in the first six weeks of the war, they supported the "just war" against fascism. Then soon afterwards, when Stalin signed his infamous Pact with Hitler, the Line was hastily changed. The CP leaders were taken completely off guard by the signing of the Hitler-Stalin Pact. Therefore, for a time, Harry Pollitt continued to push his "patriotic" Line with the usual vehemence, calling on all true patriots to support the war against Hitler and so on.

Within a few days, following orders from Moscow, the CP changed its Line to one of opposition to the war. Poor old Pollitt, who did not jump fast enough for his masters in the Kremlin, fell into disgrace and was replaced as general secretary of the British Party by Palme Dutt, an even more slavish stooge. Given the existence of the Stalin-Hitler Pact, and the carve-up of Poland between Russia and Germany, Moscow now regarded the "democracies" of Britain and France with hostility. Soon the CP was calling on the British workers to recognise "Churchill and Daladier, Attlee and Blum" as their main enemies. The British Communist Party now took a position against the imperialist war. But this was an anti-war position of a peculiar character. It was not a genuine anti-war opposition, based on a Leninist internationalist position.

Pollitt and Campbell were forced to make a humiliating recantation and confess to their "social patriotic" mistakes. They were lucky. In France, where the CP initially sought an agreement with the Germans, and even sent a delegation to request permission to publish *L'Humanite* in occupied Paris, CP leaders, who opposed the policy of the Party, were actually betrayed to the Gestapo. As reliable mouthpieces for Moscow's foreign policy, the Communist Parties dutifully attacked the "democratic" imperialist powers. In practice their position was "peace - on Hitler's terms". In other words, instead of being an agency for British imperialism they became, due to the Hitler-Stalin pact, the apologists of German imperialism. So abrupt a turn naturally provoked a certain amount of unease within their ranks. Actually they made the transition without too much difficulty, since the more proletarian elements saw the abandonment of popular frontism as a left turn. However, it meant that the best elements of the CP that we came across were more amenable to our ideas.

The way in which they changed gave rise to some amusing incidents. Dudley Edwards, a marvellous old comrade who at one time had been the secretary of the ILP's Revolutionary Policy Committee and who joined us in the 1960s, was at the time a young CP shop steward in the car factory in Oxford. He was supposed to give a speech on the war at a public meeting, and was prepared to deliver a speech on the lines of the old policy, supporting the war. Minutes before he was due to speak, someone tugged at his sleeve and whispered: "Comrade, you can't give that speech. The Line's been changed!" And in two minutes, Dudley had to improvise a different speech, putting exactly the opposite position!

The abruptness of the change of Line caused a crisis in the Party for a short time. It was not easy to explain to the workers why the enemies of yesterday had suddenly become allies, or why British "democracy" had suddenly become transformed into British imperialism. The Party lost a lot of support at this time. When Harry Pollitt presented their programme to a working class electorate at the Silvertown bye-election in February 1940, he was rejected by a vote of 12 to 1. Nevertheless, the Party held onto most of its workers, who were relieved by the abandonment of the old policy of open class collaboration. The new policy was an ultra-left caricature of a real communist policy. Most of those who left the CP were middle class types.

The CPGB had organised a "People's Convention", that was supposed to be an alternative to Parliament. We participated and sent delegates because layers of trade unionists were involved in this convention. We managed to send delegates through the trade unions to put our position. We counterposed our position against their pacifist, or semi-pacifist, peace position put forward by the *Daily Worker*. Although our position got relatively few votes, given the character of the Convention, we had a relative success and we made a certain number of CP contacts as a result.

But events were to plunge the CP into crisis yet again. On June 30 1941 Hitler's armies attacked Russia. The Germans had massed 100 army divisions on the Russian border, which struck with devastating force. Hitler's attacks on the USSR compel the Stalinists hastily to change the Line. Labour Monthly had called an industrial conference with the aim of fomenting strikes. The conference went ahead, but its content was changed. Instead of discussing how to organise strikes, they placed on the agenda the issue of how to raise productivity in industry! For the remainder of the war the Stalinists pursued an openly strike-breaking policy.

> At the 1942 CP conference, the general secretary of the CPGB, Harry Pollitt delivered a real hymn in praise of all strike-breakers: "I salute our comrade, a docker from Hull, who was on a job unloading a ship with a cargo urgently wanted... When the rest of the dockers struck work, he fought against it because he believed that the course of action he recommended would get what was wanted without a strike. What courage, what a sacred spirit of real class consciousness, to walk on the ship's gangway and resume his job.... This is not strikebreaking. That is striking a blow against fascism as vital as any blow a lad in the Red Army is striking at the present time. It sounds peculiar. It can be misunderstood. The Trotskyists and the ILP charge the party and me in particular with being strike breakers. We can face that from people whose political line is consciously helping the development of fascism." (1942 Conference CPGB).

The WIL and the war

When we received the material by Trotsky on the proletarian military policy, we were enormously enthused. Applying the policy to British conditions, our programme called for Labour to break with the wartime National Government, and for Labour to power on a socialist programme. In a socialist Britain, while we would fight fascism militarily, we would also conduct class propaganda and extend the hand of friendship to the ordinary German workers, calling on them to overthrow Hitler. The military policy also included the election of officers by the soldiers, the training of officers by the trade unions, the need for a workers' militia, the establishment of committees in the armed forces, for the workers to be trained in arms, and so on. In other words, it aimed to raise the class questions in relation to the army and the war. It attempted to show that, despite all their talk of defeating fascism, the imperialists were not in the least interested in fighting fascism, after all, and it was they who helped Hitler to power in the first place. The only class that could fight fascism was the working class, but in order to do this effectively, it was necessary to conduct an irreconcilable struggle against the ruling class in the so-called democratic countries as well as the ruling class in the fascist countries. As opposed to pacifism and conscientious objection, we were in favour of comrades going into the armed forces to conduct revolutionary work.

After the German invasion of France, the Labour Party entered a coalition government with the Conservatives and Liberals, headed by Churchill. The Labour leaders declared an electoral truce for the duration of the war. This action was endorsed by the Party conference by a massive 2,413,000 votes to 170,000. This reflected the mood of the times. The Nazi armies were already in Holland and Belgium. The Dutch had been crushed in just twenty days. The Belgian king had surrendered. The British army in France was trapped on the beaches at Dunkirk, hard pressed by the advancing Germans. Nine days later, Italy entered the war on the side of Germany. Nine days later the French bourgeoisie capitulated to Hitler without a fight. The position was desperate.

GDH Cole expressed the mood of the British workers at that time: "Momentarily, there was no time for dissention or recrimination. The workers in all essential industries worked, after Dunkirk, all hours that physical powers would permit - often many more than were wise. Gradually, some order was introduced into the organisation of the industrial war effort. The ARP services were enthusiastically performed, often by men and women who went back to work after nights spent in rescue. When the War Secretary asked for 150,000 volunteers to act as 'parashots' to watch for parachute troops, 750,000 men joined what afterwards became the Home Guard." [4]

During 1940, through the pages of *Youth for Socialism*, we tried to orientate ourselves along the lines advocated by Trotsky, explaining the role the ruling class was playing in the war in a way that would be understood by ordinary workers. We had to take into consideration the attitude of the workers towards fascism. In the factories, at that time, the working class was working 18 or even 20 hours a day for the purpose of turning out war armaments. As we were immersed in the mass movement, we instinctively understood that this approach by Trotsky, which was a development of Lenin's position, was absolutely correct. As we had the correct orientation and approach to the workers, we enthusiastically took up the position of the proletarian military policy. To give them credit, the position was also immediately taken up by the American SWP. Cannon made a number of speeches on the question, which we printed in our paper as well as in the Workers International News. However, in other sections of the International there was opposition from the sectarians to this policy. They simply wanted to repeat the position of Lenin in 1914 and the policy of revolutionary defeatism. This reflected a sectarian approach divorced from the real working class movement. They were not able to relate to the real situation on the ground in a flexible, but principled fashion.

The WIL took up Trotsky's position energetically. I wrote a *Socialist Appeal* editorial outlining the policy:

> "The British workers want to see a real end made to Hitlerism of all varieties and to the domination of one nation by another", stated the article. "They want to win the peoples of Europe to their side in a common struggle against these evils. They want to see the Soviet Union give the full measure of real assistance that will save it from destruction and enable it to reclaim and rebuild all that has been lost. They want to see China victorious over Japanese militarism. They want a genuine international 'united strategy' that will enable these tasks to be performed and bring about a truly democratic and lasting peace. But while imperialism sits in the saddle there can be no such thing.
>
> "These aims can only become a reality, that is transferred from the realm of words to that of deeds, when the workers take effective measures against imperialism. Such measures would necessarily include the granting of immediate freedom to India and the colonies, the nationalisation under workers control of the banks and all heavy industry and the armaments industry; the election of officers by the soldiers and the merging of the armed forces into the armed people. Only when such measures have been taken would Britain's war be transformed into one genuinely being fought for national liberation and in defence of the Soviet Union. Only a government of the workers can take such measures. Only a workers' government can lay the basis for a genuine 'united strategy' of a global nature. For the only force that cuts across national frontiers and continental barriers is the common interest of the working masses against capitalism." (*Socialist Appeal*, November 1942).

It was necessary to take into account the real situation of the working class in Britain. At the time of Dunkirk, when Hitler's armies swept through Norway, Netherlands, Denmark, Belgium and France, the British Army was shattered and on the retreat. This raised alarm in Britain of the danger of an immediate invasion. Under these circumstances, we raised the slogan in *Youth for Socialism* of the need to arm the British working class. If the ruling class was serious about defending Britain - which they weren't - then they must arm the population.

The French ruling class allowed Paris to fall to the Germans without a struggle. The Nazis occupied France and established a puppet government under Petain at Vichy. There was an interview by a French general in the Daily Telegraph at the time, in which he admitted that they could have defended Paris. However, that defence could only have been undertaken if they had armed and organised the population. That policy was considered too dangerous, with the memory of the 1871 Commune still fresh in their minds. The prospect of a new Paris Commune was a nightmare facing the French ruling class, and so, rather than risk the possibility of the working class taking power, they capitulated, revealing their complete rottenness and incapacity. Rather than take that chance of arming the working class, they preferred to surrender Paris to the Nazis.

When the defeated British forces in France were being evacuated from Dunkirk in 1940, an enormous wave of fear and panic - it is hard to imagine it now - swept through the working class. We argued in *Youth for Socialism* that the same thing would happen in Britain as in France if there was an invasion by Hitler. We explained that Britain could be defended, and could be an impregnable fortress against fascism, if there was the arming of workers under the control of the trade unions. Instead of the Home Guard, the workers should be armed factory by factory. On that basis, it would be entirely possible to defend Britain and render it impossible for Hitler to invade. However, as we explained, rather than risk arming the working class, the British ruling class would prefer to sell out to the Nazis if it came to the crunch. Our agitation on this question was a means of exposing the sham position of the British ruling class. We managed to get an echo for our position, which allowed us to extend our influence in the advanced sections of the working class.

Meanwhile, in early 1940, Pierre Frank, having failed to get a response from our organisation, got in touch with a tiny little grouping of Oehlerites. This was a minuscule splinter group led by a man called Hugo Oehler, which had split from the American Workers Party when they entered the Socialist Party. As in Britain, these sectarians always have an inflexible ultra-left attitude on the question of the independence of the party. Of course, the American Trotskyists were not a large party, far from it. They had a few thousand members at most. If the American SWP had been a large party, then things may have been different, and the principle of the independent party may have been correct. But as always, seeing things in terms of "principles", the sectarians lacked any sense of proportion.

There was a little fragment of this grouping in Britain, led by two chaps, called Ernie Rogers and Denis Levin. They eventually left the movement altogether, and Levin later did quite well in the business world. But at the time, they were in Coventry working in the aircraft industry, and Pierre Frank was in touch with them. He was looking round for some points of support and he gave them some brilliant advice: he told them that they should issue a leaflet demanding that the workers seize the factories! Now just imagine it. The workers, faced with the imminent prospect of an invasion by a Nazi army, were working up to twenty hours a day in arms firms, and Frank says this is the time to seize the factories. That is what you might call impeccable timing! But the ultra-lefts Levin and Rogers thought this was a brilliant idea. It appealed to them enormously. So they secretly distributed their Open Letter to British Workers leaflet. The leaflet, which was completely anonymous, without any publisher's name or address, was passed around.

A couple of days later, there was a knock on the door of the digs where Rogers and Levin were staying. In a very conspiratorial fashion, they peeped out from the top floor to see who was there. To their alarm, down below they saw a policeman clutching a copy of their leaflet. Predictably, the two heroes panicked, dashed out of the back door and went "underground". They beat it out of Coventry and came to us, asking for assistance, money, and so on. They said they were on the run from the police and everybody was after them. Well, in the meantime, the landlady got in touch with Sam Walters who was a member of the tendency also working in Coventry, and told him: "you know a policeman called around to see your friends. He said your friends had forgotten to print their name, address and authorisation on the leaflet." And that was all. The whole episode was over a small technical detail. Predictably, the sectarians got the wrong end of the stick.

Of course, we did not have the hysterical position of the ultra-lefts, but nevertheless we did pay serious attention to the question of security. When the war broke out, it wasn't at all clear within the first few weeks what was going to happen. The police had raided us before, so we weren't sure which way events were going to develop. Nobody knew whether the organisation would be declared illegal or not. As a result, in case of illegality, we decided to send certain comrades to Dublin to establish a base in Ireland for the organisation. Ireland was a neutral country, so if we had become illegal we could produce and send revolutionary material from there through sympathetic seafarers. If necessary, we would be able to set up some kind of a radio station that could broadcast to workers in Britain.

It was decided to keep Ralph, Millie and myself in Britain, and to send Jock Haston and a few other comrades to Ireland. They made contact with the left wing of the Irish Labour Party, especially with Nora Connolly O'Brien, the daughter of James Connolly. They also came into contact with the youth of the IRA. Gerry Healy without any discussion or consultation with the leadership of the tendency, unilaterally declared he was leaving Liverpool, where he was working at the time, and going back to Ireland. He was originally from Donegal. Soon afterwards, he resigned after a quarrel, the second resignation that year, but was persuaded to come back. But at any rate we managed to establish an organised group that was oriented towards the Irish Labour Party. So a base was prepared in Ireland to assist, if necessary, the movement towards socialist revolution in Britain.

> "We decided that Ralph Lee and Ted Grant would be sent to produce the paper and to train the group that we sent over and we decided to send four or six of the younger people to Ireland with them for that purpose", recalled Haston. "In the event Ralph Lee decided he wouldn't go and we took the view that Ted couldn't do the job on his own. I was sent in place of Lee and Grant to head the group that went to Ireland…
>
> "We faithfully followed the entrist line. We had contact with the left wing of the Irish Labour Party in Dublin. Our principal contact was Norah Connolly O'Brien, who was the daughter of Jim Connolly, and she was one of our best contacts then, and she fed us when we were bloody hungry from time to time…
>
> "At the same time we made contact with the youngsters in the IRA who were fairly active. In the Dublin IRA, the leadership tended to be right wing, as the youngsters tended to be socialist or labour party orientated and we made contact with them and won some of them over to the Trotskyist movement. We kept them in the IRA as a faction until they were finally thrown out, but that was part of our activity."
>
> Asked about what the IRA leadership thought about this, Haston replied, "They didn't like it very much at all. In fact, there was a classic occasion when I was running a class in Liberty Hall, which was the headquarters of the Transport Workers' Union, when a score of armed IRA guys came in and started drilling in the hall. The result was that the trade union asked us not to meet there anymore, because they were afraid there might be repercussions on them. Eventually they [the IRA] told us to 'get out, or else', and I was given forty-eight hours to get back to England or they would blow me up!" [5]

At this time we published a small daily duplicated bulletin, called *Workers Diary*, which was mainly down to the efforts of Ralph Lee, and some help from myself. This was then circulated among our members throughout the country and used effectively to supplement *Youth for Socialism* and *Workers International News*. In case we became illegal and were forced underground, we at least would have been able to turn out duplicated material. Every branch of the organisation had a silk screen printing outfit, made by the indefatigable Ralph

Lee, so that they would be able to turn out stuff if the leadership at the centre was arrested, and all connections were broken off.

At this time, our work, in the Labour Party, including the youth work in the Labour League of Youth (LLY), was dramatically tailing off. Nothing much was taking place in the Labour Party at that stage. The political truce had choked off life within the Party, and more and more we were forced into independent open work. The Labour League of Youth almost completely disappeared in 1939 as a result of the sabotage of the Stalinists. The young Ted Willis, who later became Lord Willis, had done a very good piece of fraction work for the Communist Party. The Stalinists had sent hundreds of youngsters into the League of Youth and had practically taken it over. As we had only small forces, we weren't in a position to defeat them. They succeed in taking the majority of the Labour League of Youth into the YCL, but of course, subsequently lost most of these people. In the process, the LLY was practically destroyed.

By 1940, those who were still left in the League of Youth were either conscripted into the armed forces or working long hours in the armament factories. The League of Youth had for all intents and purposes practically disappeared. All political activity ceased in the youth organisation. As for the adult party, the ward branches and constituency parties were hardly functioning at all. The trade union branches still remained and had some life during the course of the war, but this was mainly older workers and a layer from the armaments industries who were in reserved occupations.

Increasingly during 1940, we were being forced to do more and more open work. The ILP, on the basis of its anti-war activity and its pacifist stance, began to grow somewhat so we paid a certain attention to it. We were always very flexible on the question of tactics. Although we recognised the importance of the mass organisations, we never had a fetish about them. Tactics are a question of flexible attitudes, rather than principles on which one must always remain intransigent. During that period, we used our *Youth for Socialism* and *Workers International News* to turn not only towards the ILP but also towards the ranks of the Communist Party.

Tactical flexibility

Our turn towards the ILP shows the flexible way in which we dealt with things. In a review of tactics, and to show how they were developed, Jock Haston wrote a piece that is worth quoting.

> "There are no short cuts to the leadership of the working class. "Nevertheless, a correct application of tactics can assist the process of penetrating the ranks of the workers and in this way hasten the process of gaining the leadership; mistakes in tactics can condemn the revolutionary party to sterility and isolation and dissipate the energy of its cadres in fruitless activity. With every shift in the movement of the workers, the tactical tasks of the revolutionaries alter and assume new emphasis. This is particularly true of WIL. Precisely because of its lack of historical background and lack of support within the ranks of the working class, as well as the youthful and inexperienced composition of its cadres, it has had to impinge itself from the outside upon the labour organisations. But here our very weakness

allowed of extreme mobility of tactics which rapidly changing events deem it necessary to review as the need arises.

"Nevertheless, the change in organisational tactics always arouses differences of opinion within the ranks of revolutionary organisations. These differences arise from the appraisal of the political situation; from the conservatism which arises through established routine and reluctance to alter one's habits over a period; as well as from the genuine political differences ranging from ultra-left sectarianism to centrist capitulation. These are not always clearly demarcated in their lines of divergence."

"As a pre-requisite for our next step it is necessary to review our past tactics in the light of our experiences. From the time of its formation, our organisation has adopted the tactic of entry into the Labour Party. In our document entitled Tasks of the Bolshevik-Leninists in Britain presented to the 1938 Unity Conference, this position was summed up in the slogan 'Full Strength at the Point of Attack.' Here we proposed to throw the full weight of our membership into the Labour Party.

"Our argument was simple: the main task confronting us was to break down the isolation of our cadres; this could only be done by entry into the mass organisations. The British workers would enter, and were entering a new phase of radicalisation. Though delayed, this movement would be even more revolutionary than the movements of the continental workers. The mainstream of the working class would follow the historical law and pass through the Labour Party. The voluntary isolation of our comrades from the mass organisations as proposed by the lefts who raised the principle of the 'independent organisation' and the open party, was criminal at this stage. If we worked correctly for a period and dug ourselves into the mass organisations, when the swing came we would be in leading positions within the Labour Party. We would have a base among the workers who had entered in the course of their radicalisation; it was at this point that we would break down our political isolation and reap the results of consistent fraction work; it was at this point that we could contend for the leadership of the working class.

"Objectively the situation did not materialise as we expected it would. The war cut across the movement of the workers. In the ensuing period we were forced to modify our ideas.

"What were the gains of that period? What lessons are to be learned from that episode? These are the two important questions which must be answered now.

"As a prelude to answering them, it is necessary to state *that in practise we did not carry out our own tactic;* on the contrary, we even contradicted it to a large degree. The publication of WIN and Fourth Internationalist documents as well as the running of independent Trotskyist study circles, became the main axis of our work. *Youth for Socialism*, in its initial stages attempted to base itself on the entrist tactic. But when the Stalinists broke with the Labour League of Youth leaving only the husk of an organisation, *Youth for Socialism* became more and more of an open propagandist journal, finally evolving into the *Socialist Appeal*. For every ounce of energy put into the Labour Party, ten were put into direct open work for the Fourth International. At no time did we allow the work in the Labour Party to interfere with our open work. *And it was from the open field that we recruited most of the fresh members into WIL.* While it is true we did make a few organisational gains from the Labour Party, we did not succeed in embedding ourselves into its structure as we visualised. From the broader aspect of our accepted tactic, we gained nothing at all. Not a single member of our earlier cadres occupies a leading position from which to influence the local Labour Party in any area. Furthermore we have never been represented at Labour Party National Conferences where our voice could be heard. In this sense our tactic completely failed. Nevertheless, the general basis of our ideas at that period remain true. The workers have not yet broken with the Labour Party and will turn to it yet. This is the background to our transitional slogan that Labour takes power.

"The main achievements of our 'turn towards the Labour Party' lay in the field of approach and outlook. It was responsible for creating that serious attitude among our membership that we must be with the workers, that we must not isolate ourselves and make the classical blunders of the ultra-lefts in the past. It innoculated the group against the sterile sectarianism, which has isolated the British Trotskyists for years from the bloodstream of the working class.

"Eighteen months ago we substituted the conception of party in place of group in our draft constitution. This was introduced to break down the semi-conspiritorial atmosphere which pervaded our organisation as a hangover from the tactic of entry, as well as the incorrect estimate of the repression we expected would take place when war broke out which resulted in the actions taken by the organisation in preparation for 'illegality'. It also reflected the growth of the group from a local to a national organisation and corresponded to the need to broaden and co-ordinate the scope of our activity....

"But to proclaim ourselves as an independent party is not sufficient. All the arguments levelled against the ultra-lefts are as applicable today as yesterday. While it is necessary to present our tendency before the workers under the independent Trotskyist banner around a propaganda group, it is necessary at the same time to understand the limitations which our present forces impose upon our 'independence'." [6]

The death of Trotsky

During the summer of 1940 for personal and health reasons, Ralph Lee had decided to go back to South Africa. Haston and the other comrades had not long come back from Dublin. Lee's departure was certainly a blow to us at the time. He was without doubt the most important leader of the tendency, but nevertheless, despite his absence, we continued to develop the organisation. When Ralph returned to South Africa, he resumed his revolutionary work, and established a new group also called the Workers International League. The South African WIL was engaged in a number of struggles, which ended in defeat and resulted in the collapse of the organisation in 1946. Ralph, who was already ill, was terribly worn down by all these setbacks. Having spent his last penny on the revolutionary movement, he fell on extremely difficult times. Unfortunately, we, who at least could have given him some assistance, knew nothing about it until it was too late. Tragically, Ralph Lee took his own life. It was a sad end for such a giant of a man, my comrade and friend, whose historic contribution will always be remembered by our movement.

In the summer of 1940, I was called up to serve in the Pioneer Corps. This posed a dilemma. Our policy towards the armed forces was in complete opposition to the pacifist view of conscientious objection. We held to the position that revolutionaries should go with their class, and if called-up, they should go into the armed forces to conduct revolutionary work. This correct revolutionary policy, nevertheless, threatened to undermine the organisation as the call up spread. If the leadership of the organisation were called up, this would be a severe blow to the tendency. However, fortunately, you might say, I was involved in a vehicle accident and suffered a fractured skull, and was invalided out of the Forces. Haston was also relieved from the call up on medical grounds. This situation allowed us to continue to play a full role within the leadership of the organisation.

While I was recovering in hospital, I heard on the radio the fateful and heart-breaking news of Trotsky's assassination in Mexico. The comrades were all devastated by the news. Although we never raised it publicly at the time, we were deeply critical of the leadership of the American SWP, which was responsible for Trotsky's security in Coyoacan. After the first assassination attempt in May, why was Trotsky left alone in his study with a complete stranger? But we didn't raise or pursue the matter as it now served no real purpose - Trotsky was dead. It now fell on our shoulders to carry on the struggle for the socialist revolution. As a prolific writer, Trotsky had left behind a rich legacy of writings and experience from which we could draw to build a genuine revolutionary movement. In Britain, Trotsky's death and the start of the world war served to provide us with a new sense of urgency to develop and build the Workers International League. We took his last words to heart - "Go Forward! I am convinced of the victory of the Fourth International!"

The exact reverse seemed true for the RSL, the official section, which had ceased publishing any public material. In 1939, the Labour leadership had proscribed the RSL's front organisation within the Labour Party, the Militant Labour League, and it vanished immediately. It just disappeared without making a squeak. The RSL people were "intransigent revolutionaries" within the four walls of their bedroom. There, they could convince each other of their great revolutionary integrity, as opposed to the "social chauvinists", as they called us, who were putting forward a revolutionary military policy. Such a "chauvinist" policy, they claimed, was a betrayal of Lenin and a capitulation to bourgeois nationalism. The RSL were incapable of understanding anything, especially the vital question of how Lenin's position on war was to be applied to the concrete condition faced by the working class. Our genuine revolutionary opposition towards the war gave us the opportunity of working among the masses. For the RSL, such a state of affairs only existed in their heads.

After 1940, the remnants of the RSL very rapidly split into three factions. Denzil Harber, which was the centre faction, led one, another led by John Robinson was on the left, and lastly, John Lawrence led the so-called right. The Americans dubbed the latter faction the "Trotskyist Opposition" as it largely followed the correct line of the International. The proletarian military policy had been rejected by the RSL in September 1941, and this rejection had even been made a condition of membership of the organisation! Only the "Trotskyist Opposition" adhered to the official military policy. The Robinson tendency accused Lawrence and the leadership of the International of chauvinism, and true to their views, even opposed the demand for deep underground bomb shelters - as this was seen as a "defencist" policy! Nothing should be supported that assisted the war effort, including deep shelters. The fact that deeper shelters would help protect workers from Hitler's bombs was not the point! Clearly, they did not get much support in the working class for these crazy ideas. On the other hand, the WIL, having nothing to do with this ultra-left nonsense, did not hesitate to call on workers to force open the London Underground stations for use as air raid shelters.

From their comfortable armchairs, the RSL attacked the WIL for our alleged "chauvinism". "We must state that the basis for all the main political mistakes of WIL is to be found in the defencist position it has adopted with regard to the imperialist war since the fall of France first made the defeat of British imperialism a real possibility", stated the RSL. "Defencism rarely shows itself in its open form especially in a left-centrist organisation. Concealment is especially necessary in an organisation still professing to stand upon the principles of revolutionary defeatism..." [7] WIL was characterised as "an organisation, not moving politically in our direction, but moving away from us." Unfortunately for the leaders of the RSL, the International Secretariat could no longer go along with their blatant sectarianism. The International Secretariat, recognising the insane delusions from which the RSL was suffering, wrote on 21June 1942: "In our opinion your attitude towards the WIL is utterly false. Without ignoring personal differences inherited from the past, it is necessary to recognise that your false attitude flows directly from a false political appreciation of this group. You see in it a centrist group 'moving away from us'. This is an opinion which we can by no means share."

I wrote an extensive reply to the criticisms and misrepresentations of the RSL in mid-1943, which is worth quoting in order to show where we stood politically:

> "Our policy in relation to the problems of the epoch remains on the granite foundation laid down by Lenin. Our attitude towards imperialist war remains that of irreconcilable opposition. We continue the traditions of Bolshevism. But in the epoch of the decline and disintegration of capitalism a continuation, as Trotsky points out, does not mean a mere repetition. In the quarter century that has passed, the objective conditions for the socialist revolution have reached maturity and the decay and disintegration of capitalism have revealed themselves in the abortive attempts at revolution on the part of the masses, in fascism, and now in the new imperialist war. All the objective conditions of the past epoch render the proletariat responsive to the posing of the problem of the conquest of power by the working class.
>
> "As distinct from 1914-18, the cadres of Bolshevism have been trained and educated in the Leninist approach towards imperialist war. The social-chauvinism on the part of the Social Democrats and the Stalinists was anticipated and predicted by the Trotskyists long in advance. The theoretical exposure of social chauvinism is not a live issue for Bolshevism today. We build and construct our party on the Leninist internationalist basis, not least on the fundamental question of war.
>
> "As Trotsky once pointed out, war and revolution are the fundamental test for the policy of all organisations. On both these questions we continue the Leninist tradition. But Marxism does not consist in the repetition of phrases and ideas, however correct these may be. Otherwise Lenin could not have developed and deepened the conceptions first formulated by Marx. And Trotsky could not have propounded the theory of the Permanent Revolution. If all that was required of revolutionaries was to repeat *ad nauseam a* few phrases and slogans taken from the great teachers of Marxism, the problem of the revolution would be simple indeed. The SPGB would be super-Marxists instead of incurable sectarians. As Trotsky remarked of the ultra-lefts, every sectarian would be a master strategist.
>
> "In the last analysis, the basic principles of Marxism, as developed theoretically by Marx himself, have remained the same for nearly a century. The task of his successors consists, not at all in repeating a few half-digested ideas, parrot fashion, but of *using the method of Marxism* and applying it correctly to the problems and tasks posed at a particular period. It is now necessary to approach the problem of war, not only from its theoretical characterisation by Lenin, but in the task of winning the masses to the Leninist banner. For the past epoch the cadres of the Fourth International have been educated in the spirit of internationalism. We look at the war from the principled basis established by Lenin, but now from a more developed angle. We do not conduct our propaganda from the standpoint of analysing the nature of the defence of the capitalist fatherland alone but from the

standpoint of the conquest of power by the working class and the defence of the proletarian fatherland.

"As Trotsky posed the problem:

'That is why it would be doubly stupid to present a purely abstract pacifist position today; the feeling the masses have is that it is necessary to defend themselves. We must say 'Roosevelt (or Wilkie) says it is necessary to defend the country: good, only it must be our country, not that of the sixty families and their Wall Street.' (*American Problems*, August 7, 1940.)

"Only hopeless formalists and sectarians, incapable of appreciating the revolutionary dynamic of Marxism, could see in this a chauvinist deviation or an abandonment of Leninism. Our epoch is the epoch of wars and revolutions, militarism and super-militarism. To this epoch must correspond the policy and approach of the revolutionary party. War has come as a horrible retribution for the crimes of Stalinism and reformism. It came through the fact that the traitors in the workers' leadership frustrated the striving of the masses in the direction of the socialist revolution. It is a reflection of the blind alley in which imperialism finds itself, and of the historical ripeness and over-ripeness for the socialist revolution.

"The last world war was already an expression of that fact that on a world scale capitalism had fulfilled its historical mission. This objective fact leads rapidly to the subjective position where the masses of the workers are ripe for the posing of the problem of the socialist revolution, that is the problem of power. The events of the past epoch have left the working class with a psychology of frustration and bewilderment. They regarded with apprehension and horror the coming of the second blood bath in which they would expect nothing but suffering and misery. In this war, right from its inception, among the British workers, especially among the Labour workers, there has been an absence of hatred towards the German people. Even in America, where the masses are far less politically conscious than in Britain, in a recent Gallup Poll, two thirds of the people interviewed differentiated between the German people and the Nazis on the question of responsibility and punishment after the war. This, despite all the propaganda of the bourgeoisie. If this is the case in America, it is a hundred times more true of Britain.

"It is perfectly true, however, that especially among the working class there is an unclear, but deep-seated hatred of Hitlerism and fascism. But with all due respect to the leadership of the RSL, this hatred is not reactionary and chauvinist but arises from a sound class instinct. True, it is being misused and distorted for reactionary imperialist ends by the bourgeoisie and labour lackeys. But the task of revolutionaries consists in separating what is progressive and what is reactionary in their attitude: in winning away the workers from their Stalinist and Labour leaderships who misuse these progressive sentiments. And there is no other way than that mapped out by Trotsky in his last articles, of separating the workers from the exploiters on the question of war.

"The decay and degeneration of British imperialism render the masses responsive to the posing by the revolutionaries of the problem of power; to the problem of which class holds the power. Every issue which arises must be posed from this angle. Our position towards war is no longer merely a policy of opposition, but is determined by the epoch in which we live, the epoch of socialist revolution. That is, as contenders for power. Only thus can we find an approach to the working class. On paper, and in the abstract, the RSL accepts the *Transitional Programme* as the basis for our work in the present period. Trotsky points out that the objective situation demands that our day to day work is linked through our transitional demands with the social revolution. This applies to all aspects of our work. The plunging of the world into war does not in the least demand a retreat from this position, but on the contrary gives it an even greater urgency. But the same theoretical conception which forms the basis of the *Transitional Programme* and dictates the strategical orientation of all our activists forms the basis of the strategical attitude towards war in the modern epoch.

"War is part of the life of society at the present time and our programme of the conquest of power has to be based, not on peace, but on the conditions of universal militarism and war. We may commiserate with the comrades of the RSL on this unfortunate deviation of history. But alas we were too weak to overthrow imperialism and must now pay the price. It was necessary (and, of course, it is still necessary) to educate the cadres of the Fourth International of the nature and meaning of social patriotism and Stalino-chauvinism and its relation towards the war. Who in Britain in the left wing has done this as vigorously as WIL? But we must go further. The *Transitional Programme*, if it has any meaning at all, is a bridge not only from the consciousness of the masses today to the road of the socialist revolution, but also for the isolated revolutionaries to the masses.

"The RSL convinces itself of the superiority of its position over that of Stalinism and reformism. It comforts itself that it maintains the position of Lenin in the last war. This would be very good...if the RSL had understood the position of Lenin. However, for Trotsky and the inheritors of Bolshevism, *we start* (even if the RSL correctly interpreted Lenin, which it does not) where the RSL leadership finishes! We approach the problem of war from the angle of the imminence of the next period of the social revolution in Britain as well as other countries. The workers in Britain, as in America 'do not want to be conquered by Hitler, and to those who say, "let us have a peace programme" the workers will reply: "but Hitler does not want a peace programme." Therefore we say, we will defend the United States [or Britain] with a workers' army with workers' officers, and with a workers' government, etc.' (Trotsky, ibid)

"Those words of the Old Man are saturated through and through with the spirit of revolutionary Marxism, which, while uncompromisingly preserving its opposition towards the bourgeoisie, shows sympathy and understanding for the attitude of the rank and file worker and the problems which are running through his mind. No longer do we stop at the necessity to educate the vanguard as to the nature of the war and the refusal to defend the capitalist fatherland, but we go forward to win the working class for the conquest of power and the defence of the proletarian fatherland." [8]

Completely remote from public life, the only activity open to the RSL was this eternal in-fighting between the different factions. This is what passes for political activity in a sect. Of course, this did not affect the WIL, as we weren't bothered about what they were doing. The RSL was of no importance in the Labour movement, and of no importance to our tendency. After all the other splits, these new divisions with their ranks effectively paralysed them as an organisation. They were busy putting forward one internal bulletin after another and discussing among themselves as to who was holding up the true banner of internationalism, of revolutionary defeatism that had been developed by Lenin during the First World War. Meanwhile, real life passed them by completely.

The RSL maintained - behind the scenes of course - that Trotsky in the last months of his life had become a centrist, had returned to his position of the August block of 1912, and had abandoned Lenin's position of opposition to the imperialist war. As an amusing indication of the great success of this policy, John Robinson, the leader of the Left faction within the RSL (who at least should be given credit for trying to carry out their policy) gave a speech at the time of Dunkirk to one of the very few Labour Parties that was still functioning. He lectured them on the following lines: "Comrades, the victory of Hitler is a lesser evil than to support our own ruling class." He then wondered why he was immediately expelled from the Labour Party - with the full support of the rank and file! As a good sectarian, he consoled himself that he had been expelled because of his revolutionary intransigence and perhaps these workers would eventually come to understand the error of their ways.

That was the sort of policy and approach being put forward by the RSL. This policy of an absolute out-of-this-world sectarianism and ultra-leftism on the question of war was linked to an intransigent need to continue work inside the lifeless Labour Party! This gave them the opportunity in the privacy of each other's homes of carrying on what they imagined was political activity: debating the contents of internal bulletins. Whereas, in our tendency, the two things went together: activity in the working class and theoretical clarity. One without the other being useless and completely barren. This situation led to their rapid decline as a tendency.

Very quickly the WIL had come to the conclusion that entrism did not correspond to the objective situation in Britain. With the Labour Party in a national coalition government, there was no activity in the Party at all. The activity of the working class, in so far as it existed, had begun to shift towards the industrial front. Strikes began to break out after 1941, and we intervened in them with as much drive as possible. Towards the end of 1940 and the beginning of 1941, we became convinced that the main area where we could get results was in the trade unions generally, among the members of the CP where we could get a certain response, and also in the ILP, which had gained an audience thanks to its pseudo anti-war activity. As they seemed to be the only anti-war opposition, the ILP began to make gains during the course of the war. So we paid attention to it.

We were forced to answer the RSL on the question not only of the war, but also of entrism. They saw working in the Labour Party in a completely rigid fashion, and not a tactical question.

> "Making a fetish of the tactic of entrism, converting it into a mystic principle standing above time and place, sometimes lands the RSL into fantastic positions", wrote the present author. "For example, the insistence of the RSL in 'critically' supporting Labour candidates against the Stalinist and ILP anti-war candidates. By this stand they, the principled and implacable revolutionaries, found themselves in a position of critical support for the National Government, because of the coalition of Labour with the Tories! A vote for the Labour candidate could only be interpreted as a vote for the Government and thus for support of the war. Thus they placed themselves in a thoroughly opportunist position on the question of the war. (Here we may say that WIL gave critical support to the Stalinist and ILP anti-war candidates; at no time have we supported pacifist candidates as the RSL lyingly informed the IS in a letter of 7 July 1942.)
>
> "The main idea of entrism, the necessity to operate on a single field in a given set of circumstances, is summed up as in our 1938 document, in military terminology: 'Full strength at the point of attack.' Posed in this way the situation and the tasks become clearer. It is not without significance that the RSL has not posed the question to WIL from this angle: Why are we not concentrating our forces 'full strength at the point of attack' in the Labour Party at the present time? For it would raise the reply: It is ridiculous to concentrate one's army in war on a sector of the front where there are no results to be achieved. Today the 'point of attack' is the industrial field. But favourable results can be achieved by the adoption of guerrilla tactics. Owing to the development of events, magnificent opportunities for work open up before us in every direction - the trade unions, the ILP, the factories, shop stewards' movement, and... even the Labour Party.
>
> "To concentrate work inside the Labour Party...the *least* important field at the present stage, would be suicidal. In politics, as in war, a commander who fails to make the necessary changes in the strategic and tactical disposition of his men when the relationship of forces has changed, leads his army to defeat. Such are the commanders of the RSL." [9]

So we soberly came to the conclusion that nothing much could be gained by maintaining the position of entry into the Labour Party at that stage. The question of entry would inevitably arise at a certain stage in the future as events developed. But for the moment our main activity would have to be on an independent basis. This position was particularly accentuated in June 1941 when the Russians were involved in the war, and the CP did another 180-degree somersault and came out for 100 percent support of the war. They then turned into the chief strikebreaking forces for the capitalist class within the ranks of the working class. "Coal production in the industry can be increased by regular working of all shifts available", said a CP statement, "eliminating all avoidable absenteeism, continuation of work after fatal accidents, and the relaxation of overtime restrictions to ensure that all faces are cleared daily..."

Stalinist slander campaign

The Stalinists had become the loudest war-mongering chauvinists within the ranks of the working class. We therefore decided that we would have to go for open activity under our own banner, as a Fourth International tendency. As a result, we changed the name of our paper from *Youth for Socialism* to *Socialist Appeal*, not simply a youth paper but an adult paper, while continuing to publish a theoretical journal, Workers International News. We came forward publicly under the banner of the WIL, as an independent tendency within the working class. The pro-war stance of the Stalinists now provided us with great possibilities for an open Trotskyist tendency.

With this pro-war attitude, large numbers of the best workers in the armament factories, who had been supporting the CP, as well as those within the ranks of the CP, were starting to question the line and move into political opposition. They couldn't stomach the strikebreaking role and the ultra patriotism that the CP was developing at that time. So we devoted a lot of attention to the CP and we began to win some of their best members. While explaining the imperialist nature of the world war, at the same time we consistently argued, despite Stalin, for the defence of the Soviet Union. Within a short space of time, the bulk of our new members were coming from the CP. In Nottingham, for instance, we won the convenor of the Royal Ordinance Factory, John Pemberton, and then a group of shop stewards around him were won to our organisation, including Claude Bartholemew and Jack Nightingale.

At the Royal Ordinance Factory at Dalmuirs in the West of Scotland we won Alec Riach, the deputy convener, who participated in the Invergordon mutiny, and joined the Communist Party afterwards. When we met Alec, we managed to arrange a debate between himself and Jock Haston over the CP policy in the war. Feeling a bit out of his depth, he asked Campbell or one of the other CP leaders to come and debate instead. But he was told to handle it himself. The CP leaders refused to come and it was left to Alec to take on the task of trying to defend the position of the CP. At least the poor bloke was courageous. He admitted later he'd had a terrible political hammering. At any rate, we won him over and with him a number of shop stewards in the factory. So out of this approach, the WIL had begun to establish an industrial foothold in Scotland, where we later established the Clyde Workers Committee.

We had developed a base in Glasgow at that time, as well as in Edinburgh, where the communists had still stayed in the Labour Party. Of course, we still maintained a fraction in the Labour Party. We didn't have this lunatic position like all the ultra-left tendencies of leaving the Labour Party, without leaving behind reserves in case it was necessary to make a turn back to

Labour Party work. Even at that time, where the Labour Party was viable, and you could get some results, our comrades still continued to work there. But that was extremely limited at this stage. Wherever possible, we saw to it that in these Labour Parties one of our comrades would try to become the political education officer. As part of this, our comrade would have responsibility for organising literature sales. So in every meeting, there was a table for literature that would have Labour Party and working class literature, and of course, copies of the *Socialist Appeal*. So even then, our newspaper was being sold openly within the Labour Party.

However, even at this stage, we always had an orientation and approach towards Labour workers, as well as towards the workers in the trade unions. With such a sympathetic approach, free of sectarianism and ultra-leftism, we were able to win the best elements to Marxism. In fact, it would be wrong to think that even when we worked in the Labour Party that our recruits to the tendency came from the ranks of existing Labour Party members. That is completely false. While we maintained this orientation to the mass organisations, our recruits were made from fresh workers and youth, which were then taken into the Labour Party. That is the paradox, but it also contains the secret of how to build the tendency when working in the mass organisations, which our tendency alone understood.

We became a thorn in the side of the Communist Party, especially after June 1941 when Hitler invaded the USSR and they hastily changed their policy yet again. The Stalinists were getting very worried about our activity and the high profile of WIL. They began to pay serious attention to our tendency and publish articles and even pamphlets about us. They denounced us as "fascists" and "counter-revolutionaries", and spread all sorts of slanders and lies about us. One such CP pamphlet was called *Clear Out Hitler's Agents*, by William H. Wainwright. It said the Trotskyists were Hitler's agents and that we had to be physically driven out of the workers' movement.

> "There is a group of people in Britain masquerading as socialists in order to cover up their fascist activities", stated Wainwright. "They are called Trotskyists. You've heard of the fifth column. The Trotskyists are their allies and agents in the ranks of the working class… The Home Guard has been taught a quick way to deal with enemy paratroopers and spies. You must train yourself to round up these other, more cunning enemies on whom Hitler depends to do his work for him in Britain. This book is a simple training manual. It will explain to you the tactics of the strange war Hitler is waging in your factory."
>
> Wainwright continued: "Trotsky was a Russian who gathered around him an unscrupulous gang of traitors to organise spying, sabotage, wrecking and assassination in the Soviet Union… They wormed their way into important army positions, working class organisations, even Government posts. They plotted with the Nazis to hand over large tracts of their country once they had weakened it sufficiently to make its defeat quite certain… Trotsky's men are Hitler's men. They must be cleared out of every working class organisation in the country."
>
> The pamphlet then concluded: "Be on the alert for the Trotskyist disrupters. These people have not the slightest right to be regarded as workers with an honest point of view. They should be treated as you would a Nazi. Clear them out of every working class organisation."
>
> And finally, advice on *What to do with the Trotskyists:*
>
> "First: Remember that the Trotskyists are no longer part of the working class movement. Second: Expose every Trotskyist you come into contact with. Show other people where his ideas are leading. Treat him as you would an open Nazi. Third: Fight against every Trotskyist who has got himself into a position of authority, either in your trade union branch, local Labour Party or Co-op. Expose him and see that he is turned out."

Other articles accused us of acting as fascist agents within the factories, attempting to sabotage the war effort. They said that our militant demands, however reasonable, were a cover used to disrupt production and help Hitler. According to them, our agitation for the working class was simply to undermine their patriotic stand against fascism, and so on and so forth. The Stalinist pamphlets were small, but to answer them would have required books, because on every page there were so many lies. So we discussed the question of how to frame such a reply, whether we should deal with it in the detailed manner Trotsky dealt with these slanders, or use some other way. We came to the conclusion that it was not necessary under these circumstances to deal with them in such detail. We decided to choose a different tack.

In the end we found a very effective way of dealing with the Stalinist attacks which silenced the Stalinists in the factories. We published a well-produced little leaflet, entitled *Factory Workers: Be on your Guard: Clear Out the Bosses' Agents.* We intended to distribute them in tens of thousands in all the factories where we had people, and in as many workplaces as possible where the CP had an influence. And this is what we did. I must say the campaign was very effective. It really hit them where it hurt and served to throw them onto the defensive. The leaflet answered the Stalinist's lies point by point, and at the end of the reply we put out an offer of a reward: "Ten Pounds Reward!" it read. This was a great deal of money in those days, possibly a few hundred pounds in today's money. "Ten pounds reward to any member of the Communist Party who could show a single page of their pamphlet that didn't contain at least five lies", read our statement.

When we gave it out, and the workers read it, they would just laugh at the CP and their propaganda. As soon as the CPers raised their slanders, workers would ask: "Have you applied for the 10 pounds yet?" The Stalinists were mercilessly ribbed, as you can imagine, by the other workers. We of course published it not only as a leaflet, but also as a feature in the pages of the *Socialist Appeal.* And by that simple means, these lies and slanders, all this crude poison pumped out by the CP, was being cut across. Needless to say, the reward was not claimed, and we had a jolly good laugh.

Given the effect we were having, the CP had to put Wainwright, one of its leaders in charge of following our material, especially the *Socialist Appeal.* He not only wrote the pamphlet already mentioned, but most of the other stuff in the *Daily Worker* attacking our position. At the beginning of the war, the *Daily Worker* had been banned, but now as they were taking a patriotic Line, and waging a campaign in favour of the war, they were allowed to publish their paper again. In the *Daily Worker* as well as in International Press Correspondence they denounced our material with great hostility. Wainwright twisted and distorted our arguments, but found it increasingly difficult to peddle the nonsense about the WIL being pro-Hitler and all the rest of it, because obviously we were having an effect on the advanced elements of the working class.

The slander of the Stalinists having proved to be a flop, they decided to seek assistance from the worst jingoistic elements within the Tory Party, the die-hard elements in the Monday Club, and so on. They got in touch with Sir Jocelyn Lucas-Tooth the Tory MP from Portsmouth South, who I believe was also a Colonel. They gave him the April issue of the *Socialist Appeal* that was published just after Japan had entered the war. At this time, with Japan's entry, there was a tremendous campaign about the monstrous crimes of these fiends, how they cut the heads off babies, strung them up, and so on. These were the stories about the atrocities that the

Japanese had committed in Hong Kong, Singapore and elsewhere. The CP held a demonstration in Trafalgar Square, under the slogan "Remember Hong Kong". So we published a special edition of *Socialist Appeal* with the heading "Remember Hong Kong - and all the rest too". The *Appeal* carried a picture of the British troops in Burma, holding up the severed heads of Burmese guerrilla fighters. It was a repulsive and monstrous thing, of course. And it showed that the Japanese imperialists did not have a monopoly on such atrocities. The Army tops had to brutalise the British troops in order to get them to do things of this sort. We intervened in the CP demo and were selling papers like hot cakes.

Obviously, when Willie Gallacher gave Sir Jocelyn a copy of this issue of *Socialist Appeal*, he must have nearly burst a blood vessel. He sent a copy to Morrison and raised the matter in Parliament. "In view of the fact that this paper attacks our allies, and war aims, and is entirely subversive, can the Right Hon. Gentleman state any good reason for allowing it to continue?" he asked of Herbert Morrison the Home Secretary. Perhaps we were fortunate that it was Morrison who was Home Secretary in the coalition government, as he replied: "The House knows that these matters require a great deal of careful consideration, and I think it would be best that I should consider all the circumstances before intimating any decision." (*Hansard*, 30 April 1942). It was rumoured at the time that in the corridors of the House of Commons, Morrison was overheard saying, "If I do have to take action against the Trotskyists, then I'll certainly have the warm support of Mr. Gallacher." Gallacher apparently was in earshot, and said agitatedly, "What do you mean?" And Morrison replied, "You know and I know what I mean."

Not long after, in July 1942, the activities of the WIL in the British coalfields were discussed in Parliament. According to the Daily Telegraph, "Capt. Crowder raised the issue by asking Mr. Morrison what action he proposed to take regarding the distribution of subversive literature among Yorkshire miners." It was reported that "Mr. Gallacher, the Communist member, asked facetiously whether Mr. Morrison would inquire into the effect the *Daily Worker* would have. Mr. Morrison caused a laugh by remarking. 'I ask my Right Hon. Friend not to be too keen on suppressions. This organisation is only pursuing the same political policy as he and his political friends pursued up to some time ago." (*Daily Telegraph*, 17 July 1942).

Morrison, the Labour Home Minister in the wartime coalition, was clearly concerned about the Trotskyists. He made this clear in a private conversation with James Maxton, the left-wing Scottish MP, who passed the information on to us. However, Morrison had said that he knew we were misguided but honest types. Although he fundamentally disagreed with our views, he saw that we were consistent - unlike the Stalinists - and that we were anti-fascists, and that we had taken a principled position on the war. Later, a full report by Morrison about the WIL appeared in the Cabinet papers (See appendix). They must have even examined our dental records as well as everything else to try and find a way of getting rid of us! But for the moment, Morrison wasn't prepared to take action. He told Maxton to tell us that we should watch our step, but, despite the Tories pressing him hard, he hung back.

Who knows what went through Morrison's mind? He had held a pacifist anti-war position during the First World War, though he was now on the right wing of the Labour Party. Maybe he had a bit of a guilty conscience! But I do know that some years before in Hyde Park, Morrison had to have police protection because the CPers - still peddling the old social-fascist

Line - attacked him and tried to beat him up. The hooligan tactics of the Stalinists must have made a lasting effect on Morrison and now he decided to get his own back on them. He knew of all the Stalinists' twists and turns in relation to the war, and that they were dictated by Moscow. He therefore regarded them with contempt. On the other hand, as a result of our clear internationalist position, we had become a thorn in the side of the CP. Needless to say, Morrison didn't like us, but while we were politically embarrassing the CP and hammering them on every possible occasion, he must have taken malicious pleasure in the belting we gave them.

The industrial front

As the war continued, the mood of the class began to change. In 1943 there were more individual strikes in the mining industry - all of them unofficial - than in any year since the beginning of the century. If we bear in mind that the war was on and that the CP was vehemently opposed to all strikes, it is obvious that a deep mood of discontent was building up. Strikes broke out especially in the Yorkshire and South Wales areas. The exact numbers involved was not published at the time, but there were certainly far more men on strike than at any time since 1926. One hundred and twenty thousand miners were officially out in Yorkshire, one hundred thousand in Wales and several thousand more in Lancashire, Staffordshire, Durham and Scotland. Eventually the government had to back down and agree to a complete overhaul of the wage structure in the industry - which partially appeased the miners.

WIL Trotsky commemoration meeting, London
(seated: Ted Grant, Sid Bidwell and Gerry Healy)

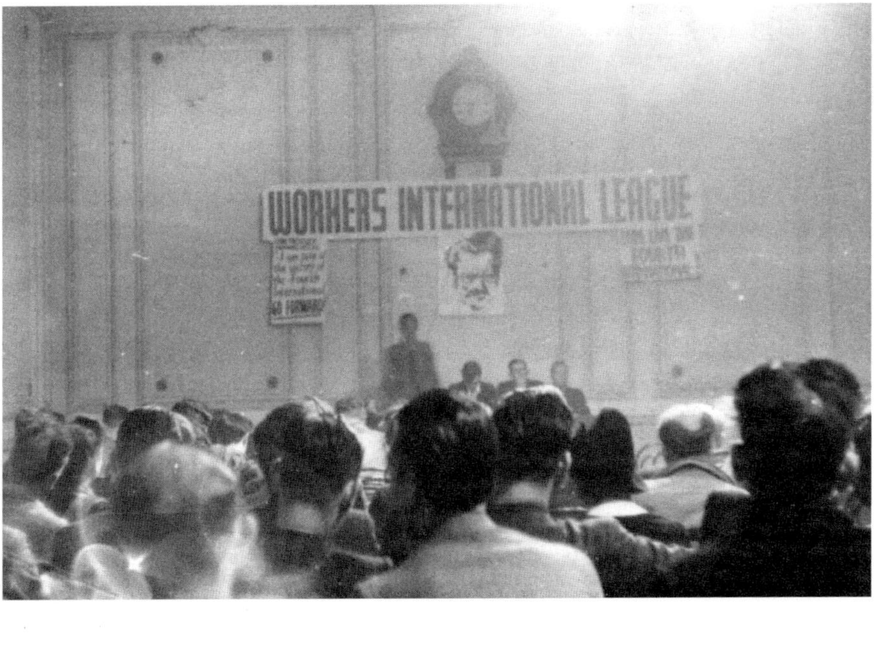

The strikes were blamed by the right wing President of the miners' union, William Lawther, on the Trotskyists. This was immediately taken up by the yellow press. The Daily Mail published a sensational "exposure" by one of its reporters who claimed to have formed a team of special investigators all over the country tracking down the Trotskyists. Ernest Bevin the ex-trade union leader who was now Minister of Labour took up the theme, accusing the followers of Leon Trotsky who, he claimed, not only had plenty of members and money, but "more influence among certain sections of the workers than His Majesty's Government and the trade union leaders combined." In his biography of Aneurin Bevan, Michael Foot recalls the panic in the trade union leadership at the time:

> "Ernest Bevin naturally watched the strike movement with growing alarm. Some other smaller unofficial strikes were taking place in other industries, among engineering apprentices and gas workers. Newspapers reported that bands of Trotskyists, who rejected the Communist Line of full support for the war effort, were among the instigators. Bevin said later that the nation was living on the edge of a volcano, which might affect three million workers. On April 5 he attended a luncheon where he underlined the peril - but chiefly the peril in the mines. The stoppage in the Yorkshire coalfield, he said, was far worse than if Sheffield had been bombed. That morning he had attended the Cabinet and that afternoon he called in at a meeting of the General Council of the TUC. He told them that as a result of the strikes, which, in his opinion, were being incited by persons outside the industry concerned, a paralysis was developing in some of the major industries in the country. Under the existing law he had no powers to deal with incitement to strike. That was the power he must have." [10]

Of course, the strikes that were taking place were not caused by "outside agitators" - either the RCP or anyone else. They were caused by the growing discontent of the miners and other workers at the bad conditions in industry, the profiteering of the employers and so on. Nevertheless, the RCP was the only organisation that supported strikes in defence of wages and conditions, while the "Communist" Party was playing a completely strike-breaking role. Therefore, Bevin's remarks were clearly directed against us. Despite our small size, they took us very seriously and we were regarded as a threat.

Bevin got his way. With the backing of the TUC, the government introduced the notorious Regulation 1AA. Its essential clause reads as follows: "No person shall declare, instigate, or make any other person to take part in, or shall otherwise act in the furtherance of, any strike among persons engaged in the performance of essential services, or any lock-out of persons so engaged." This was a draconic, catch-all piece of legislation, which effectively removed the right to strike. The penalty for violating it was five years' penal servitude or a five hundred pound fine (a fortune in those days) - or both. But in the end it proved to be a dead letter. No-one was ever prosecuted under Regulation 1AA.

We had our headquarters in a room in Millie Lee's place in Chichester Road, near Paddington. The printing press was originally stored in Jock's place in Warwick Avenue, not far from Millie's. We had used the basement for the purposes of the organisation. We then moved to a loft, at 61 Northdown Street, in Kings Cross. We considered it a great step forward at that time. When the strikes were taking place during the war we had a great deal of press coverage. If you read the pages of the capitalist press at that time, it was full of stories about this loft headquarters. We had reporters coming up to the place, from the backyard near Kings Cross Station and reporting how the class war was being waged from this dingy hide-out. They wrote spine-chilling stories in a conspiratorial and exaggerated style, as you can imagine. They were accompanied by pictures of the office taken from the road. From there, they conducted interviews with Jock Haston, Millie Lee and myself.

The WIL Centre, 61 Northdown Street, Kings Cross

With each succeeding crisis during the war, we had had the press coming to see what was going on. For instance, when the miners went on strike in the Yorkshire coalfields in the middle of 1942, Joe Hall, the president of the Yorkshire miners, launched an attack on the WIL, saying that these Trotskyist agitators were being paid £10 a week, which was a fortune in those days - for the purpose of stirring up agitation. Of course, this had no effect on the miners, but merely frightened the middle classes who were looking for reds under the bed. The capitalist press played it up and we challenged them to produce the evidence.

The *Daily Mail* reporter came around to gather material about our activities and to write an article about WIL and Joe Hall's allegations. He interviewed Haston and myself. The next day the story appeared with the heading: "Class War is Waged from Loft HQ." The article opened up: "In a bare loft above a builder's yard near Kings Cross, London, I found yesterday the home of the Trotsky organisation which has been accused by miners' leaders of subversive and pro-Nazi activities in the coalfields." (*Daily Mail*, 15 July 1942). When the *Daily Express* turned up at the loft, I showed the reporter my discharge papers and my true wage of £2/10 shillings a week. The Express described me as "...shock-headed, getting a salary of one pound a week, which is made up to two pounds ten shillings by comrades who subscribe from their own wages." I was reported as saying: "We used to have to produce the paper from our private homes but now we are getting support, membership at about 500, we have been able to take over this office for a rental of 27 shillings a week. Our sales like all other papers are on a quota basis from the Ministry of Supply and it has been cut back like all other papers. But fortunately we had in a supply." (*Daily Express*, 15 July 1942). These facts served to undercut Hall's allegations.

Between mid-1941, the time of the CP's pro-imperialist war stand, and 1944, we developed the activity of our tendency to an enormous extent. We maintained a small group in the Labour Party, as explained, ready to take advantage of the situation when it changed. However, in these years, the ILP had developed, and was a far more important field for us. We therefore maintained a fraction in the ILP, and succeeded in winning over people such as Roy Tearse, who became the Industrial Organiser of the WIL and the secretary of the Militant Workers Federation.

We also recruited T. Dan Smith, the notorious T. Dan Smith on Tyneside, who ended up on the right wing, became Labour leader in the North East of England and was subsequently jailed for corruption. Bill Hunter also came from the ILP, and after a period of good work, ended up after the break-up of the RCP as a hatchetman of Healy. Other comrades recruited from the ILP, also from the North East, were Ken Skethaway, Jack and Daisy Rawlings and Herbie Bell, all of whom remained life-long comrades of our tendency. Throughout the North East, we controlled two divisions of the ILP, in Durham and in Cumberland, which we attempted to use to maximum effect.

Herbie Bell deserves a special comment. Herbie was a courageous fighter for the working class. Born in 1885 in Northumberland, he became a farm labourer. He joined the British army and Christmas 1915 took part in the fraternisation between British and German troops. Herbie told many a tale of the victimisation and punishment he received for spreading disaffection and "mutinous" ideas among the ranks. In 1920 he joined the Independent Labour Party, and during the 1926 General Strike he was a dispatch carrier for the No.2 Central Joint Strike Committee. He was sent to Durham prison for his activities. In 1945, in protest at the expulsion of Trotskyists from the ILP, he resigned and joined the RCP. In the same year he stood as the RCP candidate for Wallsend Borough Council, his election agent being Bill Landles, who continues to support the tendency to the present day. Herbie was an active trade unionist and shop steward, and used to sell 100 copies of every issue of our paper *Militant* [established in 1964] around the pit villages until well into his retirement. He was a man very widely read and with a profound interest in Marxist theory - which he never lost. Even in his last days he was reading *Anti-Dühring* and Hegel. His dedication was a tremendous inspiration to those who knew him and his death in July 1978 at the age of 83 marked the loss of an outstanding working class revolutionary.

Important as the ILP work was, it was not our most important field of activity. Our main area of work was in the industrial field and in the main trades unions where we were beginning to recruit more and more workers. The WIL, while relatively small with around 300 members, was overwhelmingly - maybe about 90 percent - industrial working class in composition. In August 1942, the WIL held its first national conference, where for the first time we saw collected together a galaxy of working class talent. The conference sent greetings to the Fourth International and requested that WIL be accepted as the official section in Britain.

> "This, the first National Conference of the Workers International League, held under the conditions of semi-legality imposed upon us by the present war politics of the British bourgeoisie, sends greetings to the International Secretariat, expressing our solidarity with it and through it to all sections of the Fourth International throughout the world. In addressing ourselves to you, we once again express, by the unanimous vote of our membership, the desire to be acknowledged as an official section of the Fourth International.
>
> "The International Conference of 1938 rejected the appeal of the Workers International League (then only a small minority group) to be accepted as an official section of the Fourth International, or to be recognised as a sympathetic section. This decision on the part of the conference was based on an entirely incorrect estimation of the British movement and its various components. The Conference placed its trust in the 'Unified Revolutionary Socialist League', in the hands of CLR James, of Maitland and Tate, of Starkey Jackson and DD Harber. Today the 'unified' organisation has splintered into no less than five fragments; CLR James is now with the Burnham-Shachtman revisionists (his deviation had been noted by the WIL comrades in 1937); Maitland and Tait have adopted the stand of 'Conscientious Objectors' to the imperialist war on 'ethical grounds' and have decisively broken with Bolshevism; Jackson and Harber have almost completely disappeared from the political horizon of the revolutionary workers. Meanwhile, despite the loss of comrade Lee who returned to South Africa due to illness, and contrary to the prediction of the Conference that the WIL would splinter into fragments and finish in the mire, the WIL has attracted to its ranks *all* the genuine militants of our tendency in Britain and stands today as the *only* representative of the Fourth International with a voice among the British working class."

The statement recorded the fact that the RSL had "to all intents and purposes" collapsed. The last issue of its paper *Militant* appeared more than a year ago. It had produced no publications. It held no meetings. It conducted no discussion circles. "In name it retains the status of the British section of the Fourth International, in fact it has completely collapsed."

> "In contrast to this the WIL has moved slowly but steadily ahead. We have produced every important document of our international movement and sold them in thousands. The semblance of a genuine national organisation has been formed. Militants from our ranks play leading roles in workers' struggles in many parts of the country - in the trade union and shop stewards movement, particularly in heavy industry the voices of our comrades are heard at conventions of the working class. This is a new feature in British Trotskyism. Our publications have appeared with regularity under the most adverse conditions and today they are the acknowledged publications of Trotskyism in Britain."

"Preparing for power"

As the political secretary of the WIL, I was given the task of drawing up the perspectives document, which was entitled *Preparing for Power*. It is an important document, which was printed in the *WIN*, and deserves today to be reprinted and made available to a wider audience. There are those who said that the document, and its title, was out of step with the real situation. But this is false. Our task was the building of a revolutionary proletarian party, whose task was the organisation of the working class to take power. This was based upon the perspective of great revolutionary events that would arise from the war. In 1942, this remained the most likely path in front of us. Our aim was to draw out all the revolutionary possibilities inherent in the situation and to raise the sights of every member to the tasks posed by history. That was the purpose of the perspectives outlined in *Preparing for Power*.

By its very nature, the document was very optimistic as it outlined the growing upsurge in industrial militancy, and the developing mood for social change. It deals with the international situation, then analysed developments in Britain, especially in the ILP, CP and the trade unions. Together with this, it highlighted the vital role of the subjective factor, the party, as the most decisive factor.

> "In Britain, more perhaps than in any other country in the world, a correct policy towards the trade unions and factory committees is necessary for a young revolutionary party", stated the document. "Without a correct attitude on this question, our organisation would doom itself to vegetate in sectarian isolation. This is especially the case today when the workers are beginning to stir and awaken - from the period of relative 'peace' in industry which followed the debacle of the Labour Party in 1931, and when the whole of the working class is undergoing a transformation in its outlook.
>
> "This awakening of the working class is shown by the number of strikes that are taking place in formerly backward areas which were only partially organised before the war. Commencing with Betteshanger Colliery, the unrest among the miners - always a barometer of the temper of the British workers - has been followed by strikes in one coalfield after another. Small strikes have taken place among the dockers, railwaymen, engineers and shipbuilding workers. All these have for the present been limited to a local scale. But they are the first rumblings that give warning of the coming eruption.
>
> "The bourgeoisie and the Labour bureaucracy are looking with alarm on these signs of discontent among the workers, and have been compelled to retreat and compromise. They are afraid that by too stubborn opposition, they might release forces beyond their power to control. This process, however, is developing in a contradictory fashion. It can be seen, for example, that despite the terrific discontent among the highly class conscious workers in South Wales and Clydeside, no big movement is taking place in these traditional storm centres. The reason for this has not been unwillingness on the part of the workers to fight. It is the stranglehold exercised by the Stalinists over the shop stewards and leading militants in these districts. Undoubtedly, but for this feature, there would already have been a general strike on the Clydeside, at least among the shipbuilding workers. Had the Stalinists been pursuing their pseudo-left line of the 'people's government' period, they would today be at the head of a mass movement throughout the country. It is no exaggeration to say that they would probably have captured the rank and file militants in every union in industry. But the changing of the party Line after Hitler's attack on Russia, revealed the true face of Stalinism: the Communist Party has come forward as the principal strike-breaking force at the service of the ruling class.
>
> "This offers a tremendous opportunity to the Fourth International, and one which must be utilised to the fullest possible extent. Once again it must be emphasised - face to the factories, the unions, the factory committees!"

Preparing For Power went on to analyse the perspectives for the war and then concluded with great optimism for the future:

> "The possibility exists for an unprecedented growth in influence and numbers in the shortest possible time. Today the problem consists mainly in preparing the basis for a rapid increase in growth and influence. The Workers International League will grow with the growth of the left wing. It is necessary to break sharply and consciously, as the group is already doing, with

the psychology and perspectives of the past. The most difficult period is in the past - isolated membership and the hostility or indifference of the masses. Big movements and big events which we can influence are on the order of the day. The group must not be caught unawares by the development of events.

"It is necessary that the membership systematically face the workers and penetrate among the masses. Above all, it is necessary to bring the Fourth International before the masses of the workers as an independent tendency.

"It is necessary that the organisation face up critically to the most vital of all factors: the leadership and the organisation are lagging behind the development of events. Objectively, conditions are developing and have already developed, which make for the speediest and most favourable growth and entrenchment of our organisation. But the basic weakness lies in the lack of trained cadres. The membership is for the most part young and untrained and lacks theoretical education. The organisation, despite the leap in influence, still maintains for the most part the habits and attitude of mind of the past - that is, of propaganda circles rather than of branches for agitation among the masses. The difficulties and tasks of the past period of the group's life are still reflected in its ideas and work. On the basis of the new perspective a sharp break must be made with the past.

"It can be stated without exaggeration that the decisive question of whether the organisation will be able to face up to events will be determined by whether the leadership and membership can base themselves thoroughly in the shortest space of time, on these perspectives and face up to implementing them in the day to day work of the organisation. To develop deep and firm roots and to become known as a tendency and organisation throughout the country, and above all, among the advanced workers in the factories is the basic task of the organisation.

"The disproportion in the situation in Britain lies in the lack of relationship between the ripeness of the objective situation and the immaturity and weakness of our organisation. Prospects of a swift impulsion of the masses leading to a spectacular growth of the organisation on the lines of the POUM in the Spanish revolution are rooted in the situation. But only if we realise the scope of the tasks and possibilities which history has placed before us. We will rise to the situation only if *in the interim, skeleton cadres are built throughout the country.* These cadres would serve as the bones on which the body of a powerful organisation could be built up from the new and fresh recruits who will come towards us as the crisis develops.

"These tasks must be accomplished. Our untrained and untested organisation, will, within a few years at most, be hurled into the turmoil of the revolution. The problem of the organisation, the problem of building the party, goes hand in hand with the revolutionary mobilisation of the masses. Every member must raise himself or herself to the understanding that the key to world history lies in our hands. The conquest of power is on the order of the day in Britain - but only if we find the road to the masses.

"Revolutionary audacity can achieve everything. The organisation must consciously pose itself and see itself as the decisive factor in the situation. There will be no lack of possibilities for transforming ourselves from a tiny sect into a mass organisation on the wave of the revolution."

Our work in the armed forces

With many of our comrades conscripted into the armed forces, the organisation conducted energetic revolutionary activity within the army. The army was made up overwhelmingly of young conscripts. We had refused to take the pacifist position of the ILP and support the conscientious objectors. On the contrary, we had insisted that all our comrades, except for those needed for the functioning of the organisation, would have to go with their class into the forces. When they were called up they linked their fate with that of their class. This policy of revolutionary activity in the army gained really important results. The past arguments of Lenin and Trotsky had demonstrated the absolute falsity of pacifism and the tactic of conscientious objection as a method of fighting war. The main problem with conscientious objection was that the best elements, the more self-sacrificing, the more courageous elements, would simply separate themselves off from the movement of the working class and those they wanted to influence. Such a policy would leave the working class to the mercy of the reactionary officers and generals of the ruling class.

Our comrades who went into the army very quickly got a great response wherever they were stationed. The military establishment, for example, in order to boost the morale of the soldiers, organised what they called The Army Bureau of Current Affairs or ABCA. This was used by the officers to explain to the conscript soldiers exactly what was happening at the different fronts, educate them about current political events and so on, and to inspire them for their military struggle against fascism. In many cases, where our comrades were stationed, together with other lefts, we took over a number of these ABCAs. Our comrades participated in the Forces' Parliament in Cairo to such effect that the army chiefs were forced to close it down. In Cyrenaica, Arthur Leadbetter was elected Prime Minister and Home Secretary of the Benghazi Forces' Parliament, but he was posted back to Cairo and the experiment with "parliamentarism" in the armed forces terminated.

We always insisted that our comrades should be the best workers in the factories, that they should be punctual and conscientious, otherwise workers would not be prepared to listen or take you seriously. Taking the advice of Trotsky, we extended this analogy to work in the army. That is to say, in times of war we should also be the best soldiers, and demonstrate our technical capacity and proficiency in arms. At the same time, our comrades would fight for the improvement in conditions of their fellow soldiers and link this to the establishment of Soldiers' Committees and a rounded-out revolutionary position.

This tactic was very successful. So successful in fact that the officers in charge usually wouldn't know what to do with our comrades. The colonel would grumble that he couldn't have this Bolshie chap ruining the morale in his unit. So he would look around for another officer who he did not particularly like and say: "I think I'll give Percy a little present." So they would post our comrade to old Percy, or whoever, with the message: "I've got a good bloke for you, very conscientious." So they would be posted all round the place. And wherever they went, carrying on our revolutionary agitation, they succeeded in "Bolshevising" the troops, to the dismay of the officers. As a result of this revolutionary work, soldiers were getting in touch with us from all sorts of places.

A classic example of this was what happened with Frank Ward, who unfortunately later ended up on the right wing where he acted as the Labour bureaucracy's 'expert' on Trotskyism. Nevertheless at that time he did marvellous work for us in the air force. Frank, a very capable comrade at that time, was an engineer in the RAF where he created waves with his political agitation. On one occasion when Frank was busy tying the officer in charge up in knots, the officer suddenly threw up his hands and said to our comrade: "Very well then, you conduct the bloody classes." Seeing an opportunity, Frank stepped in and gave four lectures on the programme of the Fourth International - and got an amazing response from the soldiers into the bargain! Using these methods, we managed to win over whole number of soldiers to our ideas.

Finally, the bigwigs in the War Office must have got wind of what was happening. They decided that there was only one thing to do. They gave Frank Ward an "honourable discharge" from the air force and sent him home! This was not a dishonourable discharge, of course, because they had no grounds for such an action. Frank's service record was impeccable, and they didn't want any trouble. He was informed that he was "no longer suitable to requirements." Of course, we wouldn't let it end there! We waged a campaign concerning this scandalous affair. This man was healthy, we explained, and there was absolutely nothing wrong with him, mentally or physically, and yet the military bosses were kicking him out of the forces. We kicked up a terrible scandal. After his discharge, he became a professional full-time worker for the organisation.

Our revolutionary agitation within the armed forces was having a great response. It was around this time that one of the great myths was created about the alleged "chauvinism" of Ted Grant - which was peddled around by some of the sects. This arose from our attitude towards the Eighth Army stationed in North Africa. The Eighth army - or the "desert rats" as they were popularly known - was responsible for inflicting the first serious defeat on the German army in North Africa at the battle of Alamein in 1932. This is held up by British military historians as a turning point in the war. But this should be kept in proportion. At Alamein the British defeated fifteen enemy divisions. The Russians were facing one hundred and seventy six enemy divisions on the eastern front.

Anyway, the Eighth Army was regarded as the flower of the British Army, but at that time there was an enormous revolutionary ferment developing among these soldiers. In the Forces' Parliament in Cairo, as I have already mentioned, our comrades were actually elected to the positions of Prime Minister and Home Secretary. Obviously, they put forward a Trotskyist position. From the reports of our soldier comrades, the Eighth Army soldiers were saying that after the war they would refuse to disarm, and return to Britain with their guns to ensure that things would change. This was the mutinous mood that was developing amongst these troops. At the 1943 conference of our tendency, I made the point, to illustrate the thing graphically, that the military establishment though it their army, but in fact, the soldiers of the Eighth Army were in rebellion. This reflected the revolutionary developments in the army. It was our Eighth Army in that it was being transformed. It was becoming revolutionary and in the process of moving over to the side of the working class. That was the precise meaning of my remark and no other:

> "We have a victorious army in North Africa and Italy, and I say, yes", I stated to the WIL conference. "Long Live the Eighth Army, because that is our army. One of our comrades has spoken to a number of people who have had letters from the Eighth Army soldiers showing their complete dissatisfaction. We know of incidents in the army, navy and other forces that have never been reported, and it is impossible for us to report. It is our Eighth Army that is being hammered and tested and being organised for the purpose of changing the face of the world. This applies equally to all the forces." [11]

"Books have their own fate", the Romans used to say, and speeches also have a fate unintended by those who make them. The above remarks were taken completely out of context by the sectarians and twisted in order to give some credence to the false allegation concerning our supposed "chauvinism".

Militants in industry

We made great advances in the army, and we made important gains in industry. In the engineering industry we were developing an important position, particularly in the Amalgamated Engineering Union. In this union we had established a small but important influence. We had set up a network throughout the country based on key activists. Gerry Healy was our industrial organiser, but we had numerous difficulties with him. This resulted in Healy either resigning or being expelled on several occasions from the WIL. Every time Haston and myself brought him back into the leadership, against the wishes of most of the membership. We managed to convince the comrades of his organisational capacity, and we brought him back. This proved to be a big mistake. The last time this happened, in February 1943, he walked out saying he was joining the ILP. Given his track record, when we brought him back this time, we refused to bring him back into the leadership. We told him he would have to work his way back into a position of trust, which served to push him into organising an opposition to the leadership on any question he could lay his hands on. This was the start of Healy's factionalism within the WIL, which was later encouraged by the connivance of Cannon and Pablo.

Given the importance of the industrial work, and our need to sink deep roots in industry, we had no alternative but to replace Healy. Roy Tearse became our national Industrial Organiser. Tearse, who was an outstanding comrade, had a great feel for the work, and applied himself with great energy and ability. We set up the Militant Workers Federation to draw around us the best militants in industry. Tearse became its secretary and its offices were based in Nottingham near the ROF factory. It quickly involved shop stewards committees and even District Committees, especially of the engineering workers union. Wherever there were strikes, anywhere in the country, the WIL was there. As Roy Tearse stated later:

> "Essentially my basic job as the secretary of the Militant Workers Federation was to keep these militants in contact with each other. It was a question of trying to build an alternative base from the Communist Party inside industry. This is what it really meant. There was no secret made of the fact to positively push Trotskyist ideas and to support genuine militant activity on the part of the working class. For instance, this Barrow strike, which is often mentioned, the Militant Workers Federation assisted in the organisation by sending out circulars for support and so on, and collected a considerable amount of money for the strike. In those days, what was collected I don't remember exactly now, but it was a considerable amount, and it was a question of workers getting assistance, of maintaining contact, where workers needed assistance and so on, and of course arguing all the time for our point of view. This is what it all really amounted to. Its biggest activity was its involvement in the Tyneside Apprentices strike in 1944." [12]

Under wartime conditions, all strikes were unofficial and illegal. Workers had not been involved in struggle for quite a period and so our assistance was invaluable. We gave them the idea of connecting with other sections of the working class, and explained how to set up committees and how to conduct the struggle. During the Barrow engineering workers' strike of 1943, which was a solid strike affecting the shipbuilding industry, we sent over Jimmy Dean from Liverpool and Roy Tearse, who were subsequently co-opted onto the strike committee. These comrades assisted with the detailed strategy and tactics of the strike throughout its duration, and countered the barrage of attacks from the Communist Party and the government.

The strike was taking place as we held our second national conference. There was great optimism throughout our ranks at the progress we had made, and the developing situation in Britain and internationally.

> "Wonderful day, wonderful possibilities open up in front of us", stated the present author to the assembled 150 or so delegates and visitors. "You can feel revolution in the air. That attitude must permeate our conference. The correctness of our viewpoint should give us confidence in preparing ourselves for our role in the coming revolution. Whatever its fate may be, it is certain that we can, we must, we will play our part, and stamp our tendency as an influence, as a serious factor in the situation, as an organisation that will play its part in the revolution. When, twelve months ago, we called our thesis 'Preparing for Power', this was not a mad gesture. That is the serious problem with which we are faced." [13]

WIL public meeting in the Conway Hall, London. Ajit Roy speaking with Harold Atkinson and Gerry Healy seated.

After the Conference, the Barrow strike had been victorious, and was a militant example to workers everywhere. Of course, the press was nosing around the Trotskyists to see what they could dig up, but they couldn't find anything. Nevertheless, there were campaigns in the press waged by the *Sunday Dispatch*, the Sunday organ of the *Daily Mail*, and by other newspapers, with big front page headlines about these 'outside agitators', and so on. But this had little effect. When the Stalinists attempted to slander our comrades Jimmy Deane and Arthur Farrager, the whole thing backfired. Asked why they weren't doing their bit for King and Country, they replied: "I'm doing my utmost - I'm a blood donor", to cheers of delight form the workers. [14] Hundreds of *Socialist Appeal* papers were sold in the dispute.

The WIL was also involved in a number of other strikes, which were regularly covered by the *Socialist Appeal*. In the report on the WIL drawn up by Herbert Morrison, it outlines some of these interventions:

> "Trotskyists also took some part in the strikes at the Rolls Royce aircraft works, Glasgow, in August 1941 and July 1943, in a strike at the Barnbow Royal Ordnance Factory in June 1943 and in the Yorkshire Transport strike in May 1943, but their activity has consisted in advising and encouraging the strike leaders rather than in provoking the strikes."

As the resolution on industrial perspectives for our 1943 national conference explained, 1942 saw the largest number of strikes for 16 years, and in the first five months of 1943 there were one-and-a-half times as many disputes as in the same period of 1942. It highlighted the possible development of workers' committees or soviets as the industrial struggle deepened, and especially the role of the Militant Workers Federation. The resolution stated:

> "It is now possible to perceive, not only a broadening out, but a general transformation in the nature of the struggle. Whereas previously the workers who were involved in disputes were isolated, the nationwide support given to the Neptune Engine works on the Tyne, the solidarity of the miners in the South Yorkshire and South Wales coalfields over recent disputes affecting single collieries in the given areas, or the strike of 23,000 Nottinghamshire miners over the imprisonment of a lad - these are demonstrations that the workers are closing their ranks in solidarity. But the latter strike in particular, is an indication of the *political* character that the struggle is assuming.
>
> "Already the workers are realising the necessity of linking up with, and gaining support of, workers in other parts. The Committees that were established as the directing centres in these disputes are not as yet soviets, but they point to the centres in which the workers, through the efforts of the local leaders, will create fighting committees or soviets on a national scale in the future. All these factors demonstrate that the main strategy of *the revolutionary socialists in the field of industry must be to raise consciously in the minds of the industrial workers the necessity to end the industrial truce.*
>
> "All the objective conditions for tremendous explosions are maturing in the factories, mines and transport of Britain. Arising out of the struggles that have already taken place, the question of leadership is being raised more and more sharply in the minds of the working class. The workers have learned, whenever they have been forced to stand and fight, that the Labour and trade union leadership, together with the Communist Party and the National Council of Shop Stewards, have deserted them, and indeed, sabotaged their struggle at every turn."

Demise of the Comintern

In the same year, in June 1943, Stalin wound up the Communist International as a gesture to the Allies, and to demonstrate that he was not interested in world revolution. According to the Stalinist writer William Z. Foster, who was chairman of the American Communist Party,

> "It is *significant* that the historic decision was taken right at the *most crucial* moment of the fight to establish the second front. This front was very greatly needed for a quick and decisive victory; but the Western reactionaries (who also believed Goebbels' lies about the Comintern)

> were blocking it. *Undoubtedly the favourable impression all over the bourgeois world made by the dissolution of the Comintern helped very decisively to break this deadly log-jam.* It was only a few months later (in November-December 1943) that there was held the famous Teheran conference, at which the date for the second front was finally decided." [15]

In a special issue of *Socialist Appeal*, a manifesto addressed to working class internationalists was issued. I wrote an analysis in the June edition of *WIN* entitled *The Rise and Fall of the Communist International*, outlining the history of the International, from a revolutionary body under Lenin to a counter-revolutionary body under Stalin, for use by comrades in discussions with CP militants. It concluded:

> "This policy of Stalin and the 'stinking corpse' of the Comintern suffered irretrievable ruin when the Nazis invaded the Soviet Union. The Comintern had to execute a right about turn and convert itself once again into a doormat for Roosevelt and British imperialism. But with the increased dependence of Stalin on American and British imperialism, has come the increased pressure on the part of the capitalist 'allies'. American imperialism especially has demanded the ending of the Comintern as a final guarantee against the danger of social revolution in Europe after the downfall of Hitler.
>
> "The long drawn-out pretence is over. Stalin has dissolved the degenerate Comintern. In doing so he openly announces his stepping over to the side of the capitalist counter-revolution as far as the rest of the world is concerned. But the imperialists, in forcing Stalin to make this trade in return for concessions and bargains on their part, have not understood the consequences this will have. It cannot and will not prevent the coming of new revolutions throughout the world. In the less than two decades since the beginning of its degeneration, the Comintern has ruined many favourable situations in many countries.
>
> "The coming decades will witness many revolutions with the breakdown and collapse of capitalism. Even the violently disturbed epoch of the period between the wars will seem comparatively tranquil compared to the period which lies ahead. On this background of storms and upheavals a real instrument of world revolution will be created. What the workers lacked in the last decades, outside Russia, was a workers' Bolshevik Party and a Bolshevik leadership. The great days of the Comintern of 1917-23 will live again. The growth in support for the ideas of Marxism internationally, based on the traditions of Bolshevism, the rich experience of the past, and learning the lessons of defeats of the working class, can once again lead the oppressed to the overthrow of capitalism and to the world socialist republic."

The WIL had really come into its own. We had established a modest apparatus. I was the national secretary, Jock was the national organiser, and Harold Atkinson was our national treasurer. We had four full timers at this stage: myself, Jock, Andrew Scott, who was the assistant editor of *Socialist Appeal*, and Millie Lee. It was a very good team, although Scott dropped out after being called up. Our offices in Kings Cross were very modest, but they suited our purposes. By this time we must have had 300 members. Things were certainly going in our direction.

In contrast, as we explained in our statement, the official section of the International, the RSL, was in a terminal state and split into three warring factions. Its meagre forces were disintegrating before their very eyes. By the summer of 1943, the 170 members who made up the RSL at its foundation had dwindled to 23. Their paper ceased publication and they had no paid full timer. In 1943, one of their factions, the Trotskyist Opposition (TO), the so-called right wing, got in touch with us with the aim of fusing with our organisation. The Healy faction had been in regular contact with the TO, hoping, under the guidance of Cannon, to construct a stronger faction with the TO. However, just at this point when the right wing was preparing to join us, the leadership, which had become a minority in the RSL, pulled a brilliant manoeuvre by expelling the majority! That is an actual fact! They managed to pull off this trick with Harber joining up with Robertson to expel the 'social chauvinists', as they called the Trotskyist Opposition. As soon as that was complete, Harber then turned around and immediately expelled the supporters of Robertson into the bargain! So by that means the minority succeeded in expelling the majority. At any rate, the TO got in touch with us and were getting ready to enter our organisation and, at that very moment, who should arrive on the scene but Sam Gordon of the American SWP. By this time, the headquarters of the International had moved to New York as the Nazi occupation of Europe made it almost impossible for it to function. Its existence now depended completely on the American SWP. So Gordon arrived in reality as an emissary of James Cannon.

Cannon couldn't have this terrible mess in Britain. The official British section was an absolute embarrassment. It was a disaster, and they knew it. The Americans had been republishing articles from our press in the American *Militant*, particularly on our application of the military policy as well as intervention in industry. They reprinted a lot of our material because they could see the enormous progress that was being made on the basis of the policy of Trotskyism. Cannon and the rest of the leaders lamented this position and said: "It's terrible. It's unprecedented that an unofficial organisation had the official policy of Trotskyism and the official organ, the RSL, has nothing to do with Trotskyism. The RSL is completely sectarian, completely ultra-left and also completely opportunist in their attitude towards the Labour Party". So the Cannon leadership of the International sought a way out of this dilemma, but of course, in their own inimical fashion.

Firstly, they pulled back the TO from fusing with us, convincing them that their task was to re-establish the RSL, which was in ruins. So they convened a conference of all the factions of the RSL in January 1944. An IS resolution was proposed, and after some arm twisting, accepted as a means of reconstituting the RSL, which could then formally enter fusion talks with the WIL. The job of the IS was simply, as they saw it, to unify their rump grouping with the successful WIL. The International leadership forced the remnants of the RSL at gun-point to come together by threatening to expel them from the International if they weren't prepared to accept this decision. In the words of Don Corleone in *The Godfather*, they made them an offer they couldn't refuse. But before the International leadership was prepared to recognise us as the official tendency in Britain, we had to go through a farcical unification procedure. We didn't object to unification. But as we said at the time, if there is to be unity in the movement, it will not add up to much. The WIL will simply swallow up what was left of the RSL. That was our open and frank position.

We insisted that if there was going to be a unification of the organisations, then this could only take place on a principled basis. Tactical, strategic and political positions had to be laid down firmly in advance, then discussed on a democratic basis between both tendencies. This would be followed by a unity conference where the decisions would be made. The minority, whoever the minority might be, had the right to develop and put forward their position, and the organisation as a whole would consider it. But once the conference decided, then that would be the policy of the organisation. Otherwise there couldn't be any unification. We would never again allow a unification such as took place in 1938 - an unprincipled unification, which, we said, was a sure formula for future splits. In this, we were proved absolutely correct.

So they sent Sherry Mangan, another American, over to Europe to oversee the fusion. He was the correspondent for *Life* and *Time magazines*, and was in a position to travel quite extensively. He was very well off, probably earning a few thousand dollars a year, which was a lot of money in those days. He came to Britain with the purpose of getting unification at any cost. To his horror, he found we had been in touch with the Harber tendency, the old leaders of the RSL, who had informed us of the real situation in their ranks, in terms of numbers, and so on. We explained the position to Mangan and he quickly realised that we were in a very strong position. In the end, they were quite prepared to accept unity on our terms and so a conference was arranged.

Of course, before the unity conference we published all the documents. The RSL published documents on the military policy, which described us as having a chauvinist policy. We put forward our position of supporting the proletarian military policy based on the policy of Trotsky and Lenin - developed by us and applied to the present situation. This position was in complete contrast to the barren and ineffective caricature of "revolutionary defeatism" as put forward by the RSL.

On the question of entrism, we explained that in the long term, even if we had thousands of members, it would still be necessary to enter the Labour Party at a certain stage - but only under the classic conditions that had been laid down by Trotsky. These were: a pre-revolutionary situation, a ferment within the party of social democracy and a developing mass left wing opposition within the party. We explained that although this would provide a golden opportunity, it was nevertheless regarded as a short-term expedient. That was our position at that time, and that was the position of Trotsky. Events in the post war period forced us to modify this position, and, with the break-up of the RCP, we were forced to enter the Labour Party for a very lengthy period indeed. But at that time, entrism was not a viable tactic in building the organisation. It was necessary to maintain an open independent party.

Notes:

1- From *James P. Cannon, The Internationalist* by Joseph Hanson, New York, July 1980, pp.27-28.
2- Discussion/Education Documentary Collection, 1944.
3- *Writings of Leon Trotsky,* 1939-40, pp. 411-12.
4- GDH Cole, op. cit., p. 662.
5- Haston interview with Al Richardson, 30 April 1978.
6- WIL *Internal Bulletin*, 12 March 1942.
7- *Criticism by the RSL of the WIL pamphlet 'Preparing For Power'*, 22 December 1942.
8- Ibid., pp.11-12.
9- Ted Grant, *Reply to the RSL,* pp.18-19.
10- Michael Foot, *Aneurin Bevan,* vol. one, p. 388.
11- Quoted in *War and the International* by Bornstein and Richardson, London 1986, p.89.
12- Roy Tearse interview by Al Richardson, 6 July 1978.
13- Quoted in *War and the International*, pp.77-78.
14- Quoted in *War and the International*, p.73.
15- Quoted in *The Communist Movement,* Fernando Claudin, London 1975, p.23.

Public speaking at Hyde Park
Mid - 1942

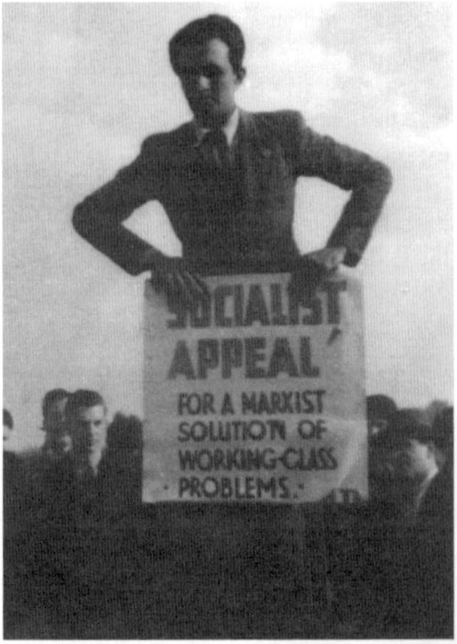

▶ Ted Grant ▼ Ajit Roy

▲ Harold Atkinson

▶ Gerry Healy

3

Making Our Mark

Revolutionary Communist Party

As a result of the fusion, the Revolutionary Communist Party was founded in March 1944. At this founding conference, all the factions were allowed to put their case. Firstly, we discussed the question of the proletarian military policy, moved by myself. Harber, and then Robinson put forward their positions, but were heavily defeated. Haston moved the resolution on entrism, which was opposed by John Archer and Robinson, but won by an overwhelming majority. Tearse then moved the industrial resolution that was passed with only the "Left" voting against. Finally, the present author moved the WIL perspectives document, *The World Revolution and the Tasks of the Working Class*. Again only the "Left" were opposed.

After a debate, the name Revolutionary Communist Party was chosen. Following elections to the Central Committee, all factions, except the Left faction of Robinson, which soon split from the party, announced their dissolution. Arthur Cooper got up as a speaker for the Trotskyist Opposition and said: "We have absolutely no political differences whatsoever with the leadership". And this was true at that time; there were no political differences. He concluded, "therefore, we can't continue as a faction and so we're dissolving the faction." This remark was greeted with laughter and jeers on the part of the delegates. The comrades had known these people for a number of years and knew the value of such speeches. Mangan, the representative of the International Secretariat, and a stooge of Cannon, stood up, holding up his hands in holy horror: "Comrades," he pontificated, "when good comrades give an undertaking like this, it is unprecedented that they should be treated in this way." Of course, we just laughed and left it at that. Nobody even bothered to reply.

Although the conference had taken very clear decisions, we didn't force everybody into line. We were never advocates of the "big stick" approach of Cannon, but were always flexible in internal Party affairs. Those who had been in the Labour Party could remain in the Labour Party for the time being. We wouldn't insist that they leave the Labour Party. On the contrary, we said they should participate in our LP fraction, which in any case had two or three times as many members in the Labour Party as the RSL had! Although they styled themselves the "Labour Party fraction" they had collapsed, for reasons I've already explained, whereas we had developed a modest base in the Labour Party in certain areas. Thus, even though we were overwhelmingly outside the Labour Party, we had succeeded with our methods where the others had failed. As long as the official position was put publicly, we accepted that these opposition comrades had the right to hold their views, continue their activity, and publish articles in the internal bulletins if they so wished.

Jock Haston, RCP general secretary, January 1945

Despite all the talk about "unity", that very same night Sherry Mangan held a secret faction meeting in his room in the Dorchester hotel. Present at the meeting was John Lawrence, Gerry Healy, John Goffe and Arthur Cooper - the leaders of the Trotskyist Opposition. And what was the purpose of this gathering? It was to decide how best to get rid of the 'anti-internationalist' leadership of the RCP, headed by Haston and Grant. Without a single political difference they were already organising an anti-leadership clique, because that is what it amounted to. Hand-in-glove with Cannon, they wanted to get rid of a leadership that had demonstrated its viability, and political correctness during the course of the war and had demonstrated that it could build a real Trotskyist movement. We had shown in practice that we were conducting possibly the most effective wartime revolutionary work of any Trotskyist organisation. But they weren't concerned with that. They were only concerned with settling personal scores. Lenin once remarked there is nothing more destructive in politics than spite.

During the war, Cannon had developed a swelled head. After the death of Trotsky, he and the other SWP leaders thought that they must control the International movement, as they had controlled the American Trotskyist movement. They therefore needed pliable people who would follow their line. They had forgotten that with these methods, the methods of Zinoviev, and later the methods of Stalin, they would build nothing. They had forgotten the main principle that Lenin had tried to teach Bukharin: that if you demand unconditional obedience from the different tendencies within the International, you will get obedient fools. Not only that, but - as we predicted in relation to Cannon and CLR James - when it comes to the first big conflict, the stooges will end up on the opposite side of their erstwhile "Leader". That actually happened with the SWP on a number of occasions.

In the 1938 unity negotiations prior to the Founding World Congress, Cannon had brought over with him a couple of young comrades from the youth organisation of the SWP, Frank Denby and Nathan Gould. We predicted at the time that the cynical manoeuvres of Cannon would have a bad effect on these youngsters, who would be completely mis-educated and start to behave in a similar fashion. We predicted that at the first serious test of opposition, they would come into collision with Cannon. And that is how it turned out. Gould entered into a bloc with Shachtman against Cannon and became a leader of the rival American Workers Party. In Britain, we saw that Cannon was spawning a monster in the person of Healy. Although Healy became an obedient tool of Cannon and Pablo, ending up as a complete political zombie and quizling, we predicted that he would come into violent opposition and the 100 percent support would turn into 100 percent opposition. As we know, after a period, that is what happened.

We deliberately took the name of the Revolutionary Communist Party - in complete contrast to the strike-breaking patriotic "Communist" Party. We wanted to contrast the genuine unblemished revolutionary programme of Trotskyism with the criminal role of Stalinism. The RCP had begun on a firm basis, continuing the revolutionary tradition of the WIL. Haston was elected general secretary of the RCP, and I was made the political secretary. Five-sixths of our membership were working class. We had a tried and tested leadership, and we had no real political rivals. It seemed that the future of our tendency and the future of the working class was assured. On the surface of it, we had solved all the problems of factionalism. We had become the official section of the Fourth International in Britain. We could now turn our attention to the really important task of building the movement. It seemed as if the situation was very favourable, and we could now begin to move forward at a rapid pace.

After the formation of the RCP, we took out a lease on a new headquarters in 256 Harrow Road, again in Paddington. Unfortunately, we didn't have the money to buy it and we didn't have a printing press. But it marked a new step forward and a new beginning for the RCP. In the Harrow Road office, we had a meeting hall that we used for party meetings. We had separate rooms for all the full-timers and some of the full-time comrades actually lived in the premises, including myself. Of course, the wages of our professionals were very small. We were earning less than one pound a week in the early stages of the war, which later went up to thirty bob and even the princely sum, in the last years of the RCP, of about £2 and 10 shillings, which was just about enough to live on.

As an amusing aside, in the early days of the RCP, the "Left" John Robinson used to say that he slept on the floor in the East End of London, and that all revolutionaries should do the same, as that is how workers lived. Well, I do not know about the workers, but we were forced to sleep on mattresses on the floor in 256 Harrow Road, not by choice, but because we didn't have the money to buy furniture! It certainly wasn't a question of so-called working-class credentials. Of course, we had Cliff Stanton of the old RSL, who became a very successful businessman, who in those days used to go round saying that he didn't take a bath, because the workers do not bath! That was the type of people who were in the old RSL - middle-class elements who had a completely false and lumpen-proletarian view of the working class.

The apprentices' strike

There was a serious shortage of coal, reflecting the lack of investment of the coal owner for a period of decades and an aging workforce. In an attempt to solve the problem in 1943 the government introduced what was known as the "Bevin boys" - a system whereby a body of young men chosen by ballot from those conscripted to serve in the army would instead be sent to the mines. This was extremely unpopular, and was aggravated by the bad conditions that the young apprentices had to put up with. The discontent surfaced in the Tyneside apprentices' strike.

In March 1944, in the middle of the founding conference of the RCP, 100,000 miners went on strike. Haston wrote a front-page article for the *Socialist Appeal*: *100,000 Miners Can't be Wrong - Horner Selling Out*. Almost within a matter of months, we had a new industrial upsurge, which reflected a new mood developing not only in the working class, but also within the army. First of all, we had the apprentices' strike in the engineering and shipbuilding industries, and particularly in the shipbuilding on Tyneside. They were striking over the introduction of the Bevin ballot scheme for conscripting youth into the coalmines. We intervened in this strike of apprentices and helped to spread it nationally. It took on a widespread character, but was especially solid in Newcastle and in the Tyneside area.

Of course, our comrades, led by Heaton Lee and Ann Keen, gave them support and assistance, and even provided important guidance to the strike through Bill Davy, the apprentices' leader. Roy Tearse explained:

> "The first contact with Bill Davy had been made by the members of Workers International League on Tyneside. It was purely a political contact at first. Bill was a political animal, at that time he was in the YCL as well as being an apprentice in industry, and the first contact that was made, was made by the comrades in Newcastle, like Heaton Lee, Jack Rawlings and so on. My first contact was really through them. By this time the apprentices' committee had been formed, Bill had become chairman of the apprentices' committee, and a possibility of a strike was in the offing. But once having made contact as secretary of the Militant Workers Federation that this meant an important link was being established. For instance, I was invited to speak to meetings of apprentices in Sunderland and elsewhere, and so the Militant Workers Federation, fairly rapidly had a considerable influence. What we were able to do as well, was that the apprentices on the Clydeside, with whom we were in contact at the same time. We put them in touch with the Tyneside people, also there were people in Huddersfield and elsewhere and so the Militant Workers Federation really had some effect in connecting these people together." [1]

SOCIALIST APPEAL

SHAMEFUL ATTACK ON TYNESIDE STRIKERS

T.U. Officials Disband Militant N.U.G.M.W. Branch By HEATON LEE

WHAT HAPPENED IN PARIS

EYE-WITNESS REPORT

National Union of General & Municipal Workers

European Trotskyist Parties Meet

Morale in the Red Army

Vickers Sack 200

No Transfers to Parent Factory

The Mid-October 1944 issue of *Socialist Appeal*, with Heaton Lee's article on the Tyneside strike

As the strike spread, the actions of the apprentices were gaining enormous sympathy amongst the older engineers in Tyneside and throughout the engineering industry. With this, the Tories and their kept press were screaming about the effects of Trotskyist agitators in the dispute. The Home Secretary, Morrison, was under pressure from the Tories to take action against these "subversives".

As always, the mouthpieces for the ruling class attempted to blame so-called subversives for the developing militancy in the working class. So, true to form, the Special Branch, MI5, swung into action, using all the information they had gathered by phone tapping, spying and the like. In the early hours of the morning, simultaneously, in a military operation, every important RCP branch in the country was raided: London, Manchester, Nottingham, Newcastle, Wallsend, Glasgow, Leeds, and elsewhere. Even smaller branches were raided. The homes of branch secretaries had visits by police at two and three in the morning and were searched from top to bottom. The police were looking in particular for documents, or any incriminating evidence that could be used in a trial of RCP leaders. Heaton Lee, the local RCP branch secretary, and Ann Keen who was also in Newcastle, were arrested. Then Roy Tearse, who was the industrial organiser of the Party, was picked up. Jock Haston, who was deeply involved in the strike, was in Edinburgh at the time on a lecture tour.

Haston knew they were looking for him when the news came on the radio and decided to play a little game of hide-and-seek with the police. So he managed to dodge them and went to a cinema to hide out. As the police searched all around Edinburgh for him, he was watching a show. In the meantime, they raided his mother's house, as well as the house of the Edinburgh branch secretary. Haston waited in the cinema until the evening. After that, he went and gave himself up at a police station with witnesses to show that it had been entirely voluntary. This was important from the point of view of possibly getting bail in the future.

Daily Sketch, 19 May 1944 Left to right: Ann Keen, Roy Tearse, Heaton Lee and Jock Haston arriving at Newcastle

Those arrested were all charged with evading the provisions of the Trades Disputes Acts of 1927, and of assisting an illegal strike. It was the very first time that this piece of vicious anti-labour movement legislation, brought in by Baldwin after the defeat of the General Strike, had been used - and scandalously used by a Labour minister into the bargain. The action was taken by the Coalition government, in which Herbert Morrison was Home Secretary. When the Tory Stanley Baldwin pushed through the Trade Disputes, he laid the onus for any action on the Attorney General. No prosecution could be taken without his permission. Of course, he would have to get clearance from the Cabinet before invoking any powers. Baldwin made sure that if the legislation was to be used, it could only be implemented with the say-so of the government.

While these arrests and attacks on our organisation rained down, our ranks stayed absolutely firm. They had been well trained and well prepared to meet these difficulties head on. There was not a single defection from the old comrades of the WIL. The majority of the old RSL membership that still remained active, also remained firm. However, there were some resignations from amongst the ex-members of the RSL. These great people of "revolutionary" principles tended to run for cover at the first shot. Ironically those defections were from the same r-r-revolutionaries, who had this intransigent policy of "revolutionary defeatism", and not at all from the ranks of the "chauvinist" Workers International League.

With the Tory anti-union laws being used against us, we immediately set up an Anti Labour Laws' Victims Defence Committee. We got in touch with Maxton, McGovern and the other ILP MPs, and through them with Nye Bevan, SO Davies and the Labour left. We succeeded in setting up a solidarity committee to raise support and money for the defence of our comrades. At the launch meeting in Conway Hall, London, there were speeches by WG Cove MP, John McGovern MP, V. Sastry, the RCP Midlands organiser, James Maxton MP, and myself. Although some of the Labour leaders, and even the left Labour leaders, supported the war, they sympathised with our support of the apprentices' struggle. Despite this, we proceeded from the contradictions of reformism and of left reformism, and sought to drive a wedge between them and the bourgeois, between them and the capitalist state. We had no puritanical ultra-left qualms about this question.

The Anti-Labour Laws Defence Committee and its campaign had an immediate success within the trade union and Labour movement. Thousands of pounds were collected to fight our case and to pay for the legal defence. We conducted a campaign above all within the trade union movement, sending speakers around as many branches and shop stewards committees as possible. We circulated nationally all the trade union branches we could reach, which amounted to thousands of branches, and the support and money actually poured in. It was quite significant that the Stalinists within these branches had to keep their mouths firmly shut when this question came up, otherwise, they would have received short shrift from the workers. It was extremely difficult for them to oppose our class appeal and come out with their poison about fascism and all the rest of it. Even the *Daily Worker* after initial stories about "saboteurs" had to tread carefully. This didn't stop the Labour MP, DN Pritt, QC, a Stalinist fellow traveller, and the other hardened Stalinists howling for our blood. "As for Grant", snarled the *Daily Worker*, "all he knows about the British working class movement in his native city, could be put on the back of a penny stamp." Tearse, in turn, was branded a "third-rate inefficient shop steward."

Despite all their sound and fury, the Stalinists were in a difficult position and were forced onto the defensive by our Anti-Labour Laws Victims Defence Committee. We took maximum advantage of the publicity surrounding the case to launch a tremendous campaign, involving every section of the organisation. Our comrades were imprisoned and we would not rest until they were released. Although those arrested were initially denied bail, on appeal they were released as long as they reported to the police station on a daily basis. This allowed them to participate in the Defence Campaign, which was of enormous benefit. Nye Bevan and the other lefts became heads of the Defence Committee, which was of great help and assistance to us in approaching Labour Parties and trade unions nationally. The Defence Campaign really put the organisation on the map. We already had a basis in the trade unions, and on the basis of these attacks by the state, our support was extended further. The influence of the RCP began to grow, and we sunk deeper roots into the working class.

The comrades were tried in camera, under the pretext that the police had not had time to complete their investigations into the alleged offences. Meanwhile, the press whipped up a tremendous hate campaign against us, spreading all manner of scare stories. They actually committed contempt of court on a massive scale, but this was war - so who cared? The Stalinists joined in the chorus against "Trotskyist wreckers" who were allegedly betraying our boys at the front. But they got their answer from the soldiers of the Eighth Army who passed a resolution pointing out: "It is the right to strike that we are fighting for".

After the trial: left to right Jock Haston, Ann Keen, Heaton Lee and Roy Tearse

The case itself was very important as it was the only time that the Trades Disputes Act was ever used, before its repeal by the post-war Attlee Labour Government. The comrades received a sympathetic response from the jury, and especially from the spectators attending the court hearing. True to form, the comrades took a very dignified and firm approach to the proceedings, and took full responsibility for all their class actions. Without any hesitation, they gave full support to the struggle of the apprentices. They refused to knuckle under, or bend under the pressure of the prosecution or the bourgeois state. However on the day, unfortunately for the authorities, the jury found them guilty only on two counts.

> "In so far as the trial and imprisonment was concerned, what was important was the political attitude of the apprentices", recalled Roy Tearse. "Now what happened was that I was,

according to the judge and the press, the main defender involved, and the prosecution called the strike committee as prosecution witnesses. The entire strike committee was called as prosecution witnesses. What they had to do during the trial was to declare every witness, except one, as hostile witnesses. They were absolutely 100 percent in solidarity with the Trotskyists during the trial, and the stand made by Bill Davy was really exceptional. He was only nineteen at the time. If you look through the transcript of the proceedings, you can see how really able he was, and I think that was most important.

"On the question of the trial, when I was first charged, I was charged with acting in the furtherance of a trade dispute, in the magistrates court. When we got to the assizes there were thirteen charges. If they can't get you on the swings, they will get you on the roundabouts. They introduced 'conspiracy' to add to 'the furtherance'. 'Aiding and abetting James William Davy to act as furtherance'. 'Conspiring to aid and abet James William Davy to act as furtherance'. By the end of it, there were thirteen counts." [2]

In the end, Mr Justice Cassels passed sentence, and Haston got six months and Roy Tearse and Heaton Lee got a year each. Ann Keen was immediately released having already served her 13-day custodial sentence. The comrades launched an immediate appeal, but in the meantime, were forced to serve their sentences while it was being considered.

"I remember what was staggering, when the jury came back, as far as I was concerned, that the first eleven were 'Not Guilty' and I thought, Jesus, what's going to happen?", recalls Tearse. "But on the last two they found us guilty. And of course, we won the appeal, and the reason why we won the appeal was because the jury had actually been contradictory, so the convictions were actually quashed, but Heaton Lee and I got a year each of two counts to run concurrently, Jock Haston got six months and Ann Keen got thirteen days which meant that she was released because she had been inside." [3]

One amusing footnote: when Haston and the other comrades went to Durham prison, they were asked to state their religious affiliation, as is normal practise in British prisons. So they answered mischievously "Dialectical Materialist". As the prison officer couldn't spell this strange-sounding religion, he simply put down "DM" as their faith!

"On another occasion", recalled Jock Haston, "it was the anniversary of Trotsky's assassination, I made an application to see the governor to have a commemoration meeting with the other two [Heaton Lee and Roy Tearse]. He denied the application and I pointed out he couldn't deny the application because it was a religious meeting, and we had a very philosophical discussion about what was meant by 'religion'. My argument was the regulations were that if there were three or more members of any denomination they gad to be given opportunities to meet together. In the end, he denied the actual application, but he said, 'I'll see that you get together during the course of the day', which he subsequently did. So we actually had a commemoration meeting in jail." [4]

While in prison, Haston spent time studying law, which allowed him to give some sound advice to his lawyers. He was so diligent that he gave the lawyers the technical information relating to previous cases, where similar points of law applied. Especially as a general principle in law, you couldn't act in furtherance of something before it actually happened. The case against them had been ill prepared. That was a fact, and shows the superiority of Marxism, even on these questions!

At the Appeal Court, which we all attended, the scene was full of amusing side issues on points of law. The prosecution lawyers, for example, indignantly produced an issue of the *Socialist Appeal* which they hoped would strengthen their case. It had a picture of Ernest Bevin, right wing leader of the TGWU, on his way to catch his train and behind him a very small porter, overloaded with huge baggage. The caption underneath was something along the lines of: look at this - two men in the same union, but Bevin is getting so many thousands a year as a cabinet minister, while the porter is on three or four pounds a week. Very indignantly, the prosecutor handed it up to the judges, evidently hoping that their Honours would be similarly outraged. However, the photo was so amusing that in spite of themselves, the judges let out a chuckle.

At the Appeal Court, our defence council argued that all the acts with which our comrades were charged concerned the period before the apprentices' strike, but "furtherance" could only apply to a strike that had already broken out. Therefore, the jury had been misdirected and the sentences should be quashed forthwith. Obviously, the point sunk home as far as the judges were concerned. At any rate, Mr. Justice Wrottesley then turned round to the prosecutor, who was obviously preparing for a long and involved speech, and asked him: "Mr. so-and-so, if we accept your submission on such and such, will you rest your case?"

The prosecutor, who was supremely confident, was beaming with satisfaction at such a request. The appeal was surely about to be rejected out of hand! On the other hand, our legal counsel had a long face - and so did we. We thought the day was totally lost and that they had already made up their minds. So the prosecutor said, "certainly, your Lordships, I accept the submission. I rest my case." When he had sat down, Justice Wrottesley turned round and said the judges did not accept his submission on this case and that they would give a full judgement in writing later. But in the meantime, they dismissed the charges on the point of law that in acting in furtherance of a strike, before the strike had taken place, was not in breach of the Act. We had won! The convictions were quashed, and our comrades were released forthwith.

The Neath by-election

After the acquittal, which was a great victory for the RCP, we won over the leader of the apprentices, Bill Davy and a number of young strikers. As soon as this battle had finished, another opportunity opened up for us. This was in a totally new area for us: the parliamentary front. South Wales remained a weak area for Trotskyism. Then, out of the blue, a by-election was called in the small mining town of Neath in South Wales as a result of the death of the Labour MP. In early 1945, after considering things fully, we took the decision to put up a candidate. The election was in a Labour stronghold that had an enormous majority, and allowed us to build upon the support we had achieved in South Wales for the Defence Committee from various miners' lodges. There was talk of an independent Communist candidate, but this did not materialise. So, we decided to use this opportunity to outline our programme and establish a base for the RCP in this important industrial area where the CP was still very strong. We had a few ILPers who were sympathetic to us in the area, but we didn't have a single member before we started the campaign.

▼ ◀

Election posters and slogans

Election headquarters, Neath 1945

▲

▼ Jock Haston (center) discussing with comrades

▼
L to R: Anne Warde, Bill Davy, Sastry, John Lawrence, Heaton Lee, Ted Grant

L to R: Anne Warde, Frank Warde, Bill Davy, (at rear) Jimmy Deane, Jock Haston, Heaton Lee, John Williams and John Lawrence. Two in front unknown.
▲

▼
Jock Haston

L to R: Heaton Lee, Jock Haston and John Lawrence
▲

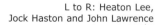

Neath by-election pictures

Four central figures: Bill Davy, John Lawrence, Sastry and Harold Atkinson

Preparing the "speaker" cars

Inside Neath headquarters: George Noseda at duplicator (far left), Harold Atkinson (seated)

Jimmy Deane in shirt

It was a foregone conclusion that Labour would win the Neath seat. However, as there was an electoral truce, the Tories obviously wouldn't oppose a Labour candidate. So we decided to put up a candidate, standing on a programme to end to the Coalition and explaining the revolutionary alternative. Given the sluggish way things worked in the by-election process, it allowed us a few months of energetic revolutionary campaigning within the Neath constituency. All the comrades who could take their holidays arranged to take them during the campaign. Comrades came from all over the country and we waged a tremendously successful campaign. It kicked off with a meeting, addressed by Jock Haston, our candidate, at the Miners' Welfare Hall in Gwaun-cae-Gurwen. We began with small meetings, ten or fifteen people, gradually building up towards the end of the campaign with meetings of a hundred, two hundred and three hundred throughout the constituency. Miners, tin-plate workers, steelworkers, transport workers and others came to hear what we had to say. We began to get a mass audience for our ideas.

To answer the attacks of the Stalinists, who raised the question of so-called "Trotsky-fascism", we challenged them to a public debate, but at first, this challenge fell on deaf ears. We conducted an energetic electoral campaign, which had nothing in common with the kind of ultra-leftism and opportunism which is always the hallmark of the sects when they engage in electoral politics. Lenin explained long ago that ultra-leftism and opportunism are head and tail of the same coin. The sects are totally incapable of approaching the labour movement, or speaking the language of the rank and file workers. They appear as something totally alien to the labour movement. But this was not at all the case with the RCP that had its finger on the pulse of the working class and knew how to present its ideas in a way that ordinary Labour workers could appreciate.

Our campaign was waged openly as an anti-war campaign. While explaining that we were opposed to Hitler and the Nazis, we put forward a class position, that we had no confidence in the British ruling class to wage the war. We also explained that the German workers were not our enemies and that it was the duty of the working class of all countries to struggle for socialism. We argued for Labour to break the Coalition government with the Tories, and for Labour to fight for power on a socialist programme to transform the situation nationally and internationally. It was an entirely internationalist case, and it connected with the mood of the workers in this solid Labour constituency. So solid was the Labour majority that they used to say that in an election in those parts they did not count the votes - they weighed them! Yet so successful was our election campaign in Neath that the Labour candidate actually started to panic. He became alarmed because, with no real campaign by the Labour Party, his own meetings were a fiasco - three men and a dog - while our meetings were the best attended in the whole campaign.

The Communist Party, of course, was foaming at the mouth. We were influencing their supporters and threatening their position in the area. True to form, they were putting forward their slanders about the Trotskyists being agents of fascism, agents of the Nazis, stooges of Hitler and all the rest of it. They constantly raised the slogan: "A Vote for Haston is a Vote for Hitler!" Of course, it had no effect at all. They only succeeded in damaging and discrediting themselves in the course of the campaign. In their delirium, they even denounced the Labour candidate, DJ Williams, who had previously been an NCLC organiser, as a "counter-revolutionary Trotskyist"! In reality, Williams was a fairly left semi-pacifist type. The Welsh

Nationalists were also standing. But they also failed to get the high attendance at meetings that we were getting.

We hired an office in the centre of Neath, a building with a shop front in the middle of the town. We had to put in a load of bed bunks so that the visiting comrades could have somewhere to sleep. There were all sorts of rumours going round the area, spread by right wingers, about these bed bunks... and strange Trotskyist agitators coming into the town from all over the country. During the campaign, we made contact with members and ex-members of the Communist Party, as well as members of the ILP. We even managed to draw a layer of ILP members around us, which we recruited and, as a consequence, formed a branch of the RCP in Neath. In the Amman Valley, in the mining village of Gwaun-cae-Gurwen, and in one or two of the other areas, we probably won about thirty new comrades in the course of that campaign. These were mostly young people, ready to fight for our ideas against all the odds.

In G-C-G, we recruited half a dozen miners, with Johnny Crown Jones as the local branch secretary. He and his three brothers, all miners, joined the organisation. He was a fine self-taught writer, and contributed often to the *Socialist Appeal*. Years later he recalled what it was like in the Trotskyist movement at the time: "Selling the *Socialist Appeal* at the pit head always ended in a punch-up with the Stalinists, who were very strong in this area. But we were tough lads", remarked Johnny.

After a gap of more than twenty years, one of those miners, Olwyn Hughes, rejoined the tendency in South Wales. He attended a Workers Educational Association class in Ammanford where Alan Woods was speaking, and introduced himself by saying "Do you know Ted Grant?" When he came back after all those years he made some very interesting remarks about the tendency. It was like coming home, after a long absence. He was absolutely delighted when we managed to contact him, thus retying the knot of history. He said that the ideas, perspectives and approach were the same as he had heard when he first joined the RCP in 1945. And that is perfectly true. The tendency has been consistent and true to itself always - right up to the present day.

The same was true of Olwyn Hughes himself, who remained true to the ideas of Trotskyism and the tendency until his death a few years ago. This was testament to the theoretical training of worker comrades in the RCP. We always understood the importance of theoretical education and of the importance of raising the political level of the workers who are drawn into the tendency. An avid reader and self-taught man, this Welsh miner never forgot the education that was given him. Thus, despite being formally separated from the tendency for many years, he was soon able to regain his bearings, to involve himself in our ranks and play an important role in attempting to re-establish a branch in the Amman Valley.

The Neath by-election campaign was pursued with great vigour and was getting a significant response. The main election leaflet distributed everywhere appealed to *Working men and women of Neath*. It outlined the nature of the war, the reactionary foreign policy pursued by Churchill, and called for the Socialist United States of Europe. It ended with a rallying call:

"In this election you can play your part; you can give a lead to the workers in the rest of the country by rejecting the policy of class collaboration and voting for class independence and class struggle.

"Down with capitalism and its bloody wars and unemployment!

"Free the colonial people from imperialist domination and brutality!

"For the unity of the workers of Britain with the workers of the world against the capitalists!

"Down with the Churchill Government!

"End the Coalition!

"For a Communist Britain as part of a Communist Europe and a Communist World!"

The Communist Party poison about "Trotsky-fascism" fell completely flat with the workers. A leading miner in the West Wales area was a man called Trevor James. He was a fine public speaker and a committed class fighter. He was the miners' agent and a member of the Labour Party, and an anti-Stalinist into the bargain. He later confirmed that although he was a member of the Labour Party, he was very sympathetic to the RCP. In fact, he was the possible independent communist candidate that was originally mooted, but he declined. He recalled that the Labour candidate complained to him: "You never attend our meetings. You are always attending meetings of the RCP. What is the matter Trevor?" He replied, "Well, they're putting forward the socialist case. You are putting forward nothing like it." This really indicated the mood of Labour workers in the area, at least the active elements in the Labour Party and the unions. It was this mood that we were connecting with. This was not only due to our approach, which was important, but our programme which was connecting with their aspirations for a better life, and the need for a fundamental change in society. Consequently, we were selling on average some 2,000 copies of *Socialist Appeal* every fortnight within the constituency.

The only argument that these active people in the unions and in the Labour Parry could come up with for refusing to vote for the RCP was, "Well, we agree with you, but you should be in the Labour Party. Your candidate should be our candidate. Haston should be the candidate of the Labour Party. We should have the same socialist ideas. They should be the ideas of the Labour Party." Generally these people were very sympathetic, even though we were standing against the Labour Party. They said quite openly that they were delighted that we came to Neath. "You have put forward a full socialist campaign, which has served to revive all the socialist aspirations of the area, not only this area, but as far as Merthyr, Swansea and other areas."

We sold over 7,500 copies of a special election issue of the *Socialist Appeal*, putting our full case in relation to the war, in relation to Germany, in relation to the Coalition, and so on. Every point was dealt with fully. It would be certainly worthwhile reproducing those issues of *Socialist Appeal* to show the way, the flexible way, the non-sectarian way we approached the working class and the Labour movement, even in an election campaign of that sort.

As a result of the campaign, we managed to establish a firm base in the West Wales area. The campaign also had repercussions nationally. The Communist Party was on the defensive and we challenged them repeatedly to debate on all the questions they raised. Of course, they were not keen about this, fearing a political roasting in front of the workers. Nevertheless, there was a crisis of confidence within their own ranks and pressure was mounting for them to do something about it. On the last day before the election, we organised an eve of poll meeting in the Gwyn Hall, where we were expecting a meeting of 800 or even a thousand. At the very last minute, the Communist Party finally took up our challenge. They would have to go through with a public debate if they were to maintain any credibility at all. We learned afterwards that the Wales CP had phoned King Street to get Pollitt, Campbell or Gallacher or some other leader to come down to debate. But again, Campbell replied, "You can handle the situation. There is no need for us to come down." In reality, they didn't want to get a public belting.

So under those last minute conditions, the CP was forced to accept the challenge. When the time came, the Town Hall was absolutely jam-packed. There may have been two thousand workers trying to get in. They had come from all around to hear this debate. In the end, given the limits of the Gwyn Hall, many were turned away at the doors. The debate took place between the CP organiser, Alun Morgan and Jock Haston. The debate ranged over a whole series of questions from the Moscow trials, the question of fascism, the nature of the war, and, of course, our whole programme for the working class. Although I wasn't speaking, I was there to assist Jock at the top table with bundles of quotes from the Communist publications, Lenin and Marx, ready to hand them to him, as they arose in the debate. "I can just remember Ted on the end of the table", recalls Frank Ward, "diving down every time the CP put the point over, and kept coming out with some selected counter-quotation..." [5] By the end of the night, the overwhelming majority of workers in the audience undoubtedly supported us as against the position that was put forward by the Communist Party.

> "We challenged them to a debate, and we spoke to the leader of the Communist Party in the area, and we slaughtered their Line on the public platform", stated Haston. "They were standing on the windows, there was an overflow meeting of a couple of hundred, and outside were even more trying to get in. It was quite an unusual thing at that stage, and we debated with him and we absolutely shattered him." [6]

While the Labour candidate was panicking, we ourselves realised that Labour would win overwhelmingly. Paradoxically, this was the result of our campaign. We had stirred up political interest for the election. If it wasn't for our campaign, there would probably have been a very low turnout. But as a consequence of our activity in the area there was a great political interest, which served to give the Labour Party a record vote of over 30,000. That the workers were sympathetic to the ideas we put forward was evident from the turnouts at our public meetings, but we recognised in advance that the result of this heightened interest in socialism would be that the vote for the Labour Party would be very high. Nevertheless, we polled a respectable 1,781 votes. If one bears in mind that these votes were cast for a revolutionary internationalist programme during the war, this was a tremendous achievement. Moreover, this was in an area where we didn't have a single member before the campaign. The electoral field is also a very difficult arena for a small revolutionary tendency. However, out of this work we established branches of the RCP in Neath, G-C-G, Pontypridd and also strengthened our position elsewhere. It was a great step forward for us.

Our whole approach and activity was in complete contrast compared to the sterile approach of the earlier Trotskyist groups. We had different methods and a different approach, a non-sectarian approach to the working class in the area. Under the prevailing conditions, we were really pleased with the result as well as the recruits we made. It was really astonishing given the fact that polling day took place a few days after Victory in Europe was announced. One would have thought that this would have provoked an enormous patriotic outburst. But this wasn't the case. Of course, the war continued in Japan, but the main brunt of the war in Europe was over. Germany was defeated. A general election was in the offing. So it was an astonishing achievement and a success for our sober internationalist attitude, and our revolutionary military policy. Above all, it was our programme of the working class taking power into its hands that contributed to our achievement. Victory in Europe didn't have the effect of swamping us, as might have been expected. The Welsh Nationalists got about five or six thousand votes, so in comparison, and under those conditions, we had done very well indeed. We had engaged in mass work and managed to connect Trotskyism with a whole layer of advanced workers.

In the Organisation Report in the *Socialist Appeal* (mid-August 1945), we read:

> "During the Neath campaign the Party distributed over 100,000 leaflets. We put up 8,000 posters and sold 15,000 copies of the *Socialist Appeal* and some hundreds of assorted pamphlets. 70 indoor public meetings were held, the two outstanding ones attracting 750 and 1,500 workers respectively.
>
> "From having practically no base in Wales at the Fusion Conference we now have three proletarian branches composed almost entirely of miners and steel workers.
>
> "The name of the Party has proved to be one of our best assets. The workers who were turning to Communism sensed that there was something wrong with the Stalinist version of 'communism' and we were able to demonstrate their role with the Stalinists on the defensive throughout."
>
> It concluded, "the result 1,781 votes for the Trotskyist programme in face of V Day, the chauvinism of the mass organisations, the first incursion into the territory by the Party - was a very fine vote."

The turn of the tide

The German army was defeated by the Soviet Union. This is proof of the colossal potential and superiority of a nationalised planned economy. When Hitler invaded the USSR in 1941 the British military strategists thought the Soviet Union would be defeated within weeks. This was a serious miscalculation. After the initial defeats, the Red Army fought back like tigers. The Soviet workers rallied to the defence of the gains of the October revolution - the nationalised planned economy. Even the peasantry, once they saw the reality of Nazi barbarism, fought heroically. At Stalingrad the German army lost 100,000 men in one week of ferocious fighting. Following this defeat, the Red Army began the biggest advance in military history. The front moved 200 miles in less than three months.

The most decisive battle of the war was fought in Kursk in July 1943. On the vast flat expanse of cornfields south of Moscow, the greatest tank battle of all times unfolded. Hitler threw everything into this titanic conflict. The Russians captured a copy of his orders: "This...[is] an offensive of such an importance that the whole future of the war may depend on its outcome. More than anything else, your victory will show the whole world that resistance to the German army is hopeless." In fact, the Wehrmacht suffered a shattering defeat at the hands of the Red Army.

Up to this point the British and Americans had been mere onlookers of the war in Europe. Apart from the bombing of German cities they played no role. The British were fighting to defend their interests in North Africa. The USA was fighting Japanese imperialism for control of Asia and the Pacific. The real war against Hitler was being fought on Russian soil.

To show the real attitude of the British imperialists, we can cite one little-known incident. While the battle of Stalingrad was raging, there was a sizable British army stationed in Persia (now called Iran). The purpose of this was to protect British oil interests. Stalin asked Churchill why he did not send these troops to fight the Germans in Stalingrad. With typical cynicism, Churchill counter-proposed that Stalin should withdraw his troops from the Persian border and send them to fight in Stalingrad, while the British army looked after the frontier with the USSR! Naturally, the "generous" proposal was refused and right throughout the war British and Soviet troops were facing each other on the Persian frontier. The real reason for Churchill's attitude was that he thought the Red Army might be defeated in Stalingrad, and he would then be able to send the British army into Soviet Azerbaijan to seize the oilfields in Baku.

In July 1943 Mussolini was overthrown by a coup in the fascist grand council, involving the king and marshal Badoglio. Churchill hastily expressed his support for Badoglio. But the overthrow of Mussolini opened the door to revolution. The workers came out onto the streets all over north Italy. Whereupon the RAF bombed hell out of the northern Italian cities of Milan, Turin, Bologna, etc., in January, February and March. Nevertheless, the power was really in the hands of the Italian CP and the partisans who set up revolutionary committees hostile to Badoglio.

The British and American landings in Sicily were hastily organised as a reaction to this. Churchill wanted to give backing to the king and Badoglio and stressed that "all surviving forces of Italian life should be rallied round their lawful government". In August the Allies again bombed Milan and other northern Italian cities, ostensibly to speed the armistice negations with the Badoglio government. But on 9 September, the king and Badoglio left Rome for Brindisi, allowing the Germans to take over.

The reactionary character of British imperialism - and also Stalinism - was shown in Greece in December 1944. At the Yalta conference, Churchill and Stalin had arrived at a cynical agreement to carve up Eastern Europe into spheres of influence. According to this deal, Greece was to be part of Britain's sphere of interest. Churchill wanted to have control of Greece because of its strategic position in the Eastern Mediterranean. The central question was control of Egypt and the Suez canal, which linked Britain to India, which was still under British rule.

The cynicism of both Stalin and Churchill was revealed with astonishing frankness by the latter in his book Triumph and Tragedy: "So far as Britain and Russia are concerned," he said to Stalin, "how would it do for you to have ninety per cent predominance in Rumania, for us to have ninety per cent predominance of the say in Greece, and go fifty-fifty in Yugoslavia?" A paper with these percentages was passed to Stalin, who wrote a tick on it and passed it back to Churchill. "It was all arranged," says Churchill, "in no more time than it takes to set down." But Churchill was concerned that this might be seen as "rather cynical" and wanted to burn the piece of paper. "No," said Stalin. "You keep it."

The Greek partisans, having fought bravely against the German invaders, were effectively in control in Athens. The most powerful group was EAM-ELAS, which was made up of left and centre forces but effectively led by the Communists. As in Italy, Churchill wanted to support the counter-revolutionary forces and particularly the monarchy. Because of the leading role of ELAS in the struggle against the Nazis, the king was compelled to make concessions to them, while plotting a coup.

Having reached his secret deal with Stalin, Churchill decided that it was time to act. On returning from Moscow in October 1944, he commented that the moment was "apt for business" to "settle our affairs in the Balkans". [7] British troops were landed in Greece in October 1944 and were greeted by the people as liberators.

On 7 November, some three weeks after the arrival of the British force, Churchill sent a message to Anthony Eden: "In my opinion, having paid the price we have to Russia [sic!] for freedom of action in Greece, we should not hesitate to use British troops to support the Royal Hellenic Government under M. Papandreou….I hope the Greek Brigade will soon arrive, and will not hesitate to shoot when necessary…. I fully expect a clash with EAM and we must not shrink from it, provided the ground is well chosen." [8]

The last phrase shows that Churchill was preparing a provocation. The British forces acted as a cover for right wing royalist troops under the fascist Colonel Grivas. Churchill sent instructions to General Scobie: "Do not hesitate to act as if you were in a conquered city where a local rebellion is in progress…We have to hold and dominate Athens. It would be a great thing for you to succeed in this without bloodshed if possible, but also with bloodshed if necessary."

On 1 December, the EAM representatives left the government and called a general strike and a mass demonstration, which led to the massacre on Constitution Square. On the same day, the provocation was staged when the police opened fire on antigovernment demonstrators in Constitution Square, Athens. Eleven demonstrators were killed and sixty-six wounded. *The Times* correspondent wrote: "Seeds of civil war were well and truly sown by the Athens police this morning when they fired on a demonstration of children and youths."

When Churchill reported the events to the British parliament he stated that the demonstrators had "collided with the police". This was a lie. The police, backed by the government and the British army, had deliberately fired on unarmed demonstrators and kept firing when they were on the ground. The aim was clearly to provoke civil war in which British troops would be used against the partisans. Between them, Stalin and Churchill plotted the downfall of the Greek revolution.

Ever since 1941, Stalin had insistently demanded that his British and American "allies" should open up a second front against Hitler. This was ignored - until events in Italy forced their hand. However, the Italian campaign was in fact a sideshow aimed at preventing the Italian workers from taking power. Only when it became clear that the Red Army was advancing into Europe with breakneck speed did the British and Americans decide to launch the invasion of France in 1944. Had they not done so, they would have met the Red Army on the English Channel instead of in Germany.

The 1945 Labour government

At this time we had a perspective, in common with the entire International, and based upon the prognosis of Trotsky, that the world war would create a revolutionary wave in Europe. This in turn would expose the counter-revolutionary role of the old organisations and lead to the creation of mass parties of the Fourth International. This perspective was based on the assumption that developments after the Second World War would be similar to the situation that arose after the First World War, when a revolutionary situation developed in Britain as in many other European countries. The short slump of 1920 prepared the way for an enormous radicalisation on the part of the working class. It was a period of tremendous upheavals and class struggles that lasted, with ebbs and flows, right up to 1939.

We believed that similar conditions would occur after 1945, and that the post-war period would be very favourable for the building of a revolutionary tendency. We also had the perspective of a Labour Government as the next stage, and we knew the masses would need to go through this experience before they would begin to draw revolutionary conclusions. We envisaged that this government would be a government of crisis as in 1929-31. Under conditions of deep capitalist crisis, there would be the crystallisation of a left wing, or a centrist current within the ranks of the Labour Party. We also understood that under those conditions, the RCP would have to enter the Labour Party and, on the basis of its ideas, win over a sizeable section of the radicalised workers. This would prepare the way for the creation of a mass Trotskyist tendency in Britain, and prepare the ground for winning the majority of the working class to the programme of socialist revolution. Unfortunately, this perspective was falsified by events, and the new situation, rather than being very favourable for our growth, produced a whole series of difficulties and problems for the revolutionary tendency.

By 1944 the mood had become more radicalised, and the coalition government was losing support among the workers and soldiers. This was reflected in the 1944 Labour Party conference, which passed very radical resolutions, including the nationalisation of the land, large-scale building, heavy industry, fuel and power and all forms of banking. The Labour leaders were mostly in favour of continuing the wartime coalition, and the CP was enthusiastically in favour of this. But the rank and file of the Party was resolutely opposed to any such proposal. The slogan of the RCP - Labour break the coalition, and carry out a socialist programme - accurately reflected the mood of the workers at that time. The mood of radicalisation, which we had detected in the armed forces, was now clear to all.

Shortly after Victory in Europe Day, the Labour Party broke with the wartime Coalition and a General Election was called for July 15. At this point, the CP was still calling for the continuation of a government of National Unity, which should include themselves! In the run up to the General Election, they had to drop that idea like a hot potato. Of course, we supported the election of a Labour Government - but based on a Socialist programme - and threw ourselves into the campaign. It is interesting to see the reaction of workers at that time. Winston Churchill, the "great" war leader put himself forward as the great statesman, the man who had won the war and could lead Britain in peace time. This was the ultimate card that was being played by the Tories and the capitalist press. They paraded Churchill all around the country as "the man of the people".

Despite the fact that Churchill had been built up as a "great war leader", his posters were everywhere and he was given four times more time on the radio than Attlee the Labour candidate, he was overwhelmingly rejected. Sure, there were tens of thousands of people who turned out, mainly out of curiously, to see the "Great War Hero". The problem was, these tens of thousands had turned out not to support Churchill but to oppose him! In London, huge crowds of hostile workers were meeting Churchill, who went round in a jeep. As expected, we participated in these protests, selling papers and so forth. Angrily, he lashed out against these "Friends of Hitler" as he put it. But that didn't save him. The Labour Party won a landslide victory, reflecting the desire for revolutionary change.

On 26 July the results of the election were announced. Labour had won 393 seats (or 397 if we add those of the ILP and Common Wealth) out of a total of 640. It had a total of 11,992,292 votes against 9,960,809 cast for the Conservative-Liberal National Alliance. True, the Party won an even higher vote number of votes in the 1951 election, but in percentage terms, the Labour Party got over 48 per cent of the vote. The Conservatives had lost 200 seats and Labour had gained as many. It was an absolute landslide.

The Labour leaders were almost as astonished as the Conservatives at this result. The stain of the defeat of 1931 was now completely wiped away. For the first time the Labour Party had a parliamentary majority. The same result was repeated a few months later in the local elections in November. The masses desired a fundamental change and expressed this by voting Labour. Had the Labour leaders wanted it, they could have carried through the socialist transformation of society through parliament. Nothing could have stopped them. But, of course, they had no intention of doing anything of the sort.

Ironically, the Labour Party organisation prior to the election was an absolute shambles. The Tory Party organisation existed simply on the basis of their paid agents. But the Labour Party, during the Coalition period was extremely weak in most areas of the country. Labour Party wards didn't meet. The Constituency Parties weren't meeting, or if they were, it was only in a skeleton form. In reality, there was hardly a Labour organisation at all. The Tory Party thought that if they could precipitate an election before the Labour Party was back on its feet, they would gain a quick victory. But they completely miscalculated. The mood of the masses was such that despite the lack of Labour organisation, the mass of workers turned out enthusiastically to vote for the Labour Party, which reflected a colossal radicalisation of the working class.

The soldiers returned home in the same militant frame of mind that we had already observed in the Eighth Army - 90 per cent of the soldiers voted Labour. This was indicative of the revolutionary mood that existed in the armed forces. The ruling class was alarmed. Churchill made demagogic speeches urgently demanding that the soldiers be demobilised as quickly as possible. When this was done, he then made speeches accusing the Labour government of leaving the country defenceless.

In August 1945 the RCP held its second Conference with over 200 delegates and visitors present. We recognised that the election of the Labour Government marked "the first wave of the radicalisation of the masses," and noted that "for the first time in any of the important capitalist countries of the West, the reformists have been returned to power with an overwhelming majority." A full-page report appeared in the *Socialist Appeal* about our conference, which concluded by saying that "the Second National Conference marked a great step forward in the history of the British Trotskyist movement, as of the working class. Despite our small forces in relation to the mass organisations of the Labour and Communist Parties, the growth of the Party and of the Trotskyist tendency in the course of the war, during which period our Party established itself as the revolutionary wing of the working class, was a heartening sight of the change which was taking place in the advanced sections of the working class... Our comrades went back to their districts with renewed determination and vigour to participate in the daily struggles of the workers and to apply the principles of our International programme which alone is the guide post for the emancipation of our class." (*Socialist Appeal*, mid-August 1945).

In September, our building worker comrades organised an unofficial mass demonstration through the Building Workers' Shop Stewards Committee over pay and conditions, which attracted 100,000 workers in Hyde Park. Jock Milligan, an outstanding worker comrade, instigated this. The Stalinists in the union succeeded in taking away his shop stewards credentials for "acting against the union", but he was reinstated within a matter of days after workers in Lewisham threatened an all-out strike over the issue. Jock had a tremendous history. He was despatched to Archangel to put down the Bolshevik Government and picked up a leaflet containing an appeal to British troops signed by Lenin and Trotsky, and drafted by the famous English author, Arthur Ransome. On his return, Jock became a founding member of the British Communist Party. Becoming disillusioned with Stalinism, he joined the Trotskyist movement. Later he joined the WIL and then the RCP. He played a key role in the union, and remained with our tendency until his death in the late 1950s.

As I have explained, we had the perspective that with the coming to power of a Labour Government, on the basis of a deep economic crisis, the situation would develop on the same lines as outlined by Trotsky before the war. Namely, once the reformists were in power, given their incapacity to deliver real reforms, they would begin to expose themselves in the eyes of the masses. However, before dealing with that perspective, I would like first to deal with the differences that had developed from 1944 in relation to the International leadership.

Our differences with the International

The period after 1945 was characterised by new developments on a world scale that had not been foreseen by the Trotskyist movement. The Stalinist and reformist leaders of the working class betrayed the mighty revolutionary tide that swept Europe from 1943 onwards. This provided the political preconditions for a revival of capitalism. Instead of the economic crisis that had been predicted by the Trotskyists, there was a period of post war reconstruction, during which the United States, which had emerged from the War with its productive capacity intact, effectively underwrote European capitalism through the Marshall Plan. This prepared the ground for a new boom and a period of relative social stability, and demanded a drastic revision of our original perspectives.

We discussed the situation within the leadership of the RCP and soon realised that important changes were taking place, which rendered the old perspective obsolete. Arising from these discussions, we amended our analysis and perspectives accordingly. The leaders of the International, however, were blind to the new developments. With the assassination of Leon Trotsky in August 1940, the leaders of the Fourth were left to their own devices, and proved woefully inadequate of analysing the new period and reorienting the Trotskyist movement. Unlike the RCP, they utterly failed to rise to the level of the tasks posed by history. James Cannon and the other leaders of the Fourth International clearly never grasped the method of Trotsky, the method of dialectical materialism. They simply repeated Trotsky's words and formulations parrot-fashion, and clung to them even after they had been falsified by events. Of course, this led them to make one blunder after another.

First of all, they refused to face facts. They refused to recognise the war was over! "We disagree", said Cannon, "with some people who carelessly think that the war is over... The war is not over." [9] Then they said there would be no economic recovery, only an economy "bordering on stagnation and decay", when all the facts indicated the opposite! [10] "It is necessary to abandon right now any juggling with a boom that has not existed and that British capitalism will never experience again", wrote Ernest Mandel. [11]

Then they insisted that there could only be military dictatorships in Europe, when in reality, as the RCP pointed out, the ruling class was carrying out a counterrevolution in a "democratic form." E.R. Frank, the official spokesperson for the SWP National Committee, talked about the "perniciousness of the theory of the renaissance of bourgeois democracy", and, in a clear reference to the RCP, that "the imperialists have succeeded beyond their wildest dreams. By covering up their military dictatorships with a little - very little - democratic veneer, they have succeeded in fooling even a few Trotskyists." [12]

Lastly, they held to the view that the USSR had emerged weakened after the war, and not strengthened as the RCP had maintained. They went so far as to state in their resolution to the International Conference (1946) that diplomatic pressure would be sufficient to overthrow the USSR: "Failing a mass movement capable of coming actively rallying to its support, the USSR incurs the risk of being destroyed in the near future", states the resolution, *"even without direct military intervention, but simply through the combined economic political and diplomatic pressure and the military threats of American and British imperialism."* (RCP internal bulletin, 12 August 1946, my emphasis). Again, "only the intervention of the proletarian revolution can save the Soviet Union from an early and fateful end."

Not one of the "leaders" of the Fourth - James P. Cannon, Michael Pablo and Ernest Mandel - proved capable of recognising reality, and this fact was to have profound consequences for the future of the International. There was not a single major question on which they did not make a fundamental mistake. Pierre Frank, for instance, advanced the "theory" that only Bonapartist regimes could exist in Europe. Frank took his own nonsense so seriously that he decided to go underground and live illegally without papers, and moreover caused the French PCI after the war to operate underground for fear of future repression! This outrageous idea was answered many times by myself and other RCP leaders. But the arguments of the British section fell on deaf ears.

Just compare this confusion to the positions adopted by the British Trotskyists, which can be read in numerous documents that we intend to make public. From a reading of this material it will immediately be clear that the RCP was able to understand and apply the Marxist method to the new situation and able to reorientate the Trotskyist movement. Unfortunately, this fact has never been recognised, and most people are completely unaware of it, since the relevant material has been unavailable for decades. Moreover, there are many people who have a vested interest in concealing the truth in order to hide their own mistakes and boost their personal prestige - a very pernicious tendency in politics.

Cliff's distortions

Tony Cliff was a second-line leader in the RCP who later became the chief proponent of the erroneous theory of state capitalism. In a recently published pamphlet entitled *Trotskyism after Trotsky*, Cliff blatantly ignored the great achievements of the RCP. In a typically dishonest fashion, he remains totally silent about the role of the main leaders of the Party - Jock Haston and myself - and our fight against the positions of Cannon and the other leaders of the Fourth International after the War.

For the readers of Cliff's account, the principled stance of the RCP simply never existed. He gives the impression we all supported the policies of the International, which is completely untrue - although, with astounding hypocrisy, the same author pontificates about the need to be "truthful"! According to Tony Cliff, it was only "the few comrades who started the International Socialist tendency" (i.e. his own group) who "in the years 1946-48" had to "wrestle with very difficult questions." [13] Nothing could be further from the truth!

"Spite plays a terrible role in politics", Trotsky once wrote. Cannon had never forgiven the Lee-Haston-Grant leadership of the WIL, for having opposed him in 1938, when it had refused to accept his terms for the unification of the Trotskyist groups in Britain. He took it very personally and from 1943 onwards secretly organised a concerted campaign to undermine and remove the British leadership. In this campaign he established an unprincipled bloc with Gerry Healy, who, for his own reasons, carried a grudge against the leadership of the organisation.

As we have seen, although Healy was an energetic organiser, he had been expelled or walked out of the WIL on six or seven occasions. On one of these occasions, in early 1943, he stormed out of a WIL central committee meeting saying he was joining the ILP. According to the CC minutes, after Healy's resignation was accepted unanimously, Ajit Roy, a CC member stated: "He was a menace to the organisation. But if he worked with us, with his energy and ability, he was of some use to us. A breach was certain in the future, but it was possible to harness him." (6 February 1943) He subsequently reapplied for membership and was once again accepted back as a member. But he returned not as a loyal member but as an incorrigible intriguer, always looking for allies in his struggle against the WIL leadership. These he found in the unscrupulous leadership of the International.

In October 1945 at a meeting of the SWP National Committee, Cannon led a verbal assault on the SWP minority led by Albert Goldman and Felix Morrow. In this Cannon linked an attack on the British RCP: "You are helping Haston and Grant to fight Healy right now. You are sending personal letters to Haston to help them in the fight against Healy - to utilise against Healy... we will fight it out and see what happens in the International." [14]

Of course, Cannon had been helping Healy from 1943 but that was not mentioned. The American SWP majority was constantly intriguing against the RCP majority, using Healy as its stooge. "The SWP members were especially helpful to us during the period between 1943 and 1949 in the struggle against the Haston clique", Healy admitted much later. "This group, which comprised a majority of the English Trotskyist organisation, was led essentially by Haston, his wife Mildred Haston and Ted Grant." [15]

In April 1953, Cannon revealed his real attitude towards the leadership of the RCP - and the reasons for it - in a private letter to Farrell Dobbs: "All the crimes and mistakes of this rotten-to-the-core Haston faction are directly traceable to its origin as an unprincipled clique in 1938. When I was in England a little later that year, on the eve of the First World Congress, I denounced the Lee-Haston faction as tainted by unprincipledness at its birth. I never had a bit of confidence in them throughout all their subsequent development, regardless of what theses they wrote or voted for at the moment." [16]

Alien methods

As far as "the theses they wrote or voted for", these were a closed book for the membership of the International. The positions of the RCP were either suppressed by the International, systematically distorted or ignored. "Early in the post-war period", states Cannon, "the Haston gang became captivated by the expansion of Stalinism and thought they saw in it 'the wave of the future.' They bestowed the honorific title of 'workers' states' on every strip of territory the

Red Army occupied the moment this occupation took place. Haston and Co. are the real godfathers of the Vern tendency which currently pollutes the atmosphere of the L.A. Local." [17]

These lines - both in form and in content - are quite typical of Cannon's methods. They are a complete distortion from the first word till the last. As far as I can see from the documents of the Vern-Ryan group within the SWP, they did not hold the position that workers' states were created as soon as the Red Army had occupied Eastern Europe. This seems to be a misinterpretation by Cannon. But we can say with certainty that this was not the view of the RCP, as Cannon knew very well. In Eastern Europe after the occupation of the Red Army, capitalist property relations remained intact. The "Peoples Democracies" that were set up were bourgeois regimes, although the Stalinists had made sure they controlled key ministries within the government, particularly interior and defence. It was only later in 1948, after the attempted introduction of the Marshall Plan, that the Stalinists leaned on the population, Bonapartist-fashion, to carry through a social overturn.

Cannon's intolerance of minority views is clearly expressed in his vitriolic tone towards the "polluter" Vern. Whether the Vern tendency was right or wrong, and they were certainly confused, Cannon's attitude was simply monstrous. It was a reflection of his whole approach to political opposition, in the USA and elsewhere. As his writings clearly show, he always tended to treat things in an organisational manner, rather than dealing with the political issues. This was reflected in the faction fight of 1939-40 with Shachtman and Burnham. Cannon's approach contrasts sharply with Trotsky's approach to internal differences.

Trotsky always dealt with things in a political fashion, including organisational issues. He always displayed the greatest tact and patience when correcting erroneous views in other comrades. His attitude to the faction fight in the American SWP was a case in point. While maintaining a firm position on the principled question of the class nature of the USSR, he never approved of Cannon's treatment of the opposition in the SWP, and was even prepared to reach an accommodation with the Shachtman/Burnham minority in 1939/40 - an "accommodation" that was sabotaged by Cannon, if the truth is to be told.

Eastern Europe

The RCP understood the nature of the changed world situation well before the so-called International leadership. The RCP recognised the strengthened position of the USSR after its victory in the War, and especially its dominant position in Eastern Europe. However, following the "Prague Coup" in February 1948, we deepened our initial analysis. Dealing with the unfolding processes in the June issue of *Socialist Appeal*, I showed that the Stalinists had leaned on the workers to carry through the expropriation of the capitalists and establish a deformed workers' state.

The same process subsequently took place throughout all the so-called Peoples Democracies. Washington attempted to use the extension of Marshall Aid to Eastern Europe to pull these states back into the orbit of world imperialism. Understanding the threat to their position, the Stalinists in Eastern Europe swept away the "shadow of the bourgeoisie" and took power into their hands, nationalising the economy and setting up regimes in the image of Moscow - not the Moscow of Lenin but of Stalin. The revolution in Eastern Europe began where the Russian revolution had ended: as a monstrous totalitarian-bureaucratic caricature of socialism.

A similar process took place in China after the victory of Mao's peasant armies and in Yugoslavia under Tito's partisans. However, the leaders of the International failed to see these revolutionary developments unfolding under their very noses, and continued to characterise these regimes as "capitalist" right up until 1951. It took until 1955 for the American SWP to characterise China as a deformed workers' state, as opposed to state capitalism. Then, they went from one extreme to another. They developed illusions in Mao as an "unconscious Trotskyist", and they remained ambivalent as to whether a political revolution was absolutely necessary to introduce workers' democracy.

At the time of the Stalin-Tito clash, these great "leaders" of the Fourth jumped overnight from a position that Yugoslavia was 'capitalist' to one where Tito was seen as the head of a relatively healthy workers' state. They capitulated to Tito and became cheerleaders for the Yugoslav regime. In an *Open Letter to Tito*, the American SWP wrote: "The confidence of the masses in it [your party] will grow enormously and it will become the effective collective expression of the interests and desires of the proletariat of its country."

The protests of the RCP, to the effect that the Tito regime was still Stalinist in nature were conveniently ignored. In a statement written in 1950 just after I was expelled by Healy, I listed as the first of three reasons for the collapse of the Fourth International in Britain, its "capitulation to Tito-Stalinism internationally." At the same time Pierre Lambert, the leader of the French PCI, was reporting enthusiastically: "I believe that I saw in Yugoslavia a dictatorship of the proletariat, led by a party which passionately seeks to combat bureaucracy and impose workers' democracy"! [18]

Degeneration of the Fourth

This degeneration and collapse of the Fourth International after Trotsky's death was partly due to objective factors - the mighty economic upswing of world capitalism, and the renewed illusions in reformism and Stalinism. This meant that, for a whole period, the forces of genuine Marxism could not expect big gains. However, the subjective factor played a crucial role. In times of war, during periods of advance, good generals are important. But in a period of retreat, they are more important still. With good generals you can retreat in good order, with a minimum of losses, keeping your forces intact, to prepare for a more favourable situation. Bad generals turn a defeat into a rout. The so-called leaders of the "Fourth" directly contributed to the undermining and destruction of the Trotskyist movement.

This is not the place to go into the details of the disastrous policies pursued by the "leaders" of the so-called Fourth International. Suffice it to say, that their personal actions and policies spelled disaster for the International, which under the leadership of the epigones, was stillborn.

The International is first and foremost a programme, perspectives, traditions and method. Only secondly is it an organisation to carry through these policies. The so-called Fourth International repeatedly trampled on these principles. In the end, nothing was left of the Fourth International founded in 1938 - except for those who kept the genuine traditions and programme alive. It was the leaders of the British section, who waged a battle to defend these principles of Trotskyism. After the destruction of the RCP, it was our tendency that kept the flame alive.

Rather than correct their mistakes or reply politically to the criticisms of the British leadership, Cannon, Mandel, Frank, Pablo and the others resorted to organisational manoeuvres and intrigue in order to undermine the British section. It was a classic case of Zinovievism, of using organisational methods to deal with political questions. First, the material of the British section was suppressed or distorted. Then the International leadership organised a secret faction inside the RCP around Healy in order to undermine and remove the leadership. These disastrous methods played a fatal role, which eventually undermined and destroyed the International movement. Obsessed with the attempt to undermine and destroy the Haston-Grant leadership at every opportunity, Cannon, Healy, Pablo, Frank and Mandel, played a wrecking role in relation to the British Trotskyist movement.

Counter-revolution in a democratic form

Up to that point, there had not been even a dot or a comma of a difference between us and the International, except the disagreement in 1938 when we refused to enter into a rotten fusion despite Cannon's insistence - an issue where we were proved to have been absolutely correct. But the situation was now different. Trotsky was no longer alive to give guidance. Moreover, because of the Nazi occupation of Europe, the International Secretariat had been transferred to America, and was in effect run by Cannon and the SWP. With the end of the war, differences began to develop in regard to the perspectives for Europe.

Pierre Frank, who had rejoined the International at the end of the war, gave a false report to the IS about the August 1945 Conference, saying the RCP was facing "grave difficulties", and, "moreover, the main responsibility for these difficulties rests with the leadership which has shown great concern, not to clarify political questions [sic], but to maintain an uncontested hold on the organisation." Soon afterwards, Haston wrote a letter to the European Executive Committee: "For our party, we did not think too highly of his capabilities." Although an understatement, it certainly must have stung Frank.

It is no accident that - despite the fact that in the World War the RCP was the largest and most important section of the Trotskyist movement in Europe - in Frank's potted "history" of the Fourth International there is not a single mention the WIL or the RCP, let alone its political views. All he says is, "After the war, the International had come out in favour of the British Trotskyists entering the Labour Party." [19] Which meant, in effect, backing Healy.

This is typical of the methods by which the leaders of the Fourth attempted to falsify the history of the International and conceal the role of the RCP. They were solely motivated by the desire for personal prestige, and laid claim to papal infallibility. The Leaders must not make mistakes! This is a recipe for the destruction of any revolutionary organisation. Lenin and Trotsky were always honest in relation to mistakes and prepared to admit them and learn from them. But Cannon and Co. could not tolerate the fact that the British Trotskyists pointed out their errors and - even worse - were consistently shown to be in the right.

Actually, Trotsky never had a good word for Pierre Frank, and wanted him expelled. "We have fought constantly against the Pierre Franks in Germany and in Spain", wrote Trotsky, "against the sceptics, and against the adventurers who wanted to perform miracles (and broke their necks in the process)." [20] This sharp criticism is a devastating comment, not just on Pierre Frank, but on the qualities of all the other leaders of the International who saw fit to promote him after the death of the Old Man.

Nevertheless, Frank, as well as his co-thinkers in the SWP, "sought to clarify political questions" by stating that what were developing in Europe were military police states.

According to them, after the fall of Hitler, the only viable way the ruling class could continue its rule in Europe was through military police regimes, or Bonapartist regimes like the Petain dictatorship, that had been established after the fall of France. The argument of Frank and Cannon was that the Anglo-American imperialists in Italy in 1944 had tried to install the dictatorship of Badoglio to replace that of Mussolini.

On behalf of the RCP leadership I wrote a reply to the arguments of Frank:

> "Frank attempts to equate all regimes in Western Europe to 'Bonapartism'. His generalisations go even further: he argues that there have been Bonapartist regimes in France since 1934; that it is impossible to have any but Bonapartist or fascist regimes until the coming to power of the proletariat in Europe. This, if you please, in the name of 'the continuity of our political analysis for more than ten years of French history'! Such complacency reduces theory to formless abstractions and conceals inevitable and episodic errors, thus making them into a system. It has no place in the Fourth International".
>
> "Comrade Frank indiscriminately mixes the terms bourgeois democracy with Bonapartism, not explaining the specific traits of either. He interchangeably speaks of 'Bonapartism', 'elements of Bonapartism' and he contrasts democratic liberties with 'a regime, which one can correctly define as democratic.' Yet the reader has to seek in vain for a definition of his ideal 'democratic regime' as distinguished from the very real bourgeois democracy. He denies the existence of democratic regimes in Europe today because 'there is literally no place for them.'"

The analysis of the RCP leadership explained that, as a result of the movement of the masses in Europe, and the class balance of forces, there would be a period of bourgeois democracy, or to give it its correct name, a period of democratic counter-revolution in Europe.

> "The British RCP has characterised the regimes in Western Europe (France, Belgium, Holland, Italy) as regimes of counter-revolution in a democratic form. Comrade Pierre Frank claims that the idea of 'democratic counter-revolution' is 'devoid of all content.' He would then be hard put to explain what the Weimar Republic organised by the social democracy in Germany was. He would be compelled to argue that what took place in Germany in 1918, was *not* the proletarian revolution which was betrayed by the 'counter-revolution in a democratic form' (by the undemocratic and bloody suppression of the January 1919 uprisings), but was a democratic revolution which overthrew the Kaiser and replaced his regime by one of 'pure' bourgeois democracy! The fact that this regime was ushered in by martial law and the conspiracy of the social democratic leaders with the General Staff of the Reichswehr, the Junkers and the bourgeoisie, validates entirely the conclusion of Lenin and Trotsky that there was a 'democratic' counter-revolution, with the bourgeoisie using the social democrats as their agents.
>
> "In advance Trotsky foresaw and prepared theoretically for a similar situation with the collapse of fascism in Italy, when he wrote in a letter to the Italian comrades in 1930:
>
> 'Following the above comes the question of the 'transitional' period in Italy. At the very outset it is necessary to establish very clearly: transition from what to what? A period of transition from the bourgeois (or 'popular') revolution to the proletarian revolution is one thing. A period of transition from the fascist dictatorship to the proletarian dictatorship is another. If the first conception is envisaged, the question of the bourgeois revolution is posed in the first place and it is then a question of establishing the role of the proletariat in it. Only after that will the question of the transitional period toward a proletarian revolution be posed.

> If the second conception is envisaged, the question is then posed of a series of battles, disturbances, upsets in the situation, abrupt turns, constituting in their ensemble the different stages of the proletarian revolution. These stages may be many in number. But in no case can they contain within them a bourgeois revolution or its mysterious hybrid: the 'popular' revolution.
>
> 'Does this mean that Italy cannot for a certain time again become a parliamentary state or become a 'democratic republic'? I consider - in perfect agreement with you, I think - that this eventuality is not excluded. But then it will not be the fruit of a bourgeois revolution but the abortion of an insufficiently matured and premature proletarian revolution. In case of a profound revolutionary crisis and of mass battles in the course of which the proletarian vanguard will not have been in a position to take power, it may be that the bourgeoisie will reconstruct its power on 'democratic' bases.
>
> 'Can it be said, for example, that the present German republic constitutes a conquest of the bourgeois revolution? Such an assertion would be absurd. There was in Germany in 1918-19 a proletarian revolution which, deprived of leadership, was deceived, betrayed and crushed. But the bourgeois counter-revolution nevertheless found itself obliged to adapt itself to the circumstances resulting from this crushing of the proletarian revolution and to assume the form of a republic in the 'democratic' parliamentary form. Is the same - or about the same - eventuality excluded from Italy? No, it is not excluded. The enthronement of fascism was the result of the incompletion of the proletarian revolution in 1920. Only a new proletarian revolution can overturn fascism. If it should not be destined to triumph this time either (weakness of the Communist Party, manoeuvres and betrayals of the social democrats, the freemasons, the Catholics), the 'transitional' state that the bourgeois counter-revolution would then be forced to set up in the ruins of its power in a fascist form, could be nothing else than a parliamentary and democratic state.' (*Problems of the Italian Revolution*, 14 May, 1930)
>
> "Events in Italy have demonstrated the remarkable foresight of Trotsky. The bourgeoisie has been compelled to allow the jettisoning of the king and the Stalinist-socialist traitors have headed off the developing proletarian revolution into the channels of a 'parliamentary and democratic state'. This of course, will not attain a stable base, but will be subject to crises and upheavals, movements on the part of the proletariat, and counter-movements of monarchists and fascists. Would Frank now deny the correctness of Trotsky's conceptions and assert that we have had a Bonapartist state since the fall of Mussolini?
>
> "Nothing saved the capitalist system in Western Europe except the betrayal of social democracy and Stalinism. When the bourgeoisie leans on its social democratic and Stalinist agencies *for the purpose of counter-revolution*, what is the 'content' of that counter-revolution? Bonapartist, fascist, authoritarian? Of course not! Its content is that of a 'counter revolution in a democratic form.'
>
> "Of course, the bourgeoisie cannot stabilise itself for any length of time on the basis of the democratic counter-revolution. Where the revolution is stemmed by the lackeys of the bourgeoisie, the class forces do not stay suspended. After a period, which can be more or less protracted according to the economic and political developments internationally and within the given country, the bourgeoisie shifts to Bonapartist or fascist counter-revolution."

Our argument was not the same as was argued by Morrow and Goldman in the SWP - who were now in opposition to Cannon - and who argued that we were in for a period of democracy, a period of "democratic revolution" in Europe, as they put it. But at least they were groping in the right direction in comparison to the rest. The differences on this question were not secondary, but of fundamental importance. It raised point blank the question of the orientation of the Trotskyist movement. How you pose questions decides your attitude, as Trotsky had explained many times. If you pose the problem correctly, you will usually get the right answer. If you pose the problem incorrectly you will invariably get the wrong answer. We pointed out that the workers in Europe were trying to make a socialist revolution, and if the Communist Party and the Socialist Party were revolutionary organisations, then inevitably the revolution would have been carried out. However, these organisations, the Communist Party in particular, but also the Social Democrats, were playing the same role now as was played by the Social Democrats between 1917 and 1920 when they betrayed the revolutionary wave that existed in Europe.

We further explained that because of a) the enormous power of the Socialist Parties and Communist Parties, and b) the revolutionary wave that was sweeping the Continent at the time, it would be impossible for the bourgeoisie to impose Bonapartist military regimes in Europe. On the contrary, for a longer or shorter period - the time scale of such events is difficult to calculate - the class balance of forces would favour the working class - and therefore, would also favour the Stalinists and Social Democrats.

In Europe, there was a movement in the direction of socialist revolution, with revolutionary developments in one country after another - Italy, Denmark, Greece, France, and even Britain - from 1943 onwards. But, as in 1918 in Germany when the Social Democrats had betrayed the revolution and carried through a counter-revolution in a democratic form, resulting in the Weimar Republic, so in the same way, the Communist Party and the Social Democrats would betray the movement. The Communist Party in particular, thanks to the role that it had played in the resistance movements in France, Italy, Belgium and Holland, would use its authority to rescue capitalism and carry through a counter-revolution. This would usher in a period not of democratic revolution - as was incorrectly put forward by Goldman and Morrow - but on the contrary, a period *of democratic counter-revolution*. This was due above all to the weakness of the revolutionary forces, which had been a decisive factor in 1917-1920 in Europe, and was an even more decisive factor in the situation that was developing in Europe after 1945.

From this false perspective of Bonapartism, the International leadership began to make one mistake after another. A whole series of disagreements between ourselves and the IS, which was symptomatic of the later degeneration that was to take place, soon opened up. I am not going to deal in detail with these questions because they are dealt with more fully elsewhere (See appendix and *Programme of the International*). However, it is necessary to explain in outline the differences that now began to appear.

Boom or slump?

The prognosis of an economic crisis after the war was one that we had in common with the entire International. However, for reasons which I have explained elsewhere (See Ted Grant, *Will there be a slump?*), things turned out differently. Rather than a short period of post-war reconstruction, then followed by a period of slump, the statistics clearly showed that a new boom or economic upturn was being prepared.

Of course, we have to say that even we did not foresee the extent of the economic upswing that was to last for some twenty five years. Nobody could predict such a development. Nevertheless, we saw that a boom was on the order of the day and certainly not a slump! In contrast, the International dogmatically stuck to the original prognosis of a post-war slump.

Not only that, but in the event of a revival, they claimed that there was a ceiling or limit on production. These ideas - primarily the inventions of Mandel and Pablo - have nothing in common with Marxism. Within a couple of months, of course, production levels had burst through this "ceiling".

Like a gramophone record with a repeating groove, Mandel, Cannon, Frank and Pablo simply repeated their original position. They never understood what Trotsky was driving at when he stated before the war that capitalism could no longer develop the productive forces. This was a conditional prognosis. In a broad historical sense, it remains correct even today, but you have to understand the limitations of any general idea. It is fundamentally false to argue that because capitalism had fulfilled its historical mission, it was not possible for capitalism to develop a boom of any kind. It was never Trotsky's position. Indeed, both he and Lenin had argued precisely the opposite against the ultra-lefts in the congresses of the Communist International. But this was a book sealed with seven seals for the leaders of the Fourth.

I wrote a reply to the arguments of the International Secretariat:

> "… With the weakness of the parties of the Fourth International, which remain small sects at this stage, the capitalists have been enabled to find a way out of the collapse and decline of economy. This has prepared the way in Western Europe for a steady and fairly rapid recovery.
>
> "If a conflict develops between Stalin and Western European capitalism and the Stalinist organisations are used to disrupt and force concessions by means of mass strikes, the situation can deteriorate for the capitalists overnight. Even the assistance of American finance would not and could not prevent the crisis that would follow. The specific position taken by the International Pre-Conference, and supported by the Minority of the British Party, that the Western European countries - France, Holland, Belgium and others - will remain on a level approaching *stagnation and slump*, and cannot reach the level of production attained pre-war, is entirely false. The Pre-Conference resolution says:
>
> 'This restoration of economic activity in the capitalist countries hit by the war, and in particular in the countries on the European continent, will be characterised by its particularly slow rhythm and these countries will thus remain on a level approaching stagnation and slump.'
>
> "Eastern Europe in particular, under the control of the Stalinist bureaucracy, will undoubtedly recover and even increase its productive resources more rapidly than after 1914-18. It is impossible for Anglo-American imperialism and the bourgeoisie of Western Europe to allow complete stagnation and decline on one half of the continent, while economic activity will develop in the other half under the domination of the Stalinist bureaucracy.
>
> "However, apart from these political considerations, there are the laws of capitalism which themselves ensure the upswing of economy and make a new 'boom' inevitable. Particularly in view of the fact that this crisis is not a crisis of over-production and that the capitalists are not being attacked in Western Europe by the mass organisations, but receive the direct assistance and support of social democracy and Stalinism, *a cyclical upswing is inevitable*. It is not excluded that particularly for Western Europe (with the exception of Germany and Austria) the productive figures can even reach and surpass the pre-war level in the next period.
>
> "Even in Germany, depending upon the relationship between the imperialists and Russia, a greater or lesser revival will take place, though here because of the conflict between the powers and the division and occupation of Germany, it is impossible that pre-war figures will be reached in the next period.

"All the factors on a European and world scale indicate that the economic activity in Western Europe in the next period is not one of 'stagnation and slump' but one of revival and boom.

"The main feature of capitalist crisis 'stagnation and slump' as revealed for example by the classic crisis of 1929-33 which assumed unexampled scope and severity on a world scale, was over-production of capital goods, consumer goods and agricultural produce. The industrial crisis was thus supplemented with a simultaneous agrarian crisis. The economic revival which followed the last world slump, as always, was achieved by the destruction and deterioration of capital goods, the deterioration and destruction of consumers' stocks, the cutting down of the areas sown with crops, etc. Though this involved immeasurable misery and suffering for the toilers, nevertheless, particularly with war preparations, by 1937-8 the production figures exceeded even the record years of 1928-9 in most countries of the world. The destruction wrought by the war has achieved similar results to those which the capitalists achieve when they consciously set out to destroy wealth in a period of crises of over-production.

"The classic conditions for boom are present in Europe today: a shortage of capital goods; shortage of agricultural produce; shortage of consumer goods. The shortages impose new miseries for the masses and new strains on the system. These conditions engendered by wilful destruction and the normal processes of decay of capitalist slump are here produced by the devastation and havoc of totalitarian war. This devastation did not lead to the overthrow of the system through the victory of the proletariat. In the same way as recovery follows a slump which does not lead to the overthrow of the system, so the restoration of the productive forces will follow the present chaos, even on a capitalist basis."

Lenin once said that politics is concentrated economics. The Labour Government came to power at a time of boom. There was also a complete crisis of confidence in the ruling class, which now found itself on the defensive. Although nominally a victor in the war against Germany, the power of British capitalism had been undermined, as can be seen by subsequent developments over the following decades. Britain no longer held a privileged position as in the past. In order to compete on the world market it was imperative to modernise at least its basic industries. For the first time in the history of British capitalism we had full employment and this situation was to be replicated in other countries.

Still the International refused to recognise reality. I remember that in 1947, there was a Polish comrade living in the Manchester area, who explained to us that there was mass unemployment in Britain. When we showed him the figures for the increase in employment, he said "Ah, yes, but this is capitalist propaganda. There are really three million unemployed in Britain." We simply scratched our heads. How could one argue seriously on that kind of level? However, that was the position of the Healy minority, which began to develop within the RCP, for reasons I will explain later.

The evolution of the Labour government was also contrary to our expectations. We had based ourselves on what Trotsky had written in *Where is Britain Going?* where he said that the moment the Labour leaders tried to nationalise even the mines, the capitalists would prepare for civil war to crush the government. Yet here was a Labour Government carrying through a programme of nationalisation of a series of bankrupt industries without any real resistance. Under the prevailing conditions, the ruling class had realised the necessity of modernising the basic industries of coal, electricity, the railways, and so on. Since it was impossible for the capitalist class to lay out such enormous sums of money, they allowed the state to intervene to solve the problem. This kind of nationalisation of bankrupt industries with lavish over-compensation to the former owners was no threat to the ruling class. On the contrary, the bourgeoisie welcomed it. This was what Marxists call state capitalism, where a minority sector of a capitalist economy is taken over by the state.

However, as far as the workers were concerned, they could see only radical reforms in the policies being implemented by the Labour Government. The active elements in the trade unions and in the Labour Party saw that the government was carrying through a radical programme, including the creation of the National Health Scheme and nationalisation of key industries. For the mass of workers, it appeared that the government was beginning to carry out the socialist transformation of society. The ideas of the reformists about a parliamentary road to socialism seemed to be correct. They were introducing the reforms that they had promised in their programme.

Harold Laski, the theoretician of Labourism, said that the Labour Party would be in power for the next 20 or 25 years and would progressively do away with capitalism by gradually socialising the economy. This experience had an enormous effect on the consciousness of the working class. Conversely, it had an extremely negative effect on our ability, as a revolutionary Trotskyist organisation, to influence the advanced workers, let alone the masses. For example, during the war our comrades could sell hundreds of copies of the *Socialist Appeal* on the docks, in the mines, and elsewhere. As a matter of fact, at one point we were selling between 12,000 and 15,000 copies of the *Socialist Appeal* a fortnight. Now with the situation changing it was becoming increasingly more difficult to sell. Even on the docks, we would be lucky if we could sell two or three papers. Workers became indifferent to the paper and our ideas,

Celebrating May Day, 1947

because as far as they were concerned the Labour Government was carrying out socialist polices.

Eastern Europe

Before the war, Trotsky advanced a conditional prognosis for the outcome of the conflict: Either the bureaucracy would be overthrown by political revolution, or the USSR would be destroyed by capitalist counter-revolution. However, events turned out differently. As Napoleon once remarked, war is the most complicated of equations. Trotsky himself had stressed the impossibility of being precise in relation to the perspectives in the war. "It would be a vain task to attempt, at this time," he wrote soon after the start of the war, "to predict the course of the war and the fate of its various participants, including those who still cherish the illusory hope of remaining outside the catastrophe. It is given to no man to survey in its entirety this vast arena and turmoil of infinitely complex material and moral forces. Only the war itself will decide the destiny of the war." [21]

In fact, things worked out differently to what Trotsky had anticipated. Instead of ending in the defeat of the USSR and capitalist restoration, the war with Hitler resulted in a spectacular victory for the Soviet Union. The Red Army advanced through Europe inflicting a crushing defeat on the fascist armies and finally raising the red flag over Berlin. The victories of the Red Army against the armies of Hitler - which were entirely unexpected to the British and American imperialists - built up colossal illusions in Stalinism and served to strengthen the Russian regime for a whole period.

The heroic defence of the Soviet Union and the tremendous sacrifices of the Russian workers and peasants in the face of the invasion of the Nazi monsters was, in reality, a defence of the gains of October Revolution: the nationalised property relations and of the planned economy. These victories meant an enormous strengthening of Stalinism internationally. This, of course, posed considerable difficulties for the Trotskyist movement, resulting in controversies and disagreements on a series of questions. These disagreements not only appeared within the ranks of the RCP, but, also within the Trotskyist movement internationally.

The new situation in Eastern Europe led the leadership of the RCP to a fundamental reappraisal of our ideas. Sometimes you can learn a great deal from a mistake, if it is honestly assessed and analysed with the Leninist method of criticism and self-criticism. The dispute over the class nature of the Eastern European regimes gave us an insight into the whole new process that was unfolding. As a matter of fact, you can trace the degeneration of the International to their refusal to analyse their mistakes on these questions.

We argued that as a result of the advance of the Red Army and the flight of the bourgeois quislings who had collaborated with the Nazi occupation, a new situation was developing in Eastern Europe. At a certain stage, we predicted, the Stalinists would inevitably carry out a social overturn, though in a caricatured form utterly different from the classical model of the October revolution. The attempt by imperialism to bolster up the capitalist elements in Eastern Europe through the use of Marshall aid immediately provoked a reaction from Moscow. The Stalinists carried through a revolution against capitalism, just as we had predicted.

This was a similar phenomenon to that which Trotsky had talked about in relation to the earlier Russian occupation of Poland and Finland. He wrote that the Red Army would provide an impulse to the socialist revolution in these countries, but then strangles all the elements of workers' democracy. In Eastern Europe, the "Communist" Parties had installed themselves in power in coalition governments under the banner of so-called People's Democracies. But these coalitions had nothing in common with the Spanish Popular Front of the 1930s. In every case, the Stalinists controlled the ministry of the interior (the police) and the ministry of defence (the army), with the Russian Red Army in the background - just in case. In such circumstances, the seizure of power was not so difficult! When it suited them, the Stalinists balanced between the classes, Bonapartist style, leaning on the working class to expropriate the weak bourgeoisie, and then establishing Stalinist regimes, or regimes of proletarian Bonapartism, on the model of Stalin's Russia.

The first such transformation took place in Czechoslovakia in April 1948. The Stalinist leader Klement Gottwald announced the elimination of the twelve bourgeois ministers from the government. The CP and its allies occupied all key ministries. The President was a CP member, and so were the two out of three deputy premiers. Simultaneously, the Stalinists organised mass rallies and demonstrations of workers. They even took the step of arming a workers' militia. Militiamen carrying guns patrolled the streets of Prague. Thus, the Stalinists leaned on the workers to crush the bourgeois and take power into their own hands.

In an article I wrote for *Socialist Appeal*, I outlined the significance of these events: the Stalinists had rested upon the workers and peasants to carry through a revolution. However, they ensured that the revolution remained within certain limits and all elements of workers' democracy were snuffed out.

> "The workers and peasants in Czechoslovakia undoubtedly gave wholehearted support to the change because of its progressive features
>
> "The workers could not but support the measures: nationalisation of all important plants that remained in private hands since the mass movement in 1945; seventy percent of the printing establishments, the whole of the chemical industry, all refrigerator plants and all building concerns employing more than fifty persons; all big hotels and the wholesale trade. No firm employing more than fifty people in any trade or industry is now allowed to be privately owned. The monopoly of foreign trade has been formally instituted.
>
> "The peasants were solidly behind the reforms. Although the Stalinists did not do as the Russian Bolsheviks did, namely nationalise the land and then hand it to the peasants, they divided the land and gave it to the peasants as their own private property.
>
> The article went on to point out: "These are the progressive features supported by the Trotskyists despite the failure to nationalise the land. They are a necessary economic foundation for a workers' state. In order to carry through these measures the Stalinists were compelled to call on the initiative and pressure of the masses.
>
> "As Trotsky pointed out in 1939, when dealing with the likely developments if Stalin invaded Poland: 'It is more likely, however, that in the territories scheduled to become a part of the USSR, the Moscow government will carry through the expropriation of the large landowners and statification of the means of production. This variant is the most probable not because the bureaucracy remains true to the socialist programme but because it is neither desirous nor capable of sharing the power and the privileges the latter entails, with the old ruling classes in the occupied territories. Here an analogy literally offers itself. The first Bonaparte halted the revolution by means of a military dictatorship. However, when the French troops invaded Poland, Napoleon signed a decree: "Serfdom is abolished". This measure was dictated not by Napoleon's sympathies for the peasants, nor by democratic principles, but rather by the fact that the Bonapartist dictatorship based itself not on feudal,

> but on bourgeois property relations. In as much as Stalin's Bonapartist dictatorship bases itself not on private property but state property, the invasion of Poland by the Red Army should in the nature of the case, result in the abolition of private capitalist property, so as thus to bring the regime of the occupied territories into accord with the regime of the USSR.
>
> "'This measure, revolutionary in character - "the expropriation of the expropriators" - is in this case achieved in a military-bureaucratic fashion. The appeal to independent activity on the part of the masses in the new territories - and without such an appeal, even if worded with extreme caution it is impossible to constitute a new regime - will on the morrow undoubtedly be suppressed by ruthless police measures in order to assure the preponderance of the bureaucracy over the awakened revolutionary masses...' (*USSR in War*, September 1939)."

Very rapidly after Czechoslovakia, the same process unfolded throughout Eastern Europe: the Stalinists leaned on the masses to sweep away the bourgeois elements. New regimes of proletarian Bonapartism were created. These events provoked a crisis in the International. The International leadership tried to insist that the regimes in Eastern Europe were state capitalist regimes, while at the same time, by paying lip service to Trotsky, insisting that Russia still remained a deformed workers state.

That was an absurd position, and one we could not accept for a moment. If the regimes in Eastern Europe were capitalist or state capitalist, then the only conclusion you could come to was that Russia was also state capitalist. However, being a serious tendency we did not immediately jump from one formulation to another. We needed to make a serious and fundamental theoretical appraisal of the question. This would require a great deal of study and thought. It was unforgivable simply to plunge light-mindedly into a characterisation as Burnham and Shachtman had done in the American SWP in 1939-40.

At first, we had a completely open mind on the question. In fact, Haston and myself originally considered the possibility that there was a state capitalist regime in Russia. But before making up our mind we considered it necessary to make a thorough analysis of the situation, and to go through the material of the great teachers, Marx, Engels, Lenin, and Trotsky. And in the light of what they had written, to study concretely the developments that were unfolding in Eastern Europe. That is the only way to approach a question of such a fundamental character. I personally spent months just going through the fundamental works of Marxism. I went through Marx's *Capital* and the political writings of Marx and Engels, Lenin and Trotsky, to see what light they could throw on the situation.

We made a thorough re-appraisal of the Marxist theory of the state, and came to the conclusion that the regimes in Eastern Europe were a form of proletarian Bonapartism. As for Russia, it was a deformed workers' state, differing in no essential way from the regimes in Eastern Europe. Of course, events had unfolded in a peculiar way. The Stalinists, having installed themselves in power proceeded to set up a new state, without capitalism and landlordism, based on a nationalised planned economy. But the revolutions that were carried out in a bureaucratic and Bonapartist way in Hungary, Poland, Czechoslovakia and Romania had nothing in common with the regime of workers' democracy established by Lenin and Trotsky 1917. They began where the Russian revolution left off: as bureaucratic, totalitarian military police states.

Not everyone was so painstaking, however, in their approach to theoretical questions. I should mention in this regard the position of Tony Cliff who arrived from Palestine in the autumn of 1946. As I have pointed out, the leadership of the RCP had originally and mistakenly considered that there was state capitalism in Russia and Eastern Europe. When Cliff arrived, we discussed our initial position with him on several occasions, when he defended the position of a workers' state. Looking back on it, Haston and myself must have played a part in convincing him that the regimes in Eastern Europe and Russia were capitalist. We must have been pretty persuasive because Cliff soon changed his position and whole-heartedly adopted the theory of state capitalism.

Cliff put his ideas down on paper, which we produced as a special internal bulletin in June 1948 entitled *The Nature of Stalinist Russia*. As soon as we examined Cliff's material our hair stood on end! He had done a 180 degree somersault and was now arguing that the bureaucracy in Russia had become a ruling class and that the last vestiges of the Russian Revolution had been destroyed. The regime - he triumphantly concluded - had been transformed into state capitalism.

I brought out a two-part reply on behalf on the RCP leadership, explaining the contradictions in Cliff's argument, and outlining the Marxist theory of the state. I was able to show that Russia remained a deformed workers' state, despite all the crimes of Stalinism. The working class had been expropriated politically, but still remained the ruling class through the nationalised planned economy. There were many times when under capitalism, the bourgeois itself had been politically expropriated, as in any Bonapartist regime, however, they remain the ruling class through their ownership of the means of production. Only a new political revolution could resolve the problem, and open the way for the movement towards socialism.

> "Innumerable references could be given to show that a capitalist state presupposes private property, individual ownership of the means of production", stated my reply to Cliff. "The state is the *apparatus of* rule: it cannot itself be the class which rules. The bureaucracy is merely part of the apparatus of the state. It may 'own' the state, in the sense that it lifts itself above society and becomes relatively independent of the economically dominant, i.e., ruling class. That was the case in Nazi Germany, where the bureaucracy dictated to the capitalists what they should produce, how they should produce it, etc., for the purposes of war. So in the war economy of Britain, USA and elsewhere, the state dictated to the capitalists what and how they should produce. This did not convert them into a ruling class. Why? Because it was in defence of private property.
>
> "Cliff argues that the bureaucracy manages and plans industry. True enough. Whose industry do they manage and plan? In capitalist society, the managers plan and manage industry in the individual enterprises and trusts. But it does not make them the owners of those enterprises and trusts. The bureaucracy manages the entire industry. In that sense it is true that it has more independence from its economic base than any other bureaucracy or state machine in the whole of human history. But as Engels emphasised and we must re-emphasise, in the final analysis the economic basis is decisive. If Cliff is going to argue that it is in their function as managers that the bureaucrats are the ruling class, then clearly he is not giving a Marxist definition of a capitalist class. He is calling the Russian bureaucracy a class, but he must work out a theory as to what class this is.
>
> "The state is the instrument of class rule, of coercion, a glorified policeman. But the policeman is not the ruling class. The police can become unbridled, can become bandits, but that does not convert them into a capitalist, feudal or slave-owning class."

The problem with Cliff's analysis is that it was based on formal logic, and did not undertake a dialectical view of the question. What we were dealing with was a workers' state which was monstrously deformed in a hostile capitalist environment. However, the existence of the nationalised planned economy, was a vital feature in determining the class nature of the regime.

Notes:

1- Roy Tearse interview with Al Richardson, 1978.
2- Ibid.
3- Ibid.
4- Jock Haston interview, op.cit.
5- Quoted in *War and the International*, p.139.
6- Jock Haston interview, op. cit.
7- Quoted by Michael Foot, op. cit. p. 417.
8- Ibid., p. 418.
9- Cannon, *Writings and Speeches 1945-47*, p.201.
10- See resolution on *The New Imperialist Peace and the Building of the Parties of the Fourth International,* April 1946.
11- Quoted in *The Unbroken Thread*, p.372
12- *Fourth International,* December 1944. See also *The Changed Relationship of Forces in Europe and the Role of the Fourth International,* by Ted Grant, March 1945
13- Tony Cliff, *Trotskyism after Trotsky, The Origins of the International Socialists,* p.23, London 1999.
14- Cannon, op. cit., p.183, New York, 1977.
15- *Trotskyism versus Revisionism*, volume 4, p.298, London 1974.
16- Cannon, *Speeches to the Party,* pp.296-7, New York, 1973.
17- Ibid., p.297.
18- Quoted in *Yugoslavia, East Europe and the Fourth international: the Evolution of Pabloist Liquidationism* by Jan Norden, New York 1993, p.13.
19- Frank, *The Fourth International: the long march of the Trotskyists*, London 1979, p.85.
20- Trotsky, *The Crisis of the French Section [1935-36]*, New York 1977, p.107.
21- *Writings of Leon Trotsky, 1939-40*, New York, 1973, p.80.

Harold Atkinson (foreground)

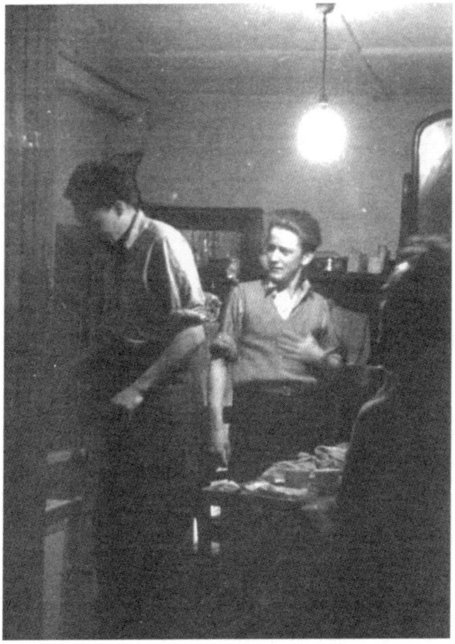

Heaton Lee in South Wales during a miners' strike

Millie Lee and George Noseda

LABOUR HATERS ATTACK OUR PARTY

SOCIALIST APPEAL

VOL. 5. No. 21. MID-APRIL, 1944 Twopence

LIES—SLANDER—PERSECUTION
Will Not Save the Boss Class

BY JOCK HASTON

DURING THE FIRST WEEK IN APRIL OUR PARTY AND ITS PRESS WAS THE OBJECT OF ONE OF THE MOST VICIOUS ANTI-RED SCARE CAMPAIGNS SINCE THE DAYS OF THE ZINOVIEV LETTER.

The capitalist press howled like dogs "hot on the scent of German gold"; the capitalist state machine and lackeys of the ruling class in the Labour and Trade Union leaderships were in the forefront fanning the flames.

Whilst the London "Evening Standard" headlined "HIDDEN HAND AGITATORS MARKED", the "Evening News" scooped the press by the information that Scotland Yard special branch had raided our headquarters.

It was all in the good old anti-working class tradition of "secret funds", "secret knocks", "mystery men" and "skilled agitators" who by some peculiar gift were bringing thousands of miners and shipbuilding apprentices out on strike.

Behind all the scare propaganda, however, there was a real crisis for the capitalist class. More so for the Trade Union leaders.

The greatest strike wave for many years was sweeping the country. Shoulder to shoulder, men and boys were demanding a living wage. Simultaneously there was a growing demand for the nationalisation of the pits. Faced with the possibility of a general strike in the key industry of the country—coal, the Government had to find a scapegoat; the Trade Union leaders had to find an excuse for their inability to control their members; and the Trotskyists were at hand.

Of course, there was another side to the question: the "Socialist Appeal" was the only paper in the country which took up a ... stand directly with the striking workers. Our party—the Revolutionary Communist Party—was the only workers' party which attempted to give the strikers a clear direction to their policy. In reporting the raid on our premises, the B.B.C. put the whole question objectively when it announced that the raid had been made because we supported the workers who were on strike. It was for this reason that we were singled out for attack.

FIRST CASE UNDER ANTI-LABOUR

SMASH BEVIN'S ANTI-LABOUR LAWS
War Crisis Used to Attack Trade Union Rights

THE NEW REGULATIONS INTRODUCED BY BEVIN ARE THE GREATEST BLOW AGAINST THE ORGANISED WORKING CLASS MOVEMENT FOR THE LAST 50 YEARS.

Extending as it does, the already infamous Trade Disputes Act, the new regulation is a direct blow against the trade union movement.

Ostensibly directed against our Party and its press the regulation is directed squarely against all militants of the working class. The Trade Disputes Act pales into insignificance as anti-labour legislation in face of this new regulation, the key section of which reads as follows:

"No person shall declare, instigate or incite any other person to take part in, or shall otherwise act in furtherance of any strike among persons engaged in the performance of essential services or any lock-out of persons so engaged."

Penal servitude and fines up to £500 or both can be imposed upon anyone

4

In Defence of Trotskyism-
Our Struggle with the International

From 1945 onwards, a whole new series of differences began to appear between the International leadership and ourselves. Firstly, they arose on the assessment of the world situation. We understood that a fundamental change had been taking place in the relationship of forces internationally. The victory of Russia in the war constituted a decisive change. After the occupation of France, the world war was really a European war between fascist Germany and Stalinist Russia, with Anglo-American imperialism as onlookers. In effect, Britain and the US were sitting on the sidelines watching this Homeric struggle between Nazi Germany and the Soviet Union. Anglo-American imperialism had calculated - or rather miscalculated - that Russia and Germany would exhaust themselves in the war, and become so debilitated, that the American and British imperialists could then step in, subjugate them both and decide the fate of the world. This miscalculation on the part of the imperialists had completely changed the world situation

In 1945 the United States had a reservoir of fresh troops, while Russia's armed forces had suffered 25 million casualties. However, the Red Army, having defeated the Germans almost single-handed, was now stationed in the heart of Europe and had occupied half of Germany. Thus, the strategic position had fundamentally changed. As a warning to the Russians, the American imperialists dropped the atom bomb on Japan. This was nothing to do with defeating Japan, as Japan was already defeated and suing for peace before the bomb was dropped. The real reason for dropping the atom bomb was fear of the Soviet Union.

Not many people realise this, but the Red Army, having smashed the Wehrmacht in the West, had gone onto the offensive against Japan in the east. Against the wishes of Anglo-American imperialism the Red Army entered Manchuria threatening to defeat the Japanese army within ten days. The American imperialists found themselves in a very difficult situation. Although their military forces were intact, and they had huge reserves of soldiers and two thirds of the world's gold supplies, they were incapable of intervening militarily against their Russian "allies". The revolutionary ferment throughout Europe, Asia and other parts of the world, as well as the general war-weariness of the Allied troops, stayed their hand. If the imperialists had attempted to intervene, their armies would not have accepted it and they would have faced a series of mutinies.

However, the IS was blind to all these developments. In a document presented by the IS to the first International Pre-Conference after the war in April 1946, it stated that as a result of the weakness of the USSR, the imperialists, by diplomatic means alone could restore capitalism in Russia. So weak was Russia supposed to be, that counter-revolution could be carried through "in the near future, even without military intervention, through the sole fact of economic, political and diplomatic pressure of American and British imperialism, and its military threats", we read in the IS document. They actually wrote such an absurdity! We were horrified when we received this material because it showed a complete lack of understanding, politically, diplomatically, and strategically. It was a completely false evaluation of the situation of the Soviet Union, which had emerged vastly strengthened, and not weakened, as they imagined.

Disagreements now opened up on a whole range of questions: perspectives for the Chinese revolution, disagreements about the world economy, disagreements over the character of the regimes that would emerge in Europe; and of the tactics and strategy that the class should pursue throughout this period. If you examine the material of the International at this time it is a catalogue of bankrupt ideas. They saw slump everywhere. Of course, if it hadn't been for the billions of dollars handed out in Marshall aid, as people like GDH Cole pointed out at the time, the standard of living of Britain would have dropped to the level of the middle of the nineteenth century. Certainly, that would have produced a revolutionary situation in Britain. But, of course, American imperialism had no alternative but to try and save capitalism in Europe and in Britain. They saw Britain as the solid anchor for its plans in Europe. If the American imperialists were compelled to intervene against the revolution in Europe, they needed Britain as a bridgehead. So they first gave some 1,500 million dollars to Britain to help prop up the economy. Soon afterwards, Marshall aid was given to West Germany, France and then the rest of Europe for the purpose of putting their economies back on their feet.

In the meantime - as is typical of this tendency - they were accusing us of all sorts of things. We were denounced as being "revisionists", "neo-Stalinists" in relation to our perspectives and characterisation of Eastern Europe, as "reformists" because we had predicted the economic boom, and as "petty-bourgeois pessimists", for failing to be as r-r-r-revolutionary as themselves! They accused us of everything instead of actually analysing and arguing on the basis of the material itself. True, in polemics it is sometimes legitimate to use terms such as "revisionist", "reformist", provided they are used in a scientific manner, and not as terms of abuse. One must argue against the ideas of an opponent, and do so honestly and loyally, showing the arguments to be false. But for these people, they were simply terms of abuse and a substitute for political argument.

What they could never forgive was the fact that on all these vital questions we were shown to be correct. Having burned their fingers with ultra-leftism, the International leadership swung over completely to opportunism, and then to an adventurist course. When the break between Tito and Stalin took place in June 1948, they argued that Yugoslavia was now a healthy workers' state - at least as healthy as the Soviet state between 1917-1921, with perhaps a little wart here and there. According to these "great Marxists", here was a transition from a capitalist state to a healthy workers' state! How this was possible, nobody knew. But that is what they now argued. The RCP leadership took a different line. We explained that the regime in Yugoslavia was a deformed workers' state that did not differ in any fundamental way from the USSR under Stalin. While of course we were prepared to give critical support to the Yugoslav people in their fight against Russian Stalinism, we had no illusions in Tito. In a pamphlet by Haston and myself, written in June 1948 entitled *Behind the Stalin-Tito Clash*, we explained:

> "The importance of the present conflict lies in the fact that it is the first important crack in the international front of Stalinism since the end of the war. It is bound to have profound effects on the rank and file members of the Communist Parties throughout the world, especially in Western Europe and Britain. It is the beginning of a process of differentiation within the Communist Parties, which in the long run will lead to splits.
>
> "The extension of the power of the Russian bureaucracy further west from the Russian borders creates new problems for them. While temporarily strengthening them, in the long run it will undermine their position.
>
> "It is clear that any Leninist must support the right of any small country to national liberation and freedom if it so desires. All socialists will give critical support to the movement in Yugoslavia to federate with Bulgaria and to gain freedom from direct Moscow domination. At the same time the workers in Yugoslavia and these countries will fight for the installation of genuine workers' democracy, of the control of the administration of the state and of industry as in the days of Lenin and Trotsky in Russia. This is impossible under the present Tito regime.
>
> *"For an Independent Socialist Soviet Yugoslavia within an independent Socialist Soviet Balkans. This can only be part of the struggle for the overthrow of the capitalist governments in Europe and the installation of workers' democracy in Russia."*

The Chinese Revolution

Meanwhile in China, the most earth-shattering events were taking place. Mao Tse-tung was leading a peasant war against the rotten, reactionary bourgeois regime of Chiang Kai-Shek. Despite the huge amounts of money and weapons given to Chiang by the Americans, the Red Army was advancing rapidly, while Chiang's army had the biggest rate of desertion of any army in history. Mao's army was made up of more than a million troops, with maybe twice that number of guerrillas in the countryside. The Chinese Red Army sliced through Chiang's armies - armed and trained by the USA - like a hot knife through butter. The feeble attempt by British imperialism to intervene by sending four warships to China ended in a humiliating defeat. The Red forces shelled the ships, which were compelled to flee under cover of darkness. The British - who are experts at making a defeat look like a victory - presented the escape of *HMS Amethyst* as a great triumph!

For Marxists, the Chinese Revolution was the second greatest event in human history, after the Bolshevik Revolution of 1917. A correct attitude to it was therefore absolutely essential. But here too the leaders of the Fourth failed miserably. They merely repeated Trotsky's pre-war position, when he thought that Mao would betray his peasant base capitulate to Chiang Kai-Shek and fuse with the capitalist elements in the cities, resulting in a "normal" capitalist development.

Their whole approach was ridiculous in the extreme. At an International Conference Cannon and the others still maintained that Mao would never cross the Yangtse river. By the time the conference was over, Chiang had crossed the Yangtse and smashed Chiang Kai-Shek's army. Max Shachtman, who had broken with the Fourth earlier, had his supporters rolling about laughing, when he joked about Cannon's "perspectives" for China - "Yes, Mao wants to capitulate to Chiang Kai-Shek. The only problem is Mao can't catch him!" Even after Mao came to power, the leaders of the Fourth said the regime was still capitalist. They actually kept that position up till the mid-1950s!

In January 1949, before Mao came to power, we predicted what would happen. Given the world balance of forces, the bankruptcy of Chinese capitalism, and the USSR in the background, Mao was able to win a victory by granting land to the peasants, and resting upon them to carry through, in a distorted fashion, a social revolution. Given the passivity and repression of the working class, the only road was the creation of a regime of proletarian Bonapartism. As I wrote at the time:

> "While supporting the destruction of feudalism in China, it must be emphasised that only a horrible caricature of the Marxist conception of the revolution will result because of the leadership of the Stalinists. Not a real democracy, but a totalitarian regime as brutal as that of Chiang Kai-Shek will develop. Like the regimes in Eastern Europe, Mao will look to Russia as his model. Undoubtedly, tremendous economic progress will be achieved. But the masses, both workers and peasants, will find themselves enslaved by the bureaucracy.
>
> "The Stalinists are incorporating into their regime ex-feudal militarists, capitalist elements, and the bureaucratic officialdom in the towns who will occupy positions of privilege and power.
>
> "On the basis of such a backward economy, a large scale differentiation among the peasants (as after the Russian Revolution during the period of the NEP) aided by the failure to nationalise the land: the capitalist elements in trade, and even in light industry, might provide a base for capitalist counter-revolution. It must be borne in mind that in China the proletariat is weaker in relation to the peasantry than was the case in Russia during the NEP owing to the more backward development of China. Even in Czechoslovakia and other Eastern European countries similarly, where the capitalist elements were relatively weaker, nevertheless the danger of a capitalist overturn existed for a time. The fact that the workers and peasants will not have any democratic control and that the totalitarian tyranny will have superimposed upon it the Asiatic barbarism and cruelties of the old regime, gives rise to this possibility. However, it seems likely that the capitalist elements will be defeated because of the historical tendency of the decay of capitalism on a world scale. The impotence of world imperialism is shown by the fact that whereas they intervened directly against the Chinese revolution in 1925-7, today they look on helplessly at the collapse of the Chiang regime."

Given the development of an independent nationalist bureaucracy in China, we predicted that it would also come into conflict with Stalin. "However, it is quite likely that Stalin will have a new Tito on his hands", continued the article. This was to come about in the Sino-Soviet conflict that developed in the late 1950s.

And the article concluded: "The shrewder capitalist commentators are already speculating on this although they derive cold comfort from it. Mao will have a powerful base in China with its 450-500 million population and its potential resources, and the undoubted mass support his regime will possess in the early stages. The conflicts which will thus open out should be further means of assisting the world working class to understand the real nature of Stalinism."

A little later in February 1949, David James, a member of the Central Committee of the RCP, questioned our analysis of what was taking place in China and Yugoslavia, and issued an internal document titled *Some Remarks on the Question of Stalinism*. This discussion served to clarify the characteristics of proletarian Bonapartism and answer some doubts about the position of the leadership. I wrote a reply to James on this question:

"Where comrade James makes the mistake here, is in assuming that once the class basis has been decided, the problems are simple, and that all tendencies which are manifest must be a *direct reflection* of the *interests of opposing classes*. But he has only to ask himself the question: what class does Stalin represent in the struggle against Tito? And what class does Tito represent when he has already agreed by definition that the class basis of the regimes are 'basically identical'? Is there a struggle between the Yugoslav working class and the Russian working class? Clearly there is something wrong here.

"First, we want to take up James's reference to Trotsky in this connection. It is true that Trotsky argued that different sections of the bureaucracy would tend to reflect class interests, one faction going with the proletariat and the other with the bourgeoisie. Butenko went over to the fascists in Italy. He did not represent any social grouping within Russia, but was merely an isolated case with no roots. Reiss represented the proletarian wing and as such found himself in the Fourth International. Trotsky did visualise the development of strong capitalist currents, as well as the strong proletarian currents at a time of crisis - that there would be a split in the bureaucracy under the pressure of class forces. But the differentiation that he expected, particularly during the war, did not take place. But Trotsky did produce arguments which were far more to the point in explaining clearly what forces are represented in the struggle within the bureaucracy, or as in the present discussion, between the two different workers' bureaucracies. We refer here to the Ukraine.

"The Old Man pointed out that in the Ukraine after the purge of the Trotskyists and Bukharinites, *nine-tenths of all Stalinist officials in the heads of the departments of government in the national republic were imprisoned, exiled and executed.* Did they represent a different class from Stalin? Of course not! They reflected the pressure and discontent of the Ukraine masses *against the national oppression of the Great Russian bureaucracy.* The Ukrainian masses were oppressed not only as workers and peasants by the bureaucracy, but as Ukrainians. Hence the struggle for national liberation in the Ukraine. This was not confined to the Ukraine. The same process took place in all the national republics of Russia, oppressed by the Russian bureaucracy. The Stalinist officialdom in all these were, to one degree or another, affected by the prevailing mood of hatred against the bureaucratic centralising tendencies of Great Russian chauvinism centred in Moscow. According to Colonel Tokaev, writing in the *Sunday Express*, there were national uprisings during the war in the Crimea, the Caucasus and some of the other national republics. After the war, the great Russian bureaucracy punished this 'disloyalty' by banishing the entire populations of some of the national republics of the Crimea and others and dissolving the republics, in violation of even the paper constitution of Stalin. Clearly this was intended as a warning against disaffection in other republics.

"*This* is the analogy with Yugoslavia. In the purge in the Ukraine, Trotsky showed that here it was not a case of different classes involved, but of different nations oppressed by the bureaucracy. *The Ukrainian Stalinists did not represent the fraction of Butenko, nor did they represent the fraction of Reiss.* What they wanted was more autonomy and more control for the Ukrainians (which meant themselves) over the national destiny of their republic. The fact that a national struggle of this character can take place after the proletarian revolution, is merely an indication of how far the revolution has been thrown back under Stalinist domination. (Here let us add that Lenin, with his far-sighted national policy, surprisingly raised in advance the possibility of clashes between different nationalities even after the abolition of capitalism. National cultures and aspirations will remain long after the proletarian revolution has taken place, even on a world scale and will constitute an important problem.)

"One can say that in Yugoslavia and Eastern Europe, Stalin has attempted to carry through a similar bureaucratic policy as in the republics in Russia. The only difference in Yugoslavia is that the Russian bureaucracy did not have as firm control over the state machine as they had in the other satellite states. This was, of course, due to the fact that while in the other countries it was the entry of the Red Army which smashed the bourgeois state and precipitated the movement of the masses, in Yugoslavia, Tito had a mass base and built up a machine which he had under control, even under the Germans. The Red Army assisted in the liberation of Belgrade, but undoubtedly Tito had a far more popular base among the masses than in the other satellite states. In the eyes of the Yugoslavs, their liberation from German imperialism was achieved under the leadership of Tito and the Yugoslav CP. Thus, Stalin's attempt to completely subordinate Yugoslavia to the Moscow bureaucracy met with resistance from the local bureaucrats, who felt confident that they would have the backing of the masses. As distinct from this, the regimes in the other satellite states felt the need to *lean on the Moscow bureaucracy*, owing to a fear of the difficulties at home in the event of a conflict.

"Stalin encountered difficulty in applying in Yugoslavia a Ukraine solution, or even a pseudo-independent solution as in Poland, where the joke circulates that Cyrankiewicz phones the Kremlin to find out if he can take the night off to go to the cinema. Stalin's attempts to intervene in Yugoslavia resulted for the first time, in the arrest of his stooges instead of vice versa. It was as if the Ukrainian Stalinists had had their own state forces and the backing of the masses, separate and powerful enough to oppose the Russian MVD [secret police], etc. On that basis, they could have resisted the demands of complete subordination to the Moscow bureaucracy.

"This explained why Trotsky considered the *national question* to be of such importance that he put forward the demand for an independent socialist soviet Ukraine. At first sight this would appear to come into conflict with the strategy of the unification of all Europe in a socialist united states. From a purely pedantic point of view it would appear that the enemy of the Ukrainian and Great Russian masses is the same and the task is a simple one of unifying their struggle for control in one unified state. Merely to find the class basis does not supply the answer. *The class basis of the Ukrainian bureaucrats is no different from that of the Russian bureaucrats.* Yet they come into conflict with one another and the victorious section savagely executes the other.

"Similarly, it is clear that the mere fact that Tito is, for the time being, victorious, no more turns him into an unconscious Trotskyist than the Ukrainian bureaucrats.

"Through the dictatorship of the Stalinist bureaucracy is expressed indirectly the rule of the proletariat. For the Soviet Union to return to a healthy basis, a new revolution, a political revolution, is necessary. The economic basis will remain the same, though of course the social consequences will result in profound changes in the overall plan, the division of income, the culture, etc. As in the case of France - where a regime of bourgeois autocracy required revolution before it could become bourgeois democracy, so in Russia, revolution will be required to transform the bureaucratic totalitarian regime into a really democratic one. The political revolution in France resulted in profound changes in its social consequences - different division of income, freer development of the productive forces, culture, etc. But the fundamental structure of the system remained the same. So in Russia, the class basis will remain: the superstructure will change. On this there is common agreement with James. But what of Yugoslavia?

"What was an unconscious process in the early stages of Stalinist degeneration in Russia, is a semi-conscious or even conscious process in Yugoslavia. The regime of Tito is very similar to the regime of Stalin during the period of 1923-8. After the experience of Russia, it is clear that where there is no democracy, where no opposition is tolerated, where a totalitarian regime exists, then developments will proceed on the same pattern as in Russia. Here precisely it is not a question of the psychology of Tito or Stalin, but the relentless interests of the differing tendencies at work within society.

"The state, as a special superstructural formation standing over society, of necessity tends to form a grouping with habits of thought, used to command, with privileges of education and culture. The tendency is to crystallise a caste with an outlook of its own, different from the class it represents. This is accentuated where the state takes over the means of production; the sole commanding stratum in society is the bureaucracy. Not for nothing did Marx and Lenin emphasise the need for the masses to retain control of the state or semi-state, because without this, new trends and tendencies are introduced which have a law of motion of their own.

"If one would assume theoretically (abstracting the Stalin regimes for the moment from the world relationships and the internal social contradictions) that such a caste could maintain itself indefinitely (the modest estimate of a leading Siberian Stalinist was 1,000 years) - *it could not lead to an amelioration of the social contradictions or to the painless withering away of the state into society.* All the laws of social evolution, of the development of the classes and castes in society speak against this. Far from developing in the direction of communism, such a society, if it depended on the will of the bureaucracy, would inevitably develop into a slave state with a hierarchy of castes such as visualised by Jack London in his picture of the oligarchy under the *Iron Heel.*

"Socialism does not arise automatically out of the development of the productive forces themselves. If it were purely a question of the automatic change in society once the productive forces are developed, revolution would not have been necessary in the changes from one society to another. As has been explained many times, the nationalisation of the productive forces alone does not abolish all social contradictions - otherwise there would be socialism in Russia. Once the bureaucracy gets a vested interest of its own, it will never voluntarily relinquish its privileged position. A further development of the productive forces will merely create new needs and open new vistas for the bureaucracy to dispose of the surplus in their interests. This is already shown by the development of the bureaucracy as a more and more rapacious and hereditary caste, instead of less and less with the development of the productive forces in Russia. (Here we are not dealing with inevitable movements of revolt on the part of the masses, the contradictions engendered by bureaucratic misrule, which must lead to explosions, etc. This whole problem requires further elaboration).

"The degeneration of Russia was not accidental. Where the proletariat has control, its position in society determines its consciousness and determines the evolution of that society in the direction of the liquidation of the state and the establishment of communism. Where the bureaucracy has control, its position in society determines its consciousness and determines the evolution of that society not towards its voluntary liquidation and communism, but to its own reinforcement. Conditions determine consciousness. And the methods, the organisation, the outlook and ideology of Tito and Mao are the same as those of the Russian Stalinists: not democratic centralism, but its opposite - totalitarian bureaucracy is what they base themselves on. The Cominform criticism of the 'Turkish terror' is well founded. All that Tito could reply in answer to the accusation that the discussion for the Party Congress was a farce, that no-one dared to oppose the resolution of the Central Committee, or even vote against it for fear of immediate arrest, that there was a dictatorship in the party and in the country - all that he could reply was to liken the criticism of the Cominform to that of the Left Opposition at the 1927 Congress of the CPSU.

"Almost word for word the description of the situation was the same, except that *in Russia in 1927 there was more democracy as a lingering survival of the past than there is in Yugoslavia today*. At least before their expulsion, the Opposition was allowed to put forward its position at the Congress, and Stalin had not yet evolved the complete totalitarian technique of suppression. There was still the faction of Bukharin, etc, in the party. Stalin still had no idea of which way he was going. Tito has taken over *in toto,* the organisation, the ideology, the technique of Bonapartist rule.

"The only difference between the regimes of Stalin and Tito is that the latter is still in its early stages. There is a remarkable similarity in the first upsurge of enthusiasm in Russia where the bureaucracy introduced the first Five-Year Plan, and the enthusiasm in Yugoslavia today.

"While Stalin can only rule through more and more unbridled terror, Tito, for the present, probably retains the support of the big majority of the population of Yugoslavia. But this is not a fundamental difference, it is a question of tempo and the experience of the masses."

And further:

"Stalinism, leaning on the proletariat can, under given conditions, balance between the opposing classes to strengthen itself for its own ends", stated the reply. "We have seen how this was accomplished in Eastern Europe. We now have a similar development taking place before our eyes in China. Whereas it would he impossible for the revolutionary Marxist tendency to make a coalition with the bourgeoisie, precisely because of the need to ensure the independent self-mobilisation of the masses in the struggle to overthrow the bourgeoisie, Stalin has no need for such inhibitions. Stalinism makes a coalition under conditions *where the back of the bourgeoisie has been broken,* in order to play off the bourgeoisie against the danger of an insurgent proletariat. Thus the coalition which the Stalinists are proposing in China will not mean the victory or even the survival of the bourgeoisie. It will be used in order to gain a breathing space for the organisation of a Stalinist, Bonapartist state machine on the lines of Moscow. Not at all a state or a semi-state on the lines visualised by the Marxists - as the free and armed organisation of the masses, but a state machine separate and apart from the masses, entirely independent and towering over them as an instrument of oppression.

"It is evident that the Chinese movement draws its viability from the 'innermost needs of the economy'. However, while a genuine revolutionary, Trotskyist leadership in a backward country would draw its strength from the proletariat, welding the peasant masses behind it, Mao rests on the peasantry and not only bases himself on the passivity of the proletariat at this stage, but ruthlessly suppresses any proletarians who dare to take measures against the bourgeoisie on the basis of independent class action. At a later stage, Mao will lean on the proletariat when he needs it against the bourgeoisie, only later to betray and ruthlessly suppress it. In this it would be far more correct to say that Mao, as Tito, is a conscious Stalinist, adopting *consciously* many of the Bonapartist manoeuvres which Stalin was forced to adopt empirically.

"While the armies of the Kuomintang have melted away under the revolutionary agrarian programme and propaganda of the Stalinists - 'land to the tiller' - one thing is clear: the programme of propaganda of Mao has not been directed to the revolutionary mobilisation of the proletariat and the organisation of soviets. Nor has it been directed to the overthrow of

> the Kuomintang regime in the towns through the conscious initiative and movement of the workers. On the contrary, it is his policy to ruthlessly crush any move in this direction. This refusal to mobilise the masses is not accidental. It expresses the fear of a mass movement in the cities at this stage. The difference between Trotskyism and Stalinism is no more strikingly illustrated than in this fact. There is an unbridgeable gulf between Marxism, which bases itself on the conscious movement of the masses, above all the proletariat, and Bonapartist Stalinism which manoeuvres between the classes and utilises the revolutionary instincts of the masses in the interests of this new caste.
>
> "Mao's regime will follow the pattern of the other Stalinist regimes. Having consolidated itself, it will become a military-police dictatorship with all the other malignant aspects of the Russian regime. The signs are already visible." [1]

The "theoreticians" of the International were tying themselves up in knots on the question of the class nature of the new regimes in China and Eastern Europe. According to them there was a healthy workers' state in Yugoslavia; capitalist states in the rest of Eastern Europe - and a deformed workers' state in Russia. This position was absolutely hopeless. It was totally incoherent even from the standpoint of formal logic, let alone Marxism. For the so-called leaders of the Fourth, however, lack of consistency presented no problem. They simply changed their position without any explanation. It was a completely dishonest method that failed to show any process of reasoning. At one conference in 1946, when we raised the question of Trotsky's prediction that in ten years not one stone upon another would be left of the Stalinist and Social Democratic organisations with one of the representatives of the SWP, he said: "Don't worry, comrades! Trotsky wrote that in 1938. There are still two years to go." That was the level of their understanding of events.

If it had been handled properly, an honest discussion on these questions could have raised the political level of the cadres of the International. But that would have undermined the prestige of the leaders. The fact that they sacrificed theoretical principle to considerations of personal prestige demonstrated the complete bankruptcy of this tendency. In fact, it is fortunate that the Fourth International did not succeed in becoming a mass tendency. At the head of mass parties of the working class, these "leaders" with their bankrupt attitudes and policies, would have quickly led to one catastrophe after another. As it turned out, the absurd antics of Mandel, Cannon, Frank, Pablo and the rest of them, served only to discredit Trotskyism in the eyes of a big layer of workers. With their fatal combination of false policies and Zinovievite organisational methods they succeeded in undermining the movement which Trotsky had built and wrecking what small forces of Trotskyism existed in Europe and elsewhere before they got the chance to build a serious base.

In Britain we were educating our cadres, raising their political level by scrupulously taking up all the theoretical questions that arose. However, within the organisation Gerry Healy commenced his disruptive activities, firstly as the agent of Cannon and the American SWP, and then as the agent of Pablo. As far as the so-called International was concerned, Healy was a very good obedient errand boy who did and said exactly what the International leadership told him to do and say. On all these key questions he could be relied upon to put forward their political line, attempting to build up a clique against the Haston-Grant leadership.

On political matters Healy had no ideas of his own. One rather amusing instance comes to mind that proves the point. In 1946, there was a discussion about the occupation of Germany and other countries by the Red Army - as well as by Allied troops. The RCP came out firmly for the withdrawal of all armies of occupation including the Red Army and for the right of national self-determination. The faction that had now begun to crystallise around Healy put forward the position that we must stand for the withdrawal of the imperialist armies from occupation areas, but not the Red Army. This was the army of the workers' state, etc. Healy waged a long campaign on this question within the organisation calling us "revisionists" for the stand we had taken. The International leadership had been silent on this question, so in order to get clarity on this issue, we wrote a letter to the International Secretariat in Paris demanding an urgent reply.

Now it just so happened that on the day this letter from the IS arrived we had invited Healy and a supporter of his called John Goffe to the Political Committee to discuss some organisational question or other. In front of Healy, Millie Lee reported that a letter had arrived from Paris and this was duly read to the committee. It was a short note that read:

Tich Shindler speaking to workers,
Naples, March 1946

"Concerning the question raised by the letter of Comrade Lee of 7 May 1946 on the subject of the interpretation of the passage of the *Manifesto* concerning the Red Army, a political reply will be made by the IS in some days specifying that our position must be in fact - 'for the withdrawal of all occupation armies, including the Red Army' - and no ambiguity must henceforth exist on this matter."

Quite naturally we all looked at Healy, like the man in the advert who sneezed. After all, he had been waging a vehement campaign for weeks and months against our alleged revisionist position. Healy turned as white as a sheet. He threw up his hands and said, "Well, so now we've got agreement." Goffe remained silent - not uttering a single word at the PB meeting on the subject. [2]

We had got agreement alright! It was agreement reached by telegraph - just like the Comintern representatives who received their marching orders by a telegraph from Moscow, without explanation of any kind. If there had been an argument or at least a document of ten, or twenty, or thirty pages, you could at least argue that Healy had been convinced by the argument or the document. But the IS letter consisted simply of a few lines! The Cannon/Pablo leadership was engaged in methods that had nothing in common with those of Lenin and Trotsky. They formed blocs not on a political basis, but on the basis of organisational manoeuvres. That is why their political stooge in London had abandoned his original position and announced that we now had agreement immediately, without hesitation, without even thinking. Indeed, no thought was required. When Paris said turn, Healy turned.

Healy's behaviour disgusted every member of the Political Committee who was present. This episode illustrated the rottenness of this tendency and also clearly indicated what the International Secretariat and the SWP really wanted to build. What they wanted in other countries were people who would bow down in front of them, and accept without question their words of wisdom as if from the mouth of the Divine Oracle. It was a disgusting method. With such means you can build nothing but political zombies - people like Healy. Their conception, even at that stage, of an International was entirely opposed to the conceptions of Lenin and Trotsky and the traditions of the best days of the Third International.

We wrote a statement about the affair in the *Internal Bulletin* which stated:

> "It is obvious that under conditions such as outlined above, political discussion with members of our Minority reduces itself to a farce. One cannot seriously discuss with an opponent who not only changes positions without motivation, and at a moment's notice, but who then denies that he ever held them. Already disgust and apathy has started to spread among the membership, who prefer to stay away from aggregates than waste their time in such farcical discussions.
>
> "We therefore appeal to all members of the Minority who have any sense of revolutionary integrity, to combat these deplorable methods. We further appeal to all members of the Party to create that necessary atmosphere of Bolshevik accounting for one's political positions, changes and transformations within the Party, as to make the use of such methods impossible in our ranks." [3]

But these words fell on deaf ears, and the Healy minority continued his intrigues as before.

The RCP and the Nuremberg trials

Following the Neath by-election campaign, we initiated an important campaign over the Nuremberg Trials and an attempt to exposed the Stalinists. Within a few months of the war ending, the Allied Powers began to put the Nazi gangsters on trial in order to put the complete responsibility for the war onto their shoulders. The RCP immediately saw them as a tremendous opportunity to expose the crimes and frame-ups of the Moscow Trials.

In the Stalinist Show Trials, the Trotskyists, and alleged Trotskyists, including Zinoviev, Kamenev, and Red Army generals like Tukhachevski, had been framed and murdered by Stalin. Nuremberg would give us an opportunity to expose the lies that the Trotskyists were Nazi agents. Above all, it would allow us to demand the rehabilitation of Trotsky and those who had perished in Stalin's Purges. In due course, this campaign would also expose those who had shamelessly supported the Moscow Trials - professional liars like Kingsley Martin of the New Statesman and a whole layer of the Labour leaders who, for the sake of their popular front with Stalinism, had gone along with their slanders against Trotskyism.

So we gathered together a committee of leading lights, intellectuals and some Labour MPs, and set up a campaign to demand that at the Nuremberg trials questions should be asked of the defendants concerning their alleged relations with Trotsky. We advocated that there should be a thorough examination of the allegations made at the Moscow trials that Trotsky had been an agent of German fascism. We wrote a letter to Labour Prime Minister Clement Attlee, and we received an acknowledgement from his secretary saying that our suggestions were noted. We conducted a campaign for months while the Nuremberg Trial were going on. Finally, we raised the demand that Natalia Sedov, Trotsky's wife, should be allowed to question the top Nazi defendants at the trial, as she had been directly involved in the slanders, and should have the opportunity to rehabilitate her husband.

We waged quite a successful campaign given the limited resources of the organisation. Every issue of *Socialist Appeal* had articles on the question. We campaigned vigorously in the labour movement and raised quite large sums of money. We also received support from the famous writer and Fabian socialist HG Wells. He deserved credit for this, particularly considering the fierce attack made on him by Trotsky in the past. Wells and a whole series of other writers and intellectuals gave valuable assistance to the campaign. We believed that Bernard Shaw probably never received our campaign material, in any case, he never replied, which was not like him. He was always polite and would have at least replied. So we figured he probably had a Stalinist secretary and never saw the material.

"The Nuremberg Campaign conducted by the Party has been one of the most important aspects of our activity in the struggle against Stalinism and the Moscow Trials", stated *The Party Organiser* (September 1946). "The Manifesto signed by prominent intellectuals had international repercussions. The campaign was taken up by our sections in other parts of the world. 40,000 leaflets were distributed throughout the country, mainly at Communist Party meetings, and a number of trade union branches were addressed on the subject."

As stated, we gave the campaign a labour movement slant and raised the issue in the trade union branches, calling for resolutions to be sent to Downing Street and to national union conferences. We even sent a letter to the Communist Party inviting them to participate, as we were sure that in the interests of truth, they would like to assist! We sent it as a registered letter, but, as expected, we got no reply. Nevertheless, we used this fact against them. In trade union branches where we had comrades, we put the Communist Party members on the spot by asking them why their party was not prepared to support this campaign. The other sections of the International, including the French, Italians, Belgians, Dutch, as well as the South American sections, reproduced material from the *Socialist Appeal* and organised their own committees on similar lines.

Incredibly, the American SWP was silent. They failed to organise any such campaign. The French comrades said that the only reason why the Americans had not done so was because of the political differences with the British section. It was due to petty spite. Towards the end of the Nuremberg trials, Shachtman of the Workers Party took up the campaign, and put the American SWP in an impossible position. Shachtman conducted an enthusiastic campaign reproducing our material on the question of Trotsky's rehabilitation. The failure of the SWP really showed the way in which Cannon conducted politics.

James Cannon was, without doubt, a workers' leader, as Trotsky said. However, he didn't have the necessary theoretical depth and neither did the other leaders of the SWP. You couldn't imagine Lenin and Trotsky, or Marx and Engels, or Luxemburg being concerned about their personal prestige - or allowing it to affect their political judgement - especially over such an issue. If Trotsky had been alive, he would have immediately taken up the Campaign and roundly condemned the SWP. The behaviour of the Americans was symptomatic of a sickness that was already prevalent in the International at that time.

Healy's intrigues

Meanwhile, behind the scenes in Britain, the little clique around Healy, Cooper and Goffe, saw it as their "internationalist duty" to get rid of the RCP leadership. Backed by the Americans, as the "real" internationalists, Healy's faction would fight to become the leadership of the tendency. At that time, John Lawrence, who had originally sided with Healy, had come over to us because we had made him a full-time organiser in Wales. Lawrence had a certain capacity and flair, and we thought he would develop his talents in a full-time capacity. But, as it turned out, we were shown to be wrong. He lacked real stamina or endurance, and was infected by the moods of pessimism that now began to affect certain layers. Healy and his group now tried to latch onto every difference they could find in their struggle with the leadership. Soon, they stumbled on our position over redundancies that affected certain industries after the war, and used that to whip up some opposition.

Obviously, the Marxist tendency is opposed in principle to redundancies in the workplaces. These attacks have to be resisted by all means possible. That is our starting point. However, where the bosses impose lay-offs upon a factory, and there is no alternative, it is the duty of activists to defend the workers' organisation in the workplace. Any attempt to transfer labour should only be undertaken under the control of the trade unions. If there are lay-offs in a factory, then they should be carried out on the basis of non-unionists first, and then on the basis of seniority, i.e. last in, first out. Such a procedure will prevent the bosses from carrying through a policy of victimisation of trade union militants.

The great Marxists always had a principled position on this question. For instance, in Where is Britain Going? Trotsky explains that it was important to defend the organised workers in any factory. He even went so far as to propose that not only should non-unionists be expelled from the workplace, but even trade unionists who refused to pay the political levy to the Labour Party. He described the latter as political blacklegs, who should be treated as such. When we explained Trotsky's position to Healy and Co., they weren't able to answer the point. Of course, they still persisted in saying we were wrong, that we had abandoned the Transitional Programme and so on.

At that time, the American SWP had a similar position to us, putting forward the idea that if there had to be redundancies, we must protect the trade union organisation, and the non-unionists must be the first to go. This had been the tradition of both the American and of the British movement on the issue of sackings. But although the SWP had the same position as ourselves, in our debate with Healy, they kept absolutely silent. They allowed their stooges in Britain to run roughshod over this important elementary position, showing once again their Zinovievist approach to principled questions.

Healy was a highly suitable stooge for Cannon. He had neither principles nor scruples, but he was a good organiser. As we have seen, Healy's intrigues and manoeuvres got him expelled from our organisation on several occasions On each occasion that Healy was expelled, we brought him back, in most cases against the wishes of the rank and file. A certain responsibility rests on Haston's shoulders and mine for allowing him to return to the organisation. We recognised that Healy had organisational ability, which we wanted to harness for the movement, and we never took a personal attitude toward these questions. We were to pay a high price for such tolerance! Between 1944 and 1947, in his struggle with the RCP leadership, Healy must have raised at least a hundred different disagreements. He was not concerned about the issues themselves either from a theoretical or a practical point of view. He was just desperate to find some key issue upon which he could galvanise some support against us within the organisation. In all of this, Healy gave unconditional support to the International leadership, and was reciprocally supported by them in their fight to replace the leadership of the RCP.

Jock, Ajit and Ted

Healy was especially encouraged and helped in his factional activity by his old friend Pierre Frank. Despite Trotsky's stern warning to keep him out of the International, Frank had managed to find a modus vivendi with the IS and later with the SWP. He now found himself in the good books of the leadership. Incredibly, he began to play the role of a "theoretician" becoming the chief exponent of entrism internationally. This tactic was entirely incorrect at the time, but Healy latched on to it to see what kind of response he would get, with the full backing of the International Secretariat, needless to say. At first, Frank favoured the dissolution of the RCP into the ILP. So Healy took up the demand for our immediate entry into the ILP. I must say, when this was raised, it was greeted with a great laugh by most of the comrades. As explained earlier, we had political control of two divisions of the ILP in the North-east. When these comrades heard the proposal that the RCP should dissolve into the ILP they were absolutely horrified. Of course, none of these comrades were prepared to support such a fantastic notion.

Immediately after the war, the ILP leaders had applied for re-affiliation to the Labour Party. Their pacifist anti-war position had not resulted in the massive gains they anticipated. There was no big anti-war backlash. On the contrary, the overwhelming mass of the population fully supported the war, which they saw as a war against fascism. In many respects, the ILP was facing the same isolation during this period as the RCP. As a result of the measures of the

Labour Government, reformist illusions within the working class were growing and being reinforced by their daily experience. Therefore, feeling the cold wind of reality, the ILP leaders wanted to go home to the Labour Party. Fenner Brockway raised the matter of the ILP's affiliation to the Labour Party in discussions with Morrison. Apparently, Morrison told Brockway that the Labour Party needed a left wing. Labour's right wing always needed a Left as a kind of shield against the anger of the working class. Morrison said he was in favour of the ILP's affiliation to the Labour Party and was sure he could get a majority on the NEC - unless, of course, the ILP was seen as "Trotskyist", and in that case there would be no agreement.

To demonstrate that the ILP was not "Trotskyist" or revolutionary, Brockway arranged for our ILP comrades in Durham and Northumberland to be expelled on trumped-up charges. Unfortunately for Brockway, he found his plans to rejoin the Labour Party blocked by the sectarianism that had been fostered in the ranks of the ILP. Although he and the rest of the ILP leadership were anxious to get into the Labour Party, and Maxton and McGovan in particular didn't want to lose their seats, the majority of the rank and file were opposed to re-affiliation. But Brockway and the rest were in too much of a hurry. Defeated over this issue, they couldn't wait to get a majority. They simply jumped ship and entered the Labour Party. The anti-affiliationists, such as Ted Fletcher in the North East and Charles Lockland who was also an MP, held out for as long as they could. But they also felt the cold winds of the objective situation. So there was a process of slow disintegration, with one layer after another, breaking from the ILP and joining the Labour Party. The rump of the ILP simply vegetated on the fringes of the labour movement - an amalgam of reformism, sectarianism and centrism, living off the (considerable) resources inherited from the past.

The RCP now found itself in a very difficult position. The objective conditions had become very difficult. During the war thousands of trade unionists were reading the *Socialist Appeal* regularly. Possibly thousands of members of the Communist Party were also reading our material on a regular basis. However, the thousands, maybe even tens of thousands that we had influenced during the course of the war, now fell into indifference. They said: "The Labour Party is doing the job. The Labour Government is carrying through its programme. What need do we have for the RCP?" Naturally, the sales of the paper declined and we found ourselves with our backs against the wall. On the other hand, those Communist Party workers, who had looked towards us sympathetically in the past in spite of the lies of the leadership, now pointed to China, Eastern Europe, and to the glittering victories of Russia: "Your case is completely discredited", they said. "The Communist Party is carrying though the revolution; the Communist Party is a revolutionary party".

We were in one of those unfortunate positions, which had been described many times by Trotsky. In his writings of 1934-35, he explained that, although the Left Opposition in Russia in the ten years between 1923 and 1933, had a correct position on all the key questions, it was shattered on the basis of the objective situation. The Opposition was isolated and defeated because of the way events developed in Russia and internationally. Similarly the Bolshevik Party was near to collapse as a result of the defeat of the 1905 Russian Revolution. Between 1908 and 1910, the Bolsheviks were reduced to a tiny handful. The black period of reaction in Russia itself inevitably isolated and shattered the revolutionary movement. This explains the dialectical relationship between the objective situation and the subjective factor - the party and the leadership. As Trotsky explained in his article *Fighting Against the Stream:* "The masses are not educated by prognostic theoretical conception, but by general experiences of their lives. It is the most general explanation - the whole situation is against us. There must be a turn in the class realisation, in the sentiments, in the feelings of the masses; a turn which will give us the opportunity for a large political success." Again, "The current is against us, that is clear. I remember the period between 1906 and 1913 in Russia. There was also a reaction. In 1905 we had the workers with us - in 1908 and even in 1907 began the great reaction." [4]

Although not experiencing a period of deep reaction as in 1908-10 in Russia, Britain was passing through an extremely difficult period that nevertheless, served to isolate the revolutionary forces. Under these conditions, it was a question of holding on to our forces, defending the fundamental ideas and raising the theoretical level of those people we could influence. It was inevitable that there would be a certain disappointment and disillusionment among comrades who had looked forward to a revolutionary development after the war. Instead of this, the old leadership of the working class had betrayed the revolution and the enormous pressures of reformism, Stalinism, and capitalism were bearing down upon our movement.

The RCP had no independent printing press during the war. The old treadle machine of the WIL had been destroyed by bombing in the war, and you couldn't get a printing press for love nor money. We had tried to buy a press when we were flush with funds from the people who printed our paper. In fact, the proprietor had agreed to give us a 51 percent discount, but unfortunately his accountant had advised him against, so he turned us down. We were quite prepared to pay him a large amount of money at that time, but the chap refused, and we couldn't budge him. Later on, we had no money anyway.

Our income was affected in many ways. Former wealthy sympathisers were no longer willing to give large sums of money. Sales of the paper and the *WIN* were dwindling. This added to the pressures on comrades, who found it more and more difficult to sell. We started to lose more comrades than we were recruiting. It was a period of retrenchment for our forces. "Towards the middle of the year", states *The Party Organiser,* "the Party was forced to retrench on the apparatus costs. In line with the general trend and drop in income after the war, the apparatus costs were out of proportion with the rate of growth and development of the organisation. Five professionals were taken off the pay-roll - two from the centre and three from the provincial areas." (September 1946) The circulation of the *Socialist Appeal* had dropped to around 10,000 copies per issue.

Although conditions were getting difficult, we still maintained our activity. We continued to make minor gains, no longer on the scale that we had made during the war. Nevertheless, we picked up the more thinking workers here and there. Between 1946 and 1947, the figures show we had gained 40 comrades and lost 48, giving us a membership of 336. There were 60 comrades in the Labour Party. In the organisational report to the national conference in 1947, we read: "Losses are recorded in Newcastle, Liverpool and Wales." The comrades were forced to cease publication of the *WIN*. The full-time professionals were: Ted Grant, Jock Haston, Heaton Lee (Wales), Roy Tearse (Glasgow), and George Smith (Business Manager). The unpaid professionals were Millie Lee, Tom Reilly, and George Nozeda.

I analysed the situation in an article comparing the Labour Government with the previous one in 1929-31, which was published in the *Socialist Appeal* in October 1947.

"The striking difference between the position in 1929 and the present", stated the article, "is that in the former case, powerful opposition developed within the Labour Party on home affairs, which assumed terrible urgency in the lives of the workers. In the previous Labour Government, the foreign policy was based on pacifist demagogy and was largely endorsed by the 'lefts'. What feeble opposition has developed in the Labour Party and Parliamentary Party today has been on the issue of foreign policy. But the opposition on foreign policy collapsed because of the weakness of British imperialism, which resulted in the forced withdrawal from India, partly from Egypt, and now the government declaration regarding its preparedness to withdraw from Palestine. Moreover, an opposition, while it is confined in the main to foreign affairs, cannot hope to attract the support of the broad masses away from the right wing. Thus, the right wing Labour leaders have been able, owing to Britain's weakness, to pose as 'liberators' of the colonial peoples with a 'socialist' foreign policy as against the blatantly imperialist policy of Churchill and the previous Tory governments, and even the previous Labour Government.

International meeting in Paris 1946. Colin de Silva speaking and to his right Jock Haston and Pierre Frank

"The policy of the Government on home affairs has been largely endorsed by the so-called opposition - a striking contrast to the situation in the Labour Party in the previous government. An instructive episode was the difference in attitude of the late James Maxton of the ILP, who welcomed enthusiastically the programme of the Third Labour Government and its suggested legislation.

"The collapse of the 'lefts' at the past two conferences of the Labour Party since the formation of the Labour Government, especially the miserable and ignominious defeat at the last one, was not at all accidental but rooted in the objective development of events. In

> contrast to the previous Labour Governments, far from the lefts gaining in support, the present period has been marked even during the dollar crisis, by a strengthening of the right wing leadership in the Labour Party. It reflects the mass consciousness in the past two years. It is a law of development within the mass organisations of the working class, that left reformist or centrist currents develop on the basis of deep-seated opposition to the right wing leadership on the part of the rank and file. Currents of opposition within the Labour movement will not flourish without mass backing. The 'leaders' are pushed from below by the pressure of the rank and file. It is thus that the processes in the country reflect themselves through the opportunist leaders inside parliament and within the mass movement. Where deep-seated processes of differentiation have not taken place, the 'opposition' can only make the feeblest of gestures."

Only on the basis of huge events would the situation change. However, in the meantime, this difficult situation was having repercussions in our ranks. The so-called leadership of the International, and Healy in particular, were attempting to feed on the understandable mood of disappointment. As always, under such circumstances, some comrades began to look for miracles or some short cut to solve our problems and offer a way out of this impasse. Then Pierre Frank - the Molinierite of yesterday (who incidentally had the delusion that we would actually win the seat in the Neath by-election), gave Healy the idea of entry into the Labour Party.

Healy moves to a split

Having been decisively defeated in the organisation on all the other questions, Healy began to beat the drum for immediate entry into the Labour Party and, given the prevailing mood, began to get an echo on this question. This was especially the case among those sections of the tendency that were faltering and becoming increasingly tired and disillusioned. These layers began to see entry into the Labour Party as a magic solution and it began to gain certain support. In the North East, T. Dan Smith and a few other ILP people went over to Healy's position. Smith was actually absorbed by the Labour Party, where he went to the right, gained a controlling position on the council and eventually achieved national notoriety in a huge corruption scandal. A similar process took place in a number of branches throughout the country. Those comrades who were worn out, and were in effect moving towards reformism, or even dropping out of the movement entirely, found in the slogan of Labour Party entry a golden excuse to pursue their inclinations. So, whereas Healy and his supporters had been a tiny minority in the past, for the first time he was now able to build a certain base inside the RCP.

We explained in the discussions that this position was entirely false. Examining the question objectively it was quite clear that the classic conditions for entry as laid down by Trotsky did not exist in any shape or form. These conditions were the development of a pre-revolutionary crisis, the capitalist regime in a blind alley, and the radicalisation of the working class. This would in turn reflect itself within the Labour Party as the development of a mass left wing, the growth of centrist tendencies, a weakening of the Labour bureaucracy, and the possibility of a rapid development of a revolutionary tendency. Of course, there had been a certain radicalisation preceding the election of the Labour Government, arising from the war, and just after the election, which stemmed from the measures that the Labour Government initially took. But this certainly was not the radicalisation Trotsky spoke of, and did not constitute even the beginnings of the classical conditions for entry into a reformist organisation.

The internal life of the party was at a very low ebb at this time. Rather than a party in the throes of crisis, the grip of reformism inside the Labour Party had been greatly increased. The Party was solidly in the grip of a right wing that was confident and moving forward. It was firmly controlled by a reinforced and strengthened bureaucracy. This was especially the case in the early post-war years. There were objective reasons for this. In contradiction to what we had predicted, the reformists, were actually carrying through reforms. From the standpoint of the Labour Party rank-and-file the reformist leadership appeared to be implementing a socialist programme of the nationalisation of the basic industries. Of course, as revolutionaries, we knew that the Government was only carrying through a certain re-organisation of the system in the interests of capitalism. Expressed in Marxist terms it was a programme of state capitalism. But this is not how the members and supporters of the Labour Party saw it.

The very first act of the Labour Government was to repeal the anti-trade union Trade Disputes Act of 1927, introduced by the Tories after the defeat of the General Strike. They also introduced the National Health Service which for the first time provided a universally free health service. In contrast to the great depression that preceded the war, there was full employment. Living standards were beginning to rise. These factors conditioned the outlook of the workers. Such was the credit extended by the working class to the Labour Government, that by 1948, both the TUC and the Labour Party Conferences had accepted without protest the need for "austerity" to assist the Government, including a wage freeze.

Knowing this to be the case, Healy and the others attempted to dress things up, presenting a completely false perspective and going from one mistake to another. Healy now maintained that the conditions for entrism would quickly develop as Britain was facing immediate slump, mass unemployment, and so on. The Healy faction spoke of the situation as if it was the beginning of the end of capitalism and the last crisis of capitalism. They echoed all the stupid arguments of the Stalinists in the "social-fascist" period. Mirroring the arguments of Mandel and Pablo, Healy really believed that we were in a classical slump. When the fuel crisis hit Britain, they repeated the same things, saying it was the end of capitalism. We had to explain to them that the fuel crisis was only temporary, and that in fact it was caused by a lack of fuel, precisely as a result of the expansion of the economy. This was clearly the opposite of what they were arguing - not a crisis of over-production, but a crisis of under-production. Britain at that time was certainly not experiencing the capitalist crisis that Marx spoke of!

Despite this, Healy wrote a document in the middle of 1946 saying that Britain was on the edge of an economic disaster:

> "In Britain itself there has been an absolute and relative decline in the conditions of industry, a deterioration of the productive apparatus and a fall in the productivity of labour, with the exception of the war industries - aviation, engineering, shipbuilding and chemicals, etc...
> "From this it is evident that British capitalism is on the edge of an abyss... the carefully patched-up internal economy will collapse into either uncontrolled inflation or later, when the competition relates to world price values, into equally disastrous deflation...
> "Our perspectives must be based upon the developing crisis which will exceed in scope and magnitude the depression that set in during the winter of 1920." [5]

The "theoreticians" of the International backed up this ridiculous view. Ernest Mandel is apparently regarded as an expert on Marxist economics, on account of a very bad book on the subject that he wrote some years ago. In fact, Mandel was a vulgar eclectic with an extremely superficial grasp of Marxist economics and Marxism in general. This will immediately become evident to anyone who takes the trouble to read what he wrote over the years, beginning with the period we are considering here.

In reply to the RCP leadership, Mandel wrote that "in the period of capitalist decadence British Industry *can no longer* overgrow the state of revival and attain one of real boom." There was "at most a boom in some isolated industries which does not determine the general aspect of the economy", and that "the situation of the British economy is *not that of a boom* if one wishes to give this term the significance that Marxists have always given to it." The history of the last fifty-five years has dealt rather harshly with his remark that "if the comrades of the RCP majority were to take their own definition seriously, they would logically conclude that we are confronting a 'boom' in ALL CAPITALIST EUROPE, because in all these countries production is 'expanding'". [6] This shows how shallow this great Marxist "economist" really was when dealing with real process, despite his later economic tomes.

Jock Haston speaking at a mass rally at the Salle des Horticulteurs, Paris March 1946

At the time, all the International leaders were peddling this line. Closing their eyes to reality, they obstinately refused to admit that capitalism had entered into a phase of economic upswing. In the IS Pre-Conference resolution, they stated that "this restoration of economic activity in the capitalist countries hit by the war, and in particular in the countries on the European continent, will be characterised by its particularly slow rhythm and these countries will thus remain on a level approaching stagnation and slump." [7]

The only ones who resolutely opposed this position was the leadership of the British section. In an amendment on economic perspectives to the World Congress, drafted by myself, the RCP explained that

> "the argument of the comrades of the American SWP, which has been echoed by the Minority of the British Party, that only after the proletariat has been decisively defeated would American imperialism give loans to assist the recovery of Western European capitalism, has already been demonstrated to be a false one. The proletariat has not been defeated, *but loans have already been granted.* Equally false is the argument that only if the proletariat is decisively defeated can economic recovery and revival take place. Such an argument lumps together political-economic problems visualising an immediate reflection of one upon the other.
>
> "Undoubtedly, a decisive defeat of the proletariat gives the bourgeoisie stability and confidence. But unless the economic pre-conditions for a boom are present, a boom would not necessarily follow even in that event. It is not a law of the development of capitalism that only the defeat of the proletariat in a revolutionary situation can lead to a boom, any more than a slump automatically leads to a revolution. History teaches us that capitalism, even in its death agony, recovers after a slump, despite the revolutionary possibilities, if the proletariat is paralysed or weakened by its organisations and rendered incapable of taking advantage of its possibilities...
>
> We also stated in the amendment that "apart from these political considerations, there are laws of capitalism which themselves ensure the upswing of economy and make a new 'boom' inevitable. Particularly in view of the fact that this crisis is not a crisis of over-production and that the capitalists are not being attacked in Western Europe by the mass organisations, but receive the direct assistance and support of social democracy and Stalinism *a cyclical upswing is inevitable.*" (*WIN*, Nov-Dec 1946)

Healy discovered economic crisis and mass unemployment at a time of full employment in Britain. He actually argued that in order to deal with mass unemployment in Britain, the government was setting up factories in Wales to build alarm clocks so that the unemployed would wake up in time to sign on the dole! Of course, it was all nonsense. The purpose of it was to convince people that a crisis was imminent and that therefore the conditions for entry would be present.

In the same way, they also tried to discover a phantom left wing in the Labour Party. When some semi-fellow traveller in the Labour Party got through a resolution about foreign policy, they made a big fuss: "there look, there's the left wing". In answer, we explained that this was an anecdote, and entirely without importance. Our comrades in the Labour Party - and we had far more than Healy's minority - were asked to give us concrete evidence of any left developments within the party. As Trotsky had suggested, the time for entry will be shown by the people that you already have inside the party. They would give you a realistic picture according to the results they were achieving, and in the mood that existed.

When we asked these comrades in the Labour Party to report on the situation, they unanimously held the opinion that the time was not right. In the report to the 1946 RCP conference, our Labour Party fraction stated "gains in this sphere have been negligible. Our Labour Party faction paper *Militant* has found no echo inside the Labour Party, and reflecting the situation within the Labour Party expresses no live movement within it..." [8] And this was also the opinion of the former Harberites, who were very keen to develop this work. There was nothing much happening in the Labour Party, and no left wing developing at that stage. So on all accounts, the time was not ripe to enter.

However, this cut no ice with the minority. Healy had the support of a minority - perhaps 20 percent of the organisation. Of these, however, a layer went out of the movement very quickly. T. Dan Smith was one of them. Healy could count on the support of 60 or 70 people out of around 350 RCP members. Healy's minority convinced very few industrial workers. He mainly attracted the more middle class elements in our ranks - the typical weathercocks of the party. Under difficult conditions, they were dropping away from the movement and they found a way out in their support for Healy's entrist platform.

The RCP was an extremely democratic party with a healthy internal regime. We did not fear differences but made use of them to educate the membership. For two years or so - from 1945 to 1947 - the conferences of the RCP had conducted full and exhaustive debates on a series of questions, and in particular on entry. Regular bulletins were published covering all the political positions. We had six to eight weeks of intensive discussion before every conference, as well as access to the internal bulletin on disputed questions. These should be reprinted at some stage. They are of great importance historically and essential for the education of the newer comrades in the history of our movement.

Throughout the whole of 1946, the International was pressing the RCP leaders to enter the Labour Party. At the June International Executive Committee (IEC) a resolution was passed urging the British section to concentrate our forces within the Labour Party. The only people to vote against this proposal at the IEC were the RCP comrades. Once again they pressed us in early 1947 to dissolve the RCP and enter the Labour Party. They were backing the Healy minority all the way along the line. In the middle of the year Healy's supporters stated that if they failed to get a majority for entry, they would urge the International to split the British

Jock with Sylvia Cozer, secretary to the Fourth International, Paris 1946

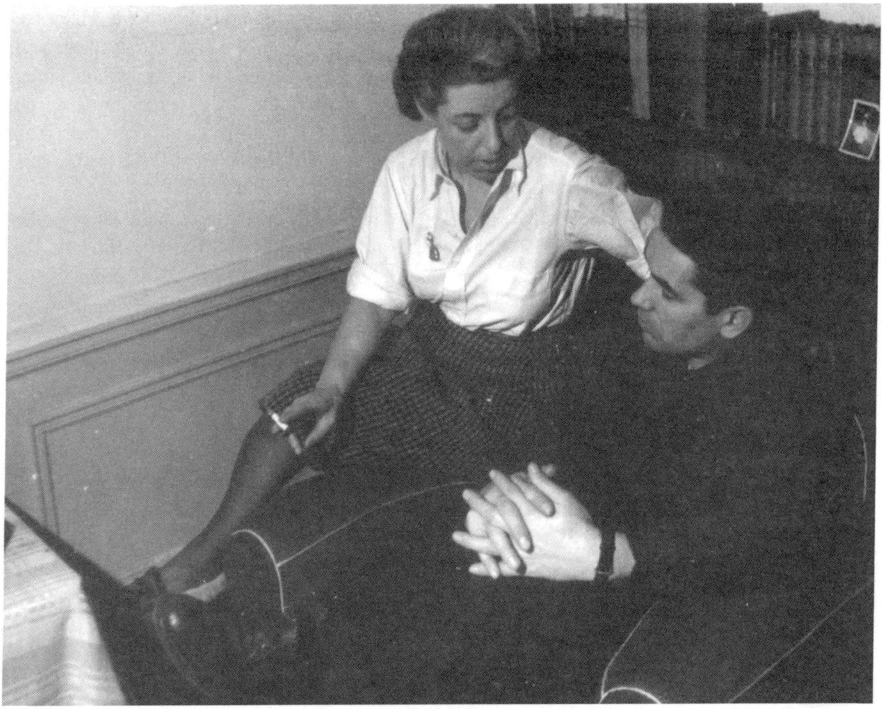

section and allow the minority to enter the Labour Party under their own discipline. The RCP leadership correctly saw this as an ultimatum and a threat to split the organisation. Our conference, which had a further discussion on the question of entry, opposed this attempted split. Positions were now entrenched and Healy failed to gain any further adherents. The factions were set and we had the overwhelming majority of the organisation supporting us - some 80 percent of the tendency. Despite the support of the International and the difficulties we faced in Britain Healy still failed to convince a majority of his position.

At the conference, we decided that we had had a full and free discussion for two years on the question of entry. It had been an exhaustive discussion and that there was no more to be said on the question for the time being. We therefore moved a resolution at the conference that the question was now closed. The discussion could only be opened again in the internal bulletin or at the following conference, when, of course, all questions were open for discussion. Healy and the others opposed this and voted against it. But it was overwhelmingly carried by the conference.

It was clear that the support for Healy had reached its peak. They weren't going to win anybody else and feared that their existing support would melt away if they remained within the organisation. It was only the Labour Party issue that gave them a basis. This was Healy's last opportunity. There was no better time to act. So Healy raised the question of a split. No doubt pre-planned, the IS intervened to back the Healy minority. Healy, now with the open support of the International, wanted to carry through the "international policy" of entrism. He demanded the separation of his tendency from the organisation. Against our wishes, and against the statutes of the International, the IS decided to separate the two organisations under the guidance of the International. Eventually, under protest, the RCP leadership had no alternative but to accept this fact as a *fait accompli.* The RCP majority accurately described this action as "a disgraceful manoeuvre to get rid of the democratically elected leadership of a section of the Fourth International."

The International supported Healy's plan for his faction to enter the Labour Party under their own banner, with their own discipline, and as a recognised official section of the International. They were to be rewarded for what they had done in later years, when Healy would turn against them, but for the time being they were united with Healy against the Haston-Grant leadership. So in October 1947 Healy and his tendency entered the Labour Party, while the RCP carried on the construction of a revolutionary party independently. "After the split took place", according to one of the leading members of Healy's group, "we were instructed to break off all personal relations with supporters of the majority!" [9] This was an indication of what was to come later. The split-off group began to operate the policy known as "deep entrism", or liquidationism, functioning clandestinely within the Labour Party, concealing their ideas and referring to themselves only as "The Club".

Paris 1946. Jimmy Deane (right) discussing with Sylvia Cozer and Dumar

In a certain sense, the departure of the Minority was greeted with great relief. We could now concentrate on building the movement free from factional activity. A thorn had been removed from our side - or so we thought. But the removal of the Minority did not change the fact that the objective situation both nationally and internationally was adverse to the building of a revolutionary tendency. Despite all our efforts we became further isolated from the working class, as illusions in the Labour government became more widespread. Of course, there were times when we would intervene in the class struggle and give a lead. There were times when we succeeded in connecting with the workers, but these successes were becoming less and less frequent. We felt ourselves getting boxed in.

Marxism and the unions

Despite all the problems, we intervened in the class struggle wherever we could - for example, in the strike in the London docks in June 1948. The union (Transport and General Workers) was under the control of the right wing. Therefore, this was a spontaneous rank and file unofficial strike. Contrary to the ultra-left attitude of the sects in strikes, we went to the dockers offering some basic class assistance and advice. We got a friendly response from the workers, who appreciated our help. Disgusted at the role of the right wing leadership of the union, thousands of dockers in all the ports were prepared to tear up their union cards. Some raised the idea of a new breakaway dockers' union, as some kind of panacea to the problems that they faced.

Jock Haston (centre) Jimmy Deane (right) discussing with comrades in Paris

We explained to any militants who would listen to us that such a road would be disastrous for the union and the workers. They should remain and fight within the ranks of the union and try to change it. They had to attend their official union meetings and their branches and start to organise an opposition that could challenge the rule of the right wing. Difficult as that might be, we told them, it was the only real way forward. If they split away from the union, they would separate the more advanced militant layers of the union from the more backward layers. This would then leave the union in the grip of the right wing. In fact it would consolidate their hold on the union. This had always been the classic position of Marxism on this question. Lenin explained this in his book *Left Wing Communism, an Infantile Disorder*. After a period of discussions with the workers and shop stewards, we managed to convince these activists of the correctness of our position.

Jimmy Deane addressing the crowd

Incidentally, a few years later, in 1954, the Healyites took the completely opposite stance. Unbelievably, they urged the dockers to leave the Transport and General Workers Union and join the so-called "Blue" Union, the NASDU. This proved disastrous, as we warned at the time. It resulted in the spread of non-unionism on the docks. The NASDU ended up on the right and was eventually absorbed into the TGWU in 1973. The same insane tactics seem to be a constant feature in the conduct of ultra left elements in the unions. Thus, in 1970 the Cliff group urged workers in the Pilkingtons Glass factory to leave the General and Municipal Workers Union, which was under the control of the rightwing, and create their own Glass Workers Union. This also ended in disaster and many workers were victimised as a result of this debacle. These sectarians never learn, and they do a great deal of damage wherever they are able to get a toe-hold in the workers' movement.

The dock strike revealed the mood in the trade union movement towards the Labour Government at that time. The strike had the sympathy of the majority of the working class. Despite the fact that the dockers - thanks to their organisation and militancy - were among the highest paid workers, there was complete solidarity from other workers. Yet when the Labour Government sent troops into the docks to break the strike and introduced a state of emergency, there were no protests within the Labour movement - except the ones that we tried to organise.

This was something that would have been unthinkable under the 1924 or 1929-31 Labour Governments. It showed the different atmosphere that now prevailed. The workers had great illusions in the Labour Government. They could be critical of the government, but the overwhelming majority still believed in it. They regarded it as their Labour Government. So the workers were not prepared to oppose the actions of the government. Even when the government sent the troops into the docks as strike-breakers, there was no question of sympathetic strike action from other sections of the working class.

Stalinism strengthened

The situation had changed, and we had a hard period in front of us. How long this would last was impossible to say, maybe a year or two, maybe longer. We certainly never expected it to last 25 years! In any case, we were caught between hammer and anvil - squeezed by the reformists on the one hand, and the Stalinists on the other. The period 1947-49 was also one of the Chinese Revolution. Although it was carried through in a distorted and deformed manner, the revolution in China nevertheless further increased the prestige of the Stalinists. True, the CP also faced difficulties arising from the successes of the Labour Government, but they could bask under the glow of the victories of the Red Army and the achievements of the Stalinists internationally. They regarded themselves as part of an international movement that was registering huge successes in China, Eastern Europe and so on.

At that time, the prestige of the Soviet Union was colossal. So they latched even more slavishly onto the strength of the USSR, which served to sustain them. They had also managed to gain two MPs in the 1945 General Election, Gallacher and Piratin, which was a high point for the Communist Party on the parliamentary plane. At this time, as the Cold War was developing apace, the support they had built up in the Labour Party was largely undermined. The CP had a number of fellow-travellers in the Parliamentary Labour Party - about 18 MP's who were either secret members of the CP or very close to the Party. But they were drastically weakened by their attempt to defend Russian foreign policy. A witch-hunt was launched against the CP within the Labour Party and the trade unions, and a number were expelled for various reasons. This included MPs such as John Platts Mills, Zilliacus, Solley, Lester Hutchinson and DN Pritt. Not only these, but a whole series of other leading people and activists in the Labour Party up and down the country were expelled. This again showed the strong position that the bureaucracy had in the Labour Party.

It is true that after 1947, the first cracks began to appear in the edifice of the Attlee government, coinciding with the beginning of counter-reforms. There was talk of 'austerity' and the first cautious attacks on the working class. At first, these attacks were not considered serious by the labour movement, which saw them as temporary setbacks in the forward march of the Labour Government. Later, the Attlee Government introduced certain charges in the National Health Service, which provoked the resignation of Nye Bevan and Harold Wilson from the government. This served to strengthen the support for Bevan and the other Lefts, and they succeeded in getting themselves elected to Labour's National Executive Committee. Bevan was regarded increasingly as the leader of the Left at this time. Nevertheless, the Left was still very weak. It represented the first rumblings of discontent within the Party. But it certainly did not represent the development of a mass left wing inside the Labour Party, as the Healy group maintained.

The betrayal of the Stalinists and reformists had provided the political preconditions for the revival of capitalism. In Britain, the Labour Government saved capitalism. In Italy and France, the Stalinists played the same role by entering the coalition governments. This effectively eliminated the threat of socialist revolution, provided a valuable breathing space, and allowed, at least in the west, a certain period of social stability. The temporary rehabilitation of western capitalism by the United States was serving to stabilise the situation. Based on huge investments from the United States, there was an enormous development of productive forces taking place in America, Japan, and in Western Europe generally. Capitalism throughout Europe was experiencing a new lease of life.

In the colonial world it was a completely different picture. The Chinese Revolution was reverberating throughout the continent of Asia. The struggle of the colonial peoples unleashed the greatest movement of social and national liberation in history. The struggle against British imperialism in India reached such a peak, that the British were forced to beat a hasty retreat, but not before dividing the living body of India and killing over a million people in the process. In Sri Lanka, formerly Ceylon, Trotskyism built a mass following. In contrast to the rest of the Communist movement, the Lanka Sama Samaja Party expelled the Stalinists from its ranks at the beginning of the war.

After their heroic struggle against British imperialism, the LSSP became the dominant working class party. In 1939, they affiliated to the Fourth International, which provided the International with a mass party. The leadership of the LSSP looked to the International for support and guidance. However, over time they became increasingly disillusioned with the false policies and antics of the International leadership. The seeds of the reformist degeneration of the LSSP, present at this stage, were accentuated by the inability of the international leadership to intervene. This was to constitute a great tragedy for Trotskyism in the Indian Sub-continent. A great part of the responsibility for this development lay with the International leadership, which was not prepared to analyse the situation or its mistakes made in the period 1945-1949.

Trotskyism had also developed a mass following in Indo-China. However, there the movement faced a crushing defeat at the hands of the Stalinists. In late 1945, with the end of the War, the Stalinists seized power in the north under Ho Chi-Minh. The Vietnamese Trotskyists were labelled counterrevolutionaries and brutally massacred by the Stalinist regime. When British troops landed in Saigon, the Stalinist chief of police, Duong bach Mai, rounded up all the Trotskyists at gunpoint. "Having carried out this operation", says Lu sanh Hanh, leader of the LIC, "Tran van Giau, with the agreement of the government in the north, ordered the systematic killing of all Trotskyist elements in the country. Tran van Thach, Ta thu Thau, Phan van Hum and dozens of other revolutionary militants were murdered in circumstances that, to this day, have not been properly established." [10]

In the underdeveloped countries, as a result of the weakness of the revolutionary forces and because of the paralysis of Stalinism and reformism, the revolution did not take place in the classical fashion as in Russia in 1917. Even the mighty Chinese Revolution, the second greatest revolution in history, could not be a pole of attraction for workers in the West because of the deformed way in which it had taken place, and the totalitarian system that had been installed. It was predominantly a peasant movement, and the workers played no independent role in it. Without this there could be no workers' democracy and the movement towards socialism in China. Based on the image of Moscow, the revolution was deformed from the very beginning. As a consequence, it had no great rallying effect on the working class in the advanced industrial countries, particularly in Britain. Thus, on an international scale, the forces of Trotskyism were extremely isolated in this period where capitalism was able to consolidate itself and Stalinism also emerged enormously strengthened.

Weakness of the Left

This situation provided the bourgeoisie with a new lease of confidence. Despite the losses they sustained in Eastern Europe and South Asia, they had managed, with the help of the Stalinists and reformists, to stabilise the situation. The confidence of the bourgeois in their system was also reflected inside the British labour movement, with the strengthening of right wing of reformism. This was later shown by the crushing domination of the Gaitskellites - the Neanderthal right wing, as I baptised them - in the Labour and trade union movement. They contemptuously referred to Marxism as an old-fashioned doctrine left over from the Victorian era. In actual fact, it was the ideas of the reformists that were pre-Marxian. They had already been answered by Marx 120 years previously. But since these ignoramuses who criticised Marx had never read a single line of his, how could they be expected to know this?

The Neanderthal rightwing had big support within the Labour Party and the trade unions. We were entering the long period of domination of the British trade union movement by extreme right wingers like Deakin, Lawther and Carron. Even the Bevanite Left was pretty muted and weak. It had support in the local Labour Parties, but did not represent any tidal movement towards the left. It was a weak and very irresolute tendency. It stood on a far lower political level than the pre-war Lefts in the Labour Party. They could not be compared to leaders like Jimmy Maxton. Even if you compare the speeches of Stafford Cripps and the Socialist League before the war, you will see that they were on a much higher level than the Bevanite Left in the post-war period.

With no mass left wing in the Labour Party the Healyites, despite all their illusions, found a very cool atmosphere within the Party. John Lawrence, who had now returned to the Minority, had made a mess of the position in Wales. From the fifty-odd members that we had there at our height after the successes of the Neath by-election, the RCP had dwindled. This was partly the objective situation, and partly because of Lawrence's own incapacity to stand up against the pressures. He complained about the lack of possibilities, and had delusions about speaking to mass movements as in the good old days of the Neath election. But instead we were reduced to a tiny movement that held small meetings in Neath every Sunday. The crowds that originally wanted to hear what we had to say had melted away. Over a period, Lawrence reduced the organisation in Wales to a shambles.

We understood that times were difficult, and that losses were inevitable, but we could at least hold the majority of our forces together until things improved. We had succeeded in consolidating the tendency nationally on the basis of Marxist education and sober perspectives and a practical explanation of the situation. We inoculated the best of our worker comrades against the pressures, and so in most areas, we had kept our forces relatively intact in the period 1947-1949.

When the Minority entered the Labour Party, they adopted a completely opportunist position. "Healy was arguing in favour of comrades concealing their political views, and the main job of comrades was to get into positions in the Labour Party, trade unions, etc., and keep one's political position as dark as possible..." relates Ellis Hillman, a supporter of Healy at the time, who later broke with him and came over to us. [11] Instead of growing, as they had expected, the Healyite organisation was suffering from stagnation and going through a crisis. From the bits and pieces of information we got, the Healyites were in the doldrums. They had no publication of their own, and were floundering in their efforts to recruit to their tendency. Despite all their boasts about a mass left wing in the Labour Party, they hadn't got the results that they had expected.

Of course, Healy and Co. tried to put the responsibility for their failings onto the shoulders of the RCP. They accused us of obstructing their work, and so on. All of which was complete nonsense. They complained that our Labour Party comrades were deliberately blocking and undermining their work in the Party. So Healy complained bitterly to his supporters in the International leadership. He cynically manipulated and used the International for his own ends, whereas the International leadership, of course, imagined that they were manipulating Healy. As a result, we had a visit from one of Pablo's faithful henchmen, Jacques Privas. He was one of the leaders of the French Trotskyists and also a member of the IS. He came to see us at our headquarters at Harrow Road. He arrived on the scene inquiring about Healy's complaints against the RCP leadership and their allegations that we were destroying their work. We could see straight away that it was just a set-up. We told him we had no interest in the Healyites or their Labour Party work. We were certainly not interested in "fingering them" to the bureaucracy and the rest of it, as they had also claimed. We scrupulously avoided even mentioning the Healy group in our public material. We let them carry on with their own devices, and we carried on with ours. But as Healy was in difficulties, he tried to put the responsibility on our shoulders.

May Day 1947

Privas, as we expected, believed Healy's story. Then he dropped his bombshell. He told us that he had an ultimatum from the IS. Unless we were prepared to withdraw our forces from the Labour Party, or place our forces in the Labour Party under Healy's control, the International would be forced to reconsider our whole position as an official section of the International. He was simply holding a gun to our head. This was a position that we could not accept. This whole business was having a demoralising effect, especially on Jock Haston, who became disorientated by the experience.

Notes:

1- In *Reply to David James,* 1948.
2- See RCP *Internal Bulletin,* 4 August 1946.
3- Ibid.
4- *Writings of Leon Trotsky, 1938-39,* p.252.
5- H. Finch, G. Healy, J. Goffe and J. Lawrence, *The Turn to Mass Work,* 17 July 1946, in *Internal Bulletin* of the RCP. Pp.1-6, quoted in *War and the International*, p.189.
6- Quoted in *War and the International,* p.190.
7- Quoted in *WIN*, Nov-Dec 1946.
8- *The Party Organiser,* No. 8, September 1946, p.7.
9- Ratner, op. cit., p.123.
10- Ngo Van, *Revolutionaries They Could not Break*, London 1995, p.162.
11- Quoted in *War and the International,* p. 210.

May Day 1947 Jimmy Hinchcliffe (under banner) Andy Sharf (far right)

5

End of an Era-
The Last Years of the RCP

In the period between 1947 and 1949 we were painfully attempting to construct a tendency piecemeal. We were gaining ones and twos, and we were also losing small numbers. In general, our forces were relatively intact, but our financial resources were constantly depleted. All our difficulties became focused largely on financial questions. When the movement is going ahead you get money from sympathisers, contacts, and supporters. But when things go badly, these sources of finance dry up to a large extent. During the war, we had had a couple of well-off sympathisers who had given us reasonable sums of money. Now, their sympathies had changed. They were influenced by the moods that were developing in society. They said, in effect, we are in business, and we only deal with results. We want to see the revolutionary movement developing. But this is no longer the case and from being enthusiastic supporters of the revolution, they now started to look towards other things.

One sympathiser I have in mind made a fortune out of paintings. It started as a hobby with him. But as his enthusiasm for the revolution waned, his attention turned increasingly towards art and paintings. Then, one day, he decided he didn't want to waste any more money on the revolution, and so this source of funds dried up. He turned his energies to paintings, and he made a fortune. Our main rich backer, however, was a hat manufacturer called Spiregen. He gave us a lot of money and sustained the movement for a long time. But that source also dried up. So, recognising our difficulties, we were forced to cut down on the number of full-time professionals from sixteen to around six or seven. The costs of the paper had to be paid for and printing costs were rising astronomically at that time. So we had to cut down the size of the *Socialist Appeal*. In the end, because of lack of resources, we had to shift from a fortnightly to a monthly paper. We still looked forward confidently to a change in the situation, even if the current position should last some years. However, at this point, we were certainly swimming against the stream.

It was at this point that Jock Haston was feeling the pressure. He was ill and was suffering from stomach ulcers at that time. He was clearly run down. He had done an enormous amount of work during the war and in the years that followed. Jock was becoming increasingly disillusioned with the leaders of the International. It must be said, he had certain illusions in the International - illusions that were not shared by other comrades, myself included. Towards the end of the war and in the immediate post war period, Jock had become increasingly despondent with the wrong perspectives that we had put forward during the course of the war, epitomised by our 1942 pamphlet *Preparing for Power*. Of course, we had corrected the perspective, and analysed the situation that was unfolding. However, Jock was sick and worn out, and tended to see things in a negative way.

The roots of our difficulties lay in the objective situation. It bore down on all of us, including the leadership. Haston was a giant of a man. I have no qualms about saying this, despite his later abandonment of Trotskyism. He had without doubt tremendous qualities. However, although he had a lot of political acumen and a certain theoretical level, he tended to be more of a political activist and an organiser than a theoretician. Under these growing pressures, by the autumn of 1948, Haston began to look for a way out. He was becoming less active. In disgust at the way things were turning out, and no doubt influenced by his subjective doubts about the movement, he raised the question of entry into the Labour Party.

In December 1948 this question was formally raised by Haston in the Political Bureau. At the meeting of the Political Bureau he maintained that this proposal was being made without the illusions of Healy. There was no suggestion that big gains could be made in the Labour Party at this time. But what it amounted to, in effect, was that Haston was throwing in the towel. There was a discussion and a vote, and he found himself in a minority of one in the Political Bureau. He was completely isolated. So Haston decided to resign from his position as general secretary in order to argue his case within the ranks of the organisation.

Harold Atkinson, who was one of the leaders and organisers of the RCP, had just returned from America from a business trip. He was very agitated by the situation. If Haston wasn't supported, it would be a disaster for the organisation, he insisted. If the truth is to be told, Atkinson was unfortunately in the same demoralised state as Haston. He put his full weight behind Haston and said we had no alternative but to enter the Labour Party. So we arranged another discussion in the Political Bureau on Haston's proposal. This time, Haston and Atkinson between them managed to gain a majority, and the proposal was taken to the Central Committee on 8 and 9 December. Their resolution concluded,

> "We propose therefore, to raise as the key question before the party, the dissolution of the RCP as an independent organisation and the entry of our members into the Labour Party.
>
> "We propose that the dissolution should be by public declaration. The supporters of our tendency should be prepared by a series of articles and the leadership of the party should approach the Labour Party with the object of securing the best results from the public entry of the RCP into the Labour Party. It follows that the IS should be informed of the proposed orientation, and if it is accepted by the majority of the party, negotiations should be opened with the object of working together with our co-thinkers." (Statement on the Perspective of the RCP, by J. Haston, H. Atkinson, R. Tearse, and V. Charles).

On the Political Bureau, only Jimmy Deane and myself were strongly opposed to entry. We were now in a minority within the leadership. The majority of the top leadership of the RCP had now gone over to a position of entrism - not the classical entrism that Trotsky had put forward, with a great perspective of growth. But entrism that would allow us just to hold our forces together within the framework of the Labour Party. The PB Majority wrote:

> "At the September 1947 Conference of the RCP, after a drawn out and bitter struggle around the tactic of entry, the Party set its course with the utmost confidence on the basis of the open tactic.
>
> "We believe we could go forward on the basis of modest gains, entrenching and consolidating our position, and thus maintaining our forces in the best possible way until the economic and political situation changed to our advantage. But the cumulative effect of our position has necessitated a reassessment of our past perspective....
>
> "In this document we hope to place before the members our positive outlook on the future perspectives and tasks of the party. We leave aside here a number of problems which have been raised, some of which have already been dealt with in the *Reply to the IS*, others which we hope to deal with in future bulletins....
>
> "It is now our opinion that it is wrong to wait until the Labour Party milieu is in ferment, then step into the left wing already formed and hope to take over the leadership. It is clearly an illusion to imagine that workers will follow us merely on the basis of our ideas. The workers will follow us when they have learned to trust us in the course of working together. An acceptance of the perspective that future political developments will centre mainly around the Labour Party, means acceptance of the need to participate in the left wing....
>
> "We cannot, of course, build the revolutionary left wing in conditions which are not favourable for its formation. But we can create a basis for our tendency by building up a cadre of national and local leaders and crystallise the left critics who undoubtedly exist in the Labour Party...
>
> "The whole nature of the objective situation determines that we face a period of hard and patient work. We hold no illusions of rapid growth. It is rather a question of building up over the next period a revolutionary trend in the labour movement which will form the basis for the future." [1]

The International lost no opportunity in sticking in the boot, accusing the Majority of liquidationism.

> "This document is the expression of liquidationist tendencies", stated the IS. It went on to denounce the RCP for taking a quick "position which helped the opponents of the International, Morrow, Shachtman... Halt! Out of the road of Shachtman, Morrow, Demaziere and other deserters of the Fourth International!.. To enable the International to cooperate with you in drawing a clear political and organisational balance-sheet of your activity which has ended in bankruptcy....", etc. etc.
>
> And again:
>
> "There is great danger because the policy of the comrades depends on nothing. Nothing is to be done because reformism is transforming the working class; nothing is to be done because Stalinism is achieving victories for the working class. They have not much hope to build the Trotskyist organisation; they have no hope in the development of the Fourth International. The proposal of entry looks like the act of a desperate man drowning himself in deep water." [2]

Jimmy Deane and myself, isolated in the leadership, were in a profound dilemma. It was clear that entry into the Labour Party could not solve our problems. That is why we originally opposed it at the Political Bureau and the Central Committee. That didn't mean that the open party was going to produce miracles either. To be honest, given the objective situation, entry or non-entry would not have made any fundamental difference. Outside the Labour Party we wouldn't gain much under the existing circumstances, but inside the Labour Party we wouldn't gain much either! Looking back on it, we made an opportunist mistake. It was difficult to see at the time. In hindsight it is much clearer.

We believed that we had a fundamental responsibility to maintain the organisation. The WIL and the RCP had shown its mettle in the period 1938-48. The organisation had been reinforced by the experience of the whole period, during and after the war, when we had been educated in the debates on a whole host of question, including entrism and revolutionary tactics. We knew that if we conducted a political struggle over this question to maintain the open party, we would undoubtedly have gained the overwhelming majority of the organisation. Haston and the majority of the Political Bureau would have certainly been isolated. But the problem that we faced was that they were the top leaders of the organisation. We had built up this leadership in a period of common work for ten years or so, and we didn't want to throw it away.

Experienced cadres are precious. They are created in the course of struggle. Our cadres had been tested in the course of the war, the Newcastle trials, the Neath by-election, and so on. They had been tested by the war itself, the pressures of capitalism, reformism, and Stalinism. They had maintained themselves under fire. They were extremely talented people. Therefore, Jimmy and I were in a terrible quandary. What were we to do? We agonised over the question and decided, rightly or wrongly, that it was a question of attempting to preserve the leadership. We wanted to maintain the leadership at all costs for the future. And so we decided not to oppose the proposals of the PB majority. This was a bad mistake, and one that had unforeseen consequences.

We stated that we wouldn't campaign on the question in the ranks of the organisation. At this point, myself, Jimmy and George Hansen, the PB minority, issued a statement to all members.

> "The discussion has not convinced us that in the present situation entry would constitute a superior tactic", it said. "However, faced with the fact that the overwhelming majority of the leadership and the trained cadres, and substantial sections of the rank and file are in favour of entering the Labour Party, and given that the objective situation will be a difficult one for the Party, we believe that a struggle would be sterile…
>
> "We do not believe that there are great opportunities for the growth of our movement at present wherever we operate. In this period the most important task consists in the maintenance of the unity of the organisation, the intensification of the education of our cadres and raising the theoretical level of the entire organisation. These tasks will pose themselves as vital for the future, whether we are inside or outside."
>
> The statement then concluded, "Under these circumstances, we do not believe it is in the best interests of the movement to wage a struggle on this issue." (*Letter to the Members* by Ted Grant, Jimmy Deane and George Hanson).

Whatever we did - in or outside the Labour Party - we might gain ones and twos and very small numbers at best. It was a hard choice. In the present climate, it was difficult to sell papers, gain contacts, and generally get an audience for revolutionary ideas. We understood that inside the Labour Party or outside the Labour Party, it wouldn't make all that much difference. Under the circumstances, we were not prepared to wage a struggle. We said quite openly that our aim was to save the leadership. If we can go into the Labour Party and keep our organisation intact, then, perhaps at a later stage when the classic conditions for entrism existed, which would inevitably arise at a certain stage, we would be able to connect with the mass left wing. The conditions for entrism would inevitably arise in the future, and if we remained outside, we would have then had to enter the Labour Party under those circumstances. So, at this stage, and from that point of view, it wouldn't matter all that much if we were inside or outside.

Our overriding aim was to maintain intact as many of the forces as possible, particularly the leadership. Had we succeeded, there would have been no problem. In any case, it would not have been as disastrous as it eventually turned out to be. But, looking back on it, it is now clear we would probably have lost Haston anyway. We may also have lost Roy Tearse, as well as Atkinson, and some other leading comrades. It is not absolutely certain what would have happened. But, at any rate, most of the forces within the movement would have been retained, particularly the active rank and file. We would have at least kept the core of the RCP and had a national organisation and profile.

On 8 and 9 January 1949, the Central Committee endorsed the PB Majority statement, signed by Haston, Atkinson, Tearse and Charles. But then in February, the younger rank and file comrades of the organisation, led by Sam Bornstein, Sam Levy, Alf Snobel, Arthur Deane - none of whom were on the Central Committee of the organisation - raised the banner of the Open Party, and declared themselves a faction. They refused to go into the Labour Party and wanted to maintain the open party at all costs. They produced a statement entitled *The Case for the Open Party* signed by 14 comrades. The statement concluded by pointing to the low level of industrial struggle, the right wing ascendancy within the Labour Party and "that the conditions are the most unfavourable for entry that we know of, and the complete negation of the conditions necessary for entry outlined by Trotsky and by our party since." It also attacked myself under the heading of *The Strange Case of Comrade Grant*, stating that my position was contradictory. That the open party was correct for this period, but given the position of the leadership, I had acquiesced.

A further document was produced by the Open Party faction entitled *Once Again - the Real Situation in Britain*, which gave a fuller explanation of their position and quoting the past position of comrades who opposed entry, who had come out now in favour of entry. In conclusion it stated, "we believe not merely that the open party can be maintained, but that there is even the possibility of small growth. They accused the entrists of "clutching at 'entry' in sheer despair."

Jimmy Deane and I were taken completely by surprise. We weren't prepared for this and were taken off our guard. If we had foreseen this development, we possibly would have taken a different attitude. Given our "neutral" position, and our unpreparedness to engage in a struggle, these comrades regarded Jimmy Deane and myself with complete hostility. Because they did not have sufficient authority in the ranks, they could not gain a majority. As far as they were concerned, we had let the party down. So they organised an Open Party faction and gained support, possibly about 25 percent support, among the rank and file. The Haston position also got around 25 percent support, while the rest were mainly undecided.

In an endeavour to frighten the organisation, and as a result maybe of inexperience, and possibly even of a certain political spite, the Open Party faction said that if the RCP decided to go into the Labour Party - and they saw this as a distinct possibility - then we would have to accept the leadership of Healy. My God! That was a terrible prospect. The Open Party comrades said Healy would have been shown to be correct in 1947. After all, he raised the question of entry into the Labour Party first, although completely incorrectly, and had pursued an opportunist path. Nevertheless, if the RCP dissolved and we entered the Labour Party, we would have to accept the leadership of Healy. Both Jimmy and myself were absolutely horrified at this idea, and we objected vehemently to this proposal, as we understood what would happen. I insisted on certain conditions otherwise we must totally oppose the fusion. But Haston, disoriented by the tiredness and ill health that was affecting his judgement, went along with this incredible idea of accepting Healy's leadership at least for a period.

We couldn't believe our ears! We had set the avalanche in motion and we couldn't stop it. There is always the danger, if you take an opportunist position, if you do not take a firm and principled attitude, even on a tactical question, you can box yourself into a corner. The Open Party faction was saying that there could not be two separate groups operating the same tactic. Although we opposed firmly the question of giving the Healyites leadership of the tendency, we couldn't stop the ground shifting under us. We argued that we had three times as many members as Healy, and it was ludicrous to accept his leadership. Then the International leadership intervened with great joy written all over their faces. Privas, following the orders of Pablo, underlined the point that the RCP would be disaffiliated from the Fourth International if they did not accept Healy's leadership. This was seized on by the Open Party faction comrades, who stressed the point that to enter the Labour Party meant to fuse with Healy on his terms, since this was the position of Pablo and the leadership of the International.

Theoretically, we could possibly have accepted the leadership of Healy - if the leading body, the national committee of the organisation represented the actual political balance within the organisation, as we had a majority of the membership. But that was certainly not Healy's idea. And he had the backing of the International. On 4, 5, and 6 June 1949, a special conference was called to discuss the question. A letter of "greetings" was addressed to the conference on behalf of the IS. After a series of attacks on the "liquidationist and pro-Stalinist" trends within the RCP, it concluded that *"a correct attitude of the RCP to the International is yet to come* and one of the main tasks of the leading comrades is to educate the organisation along these lines." The greetings also included an attack on my supposedly "soft" reply to David James. A reply was sent by the CC, drafted by myself, taking up their criticisms:

> "You complain that James' conclusions have not been dealt with by Grant. How can you say that? James has illusions in Tito and Mao. We believe Grant answered in the only convincing and educational way - by dealing with the reactionary aspects of Titoism and Chinese Stalinism. The major part of Grant's reply deals precisely with the question of whether Tito and Mao are 'unconscious Trotskyists' 'bypassing' the Fourth International in the struggle against the Stalinist (Russian) bureaucracy. We cannot fail to comment here that your uncritical letter to the Yugoslav Communist Party precisely lends weight to the point of view that Tito is an 'unconscious Trotskyist'. If you think Grant's reply inadequate, the task is for you to reply to James. Nobody can prevent you from condemning us for failing to answer James in the way you think it should have been done. But having done so, you have to realise

> that theoretical problems are not solved by denunciations, particularly when these are not accompanied with any theoretical rebuttal. You cannot expect us to counter James with your theoretical ideas, particularly in the light of your position on Eastern Europe, and, speaking frankly, we are not sure how you will build a case against James in line with your letter to the Yugoslav CP." (25 June 1949)

In the end the Special Conference voted by a majority in favour of dissolving the RCP and entering the Labour Party. On the issue of Healy's leadership of the organisation, we voted against, but we found ourselves in the minority. One of the reasons for this was that the Open Party faction voted in favour of the proposal! The last special issue of *Socialist Appeal*, announcing the dissolution of the RCP, came out in July 1949. It read as follows:

> "After a two-day debate, this fully representative Conference decided, by a substantial majority, to dissolve the organisation and call upon the members of the Party to enter the Labour Party - to which the majority already pay the trade union political levy - as individual members. Within the Labour Party they would carry on the fight for the overthrow of the capitalist system and for a socialist Britain".
>
> It concluded: "we would prefer to have the right to enter the Labour Party as an organised body, affiliated in the same manner as the Fabian Society and other organisations. But this is not possible owing to the 1946 decision of the Labour Party regarding organisations seeking affiliation. We have therefore dissolved our organisation and will fight as individual members, within the framework of the Constitution of the Labour Party, for the policy outlined above. By dissolving the Revolutionary Communist Party and entering the Labour Party as individual members we consider we will best play our part in aiding the British workers to reach their socialist goal." This was signed by Jock Haston on behalf of the Committee of Dissolution.

Looking back on things, this was a big setback for the movement. The conference set up a commission to carry through the fusion. As expected, with the backing of the International, Healy got a majority on the Political Bureau and a majority on the National Committee. Despite the size of our support, we weren't even going to get a single full-timer, as the leading bodies, which were dominated by Healy, would choose these positions. Under the fusion terms, the majority had to accept the leadership of the minority until the following conference. This conference would be organised to assess the fusion and then elect a new leadership. The problem was, Healy being Healy, he would use every rotten means to destroy the old RCP leadership and take control of the organisation. The man was a gangster and would revert to any means to get a majority, as events subsequently proved.

This was the fatal thing about entry. It wouldn't have been so damaging if we had entered with our own forces under the control of the RCP leadership. That was our position, but Haston as well as the Open Party fraction had rejected it. The other option, which also could have avoided the break-up, would have been to support the Open Party faction. But after the liquidation of the RCP, things started to unwind at a considerable speed.

Having accomplished what he had set out to do Healy received a new access of confidence. He experienced an injection of adrenaline. As far as he was concerned, he had been shown to be correct in the struggle he had started in 1943. Then he began, as one might expect, a real campaign against the RCP leaders. He wanted to make sure that he had the majority by the time of the next conference. We didn't have any full-timers, and so were compelled to seek work. Then Healy went up and down the country and for anyone who was in opposition, it was chop, chop, chop. Anyone who wasn't prepared to accept Healy's domination completely was expelled even without a report to the National Committee. This happened for instance to Bill Cleminson, a leading engineering worker in Sheffield, and a member of the Central Committee, as well as other comrades in Sheffield. They were just chopped off. In Newcastle, David James, who was in opposition in the RCP over our position on China, was also booted out. Alec Riach, and the leading comrades in Scotland, when they saw what was happening, simply left. I felt utter disgust. Our tendency was dissolving in front of our eyes. Our only hope was to muster as much opposition as possible for the Club conference.

Jock Haston

However, in the period leading up to the conference, Haston came up to me and said that he had had enough, and that he was leaving the organisation. He said he still considered himself a Trotskyist - a position he held for some time after leaving. "I still maintain my position of Trotskyism", he said, "but I can't stand the atmosphere in this organisation any longer." We pleaded to him, "For God's sake, Jock, wait until the conference itself. At least keep quiet and let us wage a struggle, while we still have the opportunity of getting a majority in the organisation. We can then put it on the same footing as the best days of the RCP. But if you walk out now, we can see what will happen. You will simply give the Healyites an opportunity to destroy the organisation altogether."

But all our efforts were in vain. Haston was obviously a broken man. He wasn't really concerned about the movement any longer; he was only interested in himself. That was what it amounted to in the end. He had completely lost his perspective and faith in the revolutionary movement. He was totally demoralised, even at that stage, though he still considered himself a Trotskyist. He refused to accept our argument to wait until the conference, and sent a letter of resignation from the organisation to the Political Bureau in February 1950. Haston was then formally expelled from the Club the following month.

This was just the opportunity Healy had been waiting for. As soon as Healy received Haston's letter of resignation, he said, "Ah! We've got them at last!" He immediately called a special meeting, an aggregate in London, and sent out a directive to the provinces to attend. At this aggregate, he and John Lawrence, the joint leaders of the tendency at that time, moved a resolution condemning Haston. The resolution stated that Haston was a renegade and a traitor, and that any member found talking to Haston, or having any relations whatsoever with Haston, would be immediately expelled from the organisation.

Of course, we fought against this hooligan attitude of Healy. It may have been possible, if we could have retained friendly relations with Haston, to have saved him politically and brought back into the movement. This has happened before, when individuals have fallen by the wayside and been drawn back in later. At least a friendly approach and sympathetic attitude could have politically neutralised Haston. But for Healy, such an approach was impossible. It was completely ruled out. Healy wanted revenge for the past. For him, Haston was now an enemy of the movement, and a traitor to the working class! Of course, treated in this fashion, branded a class traitor, Haston began to shift to the right, ending up sadly in the camp of the reformist bureaucracy.

Healy used the opportunity to carry through a widespread purge throughout the organisation. He set about creating a climate of absolute intolerance. Up and down the country he closed or amalgamated branches before the conference. In the RCP, I had been a member of the North London branch, and maintained the support of the branch. To undermine my position, Healy quite arbitrarily moved a resolution in the Political Bureau to reorganise the branch and moved me to a branch in East London, where Bill Hunter was the leading light. Hunter, who in the RCP had shown a tendency towards anarchistic and undisciplined behaviour, which we tolerated, now became an obedient tool of Healy.

Following the aggregate, Healy came down to my branch to explain his resolution against Haston. Once Healy had finished, a comrade called Dave Black objected: "But Comrade Healy, what am I to do when you are moving a resolution like that in relation to Haston? I have a wife who is a member of the IKD. [An organisation in opposition to the International] "Do you expect me to refuse to talk to my wife?" Healy's answer was typical of the man: "Well, comrade, get another wife!" This is an actual fact. Needless to say, the comrade concerned immediately left the movement. Healy was a complete hooligan. I do not need to say any more on this because I think these examples speak for themselves.

The decision to move me to another branch just before the conference was completely unprincipled. But Healy was not satisfied with this. After being forced to give up full-time work, I managed to get a job as a door-to-door salesman, which at least allowed me some free time to organise our political intervention. It allowed me the opportunity to participate actively in the pre-conference period and in the discussions that went on in the run up to the conference. So Hunter moved, through Healy, obviously on Healy's instructions, that I should give up my current job and get a job in a factory. Of course I refused to accept this proposal. I just laughed at the idea. I asked Hunter what sort of a manoeuvre was this? It was clearly an attempt to stop my political preparations before the conference. Then when I refused, Hunter moved my expulsion at the branch and they voted to expel me. It seems difficult to imagine, doesn't it? But this was absolutely typical of Healy and his stooges. However, they were forced to backtrack, under pressure from the International, which preferred to take a more cautious line on my expulsion.

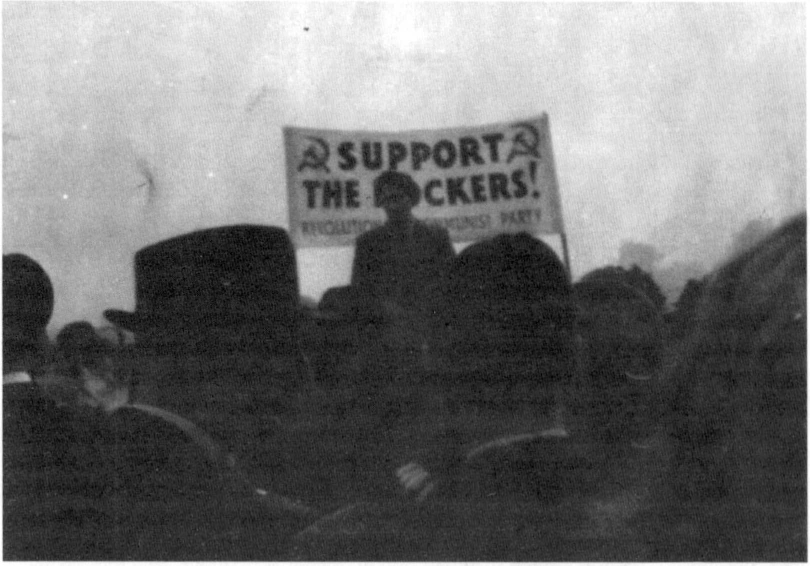

With Haston out of the way, and his hands completely freed, Healy's next move was to proceed against his "enemies", as he called them. Before the collapse of the RCP, Tony Cliff had about a dozen people supporting his state capitalist position. He now gained about twenty or thirty people out of the debacle that took place. A layer now supported Cliff as a reaction against the pro-Stalinist position of the Healy leadership. It is clear that Healy by his very nature was a totalitarian. He had nothing in common with the genuine methods of Trotskyism, and everything in common with the methods of Stalinism.

Healy decided to call an aggregate to "deal with" Tony Cliff. The supporters of Cliff put forward their views on state capitalism, and Healy was furious. I simply waited to see what line Healy would put forward. Healy turned to me and said, "why don't you answer him?" I replied, "you are supposed to be the leader, you answer him!" But they were politically incapable of answering Cliff's arguments on state capitalism. So, of course, Healy just expelled Cliff and his supporters on various charges. When Cliff's supporters wanted to present their document to the conference, they were refused. Later in the year, Cliff set up the *Socialist Review* group.

When Haston was expelled from the IEC and the International, he was accused of "shameful desertion", which was "the logical outcome of all the opportunist and liquidationist policy and of the hostility to the International which Haston, as the head of the ex-RCP, has personally shown during the whole of the last years..." The resolution asserted that his abandonment of Trotskyism was a reflection of "the pressure of the class enemy on the ideologically weaker and more confused elements in the movement." Then the IEC gave Healy the green light for an all-out purge, having approved "all the measures of revolutionary discipline taken by the English leadership against the deserters for the safeguarding of the programme and the organisation." It went on to demand "that all the British Trotskyists, loyal to revolutionary Marxism and the International, should fight with the utmost energy all complacency towards Haston and those demoralised elements who have followed him." [3]

Thus, having expelled Cliff for his ideas, they then moved a resolution that anybody in the branches who voted against the expulsion of Cliff's supporters was automatically expelled. This is an actual fact. Although I opposed them politically, I protested against this violation of their democratic rights, and I was expelled. Following this, Arthur Deane, Sam Levy, Sam Bornstein, Roy Tearse, and many others were expelled. We also heard that they had expelled Jimmy Deane and the Liverpool branch for offering opposition to their opportunist tactic in relation to the Socialist Fellowship. They were not able to answer the position put by Jimmy, and so he and the entire Liverpool branch were expelled. Many others simply dropped out in disgust.

We were left with the difficult job of organising all those who were driven out by Healy's purges, and who remained faithful to the political line and methods of the RCP. We attempted to gather together the remnants of the movement in Liverpool and London. This included people who had been lost, and people who had left the movement, as well as those who had been driven out. There were some very good comrades, worker comrades in the main, who had become completely demoralised as a result of all the things that had happened. We tried to save them. But as you can imagine, some of them placed the responsibility for this mess on the old leadership of the organisation.

We held a meeting to discuss what to do next. I was nominally a member of the International Executive Committee and, in order to appear impartial, they had suggested that I came back to the organisation. I suggested that I should go back and appeal against my expulsion and fight until I was expelled again, which would have been my third time. But the comrades said that it was a waste of time and voted against my proposal to return and fight. I believe now that the comrades were correct, and it was obviously stupid to go back under those conditions. So I accepted the decision of the group and we began the hard job of gathering together the forces once again.

To begin with, we had a small base in London and a grouping in Liverpool. All in all, we had maybe thirty comrades. But we were now operating under extremely difficult conditions, with no resources but our ideas and a faith in the future. We were under the pressures of Stalinism and reformism on the one hand, and under the pressure from Healy on the other. He had been given resources as result of the fusion, as well as the backing and recognition from the leaders of the International. We began with absolutely nothing. In a certain sense, as is always the case after a split of this character, our supporters suffered from a certain

Ted Grant 1949

demoralisation. Nevertheless, we had no alternative but to face up to the task of rebuilding the movement from scratch.

There are those who have written off the whole experience of the WIL and the RCP as a failure. They are incapable of understanding our history. Unfortunately, life does not proceed in a straight line, and neither does the revolutionary movement. We can see this not only from the period 1938 to 1949, but also from the entire history of the Marxist movement since the founding of the First International in 1864. We have to understand developments in their broad historical context; otherwise we would draw pessimistic and false conclusions concerning the future of Marxism and the revolutionary movement.

"Neither to weep nor laugh but to understand" - this was a phrase of the great philosopher Spinoza which was often quoted by Trotsky. The experience of Trotskyism in those years is a treasure-house of ideas which, taken in their totality, teaches us how a genuine Trotskyist movement can be built and sink roots in the working class. The experience that I went through personally, as the principal theoretician of British Trotskyism, added enormously to my understanding of events and served to enrich our collective knowledge that was to lay the basis for our future work. In the *Militant* tendency, we created the most powerful base for Trotskyism in Britain ever, and possibly the strongest position internationally since the days of the Russian Left Opposition. On the basis of our experience, including this period of the WIL and RCP, we will construct a movement that will put these great achievements in the shade. Trotskyism will become a mass force in Britain and internationally. Hopefully, this present work will in a modest way help to arm the new generation for the historic tasks that lie ahead.

Notes:

1- *Statement on Entry,* March 1949, pp.1 and 5.
2- *To all members of the RCP*, 5 February 1949.
3- Resolution adopted by the Eighth Plenum IEC.

Postscript on the History of British Trotskyism

By Rob Sewell

As Ted Grant's "history" finishes in 1950, the reader will obviously want to know what has happened since that time. Given its scope, writing a postscript on such a subject is a daunting task. A serious undertaking, however, would require at least another book if not several. That is a luxury that we cannot afford, but we will return to in the future. Nevertheless, I will attempt to give at least a brief outline of subsequent developments. Despite the inevitable gaps and omissions, it will, I hope, serve to set the present work in context and provide it with a certain continuity.

In 1950, after his expulsion by Gerry Healy from the Club, Ted attempted to regroup and salvage as much as possible from the wreckage of the RCP. It must be said - and was admitted by Ted later - that he had made a big mistake, in hindsight, by not backing the Open Party faction. He was still hoping to salvage the leadership - above all, Haston. It was a gamble that didn't pay off. If it had succeeded, at least the basic core of the RCP would have been kept largely intact. They would have intervened much more effectively in the crisis that hit the Communist Party in 1956. However, that opportunity was lost with the destruction of the RCP by the Healy-Cannon-Pablo-Mandel conspiracy.

By the autumn of 1950, Ted's supporters amounted to a handful of around thirty people, mainly in London and Liverpool. Given the difficult objective circumstances and the weakness of the organisation, they had no alternative but to work within the Labour Party and prepare the ground for an inevitable change in the situation. With such small forces, under the conditions prevailing in the 1950s - which resembled crossing a barren desert - it would have been madness to contemplate building an independent party outside the Labour Party. In other words, work inside the Labour Party was not based on a previously worked-out strategy or tactic, but simply a matter of necessity.

Just after his expulsion Ted issued an open letter, *Statement to the British Section of the Fourth International*, in an attempt to define his political position on a series of issues. Without any full timers or apparatus, the comrades struggled to hold things together. Minutes of their meetings record attempts to follow up contacts for the group. Visits to other areas outside of London and Liverpool were infrequent, but Ted managed to travel around to follow up some contacts. Other decisions taken were to set up a £30 "development fund" and, as a first step in establishing an apparatus, to buy a duplicator at £12 and 10 shillings. These were certainly the "dog days" of the tendency.

In May 1951, the first national conference took place in London. It was reported that there were 20 members in London and 11 in Liverpool, with a scattering of contacts around the country. Ted introduced a document entitled *Stalinism in the Post War Period* (see Appendix V), which fleshed out in a more comprehensive form the character of the new period and the perspectives for Stalinism.

> "For Marxism neither pessimism nor spurious optimism can play a role in determining the analysis of events. The first necessity is to understand the meaning of the conjuncture of historical forces leading to the present world situation.
>
> "The overthrow of Stalinism in the areas in which it holds sway will most likely be a long process. It is true that Stalinism remains a regime of permanent crisis. In it, the element of socialism, in the state economy, is in permanent contradiction to the Bonapartist state apparatus and the privileged caste whose interests it serves. Thus the regime of Stalinism in Russia itself bears a striking resemblance, even more than the Bonapartism of bourgeois origin, to the Caesarism of Ancient Rome in the epoch of the decay of the Empire. In that it bears a close resemblance to fascism. In the long run the regime of Bonapartist autocracy is incompatible with the economic base set in being by the October Revolution. That is the source of the permanent convulsions, and the endless removal of officials by the insatiable moloch in the Kremlin. The victories of Stalinism can only be a preparation for its downfall. But this only so from a long-term point of view. Undoubtedly Stalinism has been strengthened for a temporary period." [1]

This analysis provided the organisation with a more coherent perspective and was used as a basis for recruitment to the group. The conference endorsed the document unanimously and it was issued as a duplicated public pamphlet the following month. A decision was also taken to launch a theoretical magazine every two months. Figures like Jimmy Deane and his brothers Arthur Deane and Brian Deane, Alec Riach, Sam Levy and others helped to gather funds to launch the new publication. The first issue of the new magazine called *International Socialist,* with Ted as its editor, appeared in February 1952. However, the lack of resources and a paucity of funds meant that the magazine appeared only spasmodically between February 1952 and April 1954.

Healy's opportunism

For the Grant tendency, the key question was how to work in the Labour Party. The Healyites - as Ted predicted - "joined the Labour Party at the wrong time, and would inevitably leave the Labour Party at the wrong time." Within the Labour Party, the Healy group had no idea of how to work and was simply pursuing an opportunist policy. They were chasing a phantom left wing that didn't exist, while hiding their "Trotskyism" and dressing themselves in the clothes of left reformism.

Even worse, they had the false idea of "building the left" in alliance with a layer of the left reformists. Healy had set up the Socialist Fellowship in 1948 and then launched a paper called *Socialist Outlook* with such "left" luminaries as Bessie Braddock, and her husband, Councillor Jack Braddock, who moved far to the right and ruled the Liverpool Labour Party with the methods of Tammany Hall.

The Healy group was conducting a policy of "deep entrism". They simply liquidated themselves into the Labour Party. The *Socialist Outlook*, following Pablo's line, was distinctly left reformist and pro-Stalinist in character. It was no different in essence from *Tribune*, the paper of the Labour Left. For instance, its issue of 19 September 1952 had the banner headline: *For a Bevan Victory at 1952 Conference!* [Nye Bevan was one of the leaders of the Left]. The issue of 27 November 1953 thundered: *The Tories Must Resign - Let's have a petition to get them out!* And so on, and so forth.

Even so, this luke warm left reformism was still too much for the National Executive Committee of the Labour Party who banned the *Outlook* in 1954. Fearing expulsion, Healy's supporters immediately closed down the paper. When Transport House banned the Fellowship, the *Outlook* published a statement: "As loyal members of the Labour Party who have never had any interests separate and apart from the Labour Party we are obliged to accept the decision of the NEC." [2] In other words, they capitulated without a squeak.

After the closure of the Fellowship and the *Outlook*, the Healy group deepened its opportunist line within the Labour Party - which was in effect Pablo's policy of entrism of a "new type". They began to sell *Tribune* instead of their own paper. In fact, after the closure of the *Outlook*, they didn't have their own newspaper for two years. As Harry Ratner later admitted, "we wanted to help create a broad left current in the Labour Party and unions..." and "this was consistent with our strategy of deep entrism into the Labour Party." [3]

After his expulsion, Ted's "open letter" to members of the British section of the "Fourth" analysed the role of *Outlook*. "The political role of the *Socialist Outlook* was determined not by the anaemic editorials," stated Ted, "but by the leading articles of those MPs, etc., whose policies were transparently one of sweetening the bitter pills of the right wing. At the same time, the editorials were coloured by the need not to 'offend' the Stalinist fellow travellers on the Editorial Board. The editorial produced a line of 'criticism' which is worthy of the notorious 'Friends of the Soviet Union'."

He went on to quote examples from the Outlook: "The leadership... would like it to be." "We are far from suggesting that the Russian Government at all times and under all conditions supports progressive movements." "There is a distinct flavour of power politics about Moscow's attempt to secure peace in Korea in return for an extra seat on the Security Council." These were the examples of "serious Trotskyist criticism"! Amongst such statements falls the following: *"Russian foreign policy is determined by what the government of that country considers is in the interests of the Soviet Union, but that as India proved does not, by any means, always coincide with what is in the best interest of the international working class. Or even, in the long run, the best interest of the Soviet Union itself"!*

The sheer opportunism and pro-Stalinism of the Healyites went hand in hand with perspectives of immediate slump and Third World War. "Economic necessity compels the United States towards an armed showdown with the Soviet Union and the colonial revolution...", reads their 1950 conference perspectives resolution. "Imperialism is being forced to prepare for, and then embark upon a world war under extremely unfavourable conditions...But we must be ready for war - we must be organised in such a way that, despite enormous disadvantages, we can go forward to the construction of the party in war no less than in peace." [4]

From bad to worse

As was seen earlier, the leaders of the International had capitulated to Titoism and Maoism. This adaptation to Stalinism was clearly evident in the political position of the resolutions of Pablo, Mandel, Frank and co. In 1951, the Pablo leadership came out with a perspective of an impending Third World War. Under prevailing conditions, Pablo maintained that this "new reality" corresponded to "the conception of Revolution-War... upon which the perspectives and orientation of revolutionary Marxists in our epoch should rest." Instead of a struggle of classes, there was now a struggle between the camps of imperialism and Stalinism. This meant a policy of "deep entrism", where the Trotskyists would hide their identities. Cannon, Healy and the rest of them supported this position whole-heartedly. "We consider these documents to be completely Trotskyist", wrote Cannon on 29 May 1952. While Healy was organising "work brigades" to go from Britain to "socialist" Yugoslavia.

Arthur Deane, Jimmy Deane and Ted Grant in the mid - 1950's

As an aside, it is opportune to deal with a myth that has been peddled around by the Healyites over the years. Bill Hunter, a former supporter of the RCP majority, had slavishly gone over to Healy after the break-up of the RCP. A leading Healy acolyte, he was expelled from the Labour Party by the NEC in late 1954, following the proscription of *Socialist Outlook*. He was in the same Constituency Labour Party as Ted Grant, in East Islington. The local Labour Party refused on two occasions to endorse the expulsion. At a third meeting, the Labour General Management Committee (GMC) was faced with the clear choice of endorsing the expulsion or being disbanded. Under those circumstances, under protest, Ted abstained on the vote. Ever since, in order to blacken Ted's name, the Healyites have raised a hue and cry over this issue, accusing him of betrayal and supporting the right wing. Hunter repeats this story in his autobiography. Later the story was linked to the fairytale that in 1964 *Militant* supporters supported the expulsions of Healyites from the party for their political ideas - which was never the case.

Ironically, the correct stand taken by Ted was the position that Healy had endorsed a few years earlier in Manchester. When the question of disciplinary action over Salford City Labour Party was being undertaken in May-June 1951, there was a threat of closure of the Party by the

NEC. "Should we still carry on defying Transport House to the point of being expelled?", wrote Harry Ratner. "We had throughout been in touch with Gerry Healy and the Club's Executive in London [of which Bill Hunter was a member]. Their instruction was that we should avoid expulsion in view of the Club's long-term entry strategy... We had made a principled stand, and everyone would understand why it was necessary to make a tactical retreat to avoid the disbandment of the local parties and expulsion of militants." [5]

The position that Ted took in 1954 to abstain in a vote in face of disbandment of the local Labour Party was absolutely correct. While protesting against the expulsions, it was madness to allow the bureaucracy to simply close down the party and empty out all of the left wingers on a question like this. Of course, in an attempt to slander Ted Grant, the Healyites, including Ratner and Hunter, were prepared to use Ted's abstention to cast a slur on his revolutionary character.

In 1953, a split took place in the International, when Healy split away - together with the American SWP - to form their own International Committee of the Fourth International. There were no real political differences between the sides. These were manufactured later to justify the split. Cannon simply didn't want Pablo interfering in his organisation in the States. Pablo had incurred Cannon's wrath by supporting an opposition current within the SWP around Bert Cochran. So Cannon decided to split with Pablo and base everything on "his man" in Europe - Gerry Healy. This suited Healy down to the ground, since he wanted to be the "big man" in Europe. All the nonsense about "Pabloism" was simply a smokescreen. The fact is that both Cannon and Healy had previously accepted Pablo's pro-Stalinist line without question:

> "This [Pablo's] general analysis was endorsed by the Third World Congress of the Fourth International in August 1951", noted Harry Ratner. "It was at first only opposed by the majority of the French section - the Parti Communiste Internationaliste. When they were instructed by the International to enter the French Communist Party, they refused to do so. In January 1952 Michael Pablo, using his authority as Secretary of the International, suspended a majority of the PCI's Central Committee. The PCI split, and, a few months later, the majority, led by Lambert and Bleitreu, were expelled from the International.
>
> "This action and the general line of the International were generally supported, in particular by the American Socialist Workers Party and by Healy's group [the Club] in Britain. *It was only over a year later that the leaders of the SWP, faced with an internal faction fight against an opposition supported by Pablo, began to criticise 'Pabloism' as an attempt to liquidate the Fourth International and capitulate to Stalinism.* For a time, the Healy group continued to support and advocate Pablo's general line. In fact, when in July 1953 Pablo presented to the International Secretariat a draft entitled *The Rise and Fall of Stalinism* as a basis for discussion at the forthcoming Fourth World Congress, Healy agreed that it be circulated to all sections in the name of the International Secretariat, and only made minor criticisms of it." [6]

When the row broke out into the open, Ratner admits they "were taken by surprise." *So Cannon and Healy were in fact the original Pabloites.* Healy's leading collaborator and editor of *Socialist Outlook*, John Lawrence, together with his supporters, faithfully carried on with their pro-Stalinist line. Healy subsequently expelled them - not for their Stalinism, but for their support of Pablo. Lawrence, being politically consistent, broke from the International and ended up in the Communist Party. So, 1954 left Pablo and the International with nothing in Britain.

Hungary 1956

Within two years, the crisis developing within the Communist Parties following the earth-shattering revelations by Khruschev at the Twentieth Congress of the CPSU, exposing many of the crimes of Stalin, provided the Trotskyist movement with renewed possibilities. These events unfolding in the USSR served to push the International into a far more critical and correct view of Stalinism. Desperate to find new allies in Britain, Pablo went so far as to place an advertisement in the *Tribune* newspaper of the left reformists, appealing for help in the founding of a new section of the International in Britain.

Sam Bornstein, who was in touch with the International, urged Pablo to get in contact with Ted Grant's group. After some discussions, this led to a fusion with some other supporters of Pablo in London and the recognition of the new group as the official British section. In reality, Ted's original group formed the overwhelming majority of the section, the others being largely passive members who soon fell by the wayside. Nevertheless, it served to reactivate a layer of older comrades like Jock Milligan, Marion Lunt and Ann Keen.

Recognition by the International came however with the promise of resources to pay for two full timers and a new magazine. By the end of the year Ted, together with Pablo supporter, John Fairhead, became full-timers, and a new magazine, *Workers International Review*, was launched. Pablo wanted Fairhead appointed as an ally against Ted's dominant political influence within the group. However, Fairhead didn't last long and he soon left. His political evolution went originally from support for Healy's *Socialist Outlook*, into the Communist Party, through the RSL to the Cliff group, then the Posadists and into the Labour Party. From there he joined the Tory Party and became an executive member of the right wing Tory Monday Club! "I wasn't surprised", said Ted later. "He was a public school boy and from a Tory background."

This attempt to re-establish a group in Britain coincided with an unfolding political revolution in Hungary. On 23 October 1956, the events in Hungary shook the world and provoked a further deep crisis within the Communist Party. Two general strikes and two insurrections took place within six weeks. The Russian army stationed in Hungary went over to the revolutionaries. Eventually, they were withdrawn and backward troops were sent in to put down the uprising, with stories that they were going to Berlin to put down a fascist coup d'etat. The uprising was eventually put down in cold blood by Russian tanks.

The revolutionary events in Hungary created a storm of unrest within the Communist Parties internationally. The Stalinist leaders denounced the uprising as a "counter-revolutionary" movement. But large sections of the rank-and-file of the CP could not stomach this line. Peter Fryer, the British *Daily Worker* correspondent in Hungary sent back dispatches of eyewitness accounts of revolution in Hungary, which were suppressed by the leadership. They were eventually printed in the *Manchester Guardian*. In Britain, a big layer of the Communist Party was in ferment and open to the ideas of Trotskyism. Within a year, the crisis had resulted in the Communist Party losing a third of its membership.

This called for an abrupt turn by the tendency towards these possibilities in the Communist Party. A sharp debate took place within the group of how to approach these potential recruits. Ted raised the question of an open banner and the launch of an open organisation, as the only effective means of appealing to the dissidents within the CP. This was resisted by some comrades, such as Sam Levy, but was accepted by the group. In early 1957, the Revolutionary

Socialist League was launched and the *Workers International Review* issued an *Open Letter to the Communist Party* over Hungary, written by Ted, urging them to take up the struggle for genuine Leninism.

> "Comrades! New shocks lie ahead", stated the *Open Letter*. "Yesterday the 20th Congress, today Hungary, tomorrow...(?)
>
> "The intervention of Russian troops was designed to prevent the setting up of a socialist democracy on the borders of Russia, because this would have been the beginning of the end for the Russian bureaucracy. Already some Russian soldiers have deserted to the side of the Hungarian people. This is an omen of the future! The intervention of Russian troops prevented the masses establishing a socialist democracy in Hungary, but in the future when the Russian masses rise, who will defend the Russian bureaucracy then? In the coming period great events impend, in the East against Stalinism, in the West against capitalism. We can best help the workers of Russia and Eastern Europe by conducting an implacable struggle for the overthrow of capitalism and imperialism in Britain and the West.
>
> "Comrade of the Communist Party! You can best help in this task by a clear understanding of the problems of the working class and the theory and practice of Marxism and Leninism. We are convinced that you will come to understand that the revolutionary struggle can be carried through to a victorious conclusion in Britain and internationally only on the programme of Marx, Lenin and Trotsky, which your leaders have abandoned."

Flexible tactics

In a document also written by Ted, entitled *The Present Situation and Our Political Tasks* (1957), the need for flexible tactics towards Communist Party dissidents was sharply posed:

> "Large numbers of key and important cadres can be won for the Fourth International from this work. To accomplish this task, any attempt at the imposition of a line *a la Stalinism* is impermissible. For example, many of the best elements will not be prepared for an entrist perspective immediately. The first necessity is the winning of a nucleus among them to the programme and banner of the Fourth International. At a later stage, the problem of work within the mass organisations and of perspectives for the coming epoch must be discussed. But at the present stage of development, immediate entry of such a grouping into the Labour Party would mean the drowning of many excellent people in the social-democratic swamp, and the complete disillusionment of others in the possibility of real Labour Party work. Actually the best, most hardened elements in the Forum movement is at present the most antagonistic to entrism."
>
> The document continued: "The situation demands above all a flexible tactic. Entry must not be made a fetish - any more than the concept of open work. Our tactic at the given time is dictated by the opportunities open to us and the possibility of perspectives for the future. It would be greater madness to adopt a formalistic attitude and turn our backs on the immediate possibilities of work under the independent banner - the modest successes of *Workers International Review* have underlined this. The essence of tactics, in politics as in war, is to concentrate the greatest forces in that sector of the battlefield where the state of the fight most favours victory. Successful work in the open field can prepare the ground for greater successes in the future within the Labour Party, where the decisive struggles will take place." [7]

Ted and other comrades made contact and discussed with a layer of CP dissidents, but were shocked at their very low political level. "In the past," recalled Ted, "the old Stalinists would first of all ask about your programme. But the first question these people would ask is: how many are you?" After decades of miseducation by Stalinism, it was not easy to win such people to a small organisation and the results were very modest. As an example of the pernicious effects of Stalinism on worker activists, it is sufficient to cite the following example.

The Stalinists had controlled the electricians' union (ETU) from the top, by completely bureaucratic means, including ballot rigging. But in 1956, a series of important ETU leaders broke from the CP and began an opposition fighting for internal democracy within the union. Among those with whom Ted had discussions was Frank Chappel, the leader of this group, who then was still on the left. He did not join and later swung far to the right and became a reactionary witch-hunting leader of the union.

Basically, ideas, theories and principles did not attract these former Stalinists. They were more impressed by Healy's organisation, which was bigger and had far greater resources, including a printing press. As a result, Healy managed to recruit a whole layer of people, including Brian Behan (the brother of Brendan Behan, the famous Irish playwright), Peter Fryer (the former correspondent of the *Daily Worker* in Hungary) and Brian Pearce. Using Healy's resources Fryer became editor of the newly launched weekly *Newsletter*, which became the organ of the Club in 1957.

However, rather than convincing these ex-Stalinists of Trotskyism, they seemed to have recruited Healy to a version of "third period" Stalinism. Within a few years, Healy had abandoned his extreme opportunist version of work in the Labour Party and launched the Socialist Labour League early in 1959. They swung wildly from the most cowardly opportunism to the most insane ultra-leftism. But the honeymoon did not last long. Healy's internal regime of bureaucratic centralism, based on bullying and terror, soon led to the expulsion of Behan, Fryer and a whole host of others.

Years later, Healy's stooge, Bill Hunter cynically turned against his long-standing mentor. He revealed what everyone already knew - that Healy was a petty tyrant and a dictator within his organisation. "Walking out of meetings", states Hunter in his autobiography, "which he used as a deliberate method of pressure later in the 1970s, the attempt to resolve party problems with force of will, fear, administrative actions and violence..." [8]

It was clear to anyone with the slightest grasp that Healy had absolutely nothing to do with genuine Trotskyism. However much he hides, Hunter cannot escape the fact that he uncritically supported the Healy regime - until it collapsed in 1985 with the expulsion of Healy. "Healy could never have acted as he did without the support of a whole group of other people around him in the leadership", remarks Harry Ratner, "people such as Mike and Tony Banda, Bill Hunter, Cliff Slaughter and Bob Shaw, and the failure of people like myself to speak out." [9]

As already stated, Ted Grant believed that Healy entered the Labour Party at the wrong time, and would also leave the Labour Party at the wrong time. This prediction proved to be absolutely correct. Nevertheless, the zigzags of the Healyites produced a certain questioning within the tendency, so Ted used this experience to write a document in March 1959 to answer these doubts and clarify the situation. The document gave a short history of the Labour Party tactic and analysed the differences with Trotsky's conception of entrism and the long-term work that we were conducting within the mass organisations.

Clearly the classical conditions for entry, as laid down by Trotsky, did not exist in Britain at that time. The work of the Marxist tendency in the Party was based on the perspective of a future mass left wing, which would develop at a time of political and economic crisis. It was inevitable that the mass of workers, who would turn towards their traditional organisations in times of social crisis, would serve to create mass left reformist and even centrist currents. But this did not mean, as the sectarian groups tried to claim, that the Marxists were "burying themselves in the Labour Party." What was necessary was to combine Party work with independent work, fighting at all times for Marxist ideas and policies. The overwhelming majority of the new supporters came from *outside* of the Labour Party, but was won over by the clarity of our ideas and our orientation towards the mass organisations.

> "From every point of view the work is impossible without an understanding of the perspectives, whatever the momentary situation may be", explained Ted. "Otherwise the work proceeds purely empirically as with the Healyites, in a series of convulsive leaps and jumps in all directions. The tendency is at the mercy of every episodic conjuncture and turn in events, blown hither and thither by momentary favourable and unfavourable winds, instead of - while taking these into account in everyday work and explaining to the membership the meaning of all events - nevertheless fitting them into broad perspectives of the movement. It is the failure to understand the tactic of entrism, and its application, which has resulted in the new tactics of the Healyites. They will produce an abortion."

Opposition in the USFI

Although we were the official section of the International, we were always in political opposition to the leadership on a whole range of questions. Despite the fact that the Hungarian events found us on common ground, other developments produced sharp disagreements. In the Sino-Soviet dispute, for instance, rather than viewing it as a national conflict between two bureaucracies, the International decided to give critical support to the Chinese bureaucracy as allegedly more "progressive". In the meantime, Pablo, who had moved into opposition, supported the Russian bureaucracy, claiming that Khrushchev's "de-Stalinisation" campaign opened the door to the "self-reform" of the bureaucracy. Neither position had anything in common with Trotskyism.

Juan Posadas, a leader based in Argentina, went so far as to support the Chinese bureaucracy's call for a nuclear war on the United States! Eventually he set up his own "Fourth International" based in Latin America and at an Extraordinary Conference in 1962, declared:

> "We are preparing ourselves for a stage in which before the atomic war we shall struggle for power, during the atomic war we shall struggle for power and we shall be in power [sic!]. There is no beginning… there is an end to atomic war, because atomic war is simultaneous revolution in the whole world, not as a chain reaction, simultaneous. Simultaneous doesn't mean the same day and the same hour. Great historic events should not be measured by hours or days, but by periods… The working class will maintain itself, [and] will immediately have to seek its cohesion and centralisation…
>
> "After destruction commences, the masses are going to emerge in all countries - in a short time, in a few hours. Capitalism cannot defend itself in an atomic war except by putting itself in caves and attempting to destroy all that it can. The masses, in contrast, are going to come out, will have to come out, because it is the only way to survive, defeating the enemy…

> The apparatus of capitalism, police, army, will not be able to resist… It will be necessary to organise the workers' power immediately." [10]

So, in Posadas' mixed-up mind, those who are left after an atomic war, terrified and in a state of shock at millions dead, would rise up and take power! This showed how far these people had regressed theoretically and politically. These ideas have nothing in common with Trotskyism, and much more in common with the ideas emanating from the lunatic asylum. After capitulating to Stalinism, Posadas became a mouthpiece for the Maoist bureaucracy, only in an even more extreme form.

The Lanka Sama Samaja Party

The only authority that a Marxist leadership can have is a political and moral authority. This was what Lenin and Trotsky based themselves on in the formative years of the Communist International. It never occurred to them to use organisational methods to impose their ideas on the International. Only after Lenin's death, in the period of the bureaucratic degeneration, did Zinoviev begin to use the apparatus to impose the "Moscow Line" - a development that inevitably ended in the destruction of the Third International.

In the 1930s, despite all the difficulties, the colossal personal authority of Leon Trotsky kept the small forces of the Bolshevik-Leninists together. He waged a stubborn struggle to defend and preserve the genuine ideas and traditions of the October Revolution and the Bolshevik Party. But the other leaders were not at all on a similar level. Like Zinoviev, Cannon, Mandel and the others imagined that it was possible to demand authority and obedience. Lenin once warned Bukharin: "If you want obedience, you will get obedient fools". They dissipated all the political and moral authority which the Old Man had bequeathed to the Fourth International, and attempted to make up for their lack of authority by using organisational methods against their critics - as with the British section. This was a sure way to destroy the Fourth International even before it had had a chance to build a serious mass base. Most of the sections remained small and isolated from the mass movement of the working class. One of the main exceptions was Sri Lanka (Ceylon).

The Ceylonese Trotskyists in effect founded the labour movement in that country. They even invented the word for socialism, which did not exist in Sinhala. They coined the word Sama Samaja - which means literally "equal society". It is not particularly scientific, but it is the nearest equivalent they could find to "socialism".

Whereas in other countries the Stalinists expelled the Trotskyists, in Ceylon it was the other way around. The Lanka Sama Samaja Party (LSSP) was the traditional mass party of the working class in Ceylon. As a result of its courageous stand against British imperialism in the Second World War, the LSSP gained mass support, and became the second major party next to the bourgeois UNP. In 1953, it had led a successful general strike on the island, and had established Trotskyism as the leading force in the working class. However, in comparison to its successes, the failures of the leaders of the International gradually undermined their authority in the eyes of the leaders of the LSSP.

The false positions of the leaders of the Fourth International led them to make one mistake after another. This served to further undermine the credibility of the International leadership. Over a period of time, this was to have major repercussions in the largest section of the

International, the LSSP. They did not possess a shred of political and moral authority with the LSSP leaders, who had a mass organisation. Ted recalls that in meetings of the International in Paris, the LSSP leader, N.M. Pereira would sit with an ironical expression. "I believe N.M. was never a Trotskyist", says Ted. "But whereas Trotsky - one man alone - would always be listened to with respect, Mandel, Pablo and the others had no authority at all with the LSSP leaders. They would sit there thinking: 'We are mass leaders. What do these people represent? They do not have correct ideas. They do not have the masses. So what good are they?' And in fact, they had a point."

Without the check of an authoritative political leadership internationally, the opportunist pressure on the LSSP leadership inevitably took their toll. In the late 1950s, under the pressures of the adverse objective situation, the LSSP vacillated politically, taking a conciliatory attitude towards the government of the newly emerged SLFP, a split-off from the UNP. Eventually, in 1964, the LSSP voted to enter the bourgeois government. This was finally too much for the International leaders to swallow. Having failed to correct the opportunism of the LSSP leaders for years, in order not to offend them, they were compelled to condemn the Party's turn to popular frontism. Needless to say, the complaints from Paris were contemptuously dismissed by the LSSP. Then, when the damage was already done, the International Secretariat split the section, causing a deep blow to Trotskyism in Sri Lanka.

> "The International leadership played a shameful and destructive role in Sri Lanka," Ted states emphatically. "Having remained silent for years about the opportunist policies of the LSSP leaders (which was quite evident), Mandel and the others suddenly performed a somersault of 180 degrees and organised a split off of the Left led by Edmund Samorakody. He came to London and we had a friendly discussion, during which we tried to persuade him to stay in the LSSP and organise a left opposition, but he refused. He was sincere but a bit ultra-left. Naturally, the split led nowhere. Later on we contacted the left wing of the LSSP and we won a sizeable section out of it - the NSSP, which was unfortunately wrecked by the adventurism of Bahu. But that is another story."

A difficult period

From the early 1950s, a small trickle of recruits were made by the Grant tendency, including in South Wales, which was later to became an important stronghold. In early 1950 in Liverpool, Jimmy Deane drew a young 16-year old Pat Wall into the tendency. Pat had joined the Labour Party during the general election, and within two weeks had been made secretary of Garston CLP. "He was very keen to find out more about economics and the theories of Marxism, and was told by councillor Bill Sefton (who ended up in the House of Lords) to go over to Walton and ask the Deanes," recalls his life-long partner and comrade Pauline Wall. "After that he read and read and read. He devoured all the Marxist classics." Pat played a leading role for the tendency on Liverpool Trades Council and in the Labour Party (which was one body at that time), serving to develop and train up a group of younger comrades such as Terry Harrison. Terry had joined the Labour Party and disillusioned by the experience was toying with the idea of joining the Young Communist League. However, he picked up a copy of our youth paper *Rally* in a ward meeting and decided to get in touch. Pat had become a Labour councillor in Liverpool and later in Bingley, and after a battle with the right wing and an investigation by the NEC, later became Labour MP for Bradford North. He remained a committed Trotskyist until his tragic death in August 1990. He will be remembered by many for his passionate oratory at Labour Party conferences and numerous public meetings, as well as his genuinely common touch. He was truly a great man.

The experiment of the RSL was wound up after possibilities within the Communist Party dried up. The tendency issued a new publication called *Socialist Fight,* edited by Ted Grant, which appeared irregularly from January 1958 to June 1963. Others on the editorial board included Pat Wall (Liverpool), Dave Matthews (Swansea), and Muriel Browning (Llanelli). At this point, finances were in a particularly bad state. The paucity of resources resulted in the *Socialist Fight* coming out in a duplicated form during 1960, only reappearing in print in mid-February 1961.

Dave Matthews (far left), Ted (centre) and Muriel Browning (right)

In 1955, Ted had been chosen as the Labour candidate for Liverpool Walton, the Constituency Labour Party where the tendency had the strongest roots, but was blocked by the Regional Official who had the full backing of the right wing National Executive Committee. "I would have been expelled anyway", commented Ted. However, another comrade, George McCartney, an experienced comrade from the days of the WIL and RCP, was put forward instead, got selected against the then *Tribunite* (and later extreme right winger) Woodrow Wyatt. After an NEC inquiry, George finally managed to get endorsed, but failed to win the seat in the 1959 general election, as did the Labour Party nationally. Soon afterwards Eric Heffer, a former member of the CP, became the candidate and won the seat in 1964. Nevertheless, Walton was to remain a bastion for the tendency until the Walton by-election fiasco in 1991. Despite his advanced years, George remains a supporter of *Socialist Appeal* to this day.

The Labour Party bureaucracy had closed down the Labour League of Youth in 1955 and no national youth structures existed. The tendency correctly predicted on the basis of the 1959 general election defeat that a youth movement would soon be re-established, as the Labour Party would need the youth if it was to fight another general election successfully. That took place in the February of the following year with the establishment of the Young Socialists. This coincided with a ferment amongst young people, with the national apprentices' strike in 1960 and the development of a mass anti-nuclear war movement around CND.

Ultra-leftism

In 1959, the Healyites swung wildly in the direction of ultra-leftism and set up the Socialist Labour League - typically, proclaimed by Healy without any consultation with the membership of the Club. They applied for Labour Party affiliation and were swiftly and predictably (given the 1946 conference decision) proscribed by the bureaucracy. Healy was keen to provoke expulsion. He advised Ratner to "let Transport House expel you and fight to get the local party to refuse to accept it, even if it means disaffiliation." It was clear to Ratner that "Healy and the Executive Committee adopted a policy of unnecessarily provoking expulsions from the Labour Party." [11]

Despite these clear provocations by Healy, we were attacked for our alleged capitulation to the right wing by Sean Matgamna, the ex-Healyite, in a pamphlet produced by Workers' Liberty called *Seedbed of the Left*. "The Grant tendency was so venomously hostile to the Healy tendency that it refused to specifically oppose the proscription of the SLL in February 1959", states Matgamna. [12] He goes on to repeat the bile over Ted's abstention in 1954, which we have already mentioned.

However, regarding our "attitude" to the proscription of the SLL, Matgamna clearly uses Healy's old methods to manufacture a slander against his opponents. After all, why let the facts get in the way of a good story? He ignores the fact that on the front page of the *Socialist Fight* for April 1959 there was an article entitled *Socialist Labour League*. It is worth quoting in order to nail this slander.

> "The National Executive of the Labour Party has proscribed the Socialist Labour League and its journal the *Newsletter*... this is a blow against democracy in the movement. There should be room in the party for all who stand for a socialist policy. With full and fair debate, it should be left to the membership to decide what policy should be adopted. Heresy hunting and proscription can only damage the party and not assist in building it up. *All those in the party who believe in democracy will protest against this decision.* Socialist Fight *whilst disagreeing with many of the policies of the SLL, will support moves of protest against the banning."* (My emphasis).

At the beginning, as we predicted, the YS attracted a large number of young people. However, Healy, who had gone on an ultra-left binge and had just written off the Labour Party, suddenly realised the possibilities, turned 180 degrees, and threw all his resources into the YS. With Healy's strong apparatus, and youth paper *Keep Left*, the Healyites were able to take control of the YS nationally by various dubious means.

The next largest group in the YS at the time was the Cliff group, widely known as the "state caps", which produced *Young Guard*, edited by Gus Macdonald (now Lord Macdonald, and a Cabinet Minister in the Blair Government) followed by Ted Grant's group, made up of a few dozen comrades. YS Conferences became quite heated, with accusations flying around about "Healyites" and "Pabloite revisionists" and the like, to the bemusement of the NEC representatives attending the conference. One year, a puzzled Ian Mikardo, the left MP, leaned over to his colleague, and asked, "why all these attacks on Pablo Picasso and Denis Healey?"

In Liverpool, our comrades produced a duplicated magazine called *Rally* through the Walton YS branch. It was edited by Beryl Deane, and was aimed towards the youth not only in Liverpool, but had a circulation in the YS branches of London, Tyneside and Swansea. The comrades intervened in the apprentice's strike and won a number of young workers to the tendency, particularly in Liverpool.

Breakthrough among the students

Another vital area that opened up for our development was in Brighton - which was hardly the Petrograd of Britain. In 1960, my elder brother, Alan Woods had joined the YS in our home town of Swansea. Our grandfather and mother were both members of the Communist Party. Our grandfather - a tin plate worker, an active trade unionist and a veteran member of the Party - had introduced my brother to Marxism from an early age. Alan's political upbringing resulted in sharp arguments in the local YS branch, which was dominated by members of the tendency, such as Dave Matthews, Colin Tindley, Bill Smith and Phil and Alan Lloyd.

Having been regularly defeated politically at the YS, and with our grandfather running out of arguments against Trotskyism, he was eventually won over. In 1963, Alan went to Sussex University, which at the time was a new and experimental university with only 300 students. One of them was Thabo Mbeki - now President of South Africa - who had an Anti-Apartheid group around him, most of whom were won to Trotskyism through Alan's work.

At the time, Alan was the only comrade in the whole of the South of England. After consistent work in the university and later in the town, he managed to establish a powerful group of supporters, including workers such as Dudley Edwards and Ray Apps, a local bus driver and regular delegate to Labour Party conference. Dudley, an engineering worker, had a long history in the movement, and played a leading role in the Revolutionary Policy Committee in the ILP. He subsequently joined the Communist Party, but left disillusioned. He had also been in Germany just prior to Hitler's victory, and spoke to many meetings about this experience. After many discussions with Alan (he later admitted he was testing us out) he eventually joined.

The work of the comrades in Sussex was a real breakthrough for the tendency nationally. For a number of years, a large part of the tendency's finances as well as leading personnel came from the Sussex area. Without Alan's work in Sussex, we would never have been able to develop the tendency nationally as we did. Nowadays, Peter Taaffe and the leaders of the so-called Socialist Party (the rump of the old *Militant* tendency) try to belittle the role of Alan, but the record speaks for itself. "Brighton played an enormous role both financially and politically in the past period", noted the report given to the National Editorial Board in May 1965.

Student comrades won at Sussex opened up many other areas of the country for the tendency. The comrades even won over the entire active membership of the Brighton Young

Communist League, including Jim Brookshaw, a print worker and national chairman of the YCL, who remains a firm supporter. Through this work, we established a key position in the Brighton Kemptown Labour Party, with a building worker comrade, Rod Fitch, eventually becoming the parliamentary candidate in 1983.

The work in Sussex was therefore a decisive turning point in the fortunes of the *Militant* tendency.

Fusions and splits

In the early sixties, there was a move to re-unite the two Fourth Internationals - the International Secretariat based in Paris (Pablo, Mandel, Frank, and Maitan) and the US-based International Committee (Hanson, Healy and Lambert). Since the original split lacked any principled basis and was just the result of prestige and clique politics, the question of re-unification should have presented no great political difficulties.

However, as Ted always says, the pseudo-Trotskyist sects are "unlucky at fusions and lucky at splits." If you do not approach politics in a principled manner, then every attempt at unification will merely unite two groups into ten. And this was no exception. Immediately, instead of two Fourth Internationals, there were four or more. Poasdas and the South American Bureau refused to accept the unification. So did Healy in Britain and Lambert in France. Meanwhile, inside the IS, Pablo had quarreled with Mandel and the others, who soon retaliated by expelling him!

Undeterred by these problems, the International leaders began to beat the unification drum and put pressure on everyone and his uncle to unite - irrespective of political differences. It was a case of "all in together, never mind the weather." A sure recipe for disaster. In Britain, under the auspices of the International, there was an ill-advised attempt to rejoin forces with a largely Nottingham-based group around ex-CP members Pat Jordan and Ken Coates - stooges of the Paris leadership - who had launched the *Week* magazine. Coates - an adventurer who ended up as a Labour member of the European Parliament - had been briefly a member of the Healy group, but had been expelled.

These people had previously joined the Grant group in the late 1950s, and Jordan became organising secretary for a period. However, they manoeuvred with Pablo, and established a faction. This didn't last long and they left to form their own International Group - a minuscule outfit, entirely petit bourgeois in composition and in outlook. In fact, just the sort of people Mandel could feel at home with. The politics of this group were one hundred percent pure opportunism. *The Week* had an entirely reformist content, involving various left MPs and such like. They were known as the *Weak* people - a little unkind, perhaps, but entirely accurate. These were the people in whom the International placed all its hopes.

The International had a big problem in Britain. One year earlier they had reunited with the American SWP but not with Healy, for whom an International leadership based in Paris was the kiss of death, since he would no longer rule the roost in Europe as the Americans had hitherto allowed him to do. He immediately started an hysterical campaign against "Pabloism" (conveniently forgetting his close relations with Pablo in the past) and the "betrayals" of Hanson and the American SWP (conveniently forgetting his close relations with *them*).

Paris demanded that the official British section should unite with the International Group to fight Healy. This was vigorously resisted by a large part of the tendency, but was eventually pushed through. Under the pressure of the International, a shaky fusion took place at a conference at Seven Oaks in Kent in September 1964. Jimmy Deane - the then secretary of the group - mistakenly heralded this as "a very important step forward for the Trotskyist movement in Britain." He continued: "In adopting its statement on unity, the conference showed its mature attitude towards the differing experiences of comrades and towards the existence of secondary tactical differences." [13]

However, there was a lot of wish-fulfilment in this. As usual, the leadership of the International displayed bad faith, immediately commencing their manoeuvres against the British leadership. The "secondary differences" soon developed into sharp differences and things fell apart within a matter of months, with Jordan and Coates boycotting the leading bodies and eventually walking out to build their own separate International Group (later the International Marxist Group).

This was a blow to Pierre Frank, a member of the IS with a grudge against Ted and those other comrades who refused to recognise him as a great Leader and Teacher of the International. By splitting away immediately, Jordan and Coates had deprived him of the possibility of manoeuvring against the British leadership. He did not hide his displeasure at this turn of events, chiding the splitters: "You are too cowardly to fight."

The tendency had learnt a painful lesson on the impossibility of short cuts. Unification with the Mandelites turned out to be a farce. A misguided attempt to collaborate with the Cliff group in developing the *Young Guard* paper also ended in failure. In both cases, the main mover was Jimmy Deane, who had illusions in the possibilities of unification. After the failure of these attempts, Jimmy became disillusioned and moved away from active involvement in the movement, although he has always remained loyal to the ideas. He is now very ill and incapacitated after a severe stroke. But this proletarian revolutionist with his thick Liverpool accent and impressive presence was a man of tremendous ability, and is fondly remembered by all who worked with him. He was a victim not only of the period, but also of the crimes of the so-called leaders of the Fourth.

The launching of Militant

This was probably the lowest point in the fortunes of the tendency. We were a tiny, isolated group, with no paper, no money, no full timers and no centre. In the YS we were one of the smallest groups. Alan Woods recalls:

> "We faced continuous attacks not only from the bureaucracy but from the sects and from the International which was determined to crush us. But we had something more important than all these things. We had the ideas of Marxism, and we were not downcast in the slightest. We were confident in our ideas and perspectives. Ted played an absolutely key role at this time. He never lost his optimism, his unshakeable confidence or his famous sense of humour.
>
> "Paradoxically, the difficult conditions helped to train us. The young comrades who were coming into activity at that time were used to fighting for the ideas. As a result we were not afraid of anything. It made us tough and determined and also sharpened us up politically and theoretically."

In the summer of 1964, a decision was taken to launch a new publication, and after much debate, the name of *Militant* was chosen. With Jimmy Deane's departure abroad for work reasons, another decision was taken to find a replacement at the London centre. A new young recruit from Birkenhead, Peter Taaffe, was chosen to come to London on a full-time basis and help produce the paper and assist with the national work. Within a few months of launching *Militant*, the group rented three small rooms from the ILP in Kings Cross Road. It was to mark a new chapter in the development of Ted Grant's *Militant* tendency.

The Healyites, who had no idea of what to do with their control of the YS, decided to break from the Labour Party and build their own independent youth organisation. They decided to provoke expulsion from the Labour Party by using hooligan methods. Despite their intolerable conduct, involving the use of physical violence to break up meetings, they did not find this very easy. Most Labour Party members are indulgent towards young people, and not enthusiastic about expelling them.

Eventually, in 1965 after a few expulsions, their ultra-left tactics brought the youth into collision with the bureaucracy and they split the majority of the youth away. As a consequence, the official YS was closed down, and later the youth that remained were reorganised into the Labour Party Young Socialists. The hooligan provocations of the Healyites gave the Labour bureaucracy the excuse to clamp down on the youth organisation. The bureaucracy imposed severe restrictions, such as the appointment of the National Committee by the adult party, the YS Federations were banned and discussions at conference were confined to youth issues. Every effort was used to get around these bureaucratic restrictions, including a tongue-in-cheek resolution moved one year "calling for the support of all members of the Viet Cong under the age of 25"!

On their departure the Healyites spread as many lies as they could about the "Pabloite Grantists" who allegedly assisted the right wing with their expulsions. In fact, while we totally opposed hooligan methods and violence anywhere in the labour movement, we vehemently opposed political witch-hunts, bans and proscriptions against the left. However, on one occasion the line had to be drawn.

The chairman of the Wandsworth YS was a Ceylonese comrade called Mani. He was an ex-member of the Healyites who had joined the *Militant*. He became the target of an organised hate campaign, in which members of the SLL recruited raw youth from the streets ("rockers" as they were popularly known) and sent them to break up a meeting where he was in the chair. They had been told that there was a "black guy who hates the rockers". On one occasion, Mani managed to persuade them to leave quietly, but the second time they caused a riot, whereupon the Party agent called the police. At that point, Mani closed the meeting in an attempt to defuse the situation. Subsequently, the bureaucracy moved the expulsion of a number of SLL members, and Mani counter-moved the expulsion of one *who had personally been involved in violence.*

Late on the Healyites tried to make a scandal out of this. In fact, there is no place for violence inside the workers' movement, and those who resort to violence against members of the labour movement fully deserve to be driven out. Such actions cannot be justified. Trotsky explained this long ago when the Stalinists first introduced these alien methods into the workers' movement. In fact, the Healy tendency had much more in common with Stalinism than with Trotskyism.

The Healyites did colossal damage to the image of Trotskyism in Britain and internationally. They systematically miseducated their members with the crazy perspective of imminent slump, world war or fascist dictatorship for more than 50 years. Their "third period" Stalinist methods acted like a mincing machine for their new recruits, burned out with paper selling and false promises of instant revolution. They quickly destroyed all those young people they had won, and having split away from the Labour Party on an ultra-left binge, were eventually reduced to splinters.

In a statement, entitled *A Contribution on Ultra-Leftism, the Militant* editorial board stated:

> "In more recent times, we have had the activities of the ultra-lefts who, styling themselves Trotskyists, have abandoned all of Lenin's teachings on left-wing Communism, and repudiated the *Transitional Programme* of the Fourth International.
>
> "For them it is sufficient to issue ultimatums to the working class, the trade unions, the Labour Party, the Young Socialists.... To give the working class its marching orders. And when the workers and militants pass them by, they 'take off', denouncing all those who fight, practically, for a consistent revolutionary programme and policy based on Lenin's principles, as centrists, scabs, and 'Pabloites'.
>
> "Experience has taught the British comrades that those who shout loudest today about betrayals, about sell-outs, fake-lefts, etc., are precisely those 'revolutionaries' who were the deepest of deep entrists. The 'anti-Pabloites' of today were in fact the most hysterical of the 'Pabloites' of yesterday. Those who, in the past, refused to criticise Nye Bevan on the grounds that this would 'disrupt our relations with *Tribune*, are the same people who now denounce *Tribune* as the main enemy, and reserve their main fire, not - God forbid! - for the capitalist enemy, the Tories, or even for the right wing Labour leaders, but for the 'Left fakers', and, of course, the 'Pabloites'." (*The Bulletin*, August 1966).

The final break

The Grant tendency had consistently opposed the political position of Pablo and the leadership of the United Secretariat, as they were called after the fusion of 1963. There were fundamental differences over China, the Sino-Soviet dispute, Cuba, guerrillarism, and the Colonial Revolution, which are outlined in the document reproduced in the appendix, *The Programme of the International* and in Ted's book *The Unbroken Thread*. The conflict between the British section and Paris was such, that by the end of 1965, Pierre Frank, Mandel and Livio Maitan, who now called the shots in the International, decided to kick us out and recognise the Coates-Jordan group instead. This, despite the fact that that group represented less than nothing.

At the World Congress of 1965, the British comrades decided to put their views in writing. Since there was no confidence in the willingness of the USFI leadership to circulate our material, it was decided to duplicate the document Ted had written on the *Sino-Soviet Dispute and the Colonial Revolution* and send it to Paris for distribution. However, when the British delegates arrived they discovered that none of the other delegates had even seen the document. Ted commented ironically: "Lenin said that the Second International was not an International at all, but only a post office. But these people are not even a post office!"

At the International conference, Ted was given a total of seven and half minutes, excluding translation, to put the opposition case against the USFI position. A brief letter dated 19 January 1966 from Pierre Frank, who had consistently manoeuvred against the British section since it rejoined the International, informed us of our "demotion". The reply of the section simply stated that the leadership of the United Secretariat had no political authority, and was simply taking organisational measures to silence our opposition:

"The crisis of the International in part derives from a lack of understanding of this problem. For what fundamentally is the International? It is a programme, policy, method, and only lastly an organisation to carry out the former. We remain true to the ideas and methods of Trotsky." By this time Pablo had himself been expelled from the USFI (in 1964) and eventually went back to Greece and ceased active involvement in the movement. He died a few years ago in Athens at a ripe old age. Before he died he asked some of the Greek comrades to send his greetings to Ted and added: "You know, he was really the only honest man in those meetings (of the International leadership in the 1950s)."

After this experience, it was necessary to draw a balance sheet of the history of the Fourth International. Ted did this in a document called *The Programme of the International.* Thirty years of experience was surely enough to allow us to draw a clear conclusion. If a person or an organisation makes a mistake that is one thing. But if the same mistake is constantly repeated and no lessons are learned, then it is no longer a mistake, but an organic tendency. As painful as it might be, it was clear to everyone that this so-called International was dead, that any attempt to revive it was fruitless. After some discussion, it was decided that we should turn our back forever on these gentlemen and face firmly towards the mass organisations of the working class.

The opportunism of the Cliff group

By 1967, with the growing disenchantment at the Wilson Labour Government, the Cliff group (The International Socialists, who later became the Socialist Workers Party) and the International Marxist Group followed the SLL and left the Labour Party. They light-mindedly dropped everything they had said previously and ran off in all directions. In a purely opportunist fashion, they ran after the students involved in the anti-Vietnam protests, adapting their position to the prejudices of the students and petit-bourgeois layers.

The Cliff group, while holding onto their anti-Trotskyist theory of state capitalism nevertheless gave support to "state capitalist" North Vietnam. Earlier, however, they had refused to support North Korea at the time of the Korean War. The difference? In the 1960s, support for Ho Chi Min became very fashionable among the students. Later they scandalously supported the Mujaheddin Islamic fundamentalists in Afghanistan as "freedom fighters" against so-called Soviet imperialism.

In the early 1960s, Cliff had dropped any claim to Trotskyism and was even distancing himself from Leninist organisation. Rosa Luxemburg became all the rage among the petit-bourgeois enemies of Leninism - but only her weak side, of course. As crude opportunists, the Cliffites simply jumped onto whatever bandwagon was to hand. They drifted in whatever direction the wind was blowing.

A good example of this is their position on Ireland. In 1969, *Militant* opposed the sending of British troops to Ireland, and our supporters raised the issue as an emergency resolution on the floor of Labour Party Annual Conference. Although the resolution was overwhelmingly defeated, we made clear our opposition to British imperialism and the need for a united struggle of Catholic and Protestant workers based on a socialist programme as the only solution to the problems of Ireland. In contrast, the Cliff Group supported the sending of British troops to the North on the spurious grounds that they were being sent to "protect the Catholics".

The Marxist tendency represented by *Militant* explained that British troops were being sent in the interests of British imperialism, and that the working class should establish its own non-sectarian defence force based on the trade unions. But the Cliffites were "practical" people, who ended up supporting the instrument of British imperialism:

"The breathing space provided by the presence of British troops is short but vital", wrote *Socialist Worker*. "Those who call for the *immediate* withdrawal of the troops before the men behind the barricades can defend themselves are inviting a pogrom which will hit first and hardest at socialists." [14] Again, "Because the troops do not have the same ingrained hatreds of the RUC and B Specials, they will not behave with the same viciousness..." and that "The deployment of British troops in Ulster provides some sort of security against the lawlessness of the RUC and B Specials." [15] Later, in a complete *volte face*, these same people ended up supporting the campaign of individual terrorism by the Provisional IRA.

Embarrassed by these positions, they now attempt to deny or sweep them under the carpet. Eventually, Cliff, basing himself on his theory of state capitalism, would end up being neutral in the capitalist counter-revolution unfolding in the USSR and Eastern Europe. For him it was simply a shift "sideways", and was of no real significance. [16]

Ted Grant with Pat Wall in the foreground, August 1973

The IMG too gave uncritical support to guerrilla struggles everywhere while attempting to set up "red bases" [sic!] in the universities. They also supported every action of the Provos in Ireland, even going so far as to justify their bombing campaign in Britain as an "anti-imperialist struggle". "The IMG and *Red Weekly* unconditionally support the right of the Irish

Republican Movement to carry on armed actions against British Imperialism", read their press statement issued on 23 August 1973. "We do not hold that in principle such armed actions have to be confined to the other side of the Irish Channel."

In practise, the IMG had completely abandoned the position of Marx and Connolly for the methods of Bakunin and the advocates of individual terrorism. The *Militant*, on the other hand, maintained a consistent class position. We, of course, condemned the repressive rule of British imperialism in Ireland, but we also unequivocally opposed the tactics of the Provisional IRA that completely played into the hands of imperialism and intensified the sectarian gulf in the North. As opposed to this petit-bourgeois stance of the IMG, we consistently argued for a class and socialist approach to the problems of Ireland as James Connolly had always done.

This tiny Mandelite sect, which had been pursuing the deepest of deep entry, now suddenly declared that the Labour Party was a bourgeois party, and actually called on workers to abstain in the 1970 general election (not that anyone heard them). They even went so far as to recommend that people should go to Labour Party meetings and break them up. Needless to say, they never attempted to do so themselves, preferring to confine this verbal demagogy to the university coffee bars, which was their exclusive sphere of "revolutionary action".

The Militant takes off

By 1970, the only tendency of any size, which remained in the Labour Party, was ourselves. The ultra-left sects found this amusing. But in the end the laugh was on them. These vulgar empirics had no perspective whatsoever and could see no further than the end of their noses (they have not changed much today).

Superficially, they seemed to have a point. The right wing policies of the Labour government of Harold Wilson led to a growing sense of anger and disillusionment among the workers. The attempt by Barbara Castle to introduce anti-union legislation resulted in miners' lodges threatening to disaffiliate from the Party.

After the rampages of the Healyites, the LPYS had been reduced to a rump. I remember that in 1968, I was the only member left in the Swansea YS branch. Activity in the movement slumped. However, in relation to the LPYS, within a few years the Labour leadership relented and restored many of the democratic rights taken away in 1965, including the granting of a youth paper and a youth seat on the NEC.

The 1970s were a political watershed nationally and internationally. The defeat of the Wilson government and the coming to power of Heath ushered in a period of heightened radicalisation in the working class. Huge demonstrations took place against the government's anti-union legislation culminating in the imprisonment of five dockers and the threat of a general strike. Factory occupations had reached unprecedented levels and eventually the government was brought down by the miners' strike of 1974. The ruling class was on the retreat, with sections of the state preparing the ground for a future shift towards reaction, as witnessed by the views of Brigadier Kitson and others military figures at the time.

In Swansea, by turning to work among school students, we managed to win over a few young comrades, including Andy Bevan, who was to play a key role for the tendency. By 1970, democratic elections resulted in our tendency winning a majority on the national leadership of the LPYS, which started a national campaign to build up the youth organisation. Peter Doyle, chairman of the LPYS, was then elected as a youth representative on to the NEC of the party, the first time a Trotskyist was elected to such a position. We began to build up points of support within the Labour movement. Our decision to remain had been vindicated.

The mass organisations do not develop in a straight line but dialectically. Directly or indirectly, they reflect the processes at work in the working class and in society generally. The recession of 1974-75 put an end to the period of general capitalist upswing, which had lasted since 1950. This was the first serious economic recession since the war. Prior to that the cyclical recessions of the upswing had been very superficial, and had been barely noticed by the workers, while living standards generally increased. The 1970s were of a completely different character to the period that went before or even the subsequent period 1982-2000.

Internationally, the slump of 1974-75 had far reaching consequences. There were revolutionary movements in the ex-colonial world: Angola, Mozambique and elsewhere. Revolutionary developments also took place in Portugal with the overthrow of the dictatorship, in Greece with the overthrow of the military, in Spain with the end of the Franco regime. Italy experienced a pre-revolutionary ferment. In contrast to the period of "democratic" illusions in the 1950s and 1960s, the European bourgeoisie was preparing for a decisive showdown with the working class. The "Gladio" conspiracy proves beyond doubt that the ruling class was preparing for military dictatorships in Italy, Spain, Norway and Belgium. It has emerged since that sections of the ruling class and the military in 'democratic' Britain had even contemplated a coup against the Labour government of Harold Wilson in the late 1960s.

In this period the pendulum of society swung far to the left. In Portugal, after nearly half a century of fascist and Bonapartist rule, on May Day 1974, one million people demonstrated on the streets of Lisbon. Since the total population of Portugal was only 8 million, this shows the extraordinary sweep of the revolution. *The Times* published an editorial saying, "Capitalism in Portugal is dead." Once again the masses turned towards their traditional organisations. Unfortunately, it was the actions of the leaders of the Communist Party and Socialist Party - especially the Stalinists in the first instance - that again saved capitalism.

This radicalisation also reflected itself within the British Labour Party. The Left succeeded in winning a slim majority on the NEC. Official Party policy also reflected the swing to the left, when it adopted a programme containing the nationalisation of the top 25 companies. The *Militant* tendency intervened in these events in a decisive fashion and began to grow.

From fewer than 100 comrades in 1966, the tendency grew to more than 500 by 1975. We had acquired our own printing press and the *Militant* newspaper had gone weekly in 1972. The tendency gradually built up its position in the Labour movement. This was only possible because we did not succumb to the pressure of ultra-leftism, but remained within the Labour Party while others left. This was one of the secrets of the later success of the Marxist tendency in Britain - an historical breakthrough with no parallel elsewhere.

The Committee for a Workers' International

Alan Woods, who played a leading role in the British organisation since the early 1960s, became the tendency's first regional full-time professional based in South Wales, which soon became a model area. From just the two of us in Swansea in 1969, we built a thriving area, with a number of shop stewards in Fords and the deputy convener, Albert Rosser, who played a key role in the Fords strike.

We had a good base among the miners as a result of our intervention in the miners' strikes of 1970 and 1974. The paper was sold in a number of key pits. We led the bakers' strike in Swansea and also a mass rent strike. On every national demonstration the South Wales contingent was among the biggest. But we did not base ourselves on "activism". We gave a lot of attention to Marxist theory. The South Wales Summer camp became the national Summer School. We also published the *South Wales Bulletin of Marxist Studies.*

In 1974, with a tiny handful of comrades in other countries, we set up the Committee for a Workers International. At this time Alan was given a key responsibility in our international work - that of building a section of the tendency in Franco's Spain. In January 1976, Alan and his first wife Pam - who was also active in the movement - made a big personal sacrifice, and moved to Madrid with two small children (five and two years old) to build the tendency under the difficult conditions of illegal work in the Spanish underground. Within a couple of years, starting with a tiny group of just six comrades (three Spanish and three British) the Spanish organisation grew to 350, and became the second biggest section within the CWI.

But the Spanish bureaucracy had learned from the British experience. After a ferocious witch-hunt by the Socialist Party bureaucracy - the paper was banned and the majority of the comrades expelled. However, we maintained our orientation to the mass organisations, including a flexible approach, and were able to build up an important base for Trotskyism. Today, this has allowed us to wage mass struggles under the banner of the Spanish School Students Union. On several occasions since 1987, the Students Union has led national strikes of three million students.

Alan remained in Spain for eight years, till 1983, when he was obliged to return to Britain because of health problems. After returning to Britain, Alan played a leading role in the International, helping to establish our presence also in Chile, Argentina, Pakistan, Mexico and other countries. He also became editor of the theoretical magazine, the *Militant International Review*, and was expelled from the Labour Party during the purge against *Militant* supporters.

It is no accident that the tendency in Britain and Spain achieved a breakthrough precisely at this time. The success of our work in the mass organisations is determined, on the one hand, by the objective situation and, on the other hand, by the existence of patient, long-term preparatory work, which lays the basis for reaching large numbers of leftward moving workers and youth when conditions are ripe.

Marxists have never made a fetish of any organisational form or tactic. The golden rule is at all times to find a way of connecting with the working class, beginning with the active layer. This necessitates taking advantage of each and every possibility that presents itself at each stage, while keeping firmly in mind the general orientation and strategy.

The first witch hunt fails

The crisis of the Wilson-Callaghan Government of 1974-79 enabled the tendency to connect with a wide layer of radicalised workers as never before. The alarm bells were beginning to ring, not only in the bureaucracy of the Labour Party, but in the ruling class. For the first time, Trotskyism in Britain became a serious factor in the calculations of the state. The strategists of capital were alarmed by the sharp leftward turn of the Labour Party and correctly understood that the activities of the Marxists were playing a key role in pushing the Left, stiffening their resolve and urging them to go further.

Of course, this was not the main aim of our work, but a by-product. The left reformists had an ambivalent attitude to the Marxists. We were objectively allies in the struggle with the right wing, but we were also competitors and rivals, who were constantly winning ground at their expense. We were forcing them to go much further than they wished to go. Moreover, it is well known that a confused person always hates someone with clear ideas. They were at best unstable and unreliable allies.

In 1976, the witch-hunt against us began with an "exposure" in a Sunday newspaper, *The Observer*, by the well-known columnist Nora Beloff. Using material gathered by Reg Underhill, the Labour Party's National Organiser, Beloff attempted to stampede the Labour Party into a witch-hunt. This had all the hallmarks of a premeditated provocation.

Unfortunately for the organisers of the provocation, however, the mood in the Party was not favourable for a witch-hunt. The tendency had won a lot of respect among activists by its tireless work and principled stance on all questions. We never went in for the kind of abuse and hysteria that is the hallmark of the ultra-left groups and cut them off from ordinary working class people. Ted always insisted that we should stick to defending our ideas with "facts, figures and arguments", to "patiently explain" as Lenin used to say.

The "Left" majority on the NEC refused to take action, and by the end of the year, our comrade Andy Bevan, who was chair of the LPYS, was selected - after an outstanding performance in his interview and a blunder by a Party bureaucrat - as the new national Youth Officer of the Labour Party. After an initial red scare and ruckus by the Labour officials' union, Andy was eventually established in an office in Transport House, the Labour Party HQ. This gave us a tremendous opportunity to utilise our position in the LPYS to full effect, allowing us to take our ideas into wider sections of the Labour movement.

Following the 1977 national fire fighters' strike, the following year's TUC came out in opposition to the government's wages policy. A month later, at the Labour Party conference, our comrade Terry Duffy, a delegate from Wavertree CLP, moved a successful composite also rejecting the government's wages' policy. The coming months saw the biggest movement of low-paid workers in history, in the so-called Winter of Discontent. In 1979, after some prevarication, Callaghan went to the polls and was defeated by the Tory Party under Margaret Thatcher.

The Thatcher Government

Labour's defeat and the election of Thatcher resulted in a massive radicalisation in the mass organisations. The shift to the left was a reflection of the disgust with Labour's pro-capitalist policies, and took the form of the rise of Bennism within the Labour Party. Michael Foot had replaced Callaghan as leader, and in 1981 Tony Benn came within a whisker - less than one percent - of defeating Denis Healey, the right wing candidate, for the deputy leadership.

After this leadership election, a section of the right wing split away to form the SDP. This move further reinforced the leftward shift within the party. It was under these conditions that the *Militant* tendency grew quite rapidly, with 1,000 active supporters registered by 1980. The rise of Trotskyism within the Labour Party alarmed the ruling class, which had long regarded the party as an invaluable prop of the capitalist system. The ruling class was never likely to accept the loss of control over the Labour Party without a struggle. It was obvious to us that a counter-attack was just a matter of time. The capitalist press launched a new witch-hunt against the tendency, demanding our expulsion from the party.

Ted Grant appealing against expulsion at the Labour Party's closed session at 1983 Conference
Photography was banned. Thanks to Phil Lloyd for this remarkable picture.

On a personal note, I joined the tendency in Swansea in late 1966, after attending a summer YS day school where Ted was speaking on the Russian Revolution. I remember vividly a discussion in the kitchen of a comrade, where I was informed that becoming a supporter of Marxism "was a commitment for life." At that time, I believe we had about 70 or 80 comrades nationally. By the time I became full-timer, when Alan left for Spain at the beginning of 1976, we had around 600 comrades. At that time I was elected from Wales onto the National Committee of the LPYS and also onto the tendency's leading body. In early 1982, having successfully built up a powerful position for the tendency in South Wales, I went to work for the CWI, but was soon drafted into a newly formed "anti-witch hunt" department at our London headquarters.

In the fight against the witch-hunt, we organised a successful Labour movement conference of 2,000 delegates at the Wembley Conference Centre in London. Despite the protests and resolutions against the purge, eventually the "soft left" on the NEC capitulated under the pressure of the media campaign. The press was covering the activities of the tendency on a daily basis. Using the Underhill report, filled with a mixture of various documents, tittle-tattle and so-called evidence, the NEC expelled the *Militant* Editorial Board in 1983. The expulsions came just prior to the by-election in Bermondsey, South London - an apparently unassailable Labour seat which the Party lost to the Liberals.

At the end of 1983, I was appointed National Organiser of the tendency - a position I held until the end of 1991. I headed the Organisation Department responsible for Labour Party work, countering the expulsions, media relations, the MPs, councillors, co-ordination of the full timers, recruitment, organisation of the national rallies and meetings, as well as public campaigns, not least the anti-Poll Tax campaign. It was a huge operation. Massive rallies were held all over the county to protest against the expulsions, which in turn, led to greater and greater support for the tendency. This support also translated itself into the tendency's growth in the trade unions, and development of the Broad Left Organising Committee (BLOC).

The high point

In 1984 at the beginning of the miners' strike, the BLOC had become the largest left force in the trade unions and held a successful conference of more than 2,500 representatives from all the main trade unions. For the first time in history, a Trotskyist, John MacCreadie was elected to the General Council of the Trade Union Congress. During the year-long miners' strike, given our position in the mining areas, we managed to win over 500 miners to the tendency. In 1988, we filled the Alexandra Palace in London with 7,500 supporters. This was the high point of the *Militant* tendency.

Pat Wall, Marxist MP for Bradford North 1987-1990

On the political front, two of our comrades, Terry Fields and Dave Nellist were elected to parliament in 1983. These were to be followed in 1987 by Pat Wall, a marvellous comrade who had a great *rapport* with workers and youth. The *Militant* leadership of Liverpool City Council from 1983 onwards and its battle with the Tory Government also served to put the tendency firmly on the map. While our councillors in Liverpool were surcharged and banned from office, we had never been defeated at the ballot box. The *Militant* tendency had become a household name and had grown rapidly in numbers and influence. All those sects who remained outside of the Labour Party and had scoffed at our work in the party were left on the sidelines with their mouths open.

In October 1985, Kinnock, who became leader of the Party after Michael Foot had stepped down, made his infamous speech at the Labour Party conference attacking the *Militant*-led Liverpool City Council. This was the beginning of a concerted witch-hunt and a showdown with the tendency. "I think Neil's speech was of historic importance", said Denis Healey. Bob Parry, Labour MP for Liverpool Riverside, however claimed: "Kinnock showed today that he is the biggest traitor since Ramsey MacDonald."

But at the end of the day, all these measures failed. Although they made life very difficult for us (what else could you expect the bureaucracy to do?) the results were really quite poor. By the end of the decade they had only succeeded in expelling around 250 comrades out of some 8,000 supporters.

We had created the strongest Trotskyist tendency since the days of the Russian Left Opposition. From counting the pennies, we now had a turnover of over a million pounds a year, a large premises, a big web printing press, capable of printing a daily paper, and, incredibly, around 250 full time workers - which was more than the Labour Party itself. We had roots in many trade unions and Labour Parties, including about 50 councillors and three Marxist MPs. To their utter exasperation, despite their repeated attempts, the Labour leadership had still failed to separate Marxism from the Labour Party.

The poll tax

After Thatcher's third election victory in 1987, the Tory government moved to introduce a retrogressive Poll Tax in Scotland, and a year later in England and Wales. We saw this as a great opportunity to engage in mass work and lead a battle against the Tory government. In the end, our tactic of mass non-payment connected with the mood of millions of people up and down the country. At its height, around 18 million people refused to pay the hated tax. This was the biggest movement of civil disobedience in British history, led by the All-Britain Anti-Poll Tax Union, which we had established and led. 250,000 people demonstrated in London and a further 50,000 took to the streets of Glasgow. Without doubt, this mass movement, which terrified the strategists of capital, contributed to the repeal of the Poll Tax and the resignation of Thatcher in 1990.

Despite these enormous successes, there were serious problems in the tendency. The most serious was that the political level of the cadres was declining, and the leadership was doing nothing to counter this trend. In the end the reason for this became clear. Ted Grant continually stressed at editorial board meetings the need to thoroughly educate and train the new comrades who entered our ranks. Unfortunately, these calls went largely unheard. Alan Woods attempted to reverse the trend by building up the theoretical journal, but these attempts were deliberately sabotaged by the leading group around Peter Taaffe, who were already pursuing their own agenda at this time.

The Taaffe group favoured activism over theory, which they privately regarded with contempt. Given the changed objective conditions, which had become much more difficult, we had to run fast to stand still. Of course, the building of the tendency was very important, but activism began increasingly to overwhelm the tendency. The stress on growth alone served to politically dilute the tendency, weaken the cadres and open it up to all kinds of alien pressures and influences. As long as Ted's political authority in the leadership was strong, this served to hold things together. However, behind the scenes Peter Taaffe, the editor of the paper, had other ideas.

With the wisdom of hindsight it is clear that Taaffe was getting big ideas about the real significance of the tendency and his role in it. Ted had always stressed the need for "a sense of proportion and a sense of humour". But a sense of proportion was just what was missing in the leading group in *Militant*. They were intoxicated with the successes of the tendency. These were real enough, but one has to keep things in their proper context. A tendency of 8,000 was a significant force, yes. But in comparison with the multi-millioned British labour movement it was still very small. Taaffe and his supporters did not grasp this fact. They were rapidly losing contact with reality. In the immortal phrase of Stalin, they were "dizzy with success."

A very ambitious man with a morbid fear of rivals, actual or potential, Taaffe decided that his talents were not sufficiently appreciated. Actually, despite a certain flair for organisation, Taaffe was never a theoretician and was deeply jealous of people whom he saw as on a higher level than himself. He surrounded himself with a group of yes-men and yes-women, who encouraged him in his delusions of grandeur and egged him on to confront Ted. But this he could not do openly. Instead, he resorted to behind-the-scenes manoeuvres to isolate Ted, spreading rumours about his allegedly impossible character, and worse.

Slowly but surely, a clique was forming around the person of Taaffe. He took personal responsibility for the tendency in Liverpool and West of Scotland, where he assiduously cultivated certain individuals at the expense of others. Although Taaffe was a talented speaker and a capable organiser, all his ideas were taken from Ted.

As long as he worked with Ted, his abilities were put to good use in developing the tendency. However, by this time, Taaffe was clearly attempting to boost his own stature by privately undermining those around him. Taaffe worked systematically to isolate Ted in the leadership. Within the space of two years, Ted was accused of "senile dementia" or, less elegantly, of "losing his marbles". He was denounced as "another Plekhanov" (the founder of Russian Marxism who eventually ended up a Menshevik). Alan Woods, meanwhile, was described as a "mere theoretician". Yet, this phrase reveals better than anything else does the narrow organisational mentality of Taaffe and his group and their contempt for theory. They did not understand the elementary fact that our tendency was built on the solid foundation of Marxist theory. Once that foundation was removed the entire edifice would inevitably collapse - which was just what happened.

In reality, Taaffe felt particularly threatened by Alan Woods, who was certainly on a higher theoretical level and was regarded by everyone as an excellent public speaker and writer. Since Taaffe was always looking over his shoulders for rivals, he imagined (wrongly) that here was a threat to his own position. He therefore did everything in his power to isolate Alan at every step, using different means of preventing from speaking at public meetings, withholding funds from the theoretical journal and even blocking the publication of his book on the history of Bolshevism. Alan's main sin was that he was always close to Ted and consequently would never have countenanced any manoeuvres against him - or anybody else. Taaffe knew that it would be impossible to remove Ted without a battle with Alan Woods - something he feared because of the consequences, above all in the International. He therefore proceeded with great caution, concealing his intrigues as much as possible.

With the end of the Poll Tax campaign, things were coming to a head inside the tendency. Although our intervention in the Poll Tax movement was an outstanding success, because of the policy of "activism" promoted by the leadership - which at times meant that our most active people were running around aimlessly - there was a clear disproportion between the amount of effort put in and the concrete results in terms of growth. As a result, moods of frustration and impatience began to emerge within the organisation.

This even affected some of the leadership, particularly in the West of Scotland and Liverpool. They had been engaged in mass struggles and this seemed to have gone to their heads. They began to look for a short cut to success. Tommy Sheridan in Scotland in particular was keen to break from the Labour Party. Lacking a firm grounding in Marxism, and a clear perspective, they were affected by ephemeral moods in society, and the pressures of the moment. In practice, they abandoned the Marxist method in favour of eclecticism and impressionism. They had clearly lost all sense of proportion and were completely disoriented.

In April 1991, they convinced Taaffe to launch a "new turn" in Scotland. This was sold to the leadership as a temporary local "detour", allegedly intended to combat the threat from Scottish nationalism. Shortly afterwards, a violent row broke out within the international leadership with Ted and Alan accusing Taaffe of organising a clique. This led to a sharp deterioration in relations within the leadership. Then in May, with the death of Eric Heffer, the MP for Walton, the group around Taaffe came forward with the idea of standing Leslie Mahmood, who had been narrowly defeated in the selection process, against Peter Kilfoyle, the official Labour candidate and chief witch-hunter on Merseyside. The electoral challenge was depicted ridiculously as a *principled* question and the tendency was demagogically stampeded into fighting the by-election. It represented a fundamental break with our whole past orientation. Within the leadership, with Alan abroad, only Ted and myself spoke and voted against the proposal. Dave Nellist remarked later in private that "it was turkeys voting for Christmas."

All of our resources were mobilised to fight the by-election. Wildly exaggerated reports were given at national meetings to the effect that victory was within our grasp. In the end, Leslie, standing as the "Real Labour" candidate came third with a derisory 2,613 votes, while Kilfoyle won the seat with 21,317 votes. It was a humiliating defeat - bearing in mind that the *Militant* had recently led a mass movement in the city and effectively controlled the council. But Taaffe and his supporters could not admit this. Instead they resorted to blatant demagogy. *2,613 votes for Socialism*! proclaimed the *Militant* in banner headlines, in an attempt to gloss over the humiliation and to raise the demoralised spirits of the rank and file comrades.

The majority leadership proclaimed the result as a "success", which should be followed in other parts of the country! In this way, what might have been a small mistake, which could easily have been corrected, was magnified into a colossal blunder that destroyed the *Militant* tendency. The idea that a small organisation could compete with the Labour Party was ridiculous in the extreme. As we explained many times, history has shown it is not possible for small revolutionary groups to reach the mass of the working class by a direct route. But by this time, rational argument played no role in the *Militant* leadership. They were hell-bent on pushing the tendency into what Ted aptly described as "a short cut over a cliff."

The group around Taaffe was not interested in listening to anybody. The only thing that mattered now was the prestige of the leading group and the infallibility of its Leader. The conclusions they drew were quite farcical. The Merseyside organiser, Dave Cotterill, subsequently wrote: "The Labour Party would wither on the vine." This shows the absurd delusions of grandeur that characterised the mentality of these people at the time. Of course, as we predicted at the time, it was the Taaffites who would wither away to nothing.

The Walton episode merely served to intensify the Labour bureaucracy's witch-hunt against the tendency. "On the basis of photographic, and other verifiable evidence of Labour members campaigning for Mahmood in the by-election, the NEC Organisation Committee ordered 147 suspected *Militant* sympathisers to be suspended - the biggest ever crack-down against the organisation", wrote George Drower. "Proceedings were begun to expel allegedly Militant-supporting Labour MPs, Dave Nellist and Terry Fields."[17] The Taaffe leadership had deliberately placed their heads on a plate.

Within the leadership, Ted, Alan Woods and I firmly opposed this ultra-left "turn", which Ted characterised as "a threat to forty years work." As we explained in an Opposition bulletin, "After decades of successful work in the mass organisations, which have permitted us to make unprecedented gains, an attempt is being made to launch the tendency on an adventure which threatens to undermine the entire basis of the tendency." [18]

One of the things that always set us apart from the pseudo-Trotskyist sects was the extremely democratic and tolerant internal life within the tendency. Expulsions were extremely rare and dissenting views were always given a fair hearing. This was no accident. It was based on the colossal political and moral authority of the leadership, which in turn reflected that of Ted Grant, a man who was never afraid of political debate, but whom even his enemies would have to admit was always fair-minded, tolerant and loyal. But these clean traditions were trampled underfoot. Taaffe and his supporters did not possess the necessary political armoury to take on the Opposition in a fair fight. Instead they used the weight of the apparatus, the full timers, the weapon of slander, gossip and character assassination, to attempt to wear down and crush us.

In the heated faction fight, Ted and the Opposition were treated abysmally. We were presented not as comrades with arguments to be answered, but as enemies to be crushed. They resorted to the pettiest methods of harassment to undermine our morale. When we went to the centre, nobody spoke to us, not even good morning. Later, our bags were searched before we were allowed to leave the building, and so on. As Ted remarked about Taaffe: "He's got more tricks than a monkey in a box. He must think that this is what politics is all about! He has the mentality of a *provincial politician*."

The methods of the ruling clique in the faction fight were pure Stalinism. In one national meeting, which was an organised "hate session" against myself in particular, Ted made what must have been the shortest speech of his life. "I have seen these methods before. This is Healyism! This is Cannonism! This is Stalinism!" And he sat down, to a stunned silence. The fact is that the Taaffites could not tolerate opposition. They found they could not break us - as they had broken others - and so, after a farcical pretence at a "debate", we were unceremoniously expelled in January 1992.

The expulsion of the Opposition inevitably led to a split in the tendency in Britain and internationally. In Britain the Opposition had the support of several hundred mainly experienced cadres and trade union activists. The situation was far more favourable in the international. At the time of the split, the Opposition had the majority in the CWI. The Spanish, Italian, Belgian, Danish, Cypriot, Mexican, Argentinean and Pakistani organisations supported us. The Greeks were evenly divided, but all the worker comrades supported us. We had significant minorities in Sweden and Germany. In Ireland, the USA and Sri Lanka there was no debate and we were effectively prevented from putting our case. The French section had already been split by Taaffe's manoeuvres - as had the Irish, as we discovered later - the expelled comrades joined the Opposition. If we exclude Britain, this means that we almost certainly had the majority of the international tendency on our side.

In Britain, however, we were once again reduced to a relatively small group with no resources. Our apparatus was reduced to one battered old typewriter. We managed to raise enough to rent a small room and launch a monthly magazine - the *Socialist Appeal.* Nevertheless, although small in numbers, we had sizeable international support. Despite the setback, we managed to take with us the main theoreticians of the tendency, including its founder, and win over a layer of important trade union comrades. We had retained comrades who had experience in building the tendency, even in the most difficult circumstances. These qualities were, and are, a sufficient guarantee for our success.

At the time of the split, Taaffe took the big majority of the members, including the youth, almost all of whom he soon lost, the press, the money and the apparatus. He had apparently everything in his favour. By the end of the decade, the results of his stewardship were clear to all. *He has almost single-handedly managed to wreck the organisation.* The huge centre in Hepscott Road has had to be sold off as a result of a financial crisis. They are now living off the proceeds, but this money will not last forever. In the meantime, they have lost the whole of the Scottish organisation. Just as we thought, Tommy Sheridan split away on a nationalist binge fusing with the Cliff group on the way.

Most of the former leaders of the majority faction have dropped out in demoralisation. The entire leadership of the Liverpool region was booted out. Taaffe has thus succeeded in destroying the Liverpool organisation that he was in charge of for so many years, and which used to be regarded as the jewel in the crown of *Militant.* The membership has been decimated, and probably stands at no more than a couple of hundred activists (at the time of the split in 1992 they claimed 5,000). Even the name of *Militant* - which was well known in Britain and internationally - has been unceremoniously ditched and replaced with a name that nobody has ever heard of. In short, they have succeeded in destroying all that was built up through decades of work.

They light-mindedly threw away the MPs - deliberately provoking their expulsion - as well as other important points of support built up over decades of patient work. On the international front, they have lost entire sections and experienced a series of splits - which still continue. Where they retain some support, it is largely down to the political capital developed by Ted in the past. In their continuing search for a magic formula, they set up an umbrella grouping called the Socialist Alliance. When this was recently taken over by the Cliff group, the Taaffites walked out in a huff. In short, they have shown that they are only good at destroying what others have built. Ten year later, it is all quite clear. It was not the Labour Party, but the Taaffites who have "withered on the vine."

The Unbroken Thread

Over the past decade, our tendency has been rebuilt from scratch. In Britain we have built upon the important points of support we had in the trade unions and are now engaged in rebuilding our base in the youth. On an international scale we have had a number of serious successes - especially in Spain, Italy, Mexico and Pakistan, where we are now becoming a mass force.

In 1992 we launched the *Socialist Appeal* magazine, which has gained a solid reputation for serious analysis, comment and militant policies in the labour movement in Britain and internationally. Our output of high quality Marxist theoretical material is second to none. In 1995 we began the publication of books, which have made quite a spectacular impact internationally, starting with *Reason in Revolt*, by Alan Woods and Ted Grant. This was the first attempt since Engels' *Dialectics of Nature* to apply the method of dialectical materialism to the results of modern science.

This was followed by *Russia - From Revolution to Counter-revolution, Bolshevism - the Road to Revolution*, and a new expanded edition of *Lenin and Trotsky - What they really stood for*. Our books are translated into Spanish, Italian, Greek, Russian, Turkish and Urdu. *Reason in Revolt* is currently being translated into German and Dutch. Our articles and pamphlets have also been translated into French, Chinese, Vietnamese, Korean, Portuguese, Rumanian, Serbian, Macedonian, Polish, Indonesian, Hebrew and other languages.

We can say without fear of contradiction that the political authority of our tendency, both nationally and internationally, has never been greater than it is now. In 1997 we launched the extremely successful website *In Defence of Marxism* (www.marxist.com), which has had far-reaching international appeal, and has been visited by hundreds of thousands of people worldwide. In the last year alone we had over one million successful page visits, and the number of visits is constantly increasing. We deal with a voluminous correspondence from all over the world, and there is a growing number of international collaborators - many of them with sister websites - the latest being in Turkey, Serbia, Poland, Ireland, South Africa and Indonesia.

The key to our success has been our firm defence of the ideas of Marxism, which has permitted us to gain an important following in a whole series of countries where we had nothing previously. We base ourselves on the classics of Marxism, and the contribution that Ted in particular has made over the last 60 years. Thus, although we are formally a young tendency, in practice we represent an unbroken thread that can trace its past back to the days of Trotsky's International Left Opposition.

The contribution of Ted Grant, in close collaboration with Alan Woods, has been of the utmost importance. Ted's political experience has been the bedrock of the tendency. In the past his method and orientation, which are rooted in Trotsky's approach, served to make the tendency a major factor in British politics. This process was unfortunately cut across by a combination of unfavourable objective conditions and the political weaknesses of a leadership that lost its head and was blown off course by events that it did not understand.

Some people imagined that after the crisis in *Militant*, everything was lost. For our part the setback ten years ago did not dent our confidence in the slightest degree. On the contrary in many ways we have been greatly strengthened. We are more convinced than ever in the correctness of our ideas - the ideas of Marx, Engels, Lenin and Trotsky - which can be modified in this or that detail, but which remain fundamentally the same as they were 150 years ago.

Engels once said that the party becomes strong by purging itself. The split in the *Militant* was part of the crisis of the Left internationally. We have learned valuable lessons from the experience. True, in Britain above all we lost a lot of people and were thrown back. But this is not the first time such things have occurred. We have been in a small minority before, as were the great teachers of Marxism. That does not worry us. We are convinced that in the stormy period that opens up before us on a world scale, great events will propel the working class into action in one country after another. Sooner or later the new generation will begin to look for an alternative to the blind alley of capitalism and the bankrupt policies of reformism.

The collapse of Stalinism, has produced a crisis within the Stalinist or former Stalinist parties, and opened up greater possibilities for the ideas of Trotskyism than ever before. Equipped with the correct ideas, methods and approach, we can build a genuine mass Marxist tendency at home and abroad. Ten years ago, the fall of the USSR plunged the Left - and especially the Communist Parties - into a deep crisis. But now the process has turned full circle.

The introduction of the market in Russia and Eastern Europe has spelt disaster for the masses. Gradually, the workers' movement in Russia is beginning to recover, and inside the Communist Parties, there is a growing interest in the ideas of Trotsky. As we go to print, our Russian comrades will have published the book *Lenin and Trotsky - What they really stood for*, which Alan and Ted wrote in 1969, in the Russian language. In the coming period, the ideas of the Trotskyist tendency represented by the paper *Rabochaya Demokratiya* will get a mass audience in Russia, where a new edition of the October Revolution will be on the order of the day.

Events in Latin America, where the revolution in Argentina has begun, show that the so-called globalisation is expressing itself as a global crisis of capitalism. *This is the epoch of the beginning of the world revolution.* Given the weakness of the subjective factor, this process will unfold over a protracted period of time. This will provide us with a certain breathing space in which to build up our forces. We have long ago turned our back upon the myriad of sectarian groups, to whom we say: Let the dead bury the dead! We will face towards the fresh layers of the youth and the working class and its mass organisations, to find the new fighters for the revolutionary movement.

Ted Grant's great contribution was to preserve the unbroken thread of genuine Trotskyism. On this unshakeable foundation we will prepare the cadres, theoretically, politically and organisationally, for the great tasks that lie ahead. This book will undoubtedly serve to assist in this historic goal.

We draw our inspiration from that great leader, thinker and martyr of our movement, Leon Trotsky, who, at the height of the Stalinist Purge Trials, wrote the following: *"whoever seeks physical repose and spiritual comfort - let him step aside. During times of reaction it is easier to lean on the bureaucracy than on the truth. But for all those for whom socialism is not an empty phrase but the content of their moral life - forward! Neither threats, nor persecution, nor violence will stop us. Perhaps it will be on our bones, but the truth will triumph. We are paving the way for it, and the truth will be victorious. Under the terrible blows of fate, I will feel as happy as during the best days of my youth if I can join you in facilitating its victory. For, my friends, the highest happiness lies not in the exploitation of the present, but in the preparation of the future."*

Rob Sewell,
18 March 2002

Notes:

1- *Stalinism in the Post War Period,* June 1951, p. 19.
2- *Socialist Outlook,* September 1951.
3- Ratner, op. cit., p.131.
4- Ibid., pp.136-7.
5- Ibid., p.160.
6- Ibid., p.191, my emphasis.
7- *The Present Situation and Our Political Tasks* (1957), p.7
8- Bill Hunter, *Life and Times of a Revolutionary,* p. 155.
9- Ratner, op. cit., p.228.
10- Robert J. Alexander, *International Trotskyism*, pp.663-4.
11- Ratner, op. cit., p.240 and p.277.
12- Matgamna, *Seedbed of the Left*, pp.9-10, London 1993.
13- National Circular 1 October 1964.
14- *Socialist Worker*, 11 September 1969.
15- *Socialist Worker*, 21 August 1969.
16- See Ted Grant, *Russia - From Revolution to Counter-revolution,* London 1997, pp.222-226.
17- George Drower, *Kinnock,* London 1994, p.279.
18- *The New Turn,* dated 16 August 1991, p.1.

Ted Grant being filmed speaking at a youth meeting, London 2001

Appendix I

Statement of the Political Committee of the WIL on the Expulsion of Gerry Healy

The expulsion of Comrade G. Healy from our organisation will no doubt come as a shock to many of our members. The apparent suddenness of the action has made it necessary for the PB to explain the background of his expulsion from WIL.

At the conclusion of his industrial report on the second day of the National Central Committee meeting of February 6 and 7, which was attended by provincial delegates, as well as the officials of the London District Committee, Comrade Healy stated that he was resigning from the organisation and joining the ILP on the following day; his action was not motivated by political differences but his personal inability to continue further work in our organisation with J. Haston, M. Lee and E. Grant.

He then left the meeting and was thereupon unanimously expelled from WIL by the Central Committee.

The same afternoon he discussed the question of entering the ILP with two leading London [ILP] members, who imparted the information to Fenner Brockway.

His action came as a complete surprise to the Central Committee since he had not intimated his intentions in the course of the previous sitting of the CC or in his industrial report. While many of the comrades present witnessed this scene for the first fume, the majority of London CC members had witnessed a similar occurrence on numerous occasions since the beginning of 1939. In the first stages of theses ultimatums in the form of "resignations" from our organisation, there was no political issue whatsoever bound up with his actions. But in the latter stages it was usually linked up to political issues which were the subject of controversy between the EC, the PB and G. Healy.

The first "resignation" was made to the organisation when *Youth for Socialism* was, for purely technical reasons, changed from a duplicated journal to a printed one at the beginning of 1939. Comrade Healy, who was then the formal publisher of *Youth for Socialism*, took strong objection because the decision had been taken in his absence! Later, in 1939, he again "resigned" on a similar insignificant issue on the same basis of personal pique.

At the end of 1939 when he was in Eire as a member of a delegation of comrades sent there by our centre, as the result of a controversy over secondary tactical issues relating to local activity, he "resigned" from the local and stated that he intended to join the Irish Labour Party to fight our organisation. For this action he was expelled by the Irish Group. After some discussion between the National Organiser and G. Healy, and between the NC and the Irish Group, it was conceded that he be sent back to England without the publicity of denouncing him before the organisation as a whole, and thus make it possible to utilise his energy in the interest of our party in Britain.

In 1940, the first really serious breach came when his "resignation" was linked to a political issue. At that time, Comrade Healy, who was then the representative of the EC in the capacity of National Organiser, was in Scotland.

The constitution of the organisation had been redrafted by the EC with the object of bringing the statutes of the organisation into line with its development from a London local into a national organisation. As a representative of the EC he was responsible for EC policy. Having any differences with the body that elected him, it was his elementary duty to raise such differences with that body, and failing satisfaction, then taking the question up with the membership. Instead of conducting himself as a responsible official and discussing his differences with the EC, he pressed forward a series of amendments to the Constitution through a number of locals with which he had close contact in his capacity as National Organiser. These amendments were of an opportunist character, reducing the Constitution to a federal, instead of a centralised basis. When called upon by the EC to defend his policy, he failed to put up any defence whatsoever, but instead launched a slanderous and personal attack upon two of the leading comrades in the centre and "resigned" from the organisation, because of his inability to work with these comrades.

In the last instance, Comrade Healy's industrial report was to have been the subject of criticism and there is no doubt that his action was bound up with that question. Although he was invited to remain in the meeting for the political discussion on the industrial work, he refused to do this, but stated he could not work with the comrades mentioned.

On three other occasions a similar situation arose when the CC was presented with "resignations" arising out of insignificant issues.

During this period the EC made every concession to him, despite these continued disruptive acts. On each occasion, discussions were held with him in which the error of this type of ultimatum was demonstrated. During the whole of this period, the EC refrained from publicly branding these actions for what they were: crass irresponsibility, thereby allowing him to maintain a measure of authority in the organisation and afford him the possibility of continued activity in the organisation and afford him the possibility of continued activity in our ranks. This was done because it was believed that his undoubted organisational energy and ability could be harnessed in the interests of our party and that these concessions were to the benefit of both Comrade Healy personally as well as of our organisation as a whole.

The final resignation however, was the "last straw". This was particularly true, since it took place at a National Central Committee meeting. The immediate effect of his actions was one of revulsion and indignation among the provincial members and DC delegates and the outcome was to partially disrupt the work of the CC, forcing it to readjust former decisions of an organisational character. It was in these circumstances that the CC took the decision that it was now no longer possible to make concessions: the time had come to take decisive action.

Our organisation is no longer a small body with no real public activity, but a nationally growing Bolshevik organisation whose members as a whole, and in particular its leading members must conduct themselves as revolutionaries.

At the worst, this latest action was a fundamental break with Bolshevism along the road of personal opportunism and consequent political degeneration; at the best it was light-minded irresponsibility which could not be tolerated in our party in particular on its leading body in the present circumstances.

The decision of the Central Committee was unanimous.

15 February 1943

Appendix II

War Cabinet Report on Trotskyism (1944)

Trotskyism is a body of doctrine based on the teachings of Marx, as elaborated by Lenin and interpreted and applied to the conditions of the inter-war period by Trotsky. The cleavage from official Communism, or Stalinism, originated in the opposition between Trotsky's doctrinaire views and Stalin's realism. Trotsky denounced the supplanting of the "continuing world revolution" by Stalin's plan to establish Socialism in the Soviet Union as a prerequisite. He opposed the replacement of democratic discussion of party policy by the personal dictatorship of Stalin, the weakening of the influence of the Soviets (Councils) in the face of a rising bureaucracy, and the revival of economically and socially privileged classes. The Trotskyists do not regard the form of society which now exists in Russia as socialism - they believe that true socialism can be achieved only by more or less simultaneous revolution over the greater part of the globe; and they are bitterly hostile to the Stalinist regime because it has not only "betrayed the revolution" in Russia itself, but by using the national Communist parties as the instruments of its "reactionary" policy abroad has retarded the development of the working class towards world revolution.

The ultimate aim of the Trotskyists is the establishment by means of uprisings all over the world of Workers' Governments which will introduce common ownership and worker's control of the means of production. They believe that world revolution will once more become possible as a result of the war. Their immediate policy on the present "pre-revolutionary period of agitation, propaganda and organisation" is to prepare for this revolutionary moment by fostering a militant spirit among the working class and establishing themselves as its leaders. This they seek to do, according to the directions of the late M. Trotsky, by campaigning alongside the workers on the issues which most closely concern them, such as wages, employment and social conditions.

The Trotskyists, while hostile to "fascism", regard the war as a struggle between rival imperialisms, a struggle which is being used by the capitalist class as an excuse more effectively to exploit and oppress the workers. The USSR, although degenerate, is still a workers' State and must be helped in its resistance to fascism; but the Trotskyist believes that capitalist Governments cannot by their nature effectively oppose fascism, and that he can therefore only help the USSR if he first overthrows his own Government.

Organisation

The Trotskyist movement has existed in Britain since 1929, the year of Trotsky's expulsion from the USSR. The movement originally consisted of several small groups, from which there emerged in 1937 the Revolutionary Socialist League (the official British Section of the Fourth International) and the Workers International League. The Revolutionary Socialist League was stultified by internal strife and the Workers International League outdistanced it in members and activity. The two parties have for some time been urged by the International Secretariat to unite, and on the 12 March 1944, they at length did so. The new body has (to the annoyance of the Communist party of Great Britain) taken the name "Revolutionary Communist Party" and has succeeded the Revolutionary Socialist League as the British Section of the Fourth International. It is too early to say what the relations of the party with the International will be, but the International is loosely organised and is not likely to have the will or the means to do more than advise the party on broad issues; nor is the party under its present leadership likely to submit to any attempt at dictation.

The leadership remains in the hands of the former leaders of the Workers International League, James Haston, Mrs. Mildred Lee, Edward Grant, Roy Tearse and Harold Atkinson (see Appendix A). This group is in effective control of the organisation, which is strongly centralised. District Committees exist in London, Scotland, Tyneside, Merseyside, Yorkshire and the Midlands, but do not act without close consultation with Headquarters. No figures of the total membership are available, but in London, where the movement is strongest, there are 152 members, of whom thirty-two are in the forces. Outside London the party has about twenty branches. A branch rarely has more than twenty members and sometimes has less than ten, and the total number of members in the forces is unlikely to be more that a hundred. On this basis the total membership is probably well below a thousand. Membership, however, is confined to those who have served six months probation and proved themselves active workers, and sympathisers are probably more numerous than official members. Even allowing for people who are prepared to work for the movement from outside, the number of active Trotskyists in the country is very small. The party is strongest, outside London, on Clydeside, and the weakest in the Midlands and South Wales. It hardly exists outside the larger industrial areas.

The Trotskyists, like the Stalinists, attempt to increase their influence by penetrating other organisations. Attempts to penetrate Trade Unions have met with little success, but some progress has been made in the ILP, which the Trotskyists regard as the party commanding the largest following of militant workers. This progress is most marked on Tyneside, where the divisional representative on the ILP national Committee is also a member of the Central Committee off the Revolutionary Communist Party.

In the autumn of 1943 the Militant Workers Federation was formed to co-ordinate the activity of militant groups which had arisen spontaneously among dissident Communists and members of the ILP and WIL. The Federation is directed by the Revolutionary Communist Party; its secretary is Roy Tearse, who claims that it now has nine regional Committees. The most important of these are the Clyde Workers Committee and the London Militant Workers Committee. There is a committee at Sheffield and possibly also at Huddersfield, Barrow and Rugby; and there are small groups of sympathisers on Tyneside, Merseyside and in Nottingham, which Tearse may count as committees. The federation is not much more than a paper organisation, but it is useful to the Trotskyists as a source of contacts and as an instrument of their individual policy, particularly among engineering workers.

The Revolutionary Communist Party has three papers, *Socialist Appeal*, a fortnightly publication of which 8,000 to 10,000 copies are printed, Workers International News, a theoretical organ of which 2,000 copies are printed at irregular intervals, and The Militant Miner, a small local sheet which has been taken over from an independent group in Lanarkshire on its fusion with the Workers International League. The Ministry of Supply refused last October to continue to supply the Workers' International League with newsprint pending the production of satisfactory evidence of their pre-war consumption. This has not been forthcoming, and the party has been forced to reduce both the size and the circulation of *Socialist Appeal*.

Finance

There are no indications that Trotskyist organisations receive money from abroad. The members are expected to contribute liberally and are apparently prepared to do so. Haston is reported in the Daily Telegraph of the 10 April 1944, as saying: "Most of our members pay 5 shillings a week when they can, and those who can afford it pay a 25 per cent levy on their wages."

The Movement's income for 1943 was £2,654. Sales of *Socialist Appeal* brought in £781, and it is believed that Mildred Lee contributed most of her private income of £350. There were a few substantial subscriptions, including sums of £30-£50, believed to havc come from a Cumberland mill-owner, but the greater part of the total was received from branches and anonymous individuals in amounts varying from a few shillings to £5.

Policy and Methods

While the British Trotskyists follow the line of the sect in regarding the war as a struggle between rival imperialisms, their policy is not directly aimed either at stopping the war or at procuring the defeat of their country. They point out that the suffering the war brings is the fruit of the greed and cruelty of the capitalist "boss"; but they do not agitate for peace, and their programme (see Appendix B) includes a pledge of full support for the Soviet Union. Their propaganda appears to be intended rather to stir up class feeling among the workers than to have any direct effect on the war.

The main object of Trotskyist policy is to stimulate and focus discontent and to obtain the leadership of the group of militants thus formed. The party seeks not only to take the place vacated by the Communist Party as the leader of the normally discontented elements, but to attract to itself the larger body of workers who, while not yet ready to take up a militantly anti-government attitude, are suspicious of their employers, doubtful of the sincerity of the Government's promises of post-war reform, and tiring of the industrial truce and the leaders who seek to enforce it. The party's appeal to these groups is somewhat similar to that of the Communist Party before June 1941. There are the same bitter attacks on the callous, profiteering "boss," on "anti-working-class legislation," on the sacrifices demanded of the workers, and on the "imperialist war." On the latter subject the Trotskyists are, however, less persistent and less defeatist than were the Communists.

To carry out this policy they campaign on issues and in areas where there is already strong feeling among the workers. Although the party is always ready to exploit grievances in any factory or mine where it has contacts, it is too small and scattered to be able to start trouble on any considerably scale by itself, and it can make more progress by clinging to the fringes of a big strike than by leading a small one. It secures a wider field for its propaganda, a field already well prepared by the mere existence of a grievance strong enough to cause a strike; and in the bitter aftermath of a big dispute it may hope to start a new branch of the party or a committee of the Militant Workers Federation. The party's technique is accordingly to fasten on an area where a strike is threatening or has broken out; one of the leaders, or the local group if there is one, makes contacts among the strikers and sells literature; the cause and course of the strike is reported in *Socialist Appeal*; and, whatever the outcome, the moral drawn is that only by militant activity under new leadership can the workers secure their rights. But the effect is small.

Socialist Appeal devotes a good deal of its space, though by no means all, to discussing strikes and industrial grievances. It attempts to discredit the Government, the employers and the trade-union leaders; but, while it undoubtedly fans discontent and encourages strikers, it seldom explicitly incites to strike and it makes no attempt to foment sympathetic strikes. The party's slogan is not "Strike!" but "Break the coalition: Labour to power." It desires the establishment of a Labour Government because it believes than any post-war Government must fail to fulfil the workers' expectations, and that the failure of a Labour Government will produce a disillusion strong enough to throw the working class into the arms of the extremists.

Influence on Industry

The influence of the Trotskyists in industry is still slight. In connection with the recent strike of engineering apprentices, there is evidence that Roy Tearse and Heaton Lee, the party's organiser on Tyneside, advised and directed the boys' leaders and that on the Clyde the apprentices were working in conjunction with the Clyde Workers Committee. At Barrow in September 1943 Trotskyists had some part in directing the strike committee during the early days of the strike, but the cause of the strike was a strongly felt industrial grievance and not Trotskyist agitation. Trotskyists also took some part in the strikes at the Rolls Royce aircraft works, Glasgow, in August 1941 and July 1943, in a strike at the Barnbow Royal Ordnance Factory in June 1943 and in the Yorkshire Transport strike in May 1943, but their activity has consisted in advising and encouraging the strike leaders rather than in provoking the strikes.

Trotskyist influence in mining is considerably less than in engineering. There is no evidence that Trotskyists have ever started mining strikes or exercised any appreciable influence on their course. They are drawn to the coalfields by a desire to make converts and they are rarely in touch with strike leaders. In South Wales the Workers International League had at the time of this recent strike two contacts, each of a fortnight's standing, and no organisation. The intervention of the leaders was confined to two visits by Haston, one on the 10 March, four days after the strike had begun, the other on the 18 March, two days after the majority of men, including those in the area

Haston visited, had returned to work. The mid-March issue of *Socialist Appeal*, the smallest that has yet appeared, was devoted entirely to the strike but was not out until it was almost over.

In Yorkshire the Trotskyists have only two groups, at Leeds and Sheffield. Each has about twenty members, most of whom have no connection with mining. During the recent strike small-scale propaganda has been carried on in her spare time by a local leader (Betty Hamilton) with a handful of assistants. Five hundred copies of *Socialist Appeal* have been sent to the area and pamphlets have been distributed. No national leader has covered the strike, but Edward Grant, editor of *Socialist Appeal*, who is suffering from a break-down, interrupted a rest cure to address one meeting and do some canvassing. It was attended by fifty people, few of whom showed any enthusiasm. Victory Gavzey -- aged 19 -- the only other person of Trotskyist sympathies who is known to have addressed meetings, moved a resolution at one of them that the men should return to work and then ask for an increase in pay. The Trotskyists were certainly not responsible for starting the strike, and there is no evidence that they have been responsible for prolonging it. Considering their limited strength in the area and the small scale of their activity, their influence on the situation must have been very small.

The only Trotskyist mining group of any significance is that organised in Lanarkshire by Hugh Brannan, secretary of the national miners' group of the ILP and a Trade Unionist of standing. The group is, however, very small and its influence is limited.

The Trotskyists are attracting workers whose discontent and desire to hit out at the employer and the Government can find no other outlet. They have achieved a small and localised but recognisable influence; and they are confident that the appeal of their militant programme will become stronger as the strain and friction inseparable from prolonged industrial effort increases. They have a closely-knit core of energetic leaders and a membership, which makes up in enthusiasm what it lacks in numbers. They are helped by the absence of competition, except from the ILP, which they hope to use as a conscious or unconscious ally, the lack of normal political and trade-union activity, and the sense of frustration which is alleged to be produced in the absence of marked progress towards either victory in the field or reconstruction at home. These advantages are temporary and, unless the Trotskyists can exploit them much more rapidly than at present, it seems unlikely that they will ever rise to a greater position than that of sparring partners to the Communists, who would very much like to see the Trotskyists and their small paper suppressed.

H.M [Herbert Morrison - ed.]
Home Office, Whitehall
13 April 1944

Appendix A: Officials of the Revolutionary Communist Party

James Ritchie Haston, National Organiser, aged 32, describes himself variously as an aero engineer, a builder and a journalist. He has been an active Trotskyist since 1936 and from August 1941 until the amalgamation was employed as National Organiser of the Workers International League. He is in grade 4. Several attempts by the Ministry of Labour to place him in other employment have failed.

Mildred Lee, Secretary, aged 31, is a South African and a milliner's buyer by trade. She came here in 1938 with her husband, the founder of the Workers International League, and she remained as the League's Secretary when her husband returned to South Africa. She devotes most of an income of about £350 a year received from South Africa to the cause.

Edward Grant, Editor of the *Socialist Appeal*, aged 30, is also South African and has been connected with the Workers International League since its inception. He was posted to the Pioneer Corps but fractured his skull before joining up and was discharged. It has proved impossible, owing to the effects of his injury, to find him alternative employment.

Roy Tearse, Industrial organiser, is 25. He served four years in the Royal Navy and was discharged in 1937 on medical grounds. He suffers from the effects of infantile paralysis. From 1941 to 1943 he was employed as an aero engine tester at De Havillands, Edgware, but was again discharged on medical grounds and has been certified by the medical referee unfit for regular employment. He was for two years a secret member of the Workers International League under an assumed name while acting openly as an energetic member of the ILP but has lately resigned from the latter and avowed his Trotskyist allegiance. He is secretary of the Militant Workers Federation.

Harold Atkinson, Chairman and Treasurer, aged 31, has been associated with Trotskyism since 1938. He is employed as a draughtsman by Messrs. Griffin & Tatlock. He devotes most of his spare time to the business side of the organisation but does not often appear in public.

Heaton Lee and *Ann Keen*, who have been associated with Tearse in the Tyneside apprentice strike, are trusted and experienced Trotskyists; both are believed to be members of the Central Committee. Lee was born in South Africa on the 19 January 1916, and came to England in 1937 already a convinced Trotskyist. He is a civil engineer by profession and since 1938 has been employed by Messrs. Wimpey on works in London, Glasgow and Tyneside. He is reported to have met Mrs. Keen in the course of his voyage to England. She became converted to Trotskyism and has lived with Lee and collaborated in his Trotskyist activities ever since. While they were in Glasgow Lee acted as Workers International League district organiser and Keen as literature secretary; when they moved to Newcastle they continued to work in these capacities. On account of his work Lee appears little in public, and confines himself to organisation, making and developing contacts, and lecturing on political subjects under the auspices of the National Council of Labour Colleges. Mrs. Keen regularly sells *Socialist Appeal* and other literature in the streets. (Heaton Lee is not believed to be any relation of Mildred Lee's husband.)

Appendix B: Programme of the RCP

Programme of the Revolutionary Communist Party

An end to the coalition with the Bosses. Labour Trade Union Leaders must break with the Capitalist Government and wage a campaign for power on the following programme: -

Industrial and Economic Policy

1. Nationalisation of the land, mines, banks, transport and all big industry without compensation, as the prerequisite for a planned economy and the only means of ensuring full employment with adequate standards of living for the workers, and the operation of the means of production under control of workers' committees.

2. Confiscation of all war profits, all company books to be open for trade union inspection,

control of production through workers' committees to end the chaos and mismanagement.

3. Distribution of food, clothes and other consumers' commodities under the control of committees of workers elected from the Co-ops distributive trades, factories, housewives' committees, and small shopkeepers, and allocation of housing under the control of tenants committees.

4. A rising scale of wages to meet the increased cost of living with a guaranteed minimum; the rate for the job, and industrial rates for all members of the armed forces.

Democratic Demands

5. Repeal of the Essential Works Order, the Emergency Powers Act and all other anti-working class and strike-breaking legislation.

6. Full electoral and democratic rights for all persons from the age of 18 years. Full democratic and political rights for the men and women in uniform.

7. Immediate freedom and unconditional independence for India, Ireland and all the colonies of Britain; immediate withdrawal of the British armed forces from these countries; full economic and military assistance to the Indian and colonial peoples to maintain their independence against all imperialist attack.

Military policy

8. Clear out the reactionary, pro-Fascist, and anti-Labour officer caste in the armed forces and Home Guard; election of officers by the ranks.

9. Establishment of military schools by the Trade Unions at the expense of the State for the training of worker-officers; arming of the workers under the control of workers' committees elected in the factories, unions and in the streets for the defence of the democratic rights of the workers from reactionary attacks by the enemies of the working class at home and abroad.

International Policy

10. Against race hatred and discrimination of all forms (Vansittartism, Anti-Semitism, and the Colour Bar); for the fraternisation and co-operation of workers and soldiers of all countries.

11. Unconditional defence of the Soviet Union against all imperialist Powers; despatch of arms, food and essential materials to the Soviet Union under the control of the Trade Unions and factory committees.

12. A Socialist appeal to the workers of Germany, Europe, Japan and the rest of the world, on the basis of this programme in Britain, to join the Socialist struggle against Nazism, Fascism and all forms of capitalist oppression and for a Socialist United States of Europe and a Federation of Asiatic Soviet Socialist Republics.

Appendix III

Secret Service Report on Trotskyism (1944)

In 1939 the Trotskyist movement in Great Britain consisted of several small and disorganised groups. The official section of the Fourth International was the Revolutionary Socialist League, a cluster of theorists working in the Labour Party. The only other grouping of any significance was the Workers International League, an independent body founded in 1938 by two South Africans, Raphael and Mildred LEE. Raphael LEE left England before the outbreak of War, consigning the leadership of the Workers International League to his wife and James Ritchie HASTON, a young Trotskyist of some years' standing. They controlled a membership of under fifty and their monthly paper, *Workers International News*, printed 1,000 copies.

In the late summer of 1939 several of the leaders including HASTON and Cyril NOSEDA, publisher of *Workers International News,* went to Eire partly to make contact with the Irish Trotskyists and partly to avoid military service and the repressive measures which they expected to be taken against their organisation. They returned to England some months later travelling on papers procured in Eire by false representation of identity. They obtained National Registration Identity cards and Ration books in the names of JF GLOSTER and JF SMITH, and were not recognised and prosecuted until June and August 1941. Until well into 1942 the WIL continued to regard itself as a semi-legal body, and its leaders relied on assumed names, rapid changes of address, and generally furtive behaviour in order to conceal their doings.

During this period they were occupied in forming a programme, training a leadership and organising the rank and file. Until this process was well advanced, no outward activity could be attempted. The danger of premature action was shown by the Sheffield conspiracy case of August 1940 in which four members were prosecuted for stealing blank medical grade cards in order to help their associates to avoid military service. One man was discharged but the others served terms of imprisonment. It is worth noting that the culprits were reprimanded by the leadership for indiscretion and indiscipline.

The war crises of 1940 compelled the Workers International League to adopt the much-disputed Military Policy of James Cannon. This admits the necessity for workers to defend their native land from attack provided the defence is operated under their control. It departs from the traditional Marxist-Leninist policy of revolutionary defeatism and has caused bitter theoretical quarrels both in this country and in the United States of America. Party members now joined the Forces instead of trying to evade service.

This modification did not affect the general tone of the WIL's attacks on the government nor its opposition to the "imperialist" war. Passages in the July 1940 number of its paper *Youth for Socialism* caused the Ministry of Information to forward the paper to the Home Office for possible action under DR2c. There was considered to be grounds for action, but on account of the very limited circulation of the paper (2,000 copies), no measures were taken.

The period of consolidation ended in the summer of 1941, and by the time of German attack on the USSR the League was ready with - "a fighting programme to mobilise the masses for the struggle against fascism, whether of the German or the British variety, and for the defence of the Soviet Union". The main point of this was the placing in power of a Labour government. The Trotskyists held that the Labour leaders had sold themselves to the capitalists and would no longer provide a militant leadership. But to convince the masses of this, they held it necessary to have a Labour Government in power so that its alleged failures could be made the subject of propaganda. Then, it was hoped, the people would turn towards Trotskyism, which claimed to supply the only surviving militant policy for the proletariat. The rest of the programme aimed at control by the workers of all national services and of production - in fact the full Marxist programme. It was taken for granted that revolution was the only means of achieving workers' control, but as England was not yet ripe for it, the *Transitional Programme* of "Labour to Power" had to be adopted first.

1942 was notable for the first National Conference of the movement. A constitution was adopted, comprising a Central Committee, a Political Bureau, and a District organisation on classical communist lines. The "basic documents of the Fourth International" and the Transitional Programme were formally adopted as the foundations of policy.

Negotiations were then opened by the International Secretariat of the Fourth International for the union of the Workers International League with the Revolutionary Socialist League with a view to establishing a single British Trotskyist section under the discipline of the International. An American seaman representative was sent to England to report. The difficulties, personal and doctrinal, were many, and it was not until 1944 with the assistance of another American "observer" that the fusion was completed. At a conference in March 1944 the new British Section emerged under the name of "Revolutionary Communist Party". HASTON was elected General Secretary, Millie LEE organising Secretary, and Edward GRANT editor of *Socialist Appeal* (formerly *Youth for Socialism*).

Considerable importance was attached by the WIL to strikes, which they regarded is being the principal weapon of the proletariat and the beet means of preparing a revolutionary situation. They therefore endeavoured to make contact with strikers in as many parts of the country as their limited forces could reach.

In 1941 the first moves were made in the industrial world. In August 4,000 women employed at Rolls Royce, Glasgow went on strike in sympathy with a WIL member who was discharged on account of his political activities in the factory. At the Dalmuir ordnance factory in October a strike broke out following the transfer of the factory from Government to private control; a conference of Ordnance Factory Shop Stewards was called at Nottingham as a result of which the ROP Consultative Committee was set up. Two WIL stewards were elected to the controlling positions and the committee continued under Trotskyist influence for the two years or so of its existence. It only achieved a very limited influence. In 1943 WIL interference was discovered in the Yorkshire bus strike (May), the RCP Barnbow strike (June) and Rolls Royce Glasgow (July).

The Betteshanger colliery strike in December 1941 was the first of the mining stoppages in which WIL influence was brought to bear. HASTON visited the district, made contacts among the strikers by selling Trotskyist literature, and afterwards wrote up the story in *Socialist Appeal.* They used similar methods in a number of other coal strikes throughout 1942. The mining industry they regarded as a particularly fruitful field for work owing to the chronic unrest existing in the industry. A storm in a teacup blew up in 1942 when the Yorkshire Miners' agent in a somewhat exaggerated protest gave them publicity in the national press.

By this time the Workers International League found its old method of canvassing at the scenes of strikes to be too primitive, and the machinery of the ROF Co-ordinating Committee was used to put forward a more ambitious plan. At a conference of militant shop stewards summoned in Glasgow by two Trotskyist convenors a provisional "Committee for Co-ordinating Trade Union activity" was set up (June 1943). The WIL won effective control of this body and placed one of its undercover members, Roy TEARSE in the post of secretary, hoping to draw to itself the leadership of the local committees of militant workers, which were springing up in some industrial areas. The strike at Vickers Armstrong's, Barrow, in September provided the first occasion for action. TEARSE made contact with the men's leaders and undoubtedly exercised some influence on the progress of the strike. Useful publicity was also given to the existence of the committee, which had been re-named Militant Workers' Federation.

In January 1944 apprentices working in the Tyneside shipyards organised themselves into a Tyne Apprentices' Guild in order to oppose the mining ballot scheme. The boys' leader was strongly under the influence of the WIL organiser in Newcastle, Heaton LEE, and received constant advice and help from him. Having this direct contact, the WIL did not need to rely on the Militant Workers Federation. TEARSE gave his instructions direct to LEE and LEE to the boys through his protégé DAVY. In March a strike of some thousands of boys was declared.

Searches under DR39A were carried out at the Trotskyist headquarters in London, the Militant Workers Federation headquarters in Nottingham, and the houses of TEARSE, LEE and DAVY in Glasgow and Newcastle. On the evidence found, proceedings were started against TEARSE, LEE, Ann KEEN (his mistress) and Jock HASTON under the Trade Disputes and Trade Unions Act 1927. DAVY appeared as a witness for the Crown. The four were sentenced to imprisonment for one year (TEARSE and LEE), thirteen days (KEEN) and six months (HASTON), but on Appeal the sentences were quashed on a point of law.

The Revolutionary Communist Party (now so called) started Defence Committees on behalf of the accused and by working in co-operation with the ILP and other left wing organisations, improved its claim to recognition as a party of the Left. It also gained some prestige from the arrest of its leaders. The legal expenses of the trial and appeal were raised with some difficulty, but after the release of the prisoners the main object of the committees was removed and they collapsed.

The arrest of TEARSE and the coming into force of DRIAA put an end to the open activities of the Militant Workers Federation and the summer of the Second Front proved to be unpropitious for industrial agitation. The somewhat spectacular progress of the Revolutionary Communist Party in industry came to a standstill. Many discussions were held on the future of the Militant Workers Federation and of industrial work generally, but the time was not ripe for action and the future could not be usefully forecast. The party turned to purely political issues, the chief being its post-war relations with the ILP at home and with the Fourth International abroad. Party members in the Forces were instructed to seek out the Trotskyist groups in Belgium and France, and to establish an exchange of information between them and the RCP leaders. The same method was used in Italy, and also in Egypt, India and Ceylon.

In January 1945 the Revolutionary Communist Party decided that its political position had sufficiently improved to justify its contesting a Parliamentary election. At Neath there was a move to put forward a militant left wing candidate and it was arranged that this should be Jock HASTON standing openly as a representative of the RCP. Heaton LEE was made his election agent. The Party did not hope for success, but expected to consolidate its position in South Wales and to receive an amount of national publicity, which would not otherwise be obtainable. It polled 1,786 votes and forfeited its deposit.

In February 1945 the full members of the Party numbered eight hundred, with an outer circle of two thousand active associates. Twelve full time organisers were employed. All the membership must take an active part in the work and life of the organisation or they are not allowed to retain their membership.

Investigations

A small amount of work on the Trotskyist movement has been done by F2a as long as this section has formed part of the Security Services. Up to the outbreak of war most of the material in our records consisted of Special Branch reports and the products of occasional Home Office Warrants. The movement was too small and chaotic to form the subject of sustained investigation.

At the outbreak of war the Workers International League transferred much of its activity to Ireland, and those members who remained here kept quiet. Little information came to notice, and owing to extreme pressure of communist work, few enquiries were initiated about the Trotskyists. In September 1940 many of the more up to date Trotskyist records were destroyed by enemy action; they were later reconstituted with the assistance of Special Branch. Special Branch themselves however had reduced their enquiries to a minimum as they considered as we did that the groups were negligible for the time being.

When the Workers International League settled down to more regular habits, a HOW was taken out on their office at 61 Northdown Street (February 1942). This yielded a great variety of interesting information particularly on industrial activities, recruitment, Armed Forces work and organisational developments. A Censorship watch on the headquarters of the Fourth International in New York and on Irish contacts also produced good results. An agent was introduced by MS into WIL circles in the summer of 1942 and produced results, which later proved to be more valuable than was realised at the time.

Until 1942 when the Workers International League made its early appearances in industry the provincial Police forces knew little about the Trotskyist movement. In the letters which F2a began to send out to the Provinces in increasing number care was taken to add a paragraph explaining the growing security interest of Trotskyism. As a result many of the more enterprising forces undertook their own regular investigations, and by the end of the war at least five police agents had been placed in the movement. Two of these (Glasgow and Birmingham) produced first class information of general interest. Our own placing of agents was not so successful. MS's man failed in 1943 and it was not until a year later that a second was found, who only lasted a few months. In this connection may be mentioned an interesting attempt by the Revolutionary Communist Party in the autumn of 1944 to run a double-cross agent against Special Branch. The latter had approached an RCP contact who reported the fact to the secret sub-committee of the Political Bureau. They instructed him to accept the proposals of' the Special Branch officer and to report to them the kind of questions he was asked. From this they hoped to estimate the amount of information which Special Branch possessed and also to distract them with false information. The plan broke down however through the indiscretion of their go-between who spoke of it to an unauthorised person; it was then considered unsafe to continue.

In the middle of 1943 the activities of the Workers International League had increased still further, and a memorandum was drawn up in F2a recommending an enlargement of the section's powers to make inquires and record the results. The recommendations which were agreed to by DDG and DDO included a more general use of HOWs, a spell of regular observation by B6 (which had, not previously been used for Trotskyists), and the establishment of a personal link with the SB officers concerned in Trotskyist work. The historical survey attached to the memorandum was circulated to the Regional Officers, most of whom conveyed the gist of it to the Police.

Early in 1944 the Workers International League (now the Revolutionary Communist Party moved to new offices and asked for the installation of a telephone. A telephone check was taken out which proved to be of great value in revealing some of the inner workings of the organisation. Special facilities were also used which though fitful in working, produced several vitally interesting accounts of future plans and policy which could not possibly have been obtained by other means.

This brief survey will show the remarkable progress of the Trotskyist movement during the war period from being an unimportant handful of talkers to a disciplined body of some size, having programme, finance and organisation and the determination to use them. The investigations conducted by F2a expanded correspondingly.

The investigation of Trotskyism was found to differ considerably from that of the Communist Party in the latter stages of the war. The Revolutionary Communist Party used conspiratorial methods for its more important work. It only became an open organisation at all towards the end of the period. It conducted few public meetings and attached minor importance to them. Its chief work - industrial and international - was carried on clandestinely. Cover organisations such as the Militant Workers Federation were favoured in industry. As far as possible only trivial correspondence went through the post and cover addresses were resorted to. Initials instead of names were used in all Party documents. Talk on the telephone was guarded. Impending members were closely scrutinised. Communications with Fourth International headquarters were carried on by courier service and by personal visits of seaman delegates. RCP members working in the ILP used pseudonyms.

It followed that the simpler methods of investigation failed to discover any of the important aspects of Trotskyist work, and if used alone would convey a false impression. It was found that close study of the Party's methods over a period of time was necessary if an officer was to interpret at all adequately the material reaching him. Often it could not be interpreted at once and had to be put aside until later developments provided a clue. This meant that the study of Trotskyism demanded a larger proportion of the Section's time and records than the smallness of the organisation seemed at first sight to warrant.

Note:

A "HOW" is a Home Office Warrant that permits the opening of mail and phone tapping. "MS" is M Section; the organisation ran by C H Maxwell Knight, who was the former Director of Intelligence of the British Fascists.

Appendix IV

Open Letter to BSFI by Ted Grant (1950)

British Trotskyism has reached an impasse on the road which has been travelled by the official Trotskyist organisation: there is no way forward towards the development of a healthy revolutionary tendency rooted in the masses.

For three reasons, as a revolutionary tendency, the Fourth International in Britain has collapsed:

1) Capitulation to Tito-Stalinism internationally.
2) Policy and programme in Britain.
3) Lack of internal democracy.

Titoism

As a result of the development which followed World War Two an unforeseen relationship of forces has developed on a world scale between Stalinism, reformism and capitalism. The prognosis of the Fourth International before the war that the problem of Stalinism would be solved either during the war or immediately after has been falsified by events.

Owing to the viability of state ownership, the frightful decay and collapse of imperialism and capitalism, the revolutionary wave following World War Two and the weakness of the revolutionary internationalist tendency, Stalinism was enabled to take advantage of all these factors and emerged with the USSR as second world power enormously strengthened throughout the globe. Stalinism has become the mass tendency in Europe and Asia.

The collapse of capitalism in Eastern Europe enabled Stalinism as a Bonapartist tendency to manipulate the workers and manoeuvre between the classes - establishing deformed workers states of a Bonapartist character with more or less mass support. Stalinism in the present peculiar relationship of class forces, basing itself in the last analysis on the proletariat - in the sense of standing for the defence of the new economic form of society - is Bonapartism of a new type manoeuvring between the classes in order to establish a regime on the pattern of Moscow.

In China and Yugoslavia, the Stalinist parties came to power on the basis of overwhelming mass support and established regimes relatively independent of the Moscow bureaucracy.

The fact that the revolution in China and Yugoslavia could be developed in a distorted and debased character is due to the world factors of:

(a) The crisis of world capitalism.
(b) The existence of a strong, deformed workers' state adjacent to these countries and powerfully influencing the workers' movement.
(c) The weakness of the Marxist current of the Fourth International.

These factors have resulted in an unparalleled development, which could not have been foreseen by any of the Marxist teachers: the extension of Stalinism as a social phenomenon over half Europe, over the Chinese sub-continent and with the possibility of spreading over the whole of Asia.

This poses new theoretical problems to be worked out by the Marxist movement. Under conditions of isolation and paucity of forces, new historical factors could not but result in a theoretical crisis of the movement, posing the problem of its very existence and survival.

After a period of extreme vacillation and confusion throughout the International, including all tendencies, three distinct tendencies have emerged:

(a) A movement of despair and revisionism, so-called state capitalism; organisational Menshevism of Haston and the ideological disintegration of Morrow, Goldman, Craipeau, etc.
(b) A tendency in the direction of neo-Stalinism (the IS and the British Section).
(c) The Marxist current striving to carry on the best traditions of Trotskyism.

Faced with formidable problems, the I.S. and the British leadership have revealed themselves theoretically bankrupt. Without any adequate theoretical explanation or conscientious analysis of their past position, they have changed 180 degrees in true Zinovievist fashion overnight, from one maintaining that Eastern Europe and China were capitalist regimes to one where Yugoslavia - since the break with Stalin - has mysteriously changed into a healthy workers state.

In Britain, echoing the I.S. and without the least attempt at theoretical understanding, the Healy leadership gives its crudest application. Their method of reasoning follows along these lines: (a) the Fourth International has predicted that Stalinism could not make the revolution (b) Stalinism has made the revolution, therefore.... (c) it is not Stalinism! The second line of argument of which both the I.S. and the Healy leadership are guilty, is that there can only be one Stalin! Why? There can be more than one Fascist dictator because they have a class basis in the capitalist class, but Stalin, apparently, has no class basis.

Idealising and white-washing the Tito leadership because of their break with Moscow, the British leadership has suppressed all fundamental criticism of this tendency, and regards Yugoslavia in this light of a 'normal' proletarian dictatorship: i.e. a healthy workers state with this or that minor blemish of no real importance. Taking as a platform the fact that, since the break with Moscow, the Tito leadership has been compelled to borrow many of the arguments from the arsenal of Marxism in their criticism of the Moscow oligarchy, they do not see the conflict as a reflection of the national struggle against the oppression and the exploitation of the Moscow bureaucrats, and as one which was reflected throughout Eastern Europe, and even within the boundaries of the Soviet Union itself - the Ukraine, the Crimea Tartars, Volga German Republic, etc. The only important difference being the possibility of a successful resistance owing to the independent character of the state apparatus in Yugoslavia.

Despite zigzags to the left, partly demagogic partly sincere, the fundamental basis of the regime in Yugoslavia remains as before… socialism in one country (and tiny Yugoslavia at that), manoeuvring between world imperialism and the Russian bloc (only thanks to which Yugoslavia can maintain itself). The regime remains totalitarian - workers' democracy does not exist.

The attempt to apologise for these ideas as a merely secondary hangover from Stalinism is criminal and false. Some correct criticisms of the Moscow regime do not transform Tito's set-up any more than some of the correct criticisms of the Cominform change the nature of the regime in the countries where the Cominform holds power.

The crisis within Stalinism makes the problem of building the Fourth International more complex than before. The creation of new Stalinist states - independent, or semi-independent from Stalin - has added further confusion in the minds of the world working class. The Fourth International, while taking advantage of the rift within Stalinism in order to expose the real nature of this Bonapartist disease, must not make concessions to neo-Stalinism. While giving full support to the struggle for national self-determination on the part of the Yugoslav nation against the brutal attacks of Great Russian chauvinism, the Fourth International must not thereby underwrite the political position of Tito.

Whilst representing the national aspirations of the Yugoslav masses the Tito leadership - on a Lilliputian scale - use the methods and fulfil a similar role as the Kremlin clique. It must not be forgotten that the break did not come from the Yugoslav side but was forced on the Yugoslav bureaucracy by the relentless and uncompromising attempt at Moscow domination. Since the break there has been no fundamental change in the principles and methods of the Yugoslavs … How could it be otherwise? Socialism in one country remains the axis around which the ideas of the Yugoslavs revolve. To them the degeneration of the Russian bureaucracy is purely an accidental phenomenon which they do not explain from the Marxist point of view that conditions determine consciousness. Nor could it be otherwise - on a smaller scale the conditions in Yugoslavia are similar to those in the Soviet Union (backward country, small minority proletariat, hostile environment, imperialism and Stalinism). Like causes produce like results. In foreign and in domestic policy the position of the Yugoslavs is not fundamentally different to that of Stalinism in its early phases. In the long run it will have the same consequences.

Instead of taking advantage of the conflict in order to demonstrate the real nature of Stalinism and the vitally necessary attributes which a healthy workers state have converted themselves into a replica of the friends of the Soviet Union. The organisation has become the exculpatory tourist agency for Yugoslavia.

From the inception of the Socialist Fellowship by Ellis Smith, to the Korean Crisis, the organisation went through a period of collaboration and accommodation to various elements inside the Labour Party. These stretched from the social democratic left reformists such as Ellis Smith and Brockway to Stalinist fellow travellers, such as Tom Braddock and Jack Stanley. In the absence of a genuine left wing the Healy leadership helped to construct a shadow. In order to maintain this shadow they were forced to accommodate themselves to it. Thus when the Socialist Fellowship produced its policy, After the General Election, this leadership took a leading role in drafting a programme which was false and opportunistic.

At the same time, illusions were spread about the so-called working class leaders, Ellis Smith, Mrs. Braddock, etc.

At the first serious crisis when the Korea dispute arose, the inevitable splitting of this organisation took place, with Ellis Smith and Company departing. With the departure of the important left reformists, the group veered more openly in the direction of accommodating itself to the Stalinist fellow traveller wing. They remain in the rump of the Socialist Fellowship on a semi-Stalinist position.

In fact the Trotskyists form the backbone in membership, organisation and activity of the Socialist Fellowship.

The Trotskyists have expended their energy propagating an opportunist policy instead of building a revolutionary nucleus around themselves.

'Socialist Outlook'

During the period of the development of the Socialist Fellowship, the *Socialist Outlook* carried out its stated task: "to reflect the confusion of the left wing." (1949 Conference document). The political role of the *Socialist Outlook* was determined not by the anaemic editorials, but by the leading articles of those MPs, etc., whose policies were transparently one of sweetening the bitter pills of the right wing.

At the same time, the editorials were coloured by the need not to "offend" the Stalinist fellow travellers on the Editorial Board.

The editorial produced a line of "criticism" which is worthy of the notorious "Friends of the Soviet Union". "The leadership… would like it to be." "We are far from suggesting that the Russian Government at all times and under all conditions supports progressive movements." "There is a distinct flavour of power politics about Moscow's attempt to secure peace in Korea in return for an extra seat on the Security Council." These are examples of "serious Trotskyist criticism"! Amongst such statements - which have a very distinct flavour - falls the following: "Russian foreign policy is determined by what the government of that country considers is in the interests of the Soviet Union, but that as India proved does not, by any means, always co-inside with what is in the best interest of the international working class. Or even, in the long run, the best interest of the Soviet Union itself"!

On this basis of political accommodation, the Healy tendency boasts in Britain and internationally of its numerical and organisational successes in the "building of the left wing" within the Labour Party. Claims which were largely without foundation in fact.

Even with their most strenuous efforts it remains an unimportant and semi-fictitious organisation. Without their propping up it would collapse immediately.

The *Socialist Outlook* is a "forum" with no revolutionary tendency reflected in it. Neither is revolutionary criticism allowed in the paper. For instance, SL's (Sam Levy) attack on the April editorial and ML's (Marion Lunt) attack on the position of Yugoslavia were not published, whilst quantities of out and out reformist and Stalinist material was published. In this respect they compare unfavourably even with the centrist *Socialist Leader*. The important point must be borne in mind that the dominating forces in the *Socialist Outlook* are the Trotskyists.

The *Socialist Outlook* being in reality the paper of the group, should be the organiser of the Group, instead it has become a channel for Stalinist influence in the Labour Party.

The whole line of the paper and the policy of this grouping has its crassest expression in the notorious Korea supplement. There was no criticism whatsoever of the role of the Stalinist bureaucracy. There was a white-washing of the role of the Yugoslavs at UNO. Whilst correctly supporting the struggle of the North there was not a syllable on the Stalinist set-up.

In the League of Youth, where there are the most favourable conditions for work, we see not a Trotskyist concept of spreading our ideas and gaining support for them, but the concept of controlling the whole LOY organisationally. In its struggle in the LOY, while correctly fighting for democratic and organisational demands, it does so at the expense of a political position. The whole approach in the Labour Party is a Stalinist one of controlling machines, a Socialist Fellowship, a *Socialist Outlook*, an entire League of Youth, at the expense of political ideas and programme. However, it has not the saving grace that side by side with organisational appendages, the Stalinists simultaneously organise their own powerful independent party and press.

This liquidationist policy becomes the mixing of banners, policy and programme.

Lack of Internal Democracy

Without a proper sense of proportion and magnifying the dangers, the conference was held under most disadvantageous conditions. Delegates only, apart from the favoured few, were allowed to attend. Individual members, on the grounds of security, were refused the right to attend or even to know where the conference was being held.

The document of the State Capitalists was refused publication after the General Secretary had accepted it on the grounds that its author was expelled (ex poste facto). This constituted a provocation, which, of course, assisted the State Capitalists. They were a tendency represented at the conference and should have had the right to put forward a document to express their ideas even if the author was outside the organisation.

The Liverpool branch document was not published on the grounds that it was presented too late, although some of the ideas were incorporated in the last minute document, without acknowledgement.

The "amended" major document was, in fact, an entirely new document. By adding new ideas in an amalgam with the old, it could only succeed in disorientating and confusing the members. The leadership presented an entirely new document while at the same time claiming that they had only amended the old document. This is Zinovievist trickery.

At the conference the political discussion and voting took place in an atmosphere of disciplinary threats. On the resolution on reformism the delegates were told that anyone voting against its implementation would be expelled, notwithstanding the fact that some delegates disagreed with the document. In all Bolshevik organisations members have the right to vote against documents, although a majority decision determines policy, automatically. The resolution on implementation was put in order to force the minority to vote for a resolution to which they were opposed, on threat of expulsion. This ultimatistic attitude has more in common with Stalinist monolithism than Bolshevism.

They did not take the opportunity to allow the ventilation of the ideas of the State Capitalists by having a full discussion at the conference, despite the fact that growing numbers of the members were becoming sympathetic to state capitalism as a reaction to the semi-Stalinist line of the leadership.

Arbitrarily, and bureaucratically, the leadership dissolved and amalgamated branches, without taking into account the needs of the party, but only the needs of the clique. For example, the General Secretary went down to the Kilburn branch and declared the branch dissolved in order to "separate the branch from 'malign' influences". This was not ratified by the Executive Committee (EC) until a week later.

In Liverpool, there was a deliberate attempt to split the branch in two for the purposes of dividing the "Deane family" from the rest of the comrades in Liverpool.

Branches were deliberately isolated from one another in order to facilitate control from the center. There was no knowledge of what was taking place in the organisation as a whole, correspondence between branches was restricted and the statements which came through the EC had the specific purpose of rubber-stamping EC actions. Branches and individuals who disagreed were threatened with expulsion or attacked viciously as anti-party comrades.

As a consequence of this regime, political discontent was bound to reflect itself both in the infraction of disciple and dropping away of members.

The only reply to the infraction of discipline was instantaneous expulsion (Percy Downey in Birmingham). The decision to expel was taken to the branches for endorsement. Those who voted against the EC's action on the grounds that a full discussion was necessary and that these violations were a result of the lack of political discussion and the lack of democracy inside the organisation, were themselves instantly expelled (Birmingham, West London). Thus, they insisted upon the monolithic principle of unanimity.

Leading opposition comrades such as JD (Jimmy Deane) and SL (Sam Levy) who were members of the National Committee were expelled on flimsy pretexts or on technical infractions of discipline.

By restricting the rights of members, by utilizing technical points, by the dictatorial attitude of the leadership and the general intimidation of members, the group has shrunk. Due to the number of members resigning or the expulsions, it has been reduced to a shambles. In the provinces it has become a mere skeleton. In London members are losing confidence in such a leadership. These have been large losses.

Only the younger and inexperienced comrades and the hardened elements of the clique remain. The fact of an increasing number of members leaving the group, plus the fact of the expulsion of leading comrades, one a member of the National Committee and the only opposition representative on this important body, shows that it is both impossible and at the same time ceases to have any meaning, to fight for an alternative leadership in such a caricature of a Bolshevik organisation.

An Appeal

Comrades, these issues which we raise are not light ones. They are fundamental questions, which affect the fate of Trotskyism, nationally and internationally. We have not come lightly to the decision to break from this ideologically and organisationally disintegrating tendency. If the precious heritage of ideas left by Trotsky is to be preserved, expanded and developed it is necessary to break with those who trail in the wake of Stalinism. Today, groupings of the Fourth International, owing to various historical factors are small and weak. All the more necessary then, that the fundamental principles of Trotskyism should be retained intact. Today, the main task is one of ideological preparation for the development of a mass organisation at a later stage. On a programme of neo-Stalinism only disaster can be prepared. Only the training of developed revolutionary cadres can prepare the way for the future.

With the world situation and the conditions existing as they are, it is impossible to foresee the development of the mass Trotskyist movement in Britain very quickly. This will require years of patient work.

At this stage, the main activity of the group will have to lie inside the Labour movement and the mass organisations of the working class, as an entrist group. A left wing will inevitably develop in the Labour Party in the coming years. But the foolish endeavour to create a left wing out of nothing and declare that the left wing is already here has only demonstrated the impotence of the Healyites except in their own imaginings. In order to prepare for the left wing it is necessary now for serious and sober criticism of all tendencies in the Labour Party to be conducted in the press and in the Labour Party. At the same time a relentless exposure of Stalinism as well as of imperialism must be consistently carried on, in order to avert the possibility of sections in the Labour Party going over in despair to Stalinism.

For the conduct of the work scrupulous democracy and full freedom of discussion within the organisation must be maintained. Without this it will not be possible for a revolutionary grouping to be created and survive in the difficult period that lies ahead.

For all these reasons we appeal to all sincere comrades in the movement to join us in this task. Only in this way, will a fighting, living movement be created. Patient day to day work inside the Labour movement will achieve results if it is conducted on a correct basis. The years that lie ahead can be fruitful ones. The tasks are difficult, but the opportunities from a long term point of view unbounded. Forward to the building of the revolutionary tendency in Britain.

September/October 1950

Appendix V
Programme of the International
by Ted Grant

The First and Second Internationals

Without an international perspective, programme and policy, it is impossible to build a movement which can face up to the tasks of transforming society. An International is a programme, policy and a method, and its organisation is the means for carrying that through. The need for the International flows from the position of the working class internationally. This in its turn has been developed by capitalism through the organisation of world economy as one single indivisible whole. The interests of the working class of one country are the same as the interests of the workers of the other countries. Because of the division of labour established by capitalism, the basis is laid for a new international organisation of labour and planned production on a world scale. Thus, the struggle of the working class on all countries forms the basis for the movement towards socialism.

Capitalism, through the private ownership of the means of production, developed industry and smashed the local particularism of Feudalism. It broke down the archaic customs dues, tolls and exactions of Feudalism. Its great creation is the national state and the world market. But once having accomplished this task, it itself has become a fetter on the development of production. The national state and private ownership of the means of production hamper the development of society. Production possibilities can only be fully utilised by abolishing national barriers and establishing a European and World Federation of Workers' states. These, with state ownership and workers' management, are a necessary transition stage on the road to socialism. It is these factors which dictate the strategy and tactics of the proletariat, as reflected in its conscious leadership. In the aphorisms of Marx "the workers have no country and therefore 'Workers of the world unite'."

It was with these considerations in mind that Marx first organised the First International as a means of uniting the advanced layers of the working class on an international scale. In the First International were British trade unionists, French Radicals and Russian anarchists. Guided by Marx, it laid the framework for the development of the Labour movement in Europe, Britain and America. In its day, the bourgeoisie trembled before the menace of Communism in the form of the International. It established deep roots in the main European countries. After the collapse of the Paris Commune, there was an upswing of capitalism on a world scale. Under these conditions, the pressures of capitalism on the labour movement resulted in internal quarrels and factionalism. The intrigues of the anarchists received heightened impetus. The growth of capitalism in an organic upswing in its turn affected the organisation internationally. Under such circumstances, after first moving the headquarters of the organisation to New York, Marx and Engels decided that, for the time being, it would be better to dissolve the International in 1876.

The work of Marx and Engels bore fruit in mass organisations of the proletariat in Germany, France, Italy and other countries as Marx had foreseen. This in its turn prepared the way for the organisation of the International on the principles of Marxism, which embraced greater masses. Thus in 1889, the Second International was born. But the development of the Second International largely took place within the framework of an organic upswing in capitalism, and while in words espousing the ideas of Marxism, the top layers of world social democracy came under the pressure of capitalism. The leaders of the Social Democratic parties and the trade union mass organisations of the working class, became infected with the habits and style of living of the ruling class. The habit of compromise and discussion with the ruling class became second nature. The negotiation of differences through compromise moulded their habits of thought. They believed that the steady increase in the standard of living, due to the pressure of the mass organisations, would continue indefinitely. The leaders raised themselves a step higher above the masses in their conditions of existence. This affected the top layers of the Parliamentarians and the trade unions. "Conditions determine consciousness" and the decades of peaceful development which followed the Commune of 1870, changed the character of the leadership of the mass organisations. Supporting socialism and the dictatorship of the proletariat in words, and espousing internationalism in phrases, in practice the leadership had gone over to the support of the national state. At the Basle Conference of 1912, with growing contradictions of world imperialism and the inevitability of world war, the Second International resolved to oppose by all means, including general strike and civil war, the attempt to throw the peoples into senseless slaughter. Lenin and the Bolsheviks, together with Luxembourg, Trotsky and other leaders of the movement, participated in the organisation of the Second International as the means for the liberation of mankind from the shackles of capitalism.

In 1914, the leaders of Social Democracy in nearly all countries rallied to the support of their own ruling class in the First World War. So unexpected was the crisis and the betrayer of the principles of socialism, that even Lenin believed that the issue of *Vorwärts*, the central organ of the German Social Democracy, containing the support for the war credits was a forgery of the German General Staff. The International had ingloriously collapsed at its first serious test.

The Third International

Lenin, Trotsky, Liebknecht, Luxemburg, MacLean and Connolly and other Leaders were reduced to leading small sects. The Internationalists of the world in 1916, as the participants of the Zimmerwald Conference joked, could be gathered together in a few stage coaches. The unexpectedness of the betrayal led to the position where the Internationalists, isolated and weak, tended to be a little ultra-left. In order to differentiate themselves from 'social patriots' and 'traitors to socialism', they were compelled to lay down the fundamental principles of Marxism - the responsibility of imperialism for war, the right to self-determination of nationalities, the need for the conquest of power, separation from the practice and policies of reformism. Lenin had declared that the idea that the First World War was a 'war to end wars' was a pernicious fairy-tale of the Labour bosses. If the war was not followed by a series of successful socialist revolutions, it would be followed by a second, a third, even a tenth world war till the possible annihilation of mankind. The blood and the suffering in the trenches to the profit of the millionaire monopolists would inevitably provoke a revolt of the peoples against the colossal slaughter.

The principles achieved their justification in the Russian Revolution of 1917, under the leadership of the Bolsheviks. This was followed by a series of revolutions and revolutionary situations from 1917 to 1921. However the young forces of the new International, which was officially founded in 1919, were weak and immature. As a consequence, though the effect of the Russian Revolution was to provoke a wave of radicalisation in most of the countries of Western Europe and the organisation of mass Communist Parties, they were too weak to take advantage of the situation. The first waves of the radicalisation saw the masses turning to their traditional organisations and because of the inexperience, lack of understanding of Marxist theory, method and organisation, and due to their immaturity, the young Communist Parties were incapable of taking advantage of the situation. Thus capitalism was able to stabilise itself temporarily.

In the revolutionary situation in Germany in 1923, because of the policies of the leadership, which went through the same crisis as the leadership of the Bolshevik Party in 1917, the opportunity to take power was missed. After this American imperialism hastened to come to the aid of German capitalism for fear of 'Bolshevism' in the west. This prepared the way for the degeneration of the Soviet Union, because of its isolation and backwardness, and the corruption and rotting away of the Third International.

In 1923 we had the beginning of the consolidation of the Stalinist Bureaucracy and its usurpation of power in the Soviet Union. A similar process to that which had taken place in the degeneration of the Second International over the decades, took place in a short period of time in the Soviet Union. Having conquered power in a backward country, the Marxists were prepared confidently for the international revolution as the only solution to the problems of the workers of Russia and of the world. But in 1924, Stalin came forward as the representative of officialdom which had raised itself above the level of the masses of the workers and peasants.

Where "art, science and government" had remained their preserve, instead of the ideas of Marx and Lenin of the participation in Government and the running of industry by the mass of the population, the vested interests of the privileged layers came to the fore. In the autumn of 1924, Stalin in violation of the traditions of Marxism and Bolshevism, for the first time brought out the utopian theory of "socialism in one country". The Internationalists under

Trotsky fought against this theory and predicted that it would result in the collapse of the Communist International and the national degeneration of its sections.

Theory is not an abstraction but a guide to struggle. Theories, when they secure mass support, must represent the interests and pressure of groupings, castes or classes, in society. Thus the theory of "socialism in one country", represented the ideology of the ruling caste in the Soviet Union, that layer of officialdom who were satisfied with the results of the revolution, and did not want their privileged position disturbed. It was this outlook which now began to change the Communist International from an instrument of international revolution into merely a border-guard for the defence of the Soviet Union, which was supposed to be busily constructing socialism on its own.

The Left Opposition

The expulsion of the Left Opposition in the Communist Parties which stood by the principles of internationalism and Marxism, now took place. The defeat of the British General Strike and the Chinese Revolution of 1925-1927, prepared the way for this development. At this stage it was a question of "mistakes" in the policies of Stalin, Bukharin and their henchmen. It was a question of their position as ideologists of the privileged layer and the enormous pressures of capitalism and reformism. These mistakes of leadership had doomed the movement of the proletariat in other countries to defeat and disaster.

Having burned their fingers in trying to conciliate the reformists in the west and the colonial bourgeoisie in the East, Stalin and his clique zig-zagged to an ultra-left position, dragging the leadership of the Communist International with them. They split the German workers instead of advocating a United Front to prevent fascism coming to power in Germany, and thus prepared the way, by paralysis of the German proletariat, for the victory of Hitler. The degeneration of the Soviet Union and the betrayal of the Third International in its turn prepared the way for the crimes and betrayal of the Stalinist counter-revolution in the Soviet Union.

Apart from the nationalisation of the means of production, the monopoly of foreign trade and planned production, nothing remains of the heritage of October. The purge, the one sided civil war in the Soviet Union, had their counterparts in the parties of the Communist International. The victory of Hitler and the defeats in Spain and France were the results of these developments. From 1924 to 1927, Stalin had based himself on an alliance with the Kulaks and "Nepmen" in the Soviet Union, and the "building of socialism at a snail's pace". At the same time, abroad Stalinism stood for a "neutralisation" of the capitalists, and a conciliation of the Social-Democrats as a means of "warding-off" the threat of war. The defeat of the Left Opposition in the Soviet Union, with its programme of a return to workers' democracy, and the introduction of five-year plans, was due to the international defeats of the proletariat, caused by Stalinist policies.

From grovelling before the Social Democrats, and other international "Friends of the Soviet Union", the Communist International swung over to the policies of the "third period". The slump of 1929-33 was supposed to be "the last crisis of capitalism". Fascism and Social Democracy were twins, and these "theories" paved the way for the terrible defeats of the international working class.

At the same time, the policies of the Left Opposition in Russia won over the most advanced elements in the most important Communist Parties in the world. *The Lessons of October*, a work by Trotsky, dealt with the lessons of the abortive revolution of 1923 in Germany. The general programme of the opposition at home and abroad was answered by expulsions not only in the Russian Party, but in the main sections of the International. There was a rise of opposition groups in Germany, France, Britain, Spain, USA, South Africa and other countries. The programme of the opposition at this time was one of reform in the Soviet Union and the International, and the adoption of correct policies as against the opportunism of the period of 1923 to 1927, and the adventurism of the period from 1927 to 1933.

These splits, as Engels had remarked in another connection, were a healthy development in the sense of attempting to maintain the best traditions of Bolshevism and of the ideal of the Communist International. The crisis of leadership was the crisis of the International and of all mankind. Thus, these splits were a means of maintaining the ideals and methods of Marxism. In the first period of its existence, the Left Opposition regarded itself as a section of the Communist International; although expelled, and stood for the reform of the International.

The masses, and even the advanced layers of the proletariat, only learn through the lessons of great events. All history has shown that the masses can never give up their old organisations until these have been tested in the fire of experience. Up till 1933, the Marxist wing of the International still stood for the reform of the Soviet Union and the Communist International. Whether they would remain viable organisations would be shown by the test of history. Thus tenaciously the opposition maintained itself, although formally outside the ranks, as part of the International.

It was the coming to power of Hitler and the refusal of the Communist International to learn the lesson of the defeat which doomed it as an instrument of the working-class in the struggle for socialism. Far from analysing the reasons for the fatal policy of "social fascism", the sections of the Communist International declared the victory of Hitler to be a victory for the working-class, and as late as 1934 continued the same suicidal policies in France, of united action with the fascists against the "social fascists" and the "Radical fascists". Daladier, which if successful would have prepared the way for the fascist coup in France in February 1934.

The Fourth International

This betrayal and the terrible effect of the Hitler defeat led to a reappraisal of the role of the Communist International. An International which could perpetrate the treachery of surrendering the German proletariat to Hitler, without a shot being fired and without provoking a crisis within its ranks, could no longer serve the needs of the proletariat. An International which could acclaim this disaster as a victory could not fulfil its role as a leadership of the proletariat. As an instrument of world socialism, the Third International was dead. From an instrument of international socialism, the Communist International had degenerated into a complete and docile tools of the Kremlin, into an instrument of Russian foreign policy. It was now necessary to prepare the way for the organisation of a Fourth International, untarnished with the crimes and betrayals which besmirched the Reformist and Stalinist Internationals.

As in the days after the collapse of the Second International, the Revolutionary Internationalists remained small isolated sects. In Belgium they had a couple of MPs and an organisation of a thousand or two, in Austria and Holland, the same. The forces of the new international were weak and immature, nevertheless they had the guidance and assistance of

Trotsky, and the perspectives of great historical events. They were educated on the basis of an analysis of the experience of the Second and Third Internationals, and of the Russian, German and Chinese Revolutions and the British General Strike, and of the great events which had followed the First World War. In this way cadres were to be trained and educated, as the indispensable skeleton of the body of the new International.

It was this period, taking into account the historical isolation of the movement from the mass organisations of the Social Democracy and Communist party, that the tactic of "entrism" was evolved. In order to win the best workers, it was necessary to find a way of influencing them. This could only be done by working together with them in the mass organisations. Thus beginning with the ILP in Britain, the idea of entrism was worked out for the mass organisations of Social Democracy. This, where they were in a state of crisis and moving towards the left. Thus, with the developing revolutionary situation in France there was an entry into the Socialist Party. In Britain the entry of the ILP, then in a state of flux and ferment after breaking from the Labour Party, was followed by entry by many of the Trotskyists, on Trotsky's advice, into the Labour Party. In the USA there was an entry into the Socialist Party.

In the main, the pre-war period was one of preparation and orientation and selection of cadres or leading elements to be trained and steeled theoretically and practically, in the movement of the masses.

The tactic of entry was also considered as a short-term expedient, forced on the revolutionaries by their isolation from the masses, and the impossibility of tiny organisations getting the ear and finding support among the mass of the working class. It was for the purpose of working among the radical elements looking for revolutionary solutions, who would in the first place turn towards the mass organisations. But always under all conditions the main ideas of Marxism should be put forward and the revolutionary banner i.e. the ideas of Marxism, maintained and defended. It was a question of acquiring experience and understanding, of combating both sectarianism and opportunism. It was a means of developing a flexible approach, with the implacability of principle, as a means of preparing the cadres for the great events which impended.

The defeats of the working class in Germany, France and in the civil war in Spain, the defeats of the immediate post-war period, which were entirely due to the policies of the Second and Third Internationals, in their turn prepared the way for the Second World War. The paralysis of the proletariat in Europe, in conjunction with the new aggravated crisis of world capitalism made the Second World War absolutely inevitable. It was in this atmosphere that the 1938 founding conference of the Fourth International took place.

Trotsky's Perspectives

The document which was adopted at the conference itself is an indication of the reason for its foundation. The *Transitional Programme* of the Fourth International is linked to the idea of mass work, which itself is geared to the idea of the socialist revolution through transitional slogans, from today's contradictory reality. As distinct from the minimum and maximum programme of the Social Democracy is put the idea of a *Transitional Programme*, transitional from capitalism to the socialist revolution. This is an indication of the consideration of the epoch as one of wars and revolutions. Thus, all work has to be linked to the idea of the socialist revolution.

The perspective of Trotsky was that of war, which in its turn would provoke revolution. The problem of Stalinism would be resolved one way or another. Either the Soviet Union would be regenerated through political revolution against Stalinism, or the victory of the revolution in one of the important countries would resolve the situation on a world scale. With proletarian revolution victorious, the problem of the Internationals of both Stalinism and Reformism would be solved by events themselves.

This conditional prognosis, although revealing a fundamental understanding of processes in class society, was not borne out by events. Due to the peculiar military and political events of the war, Stalinism was temporarily strengthened. The revolutionary wave, during and following the Second World War in Europe was this time betrayed by the Stalinists in a worse fashion than the revolutionary wave following the First World War was betrayed by the leaders of the Second International.

The International remained, as it must even up to the present day, on the principles worked out and evolved in the first four Congresses of the Communist International and the experience of Stalinism, fascism and the great events up to the Second World War. Trotsky's idea in pushing for the foundation of the Fourth International in 1938 was because of the collapse of Stalinism and reformism as revolutionary tendencies within the working class. Both had become enormous obstacles on the path of the emancipation of the working class, and from being a means for the destruction of capitalism had become incapable of leading the proletariat to the victory of the socialist revolution.

The question of new parties and a new International was a question of the immediate perspectives which lay ahead. A new world war in its turn would provoke a new revolutionary wave in the metropolitan countries and among the colonial peoples. The problems of Stalinism in Russia and the world would thereby be solved by these revolutionary perspectives. Under these conditions it was imperative to prepare organisationally as well as politically for the great events which were on the order of the day. Thus, in 1938 Trotsky predicted that within ten years nothing would be left of the old traitor organisations, and the Fourth International would have become the decisive revolutionary force on the planet. There was nothing wrong with the basic analysis but every prognosis is conditional; the multiplicity of factors, economically, politically, socially, can always result in a different development than that foreseen. The weakness of the revolutionary forces, indeed, has been a decisive factor in the development of world politics, in the more than thirty years since Trotsky wrote. Unfortunately, the mandarins of the "Fourth International", on its leading body, without Trotsky's guidance and without Trotsky's presence interpreted this idea of Trotsky's not as a worked out thesis but as literally correct. [1]

Post War events and the Fourth International "Leaders"

The War developed on different lines to what even the greatest theoretical geniuses could have expected. The process has been explained in many documents of our tendency. The victories of Hitler in the first period of the war among other factors, was due to the policies of Stalinism in the preceding period. The attack on the Soviet Union, and the crimes and bestialities of the Nazis (fascism is the chemically distilled essence of imperialism as Trotsky once explained), without any check or balance from the working class in Germany, prostrate and without rights in front of the Nazi monsters, meant that the workers' and peasants in the Soviet Union saw as an immediate task, not the cleansing and restoration of workers' democracy in the Soviet Union through the political revolution, but the defeat of the Nazi hordes. As a consequence for a whole historical period, Stalinism was temporarily strengthened.

The war in Europe resolved itself largely into a war between Stalinist Russia and Nazi Germany. Anglo-American imperialism miscalculated the perspective completely. They had visualised that either the Soviet Union would be defeated, in which case they would then knock out a weakened Germany and emerge as the world victors, or that the Soviet Union would be so weakened in the course of the bloody holocaust on the eastern Front, that they would be enabled to dictate the course of world politics, world diplomacy and world redivision according to their whims and desires.

Trotsky's calculation proved correct in the sense that the Second World War was succeeded by an even greater revolutionary wave than after the First World War, but the masses of the different countries of Europe where, after Russia was attacked, the Communist Parties had played the major role in the resistance to the Nazis, rallied to the Communist Party and also in many countries to the Social Democrats. Already at this stage, the outline was given of the collapse of the leaders of the nascent International in the disputes which began to take place.

In 1944 it was necessary to re-orientate the movement in order to understand that a lengthy period of capitalist democracy in the West and of Stalinist domination in Russia was on the order of the day. In the documents of the Revolutionary Communist Party, it was made clear that the next period in western Europe was that of counter-revolution in a democratic form. This was because of the impossibility of the bourgeoisie maintaining their rule in Western Europe without the aid of Stalinism and of Social Democracy.

The International Secretariat (ISFI) equivocated, the American Socialist Workers Party and some of the other leaders temporised on the question and argued that on the contrary the only form of rule which the bourgeoisie could maintain in Europe was that of a military dictatorship and Bonapartism. Incapable of understanding the turn which had taken place in historical development, they could not understand that Stalinist Russia emerged strengthened out of the war, and that far from imperialism being on the offensive, it was imperialism that was on the defensive.

The alliance of Anglo-American imperialism and the Soviet bureaucracy, was dictated by mutual fear of the socialist revolution in the advanced countries of the world. At the same time the revolutionary wave sweeping over Europe and the world, made it impossible for Anglo-American imperialism, at a time when it was at its strongest in relation to Russia, and Russia at her weakest, to take advantage of the situation by an intervention on the scale even of that of 1918. They were impotent because of the revolutionary wave. Not understanding the changed relationship of forces, and the meaning of the enormous tidal-wave of revolution, the resolution drafted by the ISFI for the World Conference of 1946 even declared that "diplomatic pressure alone" could "restore capitalism in the Soviet Union"!

The Changed Relationships in Eastern Europe and China

With complete lack of perspective in relation to Western Europe, their position on the theoretical problems facing the movement in relation to Eastern Europe, was even worse. They did not understand the impulse given to the revolution by the advance of the Red Army, an impulse which was then used by the bureaucracy for their own ends. After using it, they then strangled the revolution. It was not a question of the Stalinists capitulating to capitalism under these conditions, but carrying through the revolution and then refashioning it in a Stalinist-Bonapartist form.

The "alliance" between the classes in Eastern Europe was like that in Spain of the Popular Front, an alliance not with the capitalists but with the shadow of the capitalist class. But in Spain they allowed the shadow to acquire substance. The real power in Republican Spain was handed to the capitalist class, but in all the countries in Eastern Europe the substance of power, the army and the police, were held by the Stalinist Parties, and they only allowed the shadow of power to the coalition allies.

The Stalinists used the revolutionary situation in all these countries; where the ruling class had been compelled to evacuate with the Nazi armies as they retreated, because of fear of the revenge of the masses, for their collaboration with the Nazis. As the Nazi armies retreated, the state structure collapsed. The army and the police fled or went into hiding. Thus the only armed force in Eastern Europe was the Red Army. Balancing between the classes, the Bonapartist clique proceeded to construct a state not in the image of Russia of 1917, but of the Russia of Stalin. A state in the image of Moscow 1945 was created.

These new historical phenomena, although foreshadowed in Trotsky's writings, were a closed book to the so-called leaders of the International. They declared the countries of Eastern Europe to be state capitalist, while Russia, of course, still remained a degenerated workers' state. Such a position was incompatible with any Marxist analysis. For, if Eastern Europe, where the means of production had been nationalised and a plan of production had been produced, was capitalist then it was absurd to maintain that Russia, where the same conditions of bureaucratic dictatorship were in existence, was any sort of workers' state. The conditions were fundamentally the same.

Thus, both for Western and Eastern Europe, these "leaders" were incapable of understanding the perspectives and of basing the education of the revolutionary cadres on them. Important forces in France and in other countries were frittered away in the arguments over these questions.

But their record in relation to the second greatest event in human history, the Chinese Revolution, was if anything worse. Not understanding the peasant war waged by Mao Tse-Tung and his followers, and not calculating the world relationship of forces, they were content to repeat at this time ideas which they had taken from Trotsky's work but not understood. The declared that Mao was endeavouring to capitulate to Chiang Kai-Shek, and that there was a repetition of the revolution of 1925-27. In the first place, the civil war was being waged on the question of land, and the constant offers of peace by the Chinese Stalinists were on the basis of land reform, and the expropriation of "bureaucratic capital", a programme which it was impossible for Chiang to accept. They had not understood that as a consequence of the experience of China since the 1925-27 revolution and the complete incapacity of Chinese bourgeoisie to solve the problems of the Democratic Revolution; of the national unification of China and the struggle against imperialism, as revealed in the war against Japan - that new perspectives were opening out.

On the one hand, there was the passivity of the working class in China and on the other, the peasant war, which was on the lines of those which had developed in China many times previously in the course of the last millennium. There was also the paralysis of imperialism due to the revolutionary wave following the Second World War. All these factors gave the possibility of a new direction of events. In 1947, in a document analysing the position in China, (in *Reply to David James*) the RCP foreshadowed the steps which Mao would take in the event of victory in the civil war, a victory which was inevitable under the circumstances.

At that time the leaders of the Chinese Communist Party were declaring that China stood before fifty years of "capitalist democracy". They had their alliance with the so-called "national capitalists", but Marxist analysis would not take this very seriously. Power was in the hands of the Red Army. Thus, we predicted that on the model of Eastern Europe, Mao would balance between the classes, and in the changed conditions, nationally and internationally, would construct a state in the image of that where Stalin had finished and not where Lenin had begun. Thus, right from the start of the revolution, China was heading towards a Bonapartist workers' state. The leaders of the International Secretariat and of the Chinese section maintained that Mao was capitulating to capitalism and to Chiang-Kai-Shek. Even after the complete victory of the Chinese Stalinists the ISFI did not understand its significance, but declared that China like Eastern Europe, was state capitalist, although they did not define the term.

They then declared for grandiose revolutionary perspectives in China and in Eastern Europe. Mao would not be able to maintain his "capitalist rule" for long. In Eastern Europe the "state capitalist" regimes were in a state of immediate crisis, which would lead to their overthrow. They did not understand that, leaving aside events in the main capitalist metropolitan countries or a victorious political revolution in Russia, that for a decade or two at least, the regimes in eastern Europe and in China, would remain firmly in control.

They continued to repeat that the world war was going to solve the problems of the revolution, and in the case of one leader, as the war had not solved the problems, he maintained that "the war was still on". After the war they immediately declared monotonously, that there was going to be an immediate outbreak of a new world war, each succeeding year onwards from 1945, a nuclear war was going to bring socialism. In diluted form, even today, they repeat this idea. At each crisis of imperialism, or between imperialism and the Soviet bureaucracy, they get out the tom-toms and beat out the same hoary message. To this day, they have not understood that the problems of war in the modern epoch is a problem of the relationship between the classes; that only definitive defeats of the working class in the main capitalist countries, particularly America, can lay the basis for a new world war.

Eastern Europe and the Stalinist States

As always, the hammering that their ideas received on the basis of events, coupled with their refusal to analyse their mistakes, merely pushed the ISFI into opposite and worse mistakes; from declaring China and Eastern Europe capitalist states, they now passed to the opposite extreme.

After the national bureaucracy in Yugoslavia under Tito, came into conflict with the Russian bureaucracy they now discovered that Yugoslavia was a "relatively healthy workers' state". Not understanding the nature of the conflict, in which critical support should have been given to the Yugoslavs, they began to idealise "hero Tito" and to declare that the new International could arise on Yugoslav soil.

Having been forced to change their characterisation of China from a capitalist state to that of a workers' state, they declared that China too was a "relatively healthy workers state"! They did not take into account the conditions and the way in which the revolution had taken place in China. The immeasurable backwardness of China in comparison with Russia, the fact that the working class had played no independent role in these great events, and, therefore had remained passive; that on a world scale, for a whole historical period, even though temporarily, capitalism had succeeded in stabilising itself in the west and that the socialist revolution was not imminent in the metropolitan countries of the west, meant that therefore, the Chinese Stalinists and the Chinese bureaucracy had an even greater stranglehold on the Chinese State and the Chinese people than even the Russian bureaucracy had obtained. For the socialist revolution, it requires above all, the conscious participation of the working class in the revolution, and after the revolution the conscious control and democratic participation of the workers in the running of industry and the state by the working class. To this day those "leaders" have not understood this problem and still regard China and Yugoslavia as "relatively healthy workers' states", which merely require reform, similar to that of the Russia of 1917-23, and not at all political revolution, defined and understood by Trotsky.

Thus they reinforced the errors of their previous position by violating some of the fundamental ideas of Marxism, but now at the opposite pole. They repeated this process like the Stalinists before them: at every great turn of events, zig-zagging from one position to another, and never using the Marxist method of analysing events from their original standpoint, correcting the errors and preparing the way for a higher level of thought on this basis. Each change in line, each change in tactic, abruptly brought forward like tablets from on high, to be given in resounding speeches and documents to the faithful. It is this, among other factors, which was one of the main causes of the complete incapacity to orientate correctly to the development of events. Such an honesty of purpose can be obtained only by those confident of themselves, of their ideas, and of their political authority. Only by such means can cadres of the revolutionary movement be educated, built and steeled for the great task which impends before mankind.

Having maintained that the whole of Eastern Europe and China were some peculiar form of state capitalism which was never defined, analysed or explained they now went off at a 180 degree tangent: without explanation and analysis, purely impressionistically they did a complete somersault. The Yugoslav regime having broken with Stalin because of the vested interests of the Yugoslav bureaucracy, they discovered in Tito a new saviour for the Fourth International. Yugoslavia was transformed into a "relatively healthy workers' state".

Instead of seeing on the one hand, of course, the need to give critical support to the struggle of the Yugoslav people against national oppression by the Russian bureaucracy, but at the same time explaining the vested interests of the national bureaucracy in the split, they idealised the latter. Whereas in Russia a political revolution still remained necessary (this must have been for some remote historical reason because Trotsky said so. They didn't explain the reasons. Deutscher managed to make the transition and discover that political revolution was not necessary in Russia). In Yugoslavia the ISFI now discovered that a socialist revolution had taken place during the war and the post-war period.

As a consequence of this, whereas the socialist revolution in Russia had been isolated, the revolution in Yugoslavia, because of the revolution in Russia, had not been isolated. The ISFI said the reason for the development of Stalinism in Russia was the fact that it was the only country where the revolution had been triumphant: now that the revolution had been expanded, there was no question of a similar deformation taking place. Therefore, they concluded triumphantly, there could be no repetition of Stalinism in Yugoslavia, and consequently, in Yugoslavia there was a healthy workers' state with minor deformations. They proceeded to organise international work-teams to render assistance to "building socialism" in Yugoslavia.

Their propaganda was as uncritical and laudatory as the Stalinist propaganda for visits of youth teams "to build socialism in Russia." The whole episode is an indication of the sociological "method" of this tendency. Mandel and Co. put forward the same argument for the so-called "cultural revolution" in China, and of course, to this day for Cuba. In the first place it was the backwardness of the Soviet Union together with its isolation, and the defeats of the world working class which was responsible for the rise to power of the Stalinist bureaucracy in Russia. But once having come to power, the bureaucracy itself with the state power in its hands, becomes an independent factor in the situation. The Stalinist bureaucracy in Yugoslavia was no different in fundamentals from that in Russia. The Tito clique began where Stalin ended. At no time was there workers' democracy such as that of Russia of 1917-23. The movement in Yugoslavia during the war was mainly a national peasant war of liberation. The state which was constructed was a one party totalitarian regime in the image of Russia with the perfected Stalinist apparatus.

Yugoslavia was a very backward country. Consequently in the Yugoslavian state apparatus were incorporated the elements of the old ruling class, in diplomacy, in the Army and the rest of the state apparatus.

This was the same process, of course, as that which had taken place in Russia. But without the check and control of workers' democracy, there could be no question of a healthy workers' state. A movement towards socialism in a transitional economy requires the conscious control and participation by the working class. Thus under these circumstances, like conditions and causes give and must give the same results. Leaving aside this or that peculiarity, the fundamental features of the regime in Yugoslavia were no different from those of Stalinism in Russia. It was a complete revision of Marxism to suggest otherwise.

To this day, all those tendencies which took up this position have not re-evaluated their theoretical attitude in the light of events. From Pablo, through Posadas, Healy, Mandel and Hansen, no attempt has been made to re-evaluate their theoretical errors. Consequently the most weird combinations of ideas manage to jog together in their writings. Healy finds it quite consistent to characterise Cuba as state capitalist, while hailing the so-called new version of the Paris-Commune in the Cultural Revolution in China. The *Voix Ouvriere* (now *Lutte Ouvriere*) tendency in France, still remaining on the position of the IS of 1945-47 after 35 years of events, still finds it compatible to say that Russia is a degenerated workers' state, while Eastern Europe, Yugoslavia and Cuba are capitalist states. *All of these tendencies declare Syria and Burma to be capitalist.* The United Secretariat itself, through all its zig-zags, pays the penalty of a lack of theoretical honesty by compounding the mistakes of the past.

Thus, to this day, they remain cloudy on the question of whether a political revolution is necessary in China and Yugoslavia, the majority believing that these are "relatively healthy" workers' states, and so no political revolution is necessary, but only reform.

Developments in the Stalinist States

During the course of the last quarter century, this tendency has lost completely its theoretical moorings. Caught by surprise by the development of events, they have always reacted empirically and impressionistically, capitulating to the immediate reality without seeing the future development, inevitable under the circumstances, of groupings and tendencies. Not only in relation to Tito in Yugoslavia, which arises from the incorrect analysis and lack of understanding of proletarian Bonapartism, but also in relation to all the big events in the countries of the Stalinist bloc. The movement in 1956 in Hungary, which took the form of a complete overthrow of the bureaucracy and the beginning of a political revolution in general, they supported - not to have done so would have meant abandoning any pretence to stand in the tradition of Trotskyism. But this did not prevent them from lumping the movement in Poland taking place at the same time, in the same category as the Hungarian Revolution.

They did not see that in Hungary there was almost the complete destruction of the so-called Communist Party and the beginning of an organisation of a new workers' movement. The Hungarian workers, after the experiences of Stalinist totalitarianism, were not prepared to tolerate for a single moment, the construction of a new totalitarian Stalinist state during the course of the revolution.

In Poland events developed somewhat differently. The national struggle against the oppression of the great Russian bureaucracy was derailed by a section of the Polish bureaucrats onto national Stalinist lines. Not understanding this, the leaders of the ISFI saw in Gomulka the representative of 'democratic communism'. They did not see that he represented that wing of the Polish bureaucracy which wanted to establish itself as 'master in its own house' and relatively independent of the Russian bureaucracy. That there was no fundamental difference between them and the reformist wing of the Russian bureaucracy was not clear to them. No more than Khruschev did they really wish to renew the basis of the revolution, or turn towards Russia of 1917. What was more to the point, that they were opposed to the attempt to install socialist democracy in Hungary. Therefore the potential political revolution in Poland was derailed on national Stalinist lines. Like his national Stalinist brothers in Russia, the Polish bureaucrat could only swing from repression to reform and back again while maintaining the Stalinist apparatus intact. The ISFI saw in Gomulka the beginning of a complete change in the situation in Poland, as they had illusions in the de-Stalinisation in the Soviet Union. At each stage in events, they have looked to some sort of Messiah to save them from isolation and lack of mass forces. Each time they have been doomed to disillusion and disappointment.

Not content with having burned their fingers with Maoism, the split between Russia and China, which caught them by surprise, - nevertheless resulted in a refurbishing of the illusions of Maoism. They dusted out the 'secret' idea that China was a healthy workers' state with minor blemishes, a state requiring merely reform and not overthrow. [2] Mao was to be the new saviour. They completely misinterpreted the meaning of the "cultural revolution" in China.

Trotsky had already explained that proletarian Bonapartism sometimes rested on the workers and peasants in order to purge the worse excesses of the greedy and rapacious bureaucracy. In the introduction of the five year plans in Russia, for a period Stalin leaned on the workers and peasants, and even engendered enthusiasm among the workers for what they considered to be socialist construction. But this did not alter the character, methods and policy of Stalinism. This did not change the character of the state regime. Making a scapegoat of individuals, or even a section of the bureaucracy, far from changing anything fundamentally merely reinforced bureaucratic rule. Thus Maoism and the "cultural revolution" did not change anything fundamentally in China.

Mao, resting on the basis of workers and peasants stuck blows at sections of the bureaucracy which had accumulated privileges and a material position far in excess of what the weak productive forces in China could maintain. The differentiation between workers and peasants and bureaucratic layers had reached such an extent as to provoke enormous dissatisfaction among the workers and peasants. Thus if the workers and peasants were to be harnessed for the tasks of producing heavy industry, nuclear arms and a reinforcement of production in China, it was necessary, if only temporarily, to cut down on these privileges. But the "cultural revolution" was organised from the top, from the beginning to the end. To talk of new versions of the Paris Commune in Shanghai, Peking and the other cities of China, was to bespatter with mud the tradition of the Commune and the Russian Revolution. The inevitable end of this experience, as with Gomulka in Poland, was the reinforcement of the power of the bureaucracy in China. On this road there was no way out for the Chinese or Polish masses. The ISFI's constant search for some means whereby, as if by magic, the problems would be resolved, has always been a symptom of petit-bourgeois utopianism, which replaces Marxist analysis by hysterical hopes in this or that individual or tendency.

The capitulation to various brands of Stalinism or utopianism at each stage in the development of events did enormous harm to the creation of a viable movement. Thus in Italy, it was the "Trotskyists", or to be more accurate the so-called leaders of the "Trotskyists", who helped in the formation of a large Maoist movement of 100,000 members. Enthusiastically and uncritically republishing the works of Maoism and distributing them within the Communist Party, they created the basis for Maoism in Italy. The leaders of these tendencies made special trips to the Chinese Embassy in Switzerland to get this "precious" material. The consequence of this uncritical acceptance of Maoism is that they won hardly a single member from the 100,000 but, on the contrary, have lost members to the Maoists! Thus the penalty for theoretical confusion, particularly for a weak tendency, always paid in full. Even worse is the confusion and demoralisation which is sown among their own ranks. The task under these conditions was, while offering a friendly attitude to the CP rank and file, those tending to Maoism and those against it, at the same time offering sharp criticisms not only of the opportunist pro-Moscow wing but also to the ignorant and cynical position of the Maoists, beginning with the leaders in Peking.

Colonial Revolution - Algeria

Discouraged by their lack of success (mainly due to objective circumstances, partly due to false policies) they put the responsibilities for this, as always in such conditions, on the shoulders of the working class. The workers had become corrupt and Americanised through prosperity, they said in effect. Their policies indicated that this is what they believed. They therefore looked for a new talisman which would renew and revive the fortunes of the International and the working class. This they found in the colonial revolution.

The recent documents of our tendency have explained the significance of the colonial revolution and the developments within it. It is sufficient here to say that the upheavals in the so-called Third World arise from the impasse of capitalism and imperialism to develop the productive forces in these areas to the maximum extent necessary and possible. But given the world conditions, the existence of strong Bonapartist workers' states, and the balance of forces between imperialism and non-capitalist countries, the developments in these areas have taken a peculiar pattern. Under these conditions, it is more than ever necessary to maintain with implacable determination the ideas of Trotsky on the Permanent Revolution, to learn from the experience of China, Yugoslavia and Cuba and to maintain a separation from all the tendencies, bourgeois-nationalist, petty-bourgeois-nationalist, Stalinist and reformist.

In Algeria they tied themselves almost completely to the banner of the FLN, although their position was better than that of the Lambertists (OCI in France), and Healyites (WRP), who supported the MNA which, starting from a position somewhat to the left of the FLN, ended up as an agency of the French imperialists. To give critical support to the FLN was correct, but to subordinate completely the work of their section to the nationalist movement, could only mean that the weak forces under their control would be lost in the war of liberation. While maintaining full support for the just struggle for national independence from French imperialism, at the same time it was necessary for the Algerian Trotskyists to maintain the position of internationalism. Only thus could the struggle for national liberation, be linked with the struggle of the working class in France, and the possibility of a socialist Algeria linked to a socialist France. The treachery of the Social Democrat and Stalinist organisations in France, which led to the Algerian Revolution taking a nationalist orientation was no reason to abandon the worked out ideas of Marxism-Leninism on the question.

It should have been clear, that at best after the victory over the French, it in itself an enormous step forward, it would be impossible to construct a workers' democracy in a country like Algeria. The result would be either a bourgeois or a proletarian version of Bonapartism, with hardly any industry, with a population decimated by war, no strong indigenous working class, with half the population unemployed and without a revolutionary class party. All these factors, without the aid above all of the French and international working class, meant that there could be no real solution, apart from the removal of imperialism, for the Algerian people.

The illusions that they disseminated about workers' control in the abandoned French agricultural estates showed a complete lack of theoretical grasp on this question. Workers' control by its very nature, must proceed from the industrial workers and not from the half peasant, half agricultural workers' associations which took control because the French managers had fled. At best these were primitive versions of glorified co-operatives and not examples of workers' control and workers' management. By their very nature they were temporary structures without any real future. Given that the socialist revolution did not extend to the advanced countries they were doomed as an interesting curiosity of social development, indicating the instinctive strivings of the agricultural semi-proletariat, as there had been many such movements at a time of mass awakening in many countries in the past.

The coup of Boumedienne in July 1965 came as a surprise to them, although one way or the other, a similar development of events was inevitable in Algeria. In all the colonial countries where the struggle for the expulsion of imperialist overlords has been successful, similar processes have taken place. Although political independence has been gained, economically they still remain dependent on the industrialised countries. This of course marks an enormous step forward in the development of the colonial peoples. Nevertheless, national independence with imperialist dominance of the world markets on the one side and the strength of the Stalinist Bonapartism on the other, has meant that new problems of formidable character are posed before these peoples. The native bourgeoisie are incapable of solving these problems. Thus in the former colonial territories of Africa, in semi-colonial areas of Latin America, and in most of the countries in Asia, military regimes of one sort or the other have taken power. The crisis of these regimes has forced a move either towards proletarian or capitalist Bonapartism.

While putting the emphasis on the colonial revolution as a solution to the problem of the Fourth International, at the same time blindly they have not understood the dialectic of this process. The whole development of the colonial revolution has taken a distorted form because of the lag of the revolution in the west (America and Japan are included in this). The weakness of the Marxist-Leninist forces due to the historical factors sketched previously played an enormous part in this process. It in turn meant that with the ripeness of the colonial world for social evolution, this has taken all forms of weird aberrations. It was the duty for the Marxist leadership to recognise the process and to give leadership to the young and weak forces of Marxism in the colonial world. Instead of this, the ISFI (in spite of the lessons drawn by Trotsky from the experience of the Communist Party with the Kuomintang in China, the rich experiences of Yugoslavia, China, Russia, and the countries of Africa) failing to draw the necessary conclusions, bowed down before the mighty colonial revolution. It is better to participate than to oppose. But to merge indistinguishably with the petit-bourgeois nationalists, to capitulate to middle class utopias, was to dissolve the vanguard in the nationalist miasma.

Latin America – Cuba

The complete lack of Marxist method in their approach is indicated by their attitude to the Cuban Revolution. The Cuban Revolution, the ISFI say, is an example of Marxist method. In reality, the army of Castro was gathered together on a bourgeois democratic programme and consisted in the main of agricultural workers, peasants and lumpen proletarian elements. Castro started off as a bourgeois democrat with the United States as his model society. The intervention of the working class took place when the struggle was in its final stage, when Castro was marching on Havana - the workers called a general strike in his assistance. The fall of Havana meant the collapse of the hated army and police of the Batista regime. Power was firmly in the hands of Castro's guerrillas.

The development of the regime towards the destruction of capitalism and landlordism did not take place as a result of a thought out, conscious process. On the contrary, it was the mistakes of American imperialism which pushed Castro on the road of expropriation.

With 90% of the economy owned by American capitalists, the American ruling class imposed on Cuba a blockade at a time when Castro was carrying out only bourgeois-democratic reforms. The monopolies which controlled Cuba opposed the taxes which Castro wished to impose in order to get the money for his reforms. Although these taxes were lower than the taxes they paid on the mainland, they furiously objected and appealed to Washington for support.

As a reprisal to the blockade, the Cuban regime seized American assets in Cuba. This meant that nine tenths of agriculture and industry was in the hands of the state, so the Cuban regime then proceeded to nationalise the remaining tenth. They had the model of Yugoslavia, China and Russia, and established a regime in that image. At no stage was there workers' democracy in Cuba. The Bonapartism of the regime is embodied in the rule of Castro and the meetings in the Square of the Revolution where the sole contribution of the masses is to say "Si" to Castro's exhortations. Cuba has remained throughout, a one party state, without soviets and without workers' control of industry or the state.

Consequently, more and more it has become bureaucratised. This was inevitable, given the isolation of the revolution and the way in which the revolution has developed. The workers' militia has been disarmed and differentiation between the bureaucrats - especially the higher bureaucrats - and the working class is steadily developing. The development of a state apparatus above and independent of the masses proceeds apace. Behind the scenes, Castro is attempting to negotiate an agreement with American imperialism for recognition and aid: and an agreement is probably inevitable in the next period. This will end the "revolutionary appeals" which Castro directs to Latin America. Cuba, will more and more in the thoughts of its leaders be bounded by the narrow shores of the island in the relations with the nations and classes of the world.

As it is, the Stalinist bureaucracy in Russia gives aid of a million pounds a day, without which the regime could not survive. For a regime of workers' democracy, the bureaucracy of the Soviet Union would not give one kopeck. It is only because the regime, in its basic outline, becomes more and more like that of all the other Bonapartist workers' states, that the bureaucracy can permit itself the luxury of fraternal aid to Cuba.

Given a wrong theoretical starting point, one error can only be piled upon another, Thus, the USFI is completely blind to the processes taking place on the island. They refuse to face up to the issue of the inevitable degeneration and decay of the regime on totalitarian lines, and persist in their reactionary dream of a Cuba, an agricultural and backward Cuba, moving towards socialism. Apparently, only minor reforms are needed for Cuba to be a model workers' democracy! There is no question of a political revolution which would mean the control of industry and the state by the workers, but again of mythical reforms which would install a workers' democracy. Control of industry and the state by the working classes can be gained by persuading Castro that this is necessary!

On the other hand they argue in the most obscure fashion that this already exists, in fact that Cuba is more democratic than the Russia of 1917-23. In reality, if Castro were to even attempt such actions, he would be removed by the bureaucracy. Apart from the fact that without any ideological background, Castro believes that the type of regime he is building is "socialism". He could not play the role that he does without ideological blinkers. But the sectarians without the pressure of the interests of the bureaucracy, nevertheless succumb to this variant of Stalinism and voluntarily don the blinkers themselves.

To this day, as with the experience of the entire quarter century, this tendency has learned nothing and forgotten everything. In Latin America, they repeat the mistakes in Algeria and in a different form the estimation of China, Yugoslavia and Cuba. Now Bolivia has become the magical means by which the world situation can be transformed. They merge with the petit-bourgeois guerrillas in an attempt to repeat the experience of Cuba. Castro, the "unconscious Trotskyist", the new messiah of Marxism, is the example that they wish to emulate. Not taking into account the change in circumstances, the different conditions, the awareness of the ruling class, and of imperialism, they support such adventures as those of Guevara, who attempted artificially to inject guerrilla war amongst the peasants.

The heroism of Guevara should not blind us to his theoretical bankruptcy. To endeavour to repeat in the countries of Latin America the policies of Castroism in Cuba, is to commit a crime against the international working class. The literature of Marxism is full of explanations as to the role of the different classes in Society: that of the proletariat, the peasantry, petty bourgeois and bourgeoisie. To them, apparently, this is a closed book. Marxism has explained that in the colonial revolution it is the proletariat that has played the leading role. The proletariat is forced together co-operatively in the process of production. They are compelled to combine to protect themselves against the exploiters. It is because of this that the proletariat can be the only force to achieve the socialist revolution.

But even the proletariat is only material for exploitation until it becomes not a class in itself but for itself. This consciousness is developed with the experience of the class and in its struggle for better conditions. Even here the party and leadership of the working class is needed. The peasants, the petit-bourgeois intellectuals and the lumpen proletariat can play no independent role. Where petit-bourgeois intellectuals and ex-Marxists organise the struggle on the basis of a peasant war, the level of consciousness, because of the nature of the struggle, can only be of a low character. If, nevertheless in Yugoslavia and China, the peasantry, the petit-bourgeoisie, and the lumpen proletariat organised in the armies of national and social liberation, could push aside rotted semi-feudal regimes, it is only because of the historical process that we have already explained in many of our documents.

It is true that Lenin had visualised the possibility of tribal Africa passing straight to communism. But this could only be with the aid and assistance of socialism in the advanced countries. It could not be on the basis of their own resources. The material conditions for socialism do not exist in any of the colonial countries, it is only when taken on a world scale and with the decay of the world system of capitalism that the basis is laid for the socialist revolution in the backward areas of the world. These self styled "Marxists" turn the lessons of Marxism upside down. They adopt the policy of the Narodniks and the Social Revolutionaries in Russia. Unconsciously they adapt their ideas as to the role of the different classes in society. For Bakunin the peasants and the lumpen proletariat were the most revolutionary class in Society. This conception arose from the whole method and theory of the anarchists. With this also went the idea of individual propaganda by the deed, i.e. of terror and of individual expropriations.

Guerrillaism and Marxism

It is in this whole milieu and with the even greater discrediting of the Communist Party and the reformists in Latin America, that the programme of guerrilla war in the countryside and even worse, of "urban guerrillas" has been developed. Young, weak forces of Trotskyism, disorientated by the zig-zags of the past 25 years, have been flung into this mess. In Latin America they should be teaching all the advanced elements among the intellectuals, students and above all, the working class, the fundamental and elementary ideas of Marxism. The movement for national and social liberation in Latin America, in Brazil, Argentina, Uruguay, Chile, Guatemala and the other countries in Latin America can only come from a mass movement of the working class and peasants. Desperate duels and kidnappings, bank raids etc., will only result in the extermination of young brave and sincere forces without avail. It is not for these elements to fight in a combat alone with the forces of the ruling class, of the army and the secret police, without reference to the real struggle for the overthrow of the corrupt cliques of the oligarchy and of the police.

It might seem harder, and in a sense is harder, but only by organising the working class, above all, in the struggle for national and social liberation can a socialist revolution be achieved, which would develop on healthy lines. Because of the multiplicity of historical factors and the peculiar world relationship of class forces, theoretically it cannot be excluded that a peasant guerrilla war might be successful, but then the model would be not that of the proletariat as a leading force of the revolution, leading to the victory of 1917, but at best of China and Cuba.

A mass of movement of the proletariat is entirely possible in these countries. The general strikes in Chile, Argentina and Uruguay in the recent period are proof of this. A revolutionary Marxist tendency must build with these perspectives, with the preparation of a mass insurrection as the climax of the movement in the cities. This could lead to the victory of the socialist revolution which under these conditions would rapidly spread to the whole of Latin America.

It is on the lessons of the Russian revolution that the cadres of the proletariat must be taught and developed, not to follow the examples of the Chinese, Cuban or Yugoslavian revolutions, but on the contrary that of Russia in 1917. The idea of Marx of the proletarian revolution in the cities, with the assistance of the peasant war in the rear; that must be the ideal for which they should work. The main task in these countries is to patiently explain the leading role of the proletariat in the struggle for workers' power and socialism.

It is on the lessons of the Russian Revolution that the cadres of the proletariat must be counter-posed to the capitalist state. As against military police dictatorship, the battering ram of the organised working class must be counter-posed. Once convinced of the necessity, the proletariat will acquire the necessary arms. The army, which is pitted against them, composed in the main of peasants, would split in the face of the mass movement and come over to the side of the Revolution. The peasant army could be won with the programme of the agrarian revolution and the national revolution against imperialism which is emblazoned on the banner of the proletariat.

To capitulate to all the pressures of despairing petit-bourgeois anarchism is to betray the mission of Marxism. The task of the Marxist is to polemicise, in however a friendly a fashion against the idealists, however sincere, who are leading themselves and the revolution into a fatal cul-de-sac. Against the methods and policies of anarchism an implacable struggle must be waged. Far from doing this, these besmirchers of the tradition of Trotskyism have adopted bag and baggage, the ideas of the theoretical adversaries of Marxism and their degenerate descendants, instead of the clear class ideas, rooted in the centuries of experience of the class struggle and of the national liberation movement.

It is not in the tradition of Marxism to support a movement of peasant war separate and apart from the movement of the working class, which is decisive. The efforts and work of Marxists would be largely concentrated in the cities and among the proletariat. Always of course, under all conditions, the struggle of other oppressed classes must be supported by Marxists.

The argument for peasant guerrillas at least has a semblance of sense considering the experience of the last 30 years. But even in this event, the task of Marxists is not merely to overthrow the capitalist regime, but to prepare the way for the socialist future of mankind. The destruction of capitalism and landlordism in the colonial countries is an immense step forward which raises the level of all mankind. But precisely because of the helplessness of the peasantry as a class to rise to the future socialist tasks, it nevertheless can only succeed in raising new obstacles in its path.

The victory of the peasant war, given the relationship of forces in the world and the crisis of capitalism and imperialism in the underdeveloped countries can result in a form of deformed workers' state. It cannot result in the conscious control by the workers and peasants of industry, agriculture and the state, because in the ex-colonial and semi-colonial countries, the material basis for socialism has not been created. Insofar as the possibility exists of such peculiar combinations, it is because of the world ripeness of productive forces for socialism. The necessary technique, productive capacity and resources are there on a world scale. This is what makes possible, not only a healthy dictatorship of the proletariat in the colonial areas, but also the perversions of China, Yugoslavia, and Cuba.

But where the revolution was carried through in a distorted form or, in the case of the Russian Revolution, in a healthy form but under conditions of backwardness and isolation, the retrogression of the dictatorship into Stalinist-Bonapartism means that the proletariat and the peasantry of these countries raise above them a privileged elite and a state machine independent of workers and peasants control. This means they would have to pay with a new political revolution before being able to begin the transition to socialism. In China, Yugoslavia, Cuba and Russia, the proletariat will have to pay with a political revolution before the beginning of the withering away of the state and coercion can take place. All these problems are linked with the problem of world revolution.

In Latin America, the bowing down before the alien theories and watering down of the basic ideas of permanent revolution, means an abandonment of the ideas of Marxism-Leninism. It means an abandonment of the entire Marxist tradition. Under conditions of great difficulty in Latin America, Asia and Africa, not to maintain the basic ideas of Marxism is to be lost in the swamp of petit-bourgeois nationalism, of anarchist utopianism, of Stalinist cynicism and lack of-belief in the power of the proletariat. Above all it is an abandonment of the perspective of world revolution on which our Marxist internationalism is based. The abandonment of internationalism for the petit-bourgeois deed is the abandonment of the programme of Trotskyism.

In Latin America, the proletariat, especially in Brazil, Chile, Argentina, Uruguay and Mexico, is powerful enough to play the leading role in the revolution. It is here that the forces of Marxism must be concentrated. Intellectuals and students breaking away from their middle class traditions, and understanding the impasse of capitalism and imperialism, must be educated in this spirit. It is only in a struggle against all other tendencies that Trotskyism can prepare the necessary cadres, especially among the advanced workers, to lead the revolution to success.

In the first place, a firm critique of the bureaucratic development in Cuba and of the flamboyant excesses of Castroism must become part and parcel of the ideological re-equipment of the revolutionaries in Latin America. While defending the achievements of the Cuban revolution and emphasising its positive sides, at the same time its negative features as far as the advanced workers and youth are concerned, must also be brought out. Only thus can the infantile leftism of Castroism in Latin America be combated successfully.

Mass Parties, Entrism and Methods of Work

On the problem of entrism, the policies of the US tendency are no more based on principle than any other part of the ideological baggage. In Britain, they raised the question of entry in the immediate post-war period because they saw at that time, the conditions of slump and the existence of a strong and developing left wing within the Labour Party! As against Trotsky's conception of winning over the advanced elements by standing for firm political principles, they adopted the policy of trying to win over the advanced elements without an intransigent political programme. They watered down their programme in order to find a means of adapting themselves to the left reformist leaders.

At no time did they maintain the clear programme of Marxism, but on the contrary, adopted the programme of adaptation to reformist individuals who represented no one but themselves. They adopted what they called a policy of "deep entrism". Mixing up objective and subjective factors, and in no way taking account of the process of development of mass consciousness, they explained to their members that they would organise the mass left wing. If it was a question of organising a movement purely on the basis of tricks, manoeuvres and tactics, then the Stalinist perversion of Marxism would be correct.

Leaving aside the incorrect policies, even with correct strategy, politics and tactics, the development of mass consciousness is not an arbitrary one. It follows its own laws, which are dependent on the molecular process of developing consciousness on the basis of experience and of events. The attempt (partially successful) to paint themselves as left reformists (in adaptation to the milieu) did result in their becoming to a large extent "left reformists". In the long term such policies are disastrous, and lay the seeds for the recoil in the direction of ultra-leftism - both arising from, one the one hand, the incapacity to stand on firm principles; on the other hand, to see the objective situation as it is, and to marry the subjective factor with the objective developments of events.

Events by themselves, of course, will not solve the problem of growth: and on the other hand, the Marxists will only grow stronger insofar as there is an understanding of the objective processes and an orientation of the tendency on the basis of the real movement of consciousness among the advanced workers. The left wing, as a mass tendency, will develop firstly on left reformist and centrist lines. The revolutionary forces can play a part in the development of the left wing, but with the mass movement, it is the muddled left reformists and centrists who will come to the top. Inevitably they will form the leadership in its early stages, and only the test of experience plus Marxist criticism will lead to their replacement by Marxist cadres.

To this day the "leaders" of the international have not understood the ABCs on this question. In Britain, they constantly proclaimed immediate world war every year. Echoing the opportunist propaganda of the Labour leaders in the General Election of 1951, they declared that the victory of Churchill would mean world war! Thus, instead of raising the level of the workers they could reach, they merely succeeded in confusing them. Again in 1951, it was a question of socialism or fascism in Britain within twelve months. One would imagine from reading their material, and that of their then erstwhile disciples, the Socialist Labour League (now Workers Revolutionary Party), that they had never read the material of Trotsky and other Marxist theoreticians as to the movement of class forces.

It is not a question at any particular moment of the ruling class deciding to go by car instead of by train; rather it is a question of the relationships in the middle class, working class, and the ruling class itself. Not only in Britain, where they never assimilated the lessons from their experiences, but wherever they have operated the tactic, they have failed dismally in the objects they set themselves.

This was because of the long economic upswing of the major capitalist countries which led during the quarter century to a renewal of Social Democracy in such countries as Germany and Britain, and of Stalinism in such countries as France and Italy. Due to their theoretical impasse, and the objective situation itself, the ISFI evolved a theory of general entry into the Social Democratic and Communist Parties, whichever was stronger. This was the correct tactic under the conditions. But unfortunately, as in Britain, they operated an opportunist tactic. In the Communist Parties in France and Italy, they adapted themselves to Stalinism, without putting forward a firm revolutionary Leninist line. Even under difficult conditions it should have been possible to contrast the policies of the leadership with those of Marx and Lenin.

Entrism was imposed by the objective situation and the weakness of the revolutionary forces, but they operated it in a purely opportunist fashion. As a consequence in France and Italy, no great gains were made, and they left the Communist Parties with virtually the same numbers as they entered. As always they zig-zagged from an opportunist adaptation to the leadership to an ultra-left position, thus blocking a road to the rank and file. In the Social Democratic Parties, they capitulated to left reformism; in Germany, Britain, Holland and Belgium. This could not give any results, so they in effect passed a resolution that these parties no longer existed as mass workers parties, and adopted completely ultra-left policies in relation to them. Unfortunately, the Communist Party in France and Italy and the Social Democracy in other countries still maintained the support of the overwhelming majority of the working class, and as a result, hardly noticed the displeasure of these ultra-lefts and hardly noticed that they had left.

Keynesianism instead of Marxism

In the immediate aftermath of the Second World War they were guilty on practically all questions of an infantile ultra-left attitude. They denied the possibility of an economic boom of post-war European and world capitalism, which was inevitable given the policies of Stalinism and Reformism which laid the political premises for a revival of capitalism. They declared that the economy of the capitalist countries could not be reconstituted. We were told that we were faced with the post-war slump in which capitalism was incapable of finding a way out! They ridiculed our argument when we quoted Lenin to point out that if not overthrown, capitalism always finds a way out. When their claims were falsified by events, they then solemnly pontificated "Marxistically" that there was a "ceiling" on production, that ceiling being the highest level which capitalism had reached in the pre-war period. Alas for our self-styled Marxist economists the "ceiling" was soon burst open by the rise of the world economy.

They declared it was impossible for American imperialism to render aid to its rivals. How could America prop up her rivals, they laughed ironically; were the capitalist philanthropists to bolster up their competitors? In other words they had not the faintest conception of the relationships of forces between the classes and nations, of the relationship of forces between Russia and America. Their economic analysis at this period was on the level of Stalinists of the "third period" of capitalism in the 1930s.

New periods, new gods. In the following years, as a result of the empirical crushing of their crude "theories", they now did a new somersault. Not that their analysis had been wrong, but obviously capitalism had changed. Secretly, they believed that the Marxist analysis of crisis was no longer relevant. Not daring to declare this openly, for fear of being denounced as revisionists, they accepted nevertheless the basic postulates of Keynesianism that slump could be avoided by state intervention and deficit financing. This can be demonstrated by reference to their main economic documents over a period of two decades. It is clearly stated in their 1965 World Congress document *The Evolution of Capitalism in Western Europe and the Tasks of Revolutionary Marxists* that "If this boom continues through 1965 and the first half of 1966, it is probable that no general recession will occur in western Europe. If, on the contrary, a recession breaks out in the USA in 1965 or the beginning of 1966, it is probable that this would coincide with a general recession in Western Europe, and that for the first time since the Second World War, synchronising of the economic cycles of all the important capitalist countries would occur. Even in the latter case, however, it would only be a recession, and not a serious economic crisis like that of 1929 or 1938. *The reason for this, amply considered in previous documents of the International is the possibility which imperialism has to 'amortize' crisis by increasing state expenses at the cost of continually lowering the purchasing power of money*." (Page 3, our emphasis)

This position today is universally repudiated by the serious bourgeois economists. The USFI did not explain the development of the economic upswing, but on the contrary, adapted themselves to the pressures of bourgeois "theoreticians". (For a fuller explanation, see *Will there be a Slump?* and *World Perspectives*). They will change their position on this too, now that these ideas are completely discredited. They were caught completely by surprise by economic events, and consequently adapted themselves to all the currents of Social Democracy, Stalinism and even the bourgeois currents of thought in a completely eclectic mish-mash, which they passed of as Marxist theory.

The Problems of War

In our documents in the post-World War Two period, we had explained that there was no question of an imminent inter-imperialist world war, or an immediate world war directed against the Soviet Union, because of the revolutionary wave following the Second World War. The bourgeoisie in Europe could only consolidate itself by the concession of democratic rights and as a consequence, allowing the existence and reinforcement of powerful mass organisations of the working class. Consequently, the political preconditions for an assault on the Soviet Union or on the Chinese revolution did not exist. At the same time, within a few years from the ending of the Second World War, due to the enforced de-mobilisation of Anglo-American troops by the pressure of the soldiers and of mass opinion at home, the relationship of forces, so far as conventional forces in Europe were concerned, had changed drastically in favour of the Soviet Union.

With 200 divisions mobilised, as against a little over a quarter of that in the hands of the western powers, if it came to a conventional war in Europe the Russians would sweep through far faster than Hitler's forces swept through France, and occupy the whole of Western Europe. With a crushing superiority in tanks, planes and guns, the forces which the western forces could mobilise would be swept away in a matter of days in Germany, and a matter of weeks in France by the Warsaw Bloc armies.

In Asia, China was the greatest military power on the mainland, and here too, given the power of revolutionary or semi-revolutionary war, by winning over the peasants, the Chinese forces could sweep through Asia as well. As a result, the world balance of forces had changed drastically to the disadvantage of imperialism. Having learned nothing in the school of Lenin and Trotsky, these worthy strategists could only go on repeating the cliche that "capitalism means war", which a 12-year old schoolboy having read the works of Lenin would have understood. But this formula does not tell how, and when, and under what conditions world war would break out. As a guide to strategy and tactics, this tells us nothing. Especially in the modern era, war is not only a question of the relationship between the powers, but above all a relationship between the classes. It is only with a bloody and decisive settlement with the workers that world war would be possible.

The defeats of the workers in Germany, Italy, France and Spain, and the destruction of their organisations prepared the way for World War Two. Since the Second World War, the power of the workers has been enormously enhanced and imperialists have correspondingly to be wary.

It is true that local wars against the colonial revolution and between minor powers have taken place every year since the Second World War. Similarly, after the First World War, there was a war every year till the final holocaust of 1939.

In addition to all the other factors, there is still the problem of nuclear and other terrifying means of destruction. The capitalists do not wage war for the sake of waging war. but in order to extend their power, income and profit. The idea of war is not to annihilate the enemy but to conquer him. To destroy the enemy and to be destroyed yourself is no gain. To destroy the working class, which nuclear war would mean, would be to destroy the goose that lays the golden eggs. Mutual destruction would mean also the destruction of the ruling class.

Consequently it is only totalitarian fascist regimes, completely desperate and unbalanced, which would take this road. And here again it is a question of the class struggle. The bourgeois will not lightly hand over their fate to new dictatorial maniacs like Mussolini and Hitler. In any event, before they could do so, it would require the bloody defeat of the working class.

Thus to work with a perspective of world war in reality meant not only a lack of understanding of all the multiple social and military forces involved, but was a programme of the profoundest pessimism. To imagine war would solve the problems of the socialist revolution, was to be as light minded as the Stalinists in Germany, who imagined the coming to power of the fascists in Germany would prepare the way for socialism. In reality the outbreak of world war would signify a decisive defeat for the working class. A nuclear holocaust would in more likelihood mean the mutual annihilation of countries and classes. At best, handfuls of survivors might succeed in creating some form of slave state and begin again the necessary development of the material productive forces, that with the working class, are the absolutely necessary pre-requisites of socialism. The Posadists have merely drawn to an extreme the ideas of Pablo, Hansen, Mandel, Healy and Co.

In any event, they were incapable of seeing the contradictions which still exist between the interests of the imperialists themselves. The Western European capitalist powers, including Britain, were not interested in the victory of an ideal capitalism or that of American imperialism, but of their own vested interests. A world war would at best mean the destruction of Western Europe, as Korea and Vietnam have been destroyed by American bombing. Therefore, these Imperialist powers had no interest in a war they could not win, which would be fought over their territories, and which even in the most favourable case would only be for the benefit of American imperialism.

Conventional war, for the Americans would be a daunting prospect. Starting at Calais and working across the Continent to Shanghai, Calcutta and Vladivostock would be an impossible task. Nuclear war for the first time would mean war on American soil. It would mean destruction of their home base - of the cities and the industrial power of America. Thus the theme of 'war-revolution' was not only reactionary but a fantasy as well. The position of this tendency showed a complete unawareness of the real social factors in relation to war, a problem which they have not understood to this day. At each crisis, at each conflict between the Soviet Union and American imperialism, they raised the howl of "imminent Armageddon".

In reality, both the Vietnam war and the Korean war, as well as the other wars of the post war epoch, were localised and limited by the deliberate arrangement between imperialism and the Chinese and Russian bureaucracies. For the whole period, imperialism has been on the defensive against incursions of the colonial revolution and the strength militarily, industrially and strategically of the Soviet Union and the Soviet bureaucracy.

Ultra-Leftism and Studentism

Having gained little result with their version of the policies of entrism, they now swung over to an ultra-left course in the capitalist countries in the West. Not having drawn an honest lesson from the experience of entrism in the Social Democratic and Communist Parties, they now advanced to the policies of ultra-leftism in Germany, France and Italy. However, they managed to combine this with a measure of opportunism. The Wilson Government was the advent of a "left Social Democratic government", one of their supporters wrote in Britain. His views were warmly defended by their supporters in Britain and not repudiated by them. Events were soon to disillusion them in this respect. At the same time, they succeeded in finding a fundamental difference between a Wilson Government in Britain and Willy Brandt's government in West Germany.

Eclecticism could not go further. Differences between individuals are not important, even if there were any important differences between Brandt and Wilson. In Britain, conducting an opportunist policy in the Labour Party, on the part of their protagonists, was only a step to barren adventures on the Left.

In Germany, they refused to work with the mass Social Democratic youth, turning their attention instead to the student movement. This was a tactical question, mistaken but nevertheless tactical. A certain amount of attention should have been paid to the students, but with the main purpose of educating them to understand the need to turn towards the Labour movement. The working class in Germany, like their brothers in Britain has to go through the experience of a Social Democratic government in order to understand that reformism cannot solve their problems. The German working class, which has been thrown backwards by the experience of fascism, and the policies of reformism and Stalinism, can only be educated with revolutionary ideas through testing their leaders by the experience of reformist governments.

Again, potentially valuable elements among the students were mis-educated by the USFI pandering to their prejudices, instead of undertaking the necessary work of Marxist education. This in turn means that at a later stage they will become discouraged and drop out. The tendency being to blame the working class for what are in effect their own shortcomings. In this, as in all things, this tendency managed to get the worst results from the experience. In Germany a main task should have been to get closer to the Social Democratic workers, especially the youth. A task which they are incapable of carrying out because of their failure in the past.

Not only in Germany, but in France, Italy, America and throughout the world, this tendency has indulged in what could be called Studentism. The progressive aspect of the student break from bourgeois ideology, which has become a world phenomenon, was of course to be recognised and utilised for the purpose of bringing the best of the students to the ideas of Marxism. Above all it should have been explained to the students that this phenomenon was a symptom of the social crisis of capitalism. It is a symptom of the move towards the left which in general is assuming a world scope. In colonial countries, in advanced capitalist countries, and in the Bonapartist workers' states, the same phenomenon can be observed.

It is the barometer of gathering social crisis, but unless it gains roots within the trade union and working class movements, it is doomed to be sterile and ineffective. Unless the students can gain the discipline of Marxist ideas and Marxist methods, the movement will become sterile, and degenerate into various forms of Utopianism and anarchism. Students can form a valuable leaven for the dissemination of revolutionary ideas, but only on the basis of Marxist ideas, and an understanding of the limitations of students and their role in society.

The May 1968 events in France provide a new, and perhaps decisive test, of all tendencies in the revolutionary movement. The acid test for revolutionaries is revolution. In this crucible, the gold of revolutionary ideas will soon be separated from the baser elements and alloys. Having denied the possibility of revolution in the west, for a whole historical period, they were naturally caught by surprise by events in France. Having started from the standpoint of profound pessimism as to the potential of the working class in the countries of the west, they passed to the most irresponsible ultra-leftism. The complete failure to understand that for a further historical period the Communist Parties will have a decisive role dooms them to complete sectarianism. To imagine that all the processes of the revolution, beginning to unfold in France would receive their denouncement within a matter of weeks or days, was not to understand the ABCs of revolution. The weakness of the revolutionary forces as a factor in the situation, they had not understood; nor the need to get close to the masses of the Communist Party. Instead, the need to ingratiate themselves with the wild and woolly ideas of the student left, led them to make a whole series ultra-left gestures and moves. The boycott of the elections and the boycott of the student elections which followed, was sheer irresponsibility which could only play into the hands of the Communist Party leadership, which had the overwhelming majority of the working class still supporting it.

The fact that the Communist Party would recoup its losses as an alternative to the Gaullist Party, they did not take into consideration. They have not prepared to this day their supporters for a new and inevitable period of Popular Frontism, to which the bourgeoisie will resort as a means of breaking a new offensive on the part of the working class. However, our tendency has analysed in full the development of the revolution in France, which is only in its early beginnings, so there is no need to repeat the ideas here. It only need be added that all the tendencies of the revolutionary left in France are on the decline at the moment, because of their failure to analyse and understand the ebb and flow of change in the revolution; that periods of calm, even of reaction, will prepare the way for the revolutionary mobilisation of the masses and renewed offensive on the part of the revolution.

Events indicate that not only in France, but in other countries where the Communist Party is the main party of the working class, only a mass split within the ranks of the Communist Party can prepare the way for a development of a mass revolutionary alternative party. In the countries where Social Democracy is the dominant force, similar considerations apply. The historical experience of the last five to seven decades indicates the correctness of this analysis.

The issues at their 1965 World Congress at which they expelled the Marxist opposition have been sufficiently documented. This showed their incapacity to tolerate a genuine and honest Marxist tendency within their ranks. The refusal to discuss, or to tolerate a Marxist wing within their forces, in an indication of the real processes within this organisation, and its organic tendency towards petit bourgeois sectarianism, utopianism and opportunism.

The history of the Ceylonese organisation provides an instructive lesson in what happens when the lessons of each period are not drawn by a revolutionary tendency. It was the only mass organisation of the Fourth International and the mass party of the working class in Ceylon. But precisely because of that it was prey to all tendencies of degeneration, to the pressures of hostile class forces to which mass organisations are subject. The incorrect policies over 25 years of the so-called international leadership meant that as far as Ceylon was concerned, they had no control over the MPs or the leadership. Being small groupings over the greater part of the world, they could only posses a political rather than an organisational authority. Being bankrupt at these, their feeble attempt at organisational gestures could only be treated with contempt.

It precipitated support for an immediate split when the Lanka Sama Samaja Party took an opportunist position in relation to a coalition government in 1964 which would only isolate the revolutionary elements and render them impotent and ultra-left. The consequence has been reinforcement of the position of the LSSP and decline and splits in the section that split away. The immediate task of any grouping inside or outside the LSSP should have been to face towards the mass organisation of the workers, in this case the LSSP itself. However, political authority can only be gained over a period of years and decades by demonstrating the correctness of the ideas of a revolutionary leadership, of its method, of its analysis. But of course, this is something that is conspicuously lacking. They tried to replace this real authority, a genuine authority, by means of administrative measures, which merely resulted in a series of humiliating and debilitating splits.

The Need for Marxist Theory

At their 1965 USFI Congress they put forward a "new" theory, that of capitalism and a "strong" state. This was an extension of their 1945 theory of Bonapartist states being on the order of the day in Western Europe - that capitalism could no longer allow the existence of democratic rights, and that therefore only dictatorial regimes could be established in Western Europe. They revived this theory, which was never officially repudiated in the past, with a new version of the 'strong' state. In France, Germany, Britain, everywhere, the bourgeoisie were going to replace democracy with a Bonapartist regime.

This analysis did not take into account the strength and power of working class organisations, the changed relationship of forces between the classes, the vacillation of the petty bourgeoisie, and under these conditions, far from the bourgeoisie being able to impose their will on society, society had a tendency to swing to the left. The attempt to impose Prices and Incomes policies has tended to break down in the main capitalist countries. Far from the state assuming dictatorial powers, apart from Greece (for special reasons), the tendency has been in the other direction.

In some countries there has been a tendency towards mass radicalisation, but nowhere has the bourgeoisie found it possible to impose their rule by means of installing a military police state. The movement of the students towards radicalisation, on which they place such great hopes, is a movement in the opposite direction. The only recent "strong" state in Europe, that of de Gaulle, was blown away by the first real movement of the mass of the working class. In any event, the Bonapartism of de Gaulle was the most democratic form of Bonapartism that has ever existed. Not accidentally. Its weakness was an expression of the enormous power latent in the working class.

The very development of industry has in its turn meant an enormous reinforcement of the power of the working class. Before there can be a move towards decisive reaction, there will have to be a bloody settlement with the working class. But this in its turn would mean posing the fate of the bourgeoisie as a stake in the struggle. Consequently it will be with extreme reluctance that the bourgeoisie will take this road. Nowhere are there strong fascist organisations, as existed in the pre-war period, especially in the 1930s. After the experience with the fascist maniacs, it is only with extreme reluctance that the bourgeoisie would put themselves in the power of fascism.

On the other hand, a "strong" state in its Bonapartist form is not capable of maintaining itself for any length of time without a mass basis. Hence, on the order of the day are perhaps reactionary methods and laws on the part of the bourgeois state, but not a military police dictatorship. Throughout the bourgeois world, in the twilight of capitalism, it is not "strong" states but extremely weak and paralysed states that the working class and the revolutionary movement has to face.

The whole tactics of the so-called "extra-Parliamentary opposition" in Germany, France, Italy and Britain, are manifestations of verbal opposition. They are indications of middle class and anarchist ideas, rather than those of Marxism. The task for students and radicals generally is first to educate themselves with the sober ideas of Marxism, instead of the rantings of revolutionary romanticism, and then get closer to the masses. The capitulation of the USFI to this verbal radicalisation is an expression of a complete lack of understanding of the dialectic of the class struggle and the methods of class awakening. The task is at one and the same time to maintain theoretical intransigence with flexibility of tactics in order to get closer to the working class. The whole history of this tendency is an inglorious one.

We are now thrown back to a position near to our starting point, of small groupings, struggling against the stream of opportunist tendencies. Historically, the Marxist movement has been thrown far back by isolation from the mass movement.

In one respect we are fortunate, historically. If instead of tiny sects they had organisations of 10,000 - 50,000 members in France, America and other countries, enormous damage would have been done in the mass movement, by the ultra-left course of this grouping and the various groupings around it. It would have been like the policies of the Comintern in its ultra-left phase in the '30s, when the policies, the light minded attitudes towards the mass organisations, resulted in isolation from the working class. The victory of Hitler in Germany was prepared in this way. In its own way, the antics of all the tendencies in France has enormously facilitated the regaining of prestige and power over the working class of the Communist Party leadership and reformists. In other countries, insofar as they have had any effect at all, they have helped successfully to isolate the students from the Labour Movement.

The theoretical crudities and the fundamental political errors of the clique claiming to represent the International can be traced from the period after the war. Had they conducted an honest self criticism of their errors at this time, and made a thorough analysis of their mistakes and the reasons for these mistakes, they could have built the movement on firm foundations. But having burned their fingers by repeating what they thought were the recipes of Trotsky, these cooks decided that the "Cookbook of the Revolution" was no good, and proceeded to unceremoniously dump the teachings of the great masters through the window. They abandoned the theoretical ideas of Marxism and proceeded purely on the basis of empiricism and impressionism.

Our task, nationally and internationally, remains basically the same as it has been for the last two generations. That task is the defence and extension of the basic revolutionary ideas of Marxism. The reason for the degeneration of the sects, the most important of whom are those gathered round the banner of the USFI, lies in the historical development of our times. The pressure of capitalism, reformism and Stalinism, in a period of capitalist upswing in the west, the temporary consolidation of Stalinism in the east, and the perversions of the colonial revolution, as explained in the preceding material, were causes of the degeneration of all the sects claiming to be the Fourth International.

But an explanation is not an excuse. Necessity has two sides. In preceding history, the degeneration of the Second and Third Internationals, due to objective as well as subjective factors, did not justify the leaders who had abandoned Marxism. It did not justify either reformism or Stalinism. Similarly, there is no justification for the crimes of sectarianism and opportunism which have been committed by the leaders of the so-called Fourth International for more than an entire generation. It is one thing to make an episodic mistake. Mistakes will be made by even the most revolutionary and far-sighted tendencies. But continuous repetition, a continual zig-zagging between opportunism and ultra-leftism, ceases to be a mistake and becomes a tendency. It is this tendency whose history we have analysed. A tendency which like the Stalinists and reformists before them, refuses to analyse its mistakes in order to correct them.

A tendency of this kind can never rise to the tasks posed by history. They will continue interminably with splits and manoeuvres, with dictates that they have no relation to any genuine authority gathered on the basis of political experience. A tendency of this character can never carry on the traditions of Bolshevism, the traditions of Trotskyism. They are the manure of history, which, not being ploughed into the fields cannot bear revolutionary fruit, but left in the open has begun to smell somewhat. Many of the younger elements may succeed in breaking away from this poisonous milieu and assist in building the new International. For a mass revolutionary tendency, it is necessary to have not just the tradition, method and policies of Marxism. It is necessary also to have the current of history with the tendency. Thus it was with the Bolsheviks.

However for a small revolutionary tendency it is essential, an absolute necessity to maintain the basic ideas, while adding to them consciously and openly on the basis of experience. Without this, it is the death of a tendency as a revolutionary force. If such a tendency cannot learn from the experience of events, it is doomed to remain a sect and to provoke further defeats and disintegration of the movement. From the point of view of history, there is absolutely no excuse for the continual succession of errors of the USFI. Mistakes are grievous, failure to rectify mistakes, fatal.

Lenin and Trotsky meticulously corrected even to the minutest detail any theoretical errors in order to maintain the sharpness of theory as the cutting edge of Bolshevism. A tendency like that of the USFI can never rise to the tasks posed by history. The Stalinists and the reformists have mass organisations. The Marxists have revolutionary theory which historically they will transmute from a small quality into a revolutionary quantity. With neither mass organisation nor Marxist theory, there can be no future. This tendency is doomed historically. At each stage in the development of events the British Marxists have acted generally in a correct manner. As far as the basic problems are concerned, the documents can be published and can stand as a contribution to Marxism over a period of 25 years.

The failure of the forces of Trotskyism to build a viable International can be understood on the basis of the experience of the epoch. At one and the same time, revolutionary and counter-revolutionary, with the proletariat faced with formidable obstacles in the shape of Social Democratic and Stalinist organisations, it was inevitable that great difficulties should lie in the path of creating mass revolutionary tendencies.

The new period opened out by the French Revolution begins an entirely new stage in the development of the proletariat. Mass initiative and mass action will put to the test the mighty organisations of Stalinism and Social Democracy. In these events, the mass organisations will extrude a revolutionary or quasi-revolutionary wing, but they are doomed to a whole series of catastrophic splits both to the left and to the right. During the course of this experience, the workers will put to the test, not only the reformists and Stalinist mass organisations, but the variety of sectarianism and centrist tendencies - the Maoists, Castroists, Guevaraists and other tendencies which have proliferated because there has not been a mass pole of revolutionary attraction. Events will politically expose the inadequacies and ineffectualness of all the varieties of reformism and Stalinism. The fresh forces of the new generation, not alone among the students, but far more important, among the working class, will seek the revolutionary road.

On the basis of events, mass revolutionary tendencies in the countries of the west, where Stalinism is the main current, will be formed in the Communist Parties, and where the reformists are a mass tendency, within the Social Democratic Parties. The period which Trotsky confidently foresaw in the immediate pre-war period, now opens out in different historical circumstances. The ideas of Marxism, which we have maintained for an entire generation, will begin to have a class audience.

Nationally and internationally, the ideas of our tendency can gain a mass support over the epoch. Our struggle to build the movement will have its effect internationally. Our task consists in building a viable tendency in Britain, which will have the resources and the authority to get a hearing among advanced elements throughout the world. It is impossible to detail the ways in which this will be done, but with initiative and elan, we can succeed in spreading the influence of our tendency.

In the dark days during the First World War, the Marxists were reduced to tiny handfuls but on the basis of events, they carried through a victorious revolution in Russia in 1917 and prepared the way for the building of mass revolutionary parties. Historically, the Bolsheviks maintained a rigidity of revolutionary ideas because of the influence of Lenin and Trotsky. With adverse historical currents, the ideas were swept away. In a new historical epoch the ideas will once again, reinforced by the rich experience of the last quarter century, gain a mass audience. The other tendencies claiming to be Trotskyist, will be put to the test. They will be reduced to ashes in the fire of events.

Capitalism on the one side in the developed and in the underdeveloped world, will find itself in an impasse. On the other hand, Stalinism more and more reveals its incompatibility in the non-capitalist countries with nationalisation and a planned economy. This impasse of the bourgeoisie and the Stalinist . bureaucracy, is reflected in the barrenness of their theoreticians economically and politically. The collapse of the Stalinists into warring national groupings in the countries where they have power and the countries where they are in opposition, indicates the bankruptcy of Stalinism.

Reformism on the other hand has demonstrated its baleful effects in the countries where the reformists are in the government, as well as in the countries where they are in opposition. The domination of the Labour Movement by these tendencies has extended its corrupting influences also to the small and weak tendencies of Trotskyism. For them there is no way forward, but on the basis of the great revolutionary ascent which lies ahead, youth will be attracted to the ideas of Trotskyism. The Bolsheviks in 1917, although no revolutionary International existed, carried out their revolution in the method, ideas and with the name of the International. They were internationalists through and through. The greatest international task of the revolutionary Marxists in Britain is the building of a powerful revolutionary tendency imbued with the principles and traditions of internationalism, which can assist in the building of a viable tendency internationally.

How Will the International be Organised?

Lenin and Trotsky had the occasion to point out many times that if a mistake were not corrected, it could become a tendency. The analysis of this document shows that for 25 years, the USFI has staggered from one mistake to another. From one wrong policy to its opposite, and then a higher level of mistakes back again. This is the mark of a thoroughly petit bourgeois tendency. As far as this grouping is concerned, at least its top leadership, this has now become organic. The whole outlook has been moulded by the mistakes of a quarter century, and become part and parcel of their methods of thinking, of their habits of work, and their whole outlook. Even to dignify this tendency by calling it centrist would be a compliment.

In the case of the Second International, which is a mass movement, its degeneration can be explained by the pressures of society, of the history of the latter part of the 19th Century and the beginning of the 20th. But it is also explained by the separation of the leadership by the rank and file and their remoteness from the mass base.

The 3rd International began from the most revolutionary mass tendency that the world has ever seen, an international and revolutionary mass tendency. In a revolutionary epoch (at one and the same time, revolutionary and counter-revolutionary) the degeneration of the International, leaving aside the question of the Russian Party, has been explained in many documents as the result of the pressure of the bureaucracy and its raising itself above the masses. Internationally, the degeneration of the 3rd International began with the refusal to learn from and analyse the lessons of events, and to correct the mistakes of the Stalinist leadership. This, among other factors, was not the least important.

Trotskyism, the most revolutionary and honest tendency in history, began its work above all with an analysis of this process. Starting without the broad masses, it could only succeed as a revolutionary tendency by a serious attitude to theory and events. This was the lesson from the works of Lenin, and perhaps even more so in the works and activity of Trotsky during the period of theoretical decline and degeneration. Having abandoned this precious heritage and without the corrective of mass revolutionary pressure, the USFI and other tendencies like it, became irresponsible. Questions of theory were not seriously considered, but became part of the arbitrary humours and whims of the leading clique. Twenty five years of this process has indicated that they are organically incapable of transformation organisationally and politically in the direction of Marxism.

It would be a distasteful task to document the organisational manoeuvrings of this Zinovievist tendency. Lenin contemptuously called the Second International a post office and not an International. This clique cannot even be dignified as a Post Office. Organisationally as well as politically, they are completely bankrupt.

How then will the International be built? We have pointed out many times that in Britain the movement will only be built on the basis of events. This applies with just as much force to the question of the International.

In many documents we explained how events will bring crisis to the mass Social Democratic Parties and to the mass Stalinist Parties. Events west and east will play their part. But above all, it is the development in the key industrial countries in the world that will be decisive. A new period is opening up in the history of capitalism in the west, and Stalinism in the east. The May events of 1968 in France and the present turmoil in Italy are only a beginning. The outline of the crisis in the relationship between the classes, not only in Europe but in Japan and America as well as other important centres, is already showing itself at the present time.

Under the hammer blows of events, the development of mass centrist groupings in the Stalinist and Social Democratic Parties is inevitable. Mass splits from these tendencies will be on the order of the day in the coming decade or two. Events in Russia can transform the situation internationally. Similarly, for America and other industrial countries of the west. With the developments of mass centrist groupings with large numbers of workers groping for a revolutionary lead, this will be a favourable milieu or a hot house for the reception of Marxist ideas. We must try and reach these elements internationally with the ideas and methods of Trotsky.

It is from these mass forces developing within these organisations that the mass forces of the International will come. Great events will make our ideas and policies more acceptable among these strata, especially the workers. To reach these elements will be an important part of our work in the future.

Events will also make the younger and more intelligent elements within the other tendencies claiming to be Trotskyist, amenable to our ideas. Many of the younger elements will be won over under these conditions.

It will be the Spanish Revolution all over again, but with an organic crisis of Stalinism and reformism which events will bring to the surface. The working class is far stronger, international reaction far weaker, thus preparing the basis for an offensive by the workers. Then with a period of defeats and reaction of one form or another, as well as important gains and successes, there will be an even greater surge forward by the workers, the way will be prepared for the creation of mass Centrist tendencies.

The Russian Revolution developed over nine months; this above all because of the strength of Bolshevism. The Spanish revolution developed over six to seven years. A lengthy period of revolution, because of the weakness of the revolutionary forces, is most likely as the example of France has already shown. It is in this lengthy process that the possibility is given to intervene. The revolutionary elements in the mass Centrist parties that would develop, would be looking for consistent revolutionary ideas, policies and methods of work.

It is this which makes it vital and emphasises our need to continue and expand our international work. We must develop and broaden our work among contacts, groups and even individuals that we can reach in other countries. Our criticisms and the contrast with the policy of other tendencies should give us the possibility of winning a base. Thus, this remains an important part of the activity of our tendency, nationally and internationally.

However, an important part of the international work consists of building a viable tendency in Britain. That is why the question of headquarters, press and professionals is of such vital importance, not only in our national but our international work. The main argument of the USFI and others has never been a criticism of our theoretical ideas, but a denigration of our work. Who are they? What have they built? They are incapable of building a tendency; such was the main line of the poison which they injected among young comrades, especially behind the scenes. A building of a viable and powerful tendency in Britain would demonstrate in practice not only the correctness of our ideas, but also our methods of work and of organisation. Their slanders would be refuted in practice. The collapse of the RCP dealt a blow to the movement nationally and internationally which we are now in the process of repairing.

Bolshevism grew internationally through the success of the October Revolution. This in its turn was dependent on the organisation of the Russian Party as well as the theoretical ideas and policies of Lenin and Trotsky. We are faced here with a similar process, taking things in proportion of course, in that we have yet to stand up to the test of history and to build a mass tendency.

Far more than in any other period of history, the ground is being prepared for revolutionary explosions in the industrially developed countries, and not the least in Britain. On the basis of revolutionary developments, ideas will be seized eagerly by workers groping towards Marxism. Intervention under these conditions in revolutionary situations in other countries can be very fruitful.

In one way, we are more prepared than in the past for such interventions, because we already have comrades who already speak the main European languages. Their services will undoubtedly be required more and more in the coming epoch. But it is also a question of money and resources. We have many criticisms of the American SWP, but on the basis of the revolutionary tide which is now in its early beginnings in the United States, and although principally among the students at the moment it has been reported that the SWP has sixty professionals in New York alone!

For the minimum tasks nationally and internationally, we need at least a dozen professionals. We can say that with our modest successes, the real history of the tendency is just beginning; but with our own press, our own premises and more professionals, we can really turn in a far more serious way to the development of our work on an international scale. With resources of this character, we can begin the publication of a detailed analysis of the policies of the other tendencies for the special purpose of influencing people abroad. We can commence the publication, not only in English, but in foreign languages, of this material and our own analysis and theoretical documents. We can conduct serious work. Thus the task of drawing together the elements that will form a new international goes hand in hand with the building of our own tendency.

May 1970

Notes:

1- As late as 1947, in a conversation with J. Stuart (Sam Gordon) then one of the leaders of the ISFI, while endeavouring to explain the changed conditions one of the leaders of the British Section was stopped by him saying "Ah, yes, it's only 1947 now, there is still a year to go of Trotsky's prognosis." The whole events of the war and the post-war period had been lost on him and his fellow thinkers of the ISFI.

In 1938, there had been the foundation of the Workers International League. This had been as a consequence of the expulsion of a group of comrades from the Militant Group on an organisational issue. Later that year the WIL had refused to participate in an unprincipled fusion between different groupings, some entrist, some non-entrist, with the deliberately ambiguous formula of unity on both tactics, which was calculated as the WIL stated, to produce a paralysis of the new organisation and the certainty of a split. It was a formula to unite three organisations into ten. This was subsequently confirmed by events. JP Cannon, who was instrumental in getting this "unity", and the leaders of the American SWP, pursued a vendetta against those who led the WIL.

At the 1944 founding conference of the Revolutionary Communist Party, their supporters solemnly declared that with the fusion of all Trotskyist elements there were now no political differences. Consequently, they declared that their "Internationalist" faction was dissolved. This was greeted with hoots of laughter at the conference which gained indignant protest from the representative of the International. This did not prevent the American and International representative, Phelan (Sherry Mangan) that same evening from having a secret meeting with Healy and other leaders of his clique, at his hotel, to decide how best to get rid of the RCP's anti-internationalist leadership which must be destroyed!

The RCP, of which the WIL was the principle component made rapid gains, due to, among other reasons, the support of the war-time coalition by the Labour, Stalinist and trade union leaders. It pursued flexible tactics, and with correct methods and policies, succeeded in gaining a modest but important support in all the principle industrial areas of the country. At its height, it was an important component part of the working class. The reason for its collapse is not the subject of this document, but will be dealt with when the history of British Trotskyism is produced.

Here it should be pointed out that the WIL, although it was not present at the 1938 founding conference of the Fourth International had been invited to send delegates but had been unable to do so for financial reasons. Nevertheless, it sent a statement which was falsified by Cannon in order to get the rejection of sympathetic affiliation. Despite the fact that it was outside the International formally at the time, Trotsky did not attack it but on the contrary sent a letter of congratulations for the introduction to his pamphlet on the *Lessons of Spain* and the acquiring of a small printing press.

On organisational matters, the International has been bedevilled with a heritage of Zinovievism and clique factional politics, of horse deals, of "keyman" politics, of which Cannon among others, despite his gifts as a workers' leader, was guilty. Always methods of this sort arise because of theoretical backwardness and in the last analysis, of incorrect policies. The task of a leadership, nationally and internationally, is to convince by discussion and experience. It is useless to wave the big stick of organisation.

In the days of Lenin and Trotsky, even with the immeasurable political authority that they had internationally, they always endeavoured to discuss theoretical questions, and to win people over by convincing them rather by imposing their policies. Since the death of Trotsky who always emphasised the need for a clean banner, the methods of Zinovievism have crept into the politics of the tendencies claiming to represent the Fourth International. However this document is not intended to deal with organisational questions so much as with the fundamental political divergences from the ideas of Marxism that have taken place in the last three decades.

The RCP and its forerunner the WIL provided object lessons on how organisational questions should be tackled. The RCP participated in the Labour Movement with flexible tactics. Under the given conditions, conducting its work under its own flag, but nevertheless facing always to the mass movement. The full history of the RCP and its achievements will have to be written. The leadership of the American SWP and of the International pursued the clique politics even to the extent of using the pressure of the resource that they possess, to ensure the acceptance of their ideas. Thus in a small way, continuing the policies of Zinovievism in this respect too.

2 - At the 1965 USFI World Congress, the Marxist opposition challenged the following formulation in their document *The Development of the Sino-Soviet Dispute and the Situation in the International Communist Movement*:

"In China the struggle against the bureaucracy and its regime, and for proletarian democracy, cannot be won except through an anti-bureaucratic struggle on a scale massive enough to bring about a qualitative change in the political form of government" (Page 8).

We demanded to know whether or not this meant that the International held the position that the political revolution was necessary in China before there could be the beginning of the movement towards socialism. Maitan, for the 'majority', answered that the old International Secretariat (himself, Frank, Mandel and Pablo) believed that the political revolution was not necessary while the American SWP held that it was. The formulation of the document was therefore a "Compromise". Note: the American SWP, along with Healy and Lambert, split from the ISFI in 1953. In 1963 the American SWP rejoined the ISFI, which was renamed the United Secretariat of the FI (USFI). Pablo himself split from the USFI in 1964.

Appendix VI
Obituary of Olwyn Hughes by Alan Woods-

Olwyn Hughes: worker, fighter, Marxist

I first met Olwyn in 1971 in a Marxist discussion class we had organised in the small Welsh mining town of Ammanford. But Olwyn's political life went back a lot further, to the period during and just after the War, when he first got active in politics, first in the Young Communist League, and then in the Trotskyist Revolutionary Communist Party.

For a young miner like Olwyn, it must have been difficult not to have been a Communist. Ammanford used to be known as "Little Moscow". And not accidentally. The mining valleys of South Wales had a long history of bitter class war. Memories of the General Strike and the inhuman treatment meted out to the miners and their families driven back to work by starvation by the mine owners in cahoots with Winston Churchill were burnt into the consciousness of a whole generation and passed on to the next.

The Russian Revolution offered a beacon of hope to these workers who embraced it with that passion so typical of the Welsh. The South Wales miners' union actually affiliated en bloc to the Communist International. Even in the 1970s I remember that there was still a bust of Lenin in the Ammanford workingmen's club where we held our Sunday night meetings, alongside the photographs of young men from the area killed in the Spanish Civil War.

Generation

Tragically, the Stalinist degeneration of the Russian Revolution had its effects on the British Communist Party, as all the others. A whole generation of class fighters were cynically duped and deceived. And what fighters they were! In spite of everything, one has to admire the militant spirit and dedication of the Communist workers who sincerely believed that in carrying out the orders of their leaders, they were preparing the revolutionary transformation of society. Olwyn used to speak of one of these, who would be out every evening selling the *Daily Worker*. A man of small stature, he would stride into the miners' club, plant himself firmly in the middle of the floor clutching his bundle of papers under his arm, and shout out: "Does anybody want to read the truth?"

But the real truth was that the Communist Party was no longer a weapon for changing society, but a tool in the hands of the Moscow bureaucracy. This was clearly revealed by the cynical gyrations of the CP line before and during the Second World War. Dudley Edwards, who was a marvellous old comrade. described to me one incident on the eve of the War when Stalin suddenly signed a non-aggression pact with Hitler. Prior to this, the CP line was one of "popular frontism", a class collaborationist policy, the alleged purpose of which was to secure an alliance of the Western "democracies" with Russia against Nazi Germany. Knowing nothing of the change, Dudley was preparing to mount the speakers' rostrum to defend the popular front, when someone tugged him by the sleeve and whispered "Comrade, the Line's been changed!" So he threw his notes away and delivered a speech saying the exact opposite of what he had intended. There were many such cases.

The abandonment of the policy of popular frontism and the adoption of an ultra-left policy in the first days of the War did not shake the confidence of the working class Communists, though many middle-class fellow-travellers immediately jumped ship. What really caused dismay in the ranks was the next change of Line. When in the Summer of 1941, Hitler cynically broke his pact with Stalin to attack the Soviet Union, Moscow required a totally different policy. Hitherto, the British CP had had a caricature of Lenin's policy of revolutionary defeatism, demanding, in effect, peace on Hitler's terms. They irresponsibly fomented strikes at the slightest pretext at a time when the British workers were working round the clock for the War effort. Now, at the drop of a hat, the Party called a halt to all strikes and demanded the workers step up productivity for the war.

Overnight, without any explanation, the imperialist war became a progressive war against fascism. This was too much for many Communist workers to swallow. How could such a policy be justified? What did it all mean? The only people who gave explanations were the Trotskyists of the Revolutionary Communist Party (RCP). While consistently calling for the defence of the USSR, they advocated a policy of class independence, calling on the Labour Party to break the coalition with the Tories and Liberals and take power on the basis of a socialist policy of nationalising the banks and monopolies under workers' control and management. As a result they were viciously attacked by the Stalinist leaders of the CPGB who issued a scurrilous pamphlet called *Hitler's Secret Agents*, and even called on Herbert Morrison, the Home Minister (and Labour Party member) to illegalise them - which he refused to do.

Throughout the War, the Labour Party agreed to an electoral truce with the Tories. They were all in the wartime coalition, so there were hardly any elections. An exception was the by-election in working-class Neath in 1945, when the RCP fielded a candidate in a safe Labour seat. The Stalinists were beside themselves with rage. They did everything possible to disrupt the RCP's campaign, but without success. The RCP made a big impact with its programme and ideas - not least among sections of the CP workers.

Self educated

A few miles away from Neath, along a desolate, wind-swept valley, lies the small mining town of Gwaun-cae-Gurwen, popularly known as G-C-G, or "the Waun". Here the RCP established an active branch, mainly of miners who had come over from the Communist Party. The leading spirit was one Johnny Jones, a self-educated man, like many Welsh workers at that time who took the trouble to raise themselves above the terrible conditions of life to conquer for themselves the world of culture and ideas. Johnny used to write marvellous articles for the *Socialist Appeal* from which you could get a clear idea of the lives, thoughts and aspirations of working people. Still a youth, Olwyn joined this group. He never really left it till the moment of his death.

It took some guts to be an active Trotskyist militant in a CP stronghold like that. The Stalinists looked on them as traitors or worse, and on more than one occasion criticism was not limited to verbal exchanges. Olwyn gave me the following example. One of the RCP members (I don't remember the name) was quite a tough man, although quietly spoken. Once, he and Olwyn were chatting over a pint in the local club, when a particularly fanatical Stalinist came up behind them and began taunting the alleged "Trotsky-fascists." Olwyn's companion turned round and addressed the provocateur: "Are you talking about me?" The man had scarcely had time to reply in the affirmative, when the fists started to fly. The aggressor ended up on the carpet, whereupon the victor looked challengingly round the room: "Now then. Anyone else got anything to say?" They did not.

Of course, my own acquaintance with Olwyn started many years later. Yet he always spoke of that period with the liveliest enthusiasm and affection. There was a reason for that. These were the years that gave him the education and the ideas that would shape the rest of his life. In the bleak days of the capitalist upswing, when the forces of genuine Marxism were isolated for a whole historical period, Olwyn became temporarily cut off from the movement. But unlike others he always kept faith. Not the blind faith of a religious fanatic, but the conscious faith of a working class revolutionary who has absorbed the fundamental ideas and theories of Marxism.

When I met up with him in that study group, it was as if the knot of history had been suddenly retied. He instantly recognised our ideas as his own. When he met Ted Grant again after many years he commented in amazement: "He's just the same as always". He was really delighted that we had remained firm, defending the ideas of Marxism "just the same as always". He was always a voracious reader and had a very high political level. Whenever we met, he always insisted in discussing theory. The question of the Soviet Union was one of the things that interested him most. Shortly before his death he had just read Ted Grant's new book *Russia - From Revolution to Counter-Revolution.* He regarded both this and Reason in Revolt as wonderful achievements, and "a real addition to Marxist thought."

All his life, Olwyn Hughes remained what he had always been - a working miner. In the last period, he worked in small private pits, and on one occasion he described the kind of conditions that prevailed in them. There was an explosion in a nearby mine, and Olwyn rushed to help with other miners. The first one to enter the mine, at first he could see nothing. Then, as his eyes got used to the dark, he could see a man on the ground, black all over with coal dust. Eventually, the man spoke to him in Welsh: "Olwyn. Don't you know me?" It was a friend of his. What Olwyn did not know was that, beneath the thick layer of coal dust, most of his skin had been blasted away by the explosion. He died shortly afterwards. Later, the mine owner claimed to have found a box of matches in the dead man's pocket. This version was supported by the man from the mines inspectorate who came to investigate. When I saw Olwyn in the pub, his face was ashen. "Well," he told me, "I was in that mine after the explosion. The heat was so bad, it had melted metal. Yet they say there was a box of matches!"

From this single incident you can learn more about Olwyn Hughes and thousands like him than in any book. The unshakeable loyalty to the cause of socialism and the working class he displayed all his life did not come from books, though he loved them too. It came from life itself. From hard experience. From a deep and enduring sense of rebellion against injustice. It is a matter of the most heartfelt regret that I did not manage to see Olwyn before he was taken from us. I had intended to. Now that meeting will never take place. This short tribute must stand in its place. It is the only kind of monument that I know Olwyn would want to have.

January 1998

A tribute to Herbie Bell (1895-1978)

By Bill Landles

I knew Herbie Bell from my days in the Independent Labour Party. We joined the Revolutionary Communist Party in the North East at about the same time. I was proud to be his election agent in 1945, when he stood as an RCP candidate in a local election.

Herbie Bell did not need to make an academic study of Dialectical Materialism and socialism to be the kind of man that he was. His humanity and sensitivity to the injustices perpetrated upon the working class fused into his very being. Totally committed to the eventual emancipation of all people internationally, Herbie patiently but relentlessly committed himself to their cause. It was not easy, particularly during the years of the Second World War, to sell the journal and propagate Trotskyism during the domination of Stalinism in its heyday.

Nevertheless, Herbie Bell never wavered nor lost his faith and his always cheerful demeanour inspired those of us around him. To have basked in the glow of such a sincere comrade was a privilege and by his example we had the conviction to maintain our own loyalty to our own class.

Thank you comrade Herbie Bell.

Bill Landles

▲ Herbie Bell's RCP membership card

Biographical notes

Bell, Herbie (1895 - 1978)
Left wing agitator in First World War. Joined the ILP, became a councillor in Wallsend and Northumberland. He was a despatch rider in the 1926 General Strike. In 1944 joined the RCP, and stood as the RCP candidate in Wallsend in 1945. Rejoined the Trotskyist movement in the 1960s and was active in the Labour Party.

Bornstein, Sam (1920 - 1990)
Joined the WIL shortly before the war, becoming active in the Stepney branch. Supported the majority position against Healy in the RCP. Leading figure in the Open Party faction. Linked up again with Ted Grant during the mid-50s for a period. Later worked with Al Richardson in the writing of two histories of British Trotskyism as well as helping to establish the journal *Revolutionary History*.

Brockway, Fenner (1888 - 1988)
Author and Humanist, he was a leading member of the ILP during the 1930s after its split from the Labour Party (he had been a Labour MP from 1929-31) serving as general secretary in 1928 and from 1933 up to 1939. He strongly opposed Trotsky's call for a Fourth International. Rejoined the LP later becoming a Labour MP in 1950 and from 1964 a Labour Peer.

Cannon, James P. (1890 - 1974)
American Trotskyist leader. Came to prominence as an organiser for the IWW and as a member of Eugene Debs' Socialist Party. A founding member of the Communist Labour Party in 1919 he rose to a leading position in that organisation, attending many important conferences including the Communist International in 1928 where, already in conflict with the leadership of the US party, he came into contact with Trotsky's opposition to Stalin. Breaking with the Communist Party he helped lead the Left Opposition in the USA subsequently becoming National Secretary of the American SWP. Books include *History of American Trotskyism* and *Struggle For a Proletarian Party* (1943). The transcript of his testimony at the 1941 trial of 28 members of the SWP under the Smith Act was published in book form as *Socialism on Trial* (1942).

Cliff, Tony (Ygael Gluckstein) (1917 - 2000)
Moved to Britain from Israel after the war having been influenced by Trotsky's ideas. Joining the RCP he later became a leading exponent of the theory of 'state capitalism'. Helped form

the Socialist Review Group in 1950, subsequently becoming the leading theoretician of the International Socialists and then the SWP (UK). Books include studies of both Lenin and Trotsky.

Collins, Sam
Member of the Marxist Group working in the ILP. Interviewed Trotsky in 1936 in Norway whilst on holiday (see Trotsky's *Writings On Britain* Vol. 3) but left politics after the war.

Deane, Arthur (b. 1922)
One of the younger layer of activists in the WIL and RCP, supported an Open Party position in 1949. Brother of Jimmy and Brian. Participated with Ted Grant in the launching the *International Socialist* (1952), *Socialist Fight* (1958), and then *Militant* (1964).

Deane, Gertie (1894 - 1989)
Father was in the SDF and first Labour councillor in Liverpool. Introduced to James Larkin, James Connolly and Victor Grayson. Was a Suffragett, and later convinced of Trotskyism by her sons, Jimmy, Arthur and Brian. Member of the WIL and RCP, and later with the Grant tendency.

Deane, Jimmy (b. 1921)
Recruited in Merseyside in the 1930s into the Militant Group. Along with Ted Grant and Jock Haston played a leading role in the RCP. Close collaborator of Ted Grant throughout the 1950s and first half of the 1960s, but became politically inactive. Still gives moral political support to this day.

Dewar, Hugo (1908 - 1980)
At first member of the ILP, joined the CP becoming a member of the Balham Group. Expelled from CP in August 1932. Refused with Groves to join the Trotskyists in the ILP. Later joined the RSL in 1938, and remained semi-active thereafter, writing both historical material and poetry.

Frank, Pierre (1905 - 1984)
Joined the CP in 1925. Joined the Left Opposition in 1927, later serving as Trotsky's secretary whilst he was at Prinkipo in 1932-3. A member of the International Secretariat of the Left Opposition during the 1930s he broke with this organisation as part of the Molinier Group. In the 1940s rejoined the Trotskyists and subsequently rose to become a leading member of the various post-war formations of the 'United Secretariat of the Fourth International. Published a potted history of the Fourth International in 1969, *The Fourth International: The Long March Of The Trotskyists.*

Frost, Sid (Max Basch)
One of the Johannesburg group of Trotskyists in South Africa, he travelled with Ted Grant to Europe in 1934 (changing his name to Sid Frost), joining the ILP in Britain. It is believed he returned to South Africa where he died.

Fryer, Peter (b. 1927)
As a correspondent for the paper of the British Communist Party paper the *Daily Worker*, Fryer reported on the uprising of the workers in Hungary 1956, subsequently available in book form as *The Hungarian Tragedy* (1997). These reports were censored at the time and led to Fryer breaking with Stalinism. He later joined the Healyite organisation and edited the *Newsletter*, but later resigned. Has written extensively on the struggles of Black workers.

Groves, Reg (1908 - 1988)
Like Hugo Dewar joined first the ILP and then the CP, being expelled from that organisation in 1932 for his part in the Balham Group. Joined the Labour Party in 1935, standing as a parliamentary candidate in several elections. Became leading member of the Socialist League and defended the policies of the POUM. Later became a writer and journalist. Published a history ofThe Balham Group in 1973 covering the period in which he was involved in Trotskyist politics.

Harber, Denzil Dean (1909 - 1966)
Joined the Communist League in 1932, splitting off with the minority in 1933 to enter the ILP forming the Marxist Group. Later belonged to the Bolshevik-Leninist group that worked in the Labour Party and attended as a delegate the first International Conference for The Fourth International in 1936. Ended up leading one of the three factions in the RSL in 1940. Dropped out of politics after 1950.

Haston, Jock (1913 - 1986)
A member of the same Paddington branch of the Militant Group as Ted Grant, Jock Haston later became a leading organiser of the Workers International League. He subsequently became General Secretary of the RCP and one of its most able organisers. Parliamentary candidate for the RCP at the 1945 Neath by-election. Left the movement in 1951 becoming a lecturer for the NCLC and subsequently an educational director for the EEPTU.

Healy, Gerry (1913 - 1989)
He moved to England from Ireland in 1928 becoming a Communist soon after. Following an encounter with Jock Haston in Hyde Park Corner he was won over to Trotskyism, joining the Militant Group. Active within the WIL (where he was expelled and readmitted several times) and then the RCP, he subsequently helped launch the Left-reformist Socialist Outlook in 1948. Organised around "The Club" he later formed the Socialist Labour League in 1959 which subsequently became the Workers Revolutionary Party. Expelled in 1985, he was involved with a series of subsequent splits.

Hamilton, Betty (1904 - 1994)
Became active in the French CP and joined the Left Opposition in 1929. On moving to England joined the Militant group. Later belonged to first the WIL and the RCP. Later sided with Gerry Healy remaining with his group until the 1980s, briefly supporting the Lambertists.

Hillman, Ellis (1928 - 1995)
Joined the RCP in 1946 remaining active in the Labour League of Youth after the collapse of the RCP in 1949. Briefly a member of the Healy group "The Club" he remained active thereafter in the Labour Party, serving both as a member of the LCC and its successor the GLC. He was a founding member of the editorial board of the *Militant*.

Jackson, E. Starkey (1909 - 1943)
Active member of the Labour League of Youth in Birmingham, visited Russia in 1926, joining the YCL soon after. Expelled in 1929 and soon after linked up with Harber, becoming an organiser of the Young Militant Group. Worked with Harber in the Marxist Group and later on the Bolshevik-Leninist Group in the Labour Party and then the Militant Group. Became secretary of the RSL, until called up for military service. Perished at sea.

James, Cyril Lionel Robert (1901 - 1989)
Born in Trinidad he came to Britain in 1932 where his writing skills on cricket earned him a job as assistant to Neville Cardus on the *Manchester Guardian*. His first book *The Life of Captain Cipriani* (1932) earned him a reputation as a serious commentator on Black nationalism. Having read Trotsky's *History of the Russian Revolution* he joined the Marxist Group in 1934, later becoming a editor of the journal Fight working alongside Arthur Ballard and Hilda Lane. Invited by Cannon to visit the USA he moved to that country in 1938 but subsequently broke with the SWP joining the Workers Party where he later became part of the Johnson - Forrest tendency first in the WP and then the SWP where he argued for a version of the theory of state capitalism. Having broken with Trotskyism he returned to Britain in 1953 where he became a leading radical writer on African and West-Indian affairs. His many books include *The Black Jacobins* (1938) and *World Revolution* (1937).

Lawrence, John (b. 1916)
A leading member of the RSL where he led a right-wing faction which rejected opposition to Trotsky's Proletarian Military Policy, he subsequently became a full time organiser for the RCP despite usually being in opposition to the leadership. Later went with Healy and became editor of the *Socialist Outlook*. Later joined CP.

Lee, Heaton (1915 - 1978)
South African Trotskyist (no relation to Ralph or Millie Lee) who came to Britain in 1937 joining the Militant Group. Imprisoned in 1944 for supporting an illegal apprentices' strike. Remained active until the collapse of the RCP.

Lee, Millie (Kahn) (b. 1913)
One of the original Johannesburg group of Trotskyists. Married Raff Lee in 1933) Subsequently came to Britain in 1937 where she joined the Militant Group. Later active in the leadership of the WIL and then the RCP. Became the wife of Jock Haston, and left the Trotskyist movement in 1950, but remained within the Labour Party.

Lee, Ralph (Raphael Levy) (c.1908 - c.1946)
Born in South Africa he joined the CP in 1922, but was expelled. Introduced Ted Grant to Marxist ideas. Organised a small group in Johannesburg to which Ted and Max Basch belonged and subsequently followed Ted to Britain in 1937 where he joined the Militant Group and later the WIL where he played a leading role. Returned to South Africa in 1940 and established the Workers International League.

Levy, Sam (1921 - 1995)
Joined the ILP youth section in 1938 and came into contact with members of the WIL. Member of the RCP, he became a leading member of the Open Party faction. Briefly linked to Healy he later became part of the group led by Ted Grant and Jimmy Deane who published the *International Socialist* during the early 1950s. Later helped produce the journal *Socialist Current*. He was a leading supporter of *Revolutionary History.*

Mandel, Ernest (Ernst Germain) (1923 - 1995)
Belgium Trotskyist was elected to the International Secretariat. Moved the expulsion of Ted Grant at the Fourth International's world congress of 1951. Played a leading role in the Fourth International in the 1950s and in the USFI after 1963. Writer of numerous books on economics. Keen supporter of Castroism, studentism and guerrilarism.

Mangan, Sherry (Terence Phelan) (1904 - 1961)
Leading American Trotskyist. He who participated in the discussions around the formation of the RCP on behalf of the American leadership. Served on European Secretariat during last years of war and then on the IS.

Matlow, Albert
Joined ILP in 1920s and helped form the Marxist Group in the ILP. In 1936 advocated joining the Labour Party and chaired the founding conference of the Militant Labour League in 1937. Remained active thereafter in the Labour Party.

Morrow, Felix (1906 - ?)
Leading American Trotskyist. Together with Albert Goldman (1897 - 1960) developed differences with Cannon over the perspectives for post war Europe. Convicted and imprisoned with 17 others under the Smith "Gag" Act. His 1938 account of the Spanish revolution Revolution and Counter-Revolution in Spain remains a classic account of that struggle. He was expelled from the SWP in 1946.

Pablo, Michel (Gabriel Raptis) (1911 - 1996)
A leading member of the post war Fourth International whose name would be used to describe the general tendency towards revisionism in that organisation. A leader of the International Secretariat from 1953 onwards following the split with the Fourth International. Became part of the United Secretariat in 1963 but was subsequently expelled. Later formed the AMR which rejected Trotskyism although that did not stop it from joining the USFI in the 1990s.

Reade, Arthur (1902 - ?)
Oxford graduate and lawyer. Joined the CP in the early 20s. 1924-25 member of London District committee of CPGB and business manager of Labour Monthly. One of the first defenders of Trotsky in the British Communist Party in early 1925 but isolated did not remain politically active.

Ridley, Frank (1897 - 1994)
Became active in the ILP during the 1920s, although he did not actually join until just before the Second World War. Established the Marxian League in 1929 but argued with Trotsky over perspectives for Britain (1931), later leaving Trotskyist politics, becoming an adviser to the ILP. Author of *The Assassins* (1938) and the anti-Trotskyist *At the Crossroads of History* (1935) along with many other books, pamphlets and articles.

Rosmer, Alfred (1877 - 1964)
Joined the French CP from a syndicalist background and served on the executive committee of the Communist International during the early 1920s. Known as a supporter of Trotsky rather than Trotskyism, he was expelled from the CP in 1924. Remained a friend and helper of Trotsky for the rest of his life but played little role in Trotskyist politics as such. Author of *Lenin's Moscow* (1953).

Rowe, Frank (1928 - 1994)
One of the young layer of Trotskyists who participated in the RCP having originally been a member of the YCL. Left the RCP before its demise but linked up again with Ted Grant during the early 1950s. Later supported the group around *Socialist Current* and remained active in East End community politics until his death.

Sara, Henry (1886 - 1953)
Former syndicalist who visited Russia in 1921, joining the CP in 1922. One of the Balham Group who first came into opposition with the British CP in support of Trotsky. He was chairman of the 'Unity Conference' in 1938.

Serge, Victor (V.L. Kibalchich) (1890 - 1947)
He wrote a number of important books and novels as an impassioned supporter of the Russian Revolution, working for the Comintern after 1919. Joined the Left Opposition in 1923 he was expelled from the Russian CP in 1927. Remained in Russia earning a living from writing and suffering repeated arrest until, following a campaign by Parisian intellectuals he was allowed to leave Russia. Chased out of Paris by the invading Nazi's he moved to Mexico where he continued to attack Stalinism. More libertarian than Trotskyist (although he was a friend of and corresponded regularly with Trotsky).

Shactmann, Max (1903 - 1972)
He became first a leading member of the CP in the USA and then a founding member of the Left Opposition. Attended a meeting in London in 1931 to establish the Left Opposition in Britain. Broke with Trotskyism in 1940 joining the Workers Party. Later joined the Socialist Party in 1958.

Tearse, Rawling (Roy) (1919 - 1986)
Joined the WIL from the ILP, subsequently becoming Scottish Organiser and then Industrial Organiser during the Second World War. Jailed in 1944 for his part in the illegal apprentices' strike. Expelled by Healy from the Club in 1950, he left the movement.

Wall, Pat (1933 - 1990)
Joined the Labour Party and then Ted Grant's group in 1950. Liverpool Trades Council 1951-64. Active in the apprentices movement in Merseyside in 1960. Played an important role in launching and building both *Socialist Fight* (1958 - 63) and *Militant* (1964 onwards) as well as a Marxist youth journal *Rally* which was produced by Walton Labour Youth League during the 1950s. President of Bradford trades council 1972-87. Fought Bradford North for Labour in 1983, but vote split by SDP defector. Won the seat in 1987. Frequent delegate and speaker at Labour Party Conference.

Wicks, Harry (1905 - 1989)
Born in London, became an active trade unionist on the Railways. Joined the YCL and later visited Russia where he attended the Lenin School for several years. Becoming aware on his return to Britain of the Stalinist consolidation in the British CP he spoke out and was expelled in 1932 for Trotskyism. Helped to form the Marxist League, publishing *The Red Flag*. Remained active in various groups up until his death.

wellred.marxist.com

Wellred Books Online Bookshop

Welcome to Wellred Books, the Internet's premier source of Marxist literature. We can deliver anywhere in the world, and we accept all currencies. Orders can be placed securely online with one of the following cards:

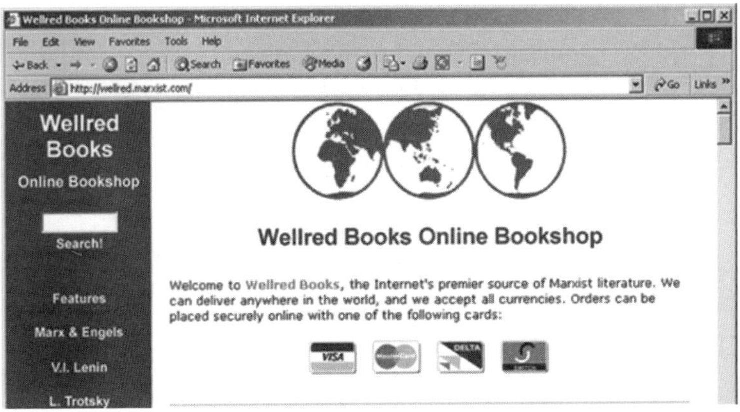

Bolshevism - The Road to Revolution

Alan Woods

There have been many books and potted histories of Russia, either written from an anti-Bolshevik perspective, or its Stalinist mirror image, which paint a false account of the rise of Bolshevism. For them, Bolshevism is either an historical "accident" or "tragedy". Or it is portrayed erroneously as the work of one great man (Lenin) who marched single-minded towards the October Revolution. Alan Woods, in rejecting these false ideas, reveals the real evolution of Bolshevism as a living struggle to apply the methods of Marxism to the peculiarities of Russia. Using a wealth of primary sources, Alan Woods uncovers the fascinating growth and development of Bolshevism in pre-revolutionary Russia.

Publisher: Wellred Publications
Pub. Date: 1999
Format: Paperback
No. Pages: 636
ISBN: 1900007053

List Price £15.00
Our Price £9.95

Lenin and Trotsky - What they really stood for

Alan Woods & Ted Grant

The ideas of Lenin and Trotsky are without doubt the most distorted and slandered ideas in history. For more than 80 years, they have been subjected to an onslaught from the apologists of capitalism, who have attempted to present their ideas - Bolshevism - as both totalitarian and utopian. An entire industry was developed in an attempt to equate the crimes of Stalinism with the regime of workers' democracy that existed under Lenin and Trotsky.

It is now more than thirty years since the publication of the first edition of this work. It was written as a reply to Monty Johnstone, who was a leading theoretician of the Communist Party of Great Britain. Johnstone had published a reappraisal of Leon Trotsky in the Young Communist League's journal Cogito at the end of 1968. Alan Woods and Ted Grant used the opportunity to write a detailed reply explaining the real relationship between the ideas of Lenin and Trotsky. This was no academic exercise. It was written as an appeal to the ranks of the Communist Party and the Young Communist League to rediscover the truth about Trotsky and return to the original revolutionary programme of Lenin.

Also included in this new edition is Monty Johnstone's original Cogito article, as well as further material on Lenin's struggle with Stalin in the last month of his political life. The foreword is written by Trotsky's grandson, Vsievolod Volkov.

Publisher: Wellred Publications
Pub. Date: 2000
Format: Paperback
No. Pages: 221
ISBN: 8492183268

List Price £8.95
Our Price £5.95

Reason in Revolt -
Marxist Philosophy and Modern Science

Alan Woods & Ted Grant

As we enter the 21st Century science and philosophy are at the crossroads. The achievemenrs of science and technology in the 20th Century are unparalleled in history. Yet amongst today's leading scientists there is a growing tendency towards mysticism. An example is the "Big Bang" theory of the origin of the Universe which is being used to justify the existence of a Creator, as in the book of Genesis. For the first time in centuries, science appears to lend credence to religious obscurantism. But a growing number of scientists are becoming discontented with the old outlook.

The rapid rise of the theory of Chaos and Complexity is one of the most significant developments in science at the end of the 20th Century. A significant part of this book is devoted to an exploration of the relationship between Marxist philosophy and these new theories. Will this encounter provide the basis for a new and exciting breakthrough in the methodology of science?

With a foreword by Eric Lerner, author of The Big Bang Never Happened.

Publisher: Wellred Publications
Pub. Date: 1995
Format: Paperback
No. Pages: 443
ISBN: 1900007002

Price £9.95

Russia - From Revolution to Counter-Revolution

Ted Grant

The Russian Revolution changed the course of world history. The entire 20th century was dominated by its consequences - this fact is recognised even by the most conservative commentators.

For the best part of three generations, the apologists of capitalism vented their spleen against the Soviet Union, no effort or expense was spared in the attempt to blacken the image of the October Revolution and the nationalised planned economy that issued from it. In this campagin the crimes of Stalinism came in very handy. The trick was to identify socialism and communism with the bureaucratic totalitarian regime of Stalin. But these slanders are baseless; the regime established by the revolution was neither totalitarian nor bureaucratic, but the most democratic regime yet seen on earth - a regime in which, for the first time, millions of ordinary men and women overthrew their exploiters, took their destiny in their hands, at begun the task of transforming society. Now the collapse of Stalinism has ushered in any attempt to put the clock back 80 years.

Ted Grant traces the evolution of Russia from the Bolshevik victory in 1917, through the rise of Stalinism, its emergence as a super power after the second world war, and the crisis and collapse of the regime. Given the turmoil and the political and social upheavals that charaterise Russia today, Ted Grant asks where Russia is heading? With a "democratic" path ruled out, what are the perspectives for a military dictatorship or a new workers revolution?

Publisher: Wellred Publications
Pub. Date: 1997
Format: Paperback
No. Pages: 585
ISBN: 1900007029

List Price £11.95
Our Price £9.95

Partition - Can it be undone?

Lal Khan

The partition of India was one of the greatest crimes of British Imperialism. This was not to an act to defend the Muslims or the Hindus but to split and wreck the national liberation movement which they had failed to defeat by force of arms. The present states of India and Pakistan were created over the bones of the millions who died during the bloodshed unleashed. Lal Khan's book covers the history of the subcontinent from the Raj to the present day and demonstrates that a socialist federation of the subcontinent is the only way forward.

Publisher: Wellred Publications
Pub. Date: 2001
Format: Hardback
No. Pages: 290
ISBN:

Price £8.95

Germany - From Revolution to Counter-Revolution

Rob Sewell

The barbarity of the Nazis is well documented. Less well known are the events that preceeded Hitler's rise to power. This book is a history of the German workers' struggles between 1918 and 1933; from the revolution of 1918 and the downfall of the Kaiser, to the rise to power of Hitler. How was it possible for the mightiest labour movement in Europe to be trampled under the iron heel of fascism?

Publisher: Fortress Books
Pub. Date: 1988
Format: Paperback
No. Pages: 93
ISBN: 1870958047

Price £2.50

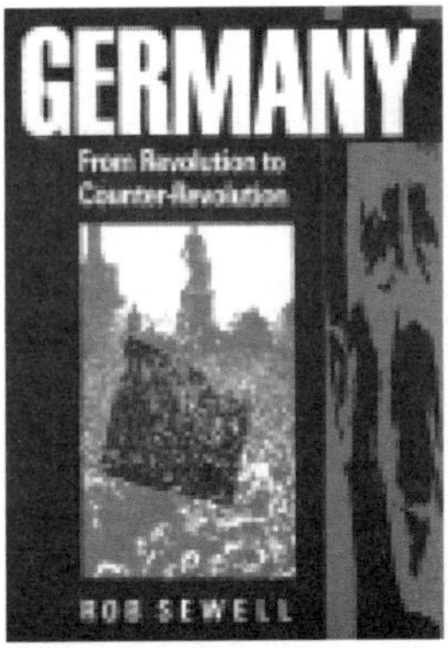

In Defence of Marxism

www.marxist.com

The ideas represented by Marxist.com have gained a considerable audience over the last seven years. The launching of Marxist.com was an important initiative. This was a big step forward, which has made possible big advances in getting our ideas known and entering new areas. The sheer volume of our theoretical production has never been greater. This has enabled us to break into new areas: Indonesia, Turkey, Ireland, the Balkans, Russia, North America and others.

Few would dispute the fact that our website is the best in the world. It is increasingly a point of reference for communist and socialist activists everywhere. In 2001 alone we had over a million successful page requests. This is a guarantee of our future success. It should fill all our comrades with a sense of pride and confidence in the Marxist tendency in Britain and internationally.

We are determined that our theoretical work will be continued and stepped up, and our use of the Internet maximised. The work of educating and training Marxist cadres and integrating them in the mass organisations of the working class is the prior condition for the creation, first of a mass Marxist tendency, and then a mass Marxist party and an International which is really capable of leading the working class to the socialist transformation of society, nationally and internationally.

by Alan Woods

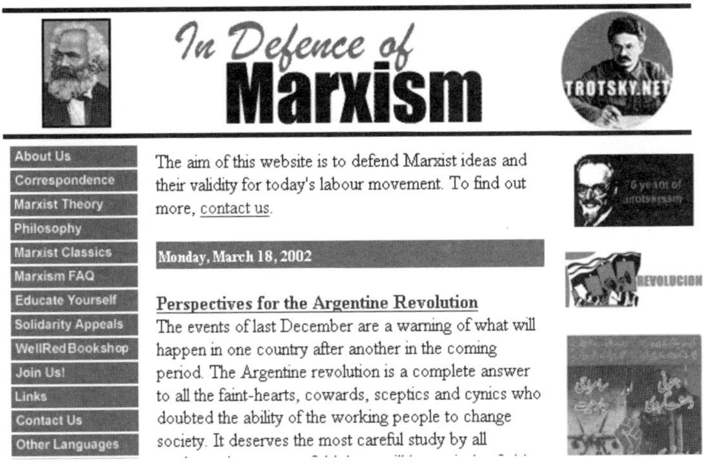

In Defence of
Marxism
TROTSKY.NET
About Us
Correspondence
Marxist Theory
Philosophy
Marxist Classics
Marxism FAQ
Educate Yourself
Solidarity Appeals
WellRed Bookshop
Join Us!
Links
Contact Us
Other Languages
The aim of this website is to defend Marxist ideas and their validity for today's labour movement. To find out more, contact us.
Monday, March 18, 2002
Perspectives for the Argentine Revolution
The events of last December are a warning of what will happen in one country after another in the coming period. The Argentine revolution is a complete answer to all the faint-hearts, cowards, sceptics and cynics who doubted the ability of the working people to change society. It deserves the most careful study by all
REVOLUCION